Peremptory Norms of General International Law (*Jus Cogens*) and the Prohibition of Terrorism

Peremptory Norms of General International Law (*Jus Cogens*) and the Prohibition of Terrorism

By

Aniel Caro de Beer

BRILL
NIJHOFF

LEIDEN | BOSTON

Library of Congress Cataloging-in-Publication Data

Names: De Beer, Aniel Caro, author.
Title: Peremptory norms of general international law (jus cogens) and the prohibition of terrorism / by Aniel Caro de Beer.
Description: Leiden ; Boston : Brill Nijhoff, 2019. | Based on author's thesis (doctoral – University of Pretoria, 2018). | Includes bibliographical references and index.
Identifiers: LCCN 2019000987 (print) | LCCN 2019001832 (ebook) | ISBN 9789004391543 (ebook) | ISBN 9789004391536 (hardback : alk. paper)
Subjects: LCSH: Terrorism (International law) | Jus cogens (International law) | Terrorism—Prevention—Law and legislation.
Classification: LCC KZ7220 (ebook) | LCC KZ7220 .D43 2019 (print) | DDC 344.05/325–dc23
LC record available at https://lccn.loc.gov/2019000987

Typeface for the Latin, Greek, and Cyrillic scripts: "Brill". See and download: brill.com/brill-typeface.

ISBN 978-90-04-39153-6 (hardback)
ISBN 978-90-04-39154-3 (e-book)

This book is printed on acid-free paper and produced in a sustainable manner.

Contents

Foreword

Academia sometimes can be very rewarding. Perhaps the most rewarding moments are encounters with committed and motivated students. My encounter with Aniel de Beer, Dr de Beer, was very rewarding. When I first met her as an LLM student in 2015, Aniel was a highly-motivated and hardworking student, always eager to engage in interesting discussion on international law. Already at that stage she exhibited a deep interest in the subject of this book, peremptory norms of general international law (*jus cogens*). I therefore was not surprised when, at the end of 2015, she hinted – much to my great joy, I must admit – that she was interested in pursuing a PhD under my supervision.

Aniel eventually wrote an excellent PhD thesis. I say eventually, but the thesis was actually completed in two years. Even though it was completed in such a short time, her thesis was excellent. What is more remarkable is that during the time she wrote this thesis, Aniel was employed full-time as an executive in a sector unrelated to her field of study (telecommunications) while engaged in other extracurricular activities, including learning Chinese and continuously trying to improve her French. This book is a testament to Aniel's continuing hard work, dedication and commitment to the study of international law.

Aniel's interest in the subject of *jus cogens*, and this book, flows from her concern for the human condition and a deep-seated desire to deal with human suffering. I believe – and I think so does Aniel – that norms of *jus cogens* are developed to address these ends: to prevent human suffering and promote humane conditions for the inhabitants of our planet. These objectives are at the heart of the most widely-accepted list of norms of *jus cogens*: prohibition of genocide; slavery; crimes against humanity; the aggressive use of force; apartheid; torture; self-determination; and enforced disappearance. This concern for the human condition flows through the pages of this book.

In this book Aniel tackles themes that in the most direct, but different, ways negatively affect the human condition. Few things today wreak more havoc on human security globally than terrorism. The growth in the number and intensity of terrorist acts worldwide is a serious cause for concern. This book has as its central theme the existential threat of terrorism for human society as we know it. While terrorism threatens humans as a collective, other principles covered in this book, including the prohibition of torture and the right to a fair trial, affect human beings at an individual but no less serious level. All the themes of the book, therefore, directly concern the human condition and the search for security of the human being.

Yet, Aniel is all too aware of the fact that the concern for the human condition is very often used by lawyers as a pretext for policy preferences in law and a justification for lack of rigour. Human suffering all too often is advanced to camouflage a lack of reasoning and argumentation. In her book she is careful to avoid making the human condition and the desire to deal with human suffering the argument. It certainly is a motivation for the argument, but it is not the argument. Relying on the ongoing work of the International Law Commission, which itself carefully and explicitly avoids the positivism-natural law debate, she adopts a rigorous approach to the identification of both customary international law and *jus cogens* but at the same time gives content to the humanist ideals that clearly inspire her.

The book adopts the two-pronged criteria for the identification of *jus cogens*, namely, first, that there should be a norm of general international law, typically a rule of customary international law, and, second, that this norm of general international law must be accompanied by what may be termed *opinio juris cogentis*. She applies these criteria in a rigorous manner to each norm of which the *jus cogens* status is under consideration, that is, the prohibition of terrorism; the right to a fair trial; the prohibition of torture; and the prohibition of the use of force.

However, the book does more than merely establishing the *jus cogens* status of these norms. It also – and in my view this is its most important contribution to securing the human condition – studies the interaction between the prohibition of terrorism and these other norms of international law that arguably rise to the level of *jus cogens*. In a world where terrorism is such a global threat to the human condition, there is always a danger that in our desire to address and defeat it, we may lose perspective and seek solutions that cause greater harm to the human condition by attacking those values that protect the individual, such as the prohibition of torture and the right to a fair trial. A 2010 film, *Unthinkable*, shockingly brings to the fore this dilemma. It asks us to consider whether attacking individual human security is consistent with the ideals that inspire the evolution of norms of *jus cogens* – and I am sure they inspire Aniel de Beer. While *Unthinkable* does not offer the answer, I hope the message that readers take from Aniel's book is that we ought not to attack individual security.

This of course is a normative argument, and Aniel, although clearly driven by normative and value-laden concerns, seeks to make a doctrinal argument. She makes the argument by rigorously assessing the practice of states.

It has been a pleasure knowing Aniel de Beer. A pleasure to teach her. A pleasure to guide her through her a doctoral thesis. It has been pleasure to celebrate her achievements with her. And it is a pleasure to watch her begin what I hope will be her second career as an academic, launching this career with a very important book, on a very important subject, which I think will be influential in international law.

Dire Tladi
University of Pretoria
UN International Law Commission
Special Rapporteur on Peremptory Norms of General International Law (*Jus Cogens*)
2018

Foreword

On the occasion of accepting an honorary degree from the University of Tilburg in 2002, Kofi Anan, then Secretary-General of the United Nations, cautioned that after 9/11 the world faces a nearly unsolvable conflict between protecting individual liberties of citizens and ensuring their safety from terrorist attacks with potentially catastrophic consequences. At the time, and following the near universal condemnation of the twenty-first century's transnational terrorist movements and their methods and practices, there was good reason to fear over-zealous responses by states that could threaten the very civil liberties states were supposed to protect. The global counter-terrorism strategy that evolved in response to the post-9/11 world of security threats has duly taken note of these concerns with the result that rule of law and human rights guarantees have become crucial elements of the United Nations' comprehensive counter-terrorism strategy.

It is precisely these developments that form the wider context of Aniel de Beer's monograph on *jus cogens* norms and the prohibition of terrorism. The rapid development of a new body of law, internationally, regionally and nationally, and concomitant state practice in this area of international law, are skillfully and systematically analysed and argued in explaining the status of the prohibition of terrorism as a *jus cogens* norm and the legal consequences of its relationship with other *jus cogens* norms, such as the prohibition of torture, the legal entitlement to core fair trial rights, and the prohibition on the use of force. In a text that demonstrates commendable scholarship, extensive research and clarity of argument the reader will find much to ruminate about concerning a phenomenon that has left such an indelible mark on the twenty-first century. To the extent that Aniel's work also alerts us to the consequences of classifying a norm in international law as *jus cogens*, there is, coincidentally, the publication in 2018 of the International Law Commission's third report on peremptory norms of general international law (*jus cogens*) by the Special Rapporteur, which considers the consequences and legal effects of *jus cogens* norms. This report duly admits that the issue of consequences is most important, but at the same time most challenging and complex.

Hennie Strydom
Professor of Public International Law and incumbent of the National Research Foundation Chair in International Law, University of Johannesburg
2018

Table of Statutes

Domestic

Afghanistan Interim Criminal Procedure Code 2004
Alien Torts Claims Act 28 USC § 1350
Algeria Code of Criminal Procedure 1966
Andorra New Penal Code 2005
Antigua and Barbuda Prevention of Terrorism Act 2001
Arabia Law of Criminal Procedure 2001
Armenia Criminal Code 2003
Australia Criminal Code Act 1995
Bahamas Anti-Terrorism Act 2004
Bahrain Penal Code 1976 (as amended)
Bangladesh Anti-Terrorism Ordinance 2008
Bangladesh Torture and Custodial Death (Prevention) Act 2013
Basic Law for the Federal Republic of Germany 1949
Basic Law of Israel 1958
Belgium Organic Law on the Intelligence and Security Services 1998
Botswana Counter-Terrorism Act 2014
Brazil Anti-Terrorism Law 2016
Brazil Law No 9.455 1997
Cambodia Code of Criminal Procedure 2007
Cambodia Law on the Establishment of the Extraordinary Chambers 2001 (as amended)
Cameroon Law on the Suppression of Acts of Terrorism in Cameroon 2014
Cameroon Prevention and Prohibition of Torture Act 1997
Cameroon Penal Code 1967, as amended by Act 97/009
Canada Criminal Code C-46 1985
China Criminal Procedure Law 1979 (as amended)
Columbia Penal Code Law 2000
Constitution of the Bolivarian Republic of Venezuela 1999
Constitution of Cameroon 1972 (as amended)
Constitution of Colombia 1991
Constitution of the Democratic Republic of the Congo 2005
Constitution of the Dominican Republic 2015
Constitution of Ghana 1992
Constitution of Greece 1975 (as amended)

Iraq's Law of the Supreme Iraqi Criminal Tribunal 2005
Iraq Penal Code 1969
Israel Criminal Procedure (Enforcement Powers – Detention) Law 5756 1996
Italian Criminal Code (as amended by Law 155 of 2005)
Jamaica Terrorism Prevention Act 2005
Kenya National Intelligence Service Act 2012
Kenya National Police Service Act 2011
Lebanese Penal Code 1943
Lesotho Penal Code Act 2010
Malaysia Penal Code 2015
Mexico's Federal Act on the Prevention and Punishment of Torture 1991
Morocco Penal Code 1962
New Zealand Terrorism Suppression Act 2002
Nigeria Terrorism (Prevention) Act 2011
Penal Code of Algeria 1966
Penal Code of the Democratic Republic of Timor Leste Decree Law No 19/2009
Penal Code of Bhutan 2004
Penal Code of Peru 1991
Penal Code of Spain 1995
Peru New Code of Criminal Procedure 2004
Phillipines Anti-Torture Act 2009
Philippines Revised Rules of Criminal Procedure 2000
Restatement (Third) of Foreign Relations of the United States 1987
Saudi Arabia Penal Law for Crimes of Terrorism and its Financing 2013
Saudi Law of Criminal Procedure 2001
Seychelles Prevention of Terrorism Act 2004
Sixth Amendment to the US Constitution 1789
South Africa Prevention of Combating and Torture of Persons Act 2013
South Africa Protection of Constitutional Democracy Against Terrorist and Related Activities 2004
Sri Lanka Convention Against Torture And Other Cruel, Inhuman or Degrading Treatment or Punishment 1994
Sudan Criminal Code 1991
Tanzania Prevention of Terrorism Act 2002
The Netherlands Crimes of Terrorism Act 2004
Torture Victim Protection Act 1992
Trinidad and Tobago Anti-Terrorism Act 2005 (as amended by Act 13 of 2018)
Tunisia Anti-Terrorism Law 26 2015
Tunisia Criminal Code 1968 (as amended)
Uganda Anti-Terrorism Act 2002

Uganda Prevention and Prohibition of Torture Act 2012
United Kingdom Counter-Terrorism and Security Act 2015
United Kingdom Criminal Justice Act 1988
United Kingdom Human Rights Act 1998
United Kingdom Prevention of Terrorism Act 1984
United States of America 18 USC 2331 2004
Vanuatu Penal Code (Cap 135) 1981

International Statutes and Rules of Procedure

International Criminal Tribunal for Rwanda, Rules of Procedure and Evidence UN Doc ITR/3/REV.1 (1995)
International Tribunal for the Prosecution of Persons Responsible for Serious Violations of International Humanitarian Law Committed in the Territory of the Former Yugoslavia Since 1991, Rules of Procedure and Evidence, UN Doc IT/32/Rev.11 (1997)
Rome Statute of the International Criminal Court (1998)
Statute of the International Criminal Tribunal for Rwanda (as amended) (8 November 1994) UN Doc. S/Res/955 (1994)
Statute of the International Tribunal for the Prosecution of Persons Responsible for Serious Violations of International Humanitarian Law Committed in the Territory of the Former Yugoslavia Since 1991, UN Doc S/25704 (1993) (as amended)
Statute of the International Court of Justice (1946)
Statute of the Special Court for Sierra Leone (2002)
Statute of the Special Tribunal for Lebanon (2007)

Table of Cases

Permanent Court of International Justice

Oscar Chinn (*United Kingdom v Belgium*) Judgment, PCIJ series A/B No 63, ICGJ 313 (PCIJ 1932) (1934)
The SS Lotus Case (*France v Turkey*) (7 September 1927) (1927) PCIJ Ser A No 10

International Court of Justice

Advisory Opinion Concerning Reservations to the Genocide Convention ICJ (28 May 1951) (1951) ICJ Reports 23
Advisory Opinion OC-18/03 of September 17, 2003, Requested by the United Mexican States Juridical Condition and Rights of Undocumented Migrants
Application of the Convention on the Prevention and Punishment of the Crime of Genocide (*Bosnia and Herzegovina v Serbia and Montenegro*) (26 February 2007) (2007) ICJ Reports 43
Armed Activities on the Territory of the Congo (*DRC v Rwanda*), Preliminary Objections (3 February 2006) (2006) ICJ Reports
Armed Activities on the Territory of the Congo (*Democratic Republic of the Congo v Uganda*) 19 December 2005 (2005) ICJ Judgment
Arrest Warrant of 11 April 2000 (*DRC v Belgium*) (14 February 2002) (2002) ICJ Reports 3; 41 ILM 536
Barcelona Traction Light and Power Company Ltd (5 February 1970) (1970) ICJ Reports 3
Belgium v Senegal (Questions Relating to the Obligation to Prosecute or Extradite) (20 July 2012) (2012) ICJ Reports
Constitution of the Maritime Safety Committee of the Intergovernmental Maritime Consultative Organization Advisory Opinion (8 June 1960) 1960 ICJ Reports 150
Corfu Channel Case (*United Kingdom v Albania*) Merits ICJ (9 April 1949) (1949) ICJ Reports 22
Delimitation of the Maritime Boundary in the Gulf of Maine Area (*Canada v United States*) (12 October 1984) (1984) ICJ Reports 246
East Timor (*Portugal v Australia*) (30 June 1995) (1995) ICJ Reports 90
Fisheries Jurisdiction (*UK v Iceland*) Merits (25 July 1974) (1974) ICJ Reports 3

International Criminal Tribunals

Other Courts and Tribunals

Garb v Republic of Poland 207 F Supp 2d 16 (EDNY 2002)
Hamdan v Rumsfeld 548 US 557 (29 June 2006)
Hamdi v Rumsfeld 296F3d 278, 281 (4th Cir 2002)
Hamdi v Rumsfeld 124 S Ct 2635 (2004)
Heaney and McGuinness v Ireland (1996) 1 IR 580
Hilao v Marcos 25 F3d 1467, 1475 (9th Cir 1994)
Hwang Geum Joo v Japan 172 F Supp 2d 52 (DC 2001)
In re Estate Ferdinand E Marcos 978 F2d 493 (9th Cir)
John Fairfax Publications Pty Ltd v Hitchcock (2004) 61 NSWLR 344
Jones v Ministry of Interior for the Kingdom of Saudi Arabia & Others (2007) 1 AC 270 (HL) 1 All ER 113
Kadic v Karadzic 70 F3d 232, 239–40, 243 (2d Cir 1995)
Kazemi Estate v Islamic Republic of Iran 2014 SCC 62
Kaunda & Others v President of the Republic of South Africa & Others (*Society for the Abolition of the Death Penalty in South Africa intervening as Amicus Curiae*) 2005 (4) SA 235 (CC)
Khouzam v Ashcroft 361 F3d 161, 171 (2d Cir 2004)
Koigi Wamwere v the Attorney-General (2015) eKLR 6
Loizidou v Turkey (23 March 1995) Series A No 310, 26
Madan Singh v State of Bihar (2004) INSC 225
Mann v Republic of Equatorial Guinea (2008) 1 ZWHHC 12
Marcelino Tineo Silva and Others Peru Constitutional Court Case No 010-2002-AI/TC (3 January 2003)
Marcos Manto v Thajane 508 US 972, 125L Ed 2d 661, 113 S Ct 2960
Mazzeo Julio Lilo & Others (Judgment of 13 July 2007) 2007-III-573 (Arg Supreme Court)
Mohamed & Another v President of the Republic of South Africa & Others CCT 17/01 (28 May 2001) 2–18
Mohammed v Obama 704 F Supp 2d 1, 28–29 (DDC 2009)
Mukoko v Attorney-General (2012) JOL 29664 (ZS)
Mullane v Central Hanover Trust Co 339 US 306, 313 (1950)
Nulyarimma v Thompson (1999) FCA 1192 (1 September 1999) 145
Pablo Nájera (France) v United Mexican States Decision No 30-A (19 October 1928) UN Reports of International Arbitral Awards vol 5 466
Princz v Federal Republic of Germany 813 F Supp22 (DDC 1992) 1168
Prosecutor v Rajko Radulović & Others K-15/95 (Judgment of 26 May 1997)
Public Committee against Torture v State of Israel HCJ 5100/94 (1999)
Rasul v Bush 215 F Supp 2d 55 (DC 2002)
Rasul v Bush 124 S Ct 2686 (2004)

Re BC Motor Vehicle Act (1985) 2 SCR 486, 503
R v Bartle and Commissioner of Police, Ex parte Pinochet (1999) UKHL 17
R v Bow Street Metropolitan Stipendiary Magistrate, Ex parte Pinochet Ugarte (No 3) (2000) 1 AC 147
R v Oakes (1986) 26 DLR (4th) 200
R (Mohamed) v Secretary of State for Foreign and Commonwealth Affairs (2009) 1 WLR 2579
Sampson v Federal Republic of Germany & Claims Conference 250 F3d 1145 (7th Cir 2001) 1150
Sabbithi v Al Saleh 623 F Supp 2d 93 (DDC 2009)
Sarei v Rio Tinto PLC 671 F 3d 736 (9th Cir 2010)
Sentencia del Pleno Jurisdiccional del Tribunal Constitucional del Perú Exp n 0024-2010-PI/TC
Siderman de Blake v Republic of Argentina 965 F 2d 699 (9th Cir 1992)
Smith v Socialist People's Libyan Arab Jamahiriya 101 F 3d 239 (2nd Cir 1996)
Snyder v Massachussets 291 US 97 (1934) 201
Suresh v Canada (Minister of Citizenship and Immigration) (2002) 1 SCR 3
S v Makwanyane 1995 (6) BCLR 665 (CC)
S v Mthembu (379/07) (2008) ZASCA 51
S v Wouter Basson (2004) (Judgment) CCT 30/03
Tachiona v Mugabe 169 F Supp 2d 259 (SDNY 2001) 316
Tel-Oren v Libyan Arab Republic (Judgment of 3 February 1984) 726 F2d 774, 233 (US App DC) 384
The Prosecutor v Saif Al-Islam Gaddafi Appeal No 00-87215 Decision No 64 2001 125 ILR 490 (2001)
Trial of Shigeki Motomura and 15 Others 13 Law Reports of Trials of War Criminals (1947) 138 (Netherlands)
Tyrer v the United Kingdom 25 April 1978, Series A No 26
United States v Ghailani 2010 US Dist LEXIS 107830 (SDNY) (6 October 2010)
United States v Matta Ballesteros 71 F 3d 754 (10th Cir 1995)
United States v Reid 206 F Supp 2d 132 (D Mass 2002)
United States v Yousef 327 F 3d 56 (2d Cir 2003)
Xuncax v Gramajo 886 FSupp (D Mass 1995) 162, 174, 178
Youssef v Secretary of State for Foreign and Commonwealth Affairs (2014) QB 728 53 and (2016) 2 WLR 509 17
Zheng v Ashcroft 332 F3d 1186, 1194 (9th Cir 2003)
Zubeda v Ashcroft 333 F3d (3rd Cir 2003)

European Court of Justice

Yusuf and Al Barakaat International Foundation v Council and Commission (21 September 2005) ECR II-3533 282

European Court of Human Rights and European Commission of Human Rights

Aksoy v Turkey Application No 21987/93 (1996) ECHR 23 (1997) EHRR 553 paras 50, 76
Al-Adsani v United Kingdom Application No 35763/97 ECHR (21 November 2001) 761, 30
Al-Dulimi and Montana Management Inc v Switzerland (21 June 2016) ECHR 576
Allenet de Ribermont v France Application No 15175/89 20 EHRR 557
Al Nashiri v Poland Application No 28761/11 (24 July 2014) ECHR section B
Aydin v Turkey Communication 23178/94, ECHR 25 September 1997
Brogan & Others v the United Kingdom ECHR (29 November 1988) Ser A No 145-B 1
Case of *Ibrahim & Others v The United Kingdom* Applications No 50541/08, 50571/08, 50573/08 & 40351/09) ECHR (13 September 2016)
Chahal v United Kingdom Application No 22414/93 ECHR (5 November 1996)
Debboub alias Husseini Ali v France Application No 37786/97 (Judgment of 9 November 1999)
Ekin Association v France Application No 39288/98 ECHR (17 July 2001)
Funke v France (1993) 16 EHRR 297
Gäfgen v Germany Application No 22978/05 (1 June 2010) 87
Gérard Bernard v France Application No 27678/02 (judgment of 26 September 2006)
Hilal v The United Kingdom Application No 45276/99 ECHR (6 June 2001) para 28
Ireland v The United Kingdom Application No 5310/71 ECHR (1978) 602 Yearbook of European Convention on Human Rights
Ireland v The United Kingdom EC (1976) 512 Yearbook of European Convention on Human Rights 489–491
Kadi v Council & Commission (2005) ECR II-3649 Case No T-315/01, joined cases C-402/05 P & C-415/05P
Kadi v Commission Judgment of the General Court (Seventh Chamber) (30 September 2010) T-85/09
Kennedy v United Kingdom Application No 26839/05 ECHR (18 May 2010)

Kurt v Turkey Application No 24276/94 ECHR (25 May 1998)
Labita v Italy Application No 26772/95 ECHR (6 April 2000)
Morgani v France Application No 17831/91 EC (report of 30 November 1994)
Mouesca v France Application No 52189/99 ECHR (judgment of 3 June 2003)
Murray v UK (1996) 22 EHRR 29
Othman (Abu Qatada) v The United Kingdom Application No 8139/09 ECHR (17 January 2012) 183–184 para 260
Opuz v Turkey Application No 33401/02 ECHR (9 June 2009) para 176
Ramirez Sanchez v France Application No 59450/00 (4 July 2006) ECHR paras 116, 165 & 179
Saadi v Italy Application No 37201/06, Council of Europe: ECtHR (28 February 2008)
Saunders v UK (1997) 23 ECHRR (ECHR) 313
Selmouni v France Application No 25803(94) ECHR (1 December 1977)
Soering v United Kingdom Application No 14038/88 ECHR (7 July 1989) para 91
The Greek Case Report of the Commission: Application No 3321/67 – *Denmark v Greece*, Application No 3322/67 – *Norway v Greece*, Application No 3323/67 – *Sweden v Greece*, Application No 3344/67 – *Netherlands v Greece* (1970) EC
Z & Others v United Kingdom (Application No 29392/95) (31 May 2001) ECHR

Inter-American Court of Human Rights and Inter-American Commission of Human Rights

Durand and Ugarte v Peru Inter-American Commission for Human Rights, IAm Comm of HR (16 August 2000) Ser C No 68 59
Jorge A Giménez v Argentina Inter-American Commission for Human Rights, IAm Comm of HR (1 March 1996) Case 11.245 Report No 12/96 OEA/Ser.L/V/II.91 Doc 7, 33
Loayza-Tamayo v Peru, IACtHR (17 September 1997) Series C No 33 para 57
Maritza Urrutia v Guatemala Inter-American Commission for Human Rights, IAm Comm of HR (27 November 2003) Ser C No 103
Martin de Mejia v Peru Inter-American Commission for Human Rights, IAm Comm of HR (1 March 1996) Case 10.970, Report No 5/96 OEA/Ser.L/V/II.91
Mendoza et al v Argentina Inter-American Commission for Human Rights, IAm Comm of HR (14 May 2013) Ser C No 260
Michael Domingues v US (Merits) (22 October 2000) Report No 62/02, case 12.285
Morales v Guatemala Inter-American Commission of Human Rights, IAm Comm of HR (8 March 1998) Ser C No 37 134

Suárez Rosero v Ecuador IACtHR (12 November 1997) Series C No 35
Tibi v Ecuador Inter-American Commission for Human Rights, IAm Comm of HR (7 September 2004) Ser C No 114, IHRL 1497

African Court on Human and Peoples' Rights and African Commission on Human and Peoples' Rights Reports and Decisions

Abdel Hadi, Ali Radi & Others v Republic of Sudan Communication 368/09 (5 November 2013)
Constitutional Rights Project & Others v Nigeria (2000) AHRLR 227 (ACHPR 1999)
Good v Botswana (2010) AHRLR 43 (ACHPR 2010
Mohammed Abdullah Saleh Al-Asad v The Republic of Djibouti Communication 383/10 ACHPR (12 May 2014)
Pagnoulle v Cameroon (2000) AHRLR 57 (ACHPR 1997)
Regina (David Miranda) v Secretary of State for the Home Department & Others (2016) EWCA Civ

UN Human Rights Committee

Acosta v Uruguay Communication 110/1981 UNHR Committee (12 August 1981) UN Doc Supp no 40 (A/39/40) 1984
Ahani v Canada Communication 1051/2002 UN Doc CCPR/C/80/D/1051/2002 (2004)
Bequio v Uruguay Communication 88/1981 UNHR Committee (14 March 1981) UN Doc CCPR/C/OP/2 (1990
Cabreira v Uruguay Communication 105/1981 UNHR Committee (7 August 1981) UN Doc CCPR/C/OP/2 (1990)
Gilboa v Uruguay Communication 147/1983 UNHR Committee (1 November 1985) UN Doc Supp no 40 (A/41/40) (1986)
Gómez v Spain Communication 701/1996 HRC (6 April 1998) UN Doc GAOR, A/55/40 (vol II) 109
Gridin v Russia Communication 770 UNHR Committee (20 July 2000) UN Doc CCPR/C/69/D/770/1997 (2000)
Khalilov v Tajikistan Communication 973/2001 UNHR Committee (13 April 2005) UN Doc CCPR/C/83/D/973/2001
Lafuente Peñarrieta et al v Bolivia Communication 176/1984 UNHR Committee (2 November 1987) UN Doc CCPR/C/OP/2 201 (1990)

Miguel Angel Estrella v Uruguay Communication 74/1980 UNHR Committee (17 July 1980) UN Doc Supp No 40 (A/38/40) 150 (1983)
Rodríguez v Uruguay Communication 322/1988 UNHR Committee (23 July 1988) UN Doc CCPR/C/51/D/322/1988
Saidova v Tajikstan Communication 964/2001 UNHR Committee (20 August 2006) UN Doc CCPR/C/81/D/964/2001

Human Rights Committee Reports and Resolutions

Commission on Human Rights Summary Records of the 325th meeting E/CN4/325 (13 June 1949)
General Comment No 29: Derogations from Provisions of the Covenant During a State of Emergency, General Comment on article 4, UNHR Committee, CCPR/C/21/Rev1/Add11 (31 August 2001)
General Comment No 32, Right to Equality before Courts and Tribunals and to a Fair Trial, UNHR Committee 90th session, Geneva (9 to 27 July 2007) UN Doc CCPR/C/GC/32
Human Rights Committee Commission of Inquiry on Lebanon Implementation of General Assembly Resolution 60/251 of 15 March 2006 entitled 'Human Rights Council': Report of the Commission of Inquiry on Lebanon Pursuant to Human Rights Council Resolution S-2/1 UN Doc. A/HRC/3/2 (23 November 2006)
Report of the United Nations High Commissioner for Human Rights on the Protection of Human Rights and Fundamental Freedoms while Countering Terrorism (A/HRC/22/26)
Report of the United Nations Working Group on Arbitrary Detention – Basic Principles and Guidelines on the Right of Anyone Deprived of their Liberty to Bring Proceedings before a Court A/HRC/30/37 (6 July 2016)
Third Periodic Report to the Human Rights Committee, Azerbaijan, 10 December 2007, UN Doc CCPR/C/AZE/3 (submitted 4 October 2007)

Committee Against Torture

Committee Against Torture *Dragan Dimitrijevic v Serbia and Montenegro*, Communication 207/02 (24 November 2004)
Committee Against Torture *Jovica Dimitrov v Serbia and Montenegro* UN Doc CAT/C/34/D/171/2000 (3 May 2005)

Committee Against Torture: Reports by and Submitted to the Committee

Committee Against Torture Consideration of Reports Submitted by States Parties under article 19 of the Convention Third Periodic Reports of States Parties due in 1996 CAT/C/34/add.19 (France) (10 January 2005)

Committee Against Torture, General Comment No 2: Implementation of Article 2 by States Parties (24 January 2008) CAT/C/GC/2

Committee against Torture Report on Argentina UN Doc A/45/44 1990

Concluding Observations on Yugoslavia, Committee Against Torture (1999) UN Doc A/54/44

Consideration of Reports Submitted by States Parties Under Article 19 of the Convention: Conclusions and Recommendations of the Committee Against Torture, UN Doc A/52/44 (5 September 1997)

US Department of State 'Initial Report of the United States of America to the UN Committee Against Torture' (1999)

US Department of State 'Second Periodic Report of the United States of America to the UN Committee Against Torture' 6 (2005)

Committee on Civil and Political Rights

Communication 973/01, *Khalilova v Tadjikistan*, Committee on Civil and Political Rights (18 October 2005)

Communication 124/82, *Muteba v Zaire*, Committee on Civil and Political Rights (24 March 1983)

Communication 28/1978 *Weinberger v Uruguay*, Communication Committee on Civil and Political Rights (29 October 1980)

Table of Treaties and Other Instruments

Additional Protocol to the South Asian Association for Regional Co-operation Regional Convention on Suppression of Terrorism, 2004

African Charter on Human and Peoples' Rights, 1981

American Convention of Human Rights, 1969

American Declaration of the Rights and Duties of Man, 1949

Arab Charter of Human Rights, 2004

Arab Convention for the Suppression of Terrorism, 1998

ASEAN Convention on Counter-Terrorism, 2007

ASEAN Human Rights Declaration, 2012

ASEAN Convention on Counter-Terrorism, 2007

Cairo Declaration on Human Rights in Islam, 1990

Charter of the Organization of American States, 1948

Charter of the United Nations, 1945

Code of Conduct for Law Enforcement Officials, 1979

Common Defence Pact of the African Union, 2005

Commonwealth of Independent States Treaty on Cooperation in Combating Terrorism, 1999

Convention Against Torture and Other Cruel, Inhuman or Degrading Treatment or Punishment, 1984

Convention for the Prevention and Punishment of the Crime of Terrorism, 1937

Convention for the Suppression of Unlawful Acts Against the Safety of Civil Aviation, 1973

Convention on the Suppression of Unlawful Acts Relating to International Civil Aviation (Beijing Convention), 2010

Convention for the Suppression of Unlawful Acts Against the Safety of Maritime Navigation, 1988

Convention for the Suppression of the Unlawful Seizure of Aircraft, 1970

Convention for the Unification of Certain Rules for International Carriage by Air, 1999

Convention of the Cooperation Council for the Arab States of the Gulf on Combating Terrorism, 2008

Convention of the Organization of the Islamic Conference on Combating International Terrorism, 1999

Convention on Offences and Certain Other Acts Committed on Board Aircraft, 1963

Convention on the Prevention and Punishment of Crimes Against Internationally Protected Persons, Including Diplomatic Agents, 1973
Convention on the Prevention and Punishment of the Crime of Genocide, 1948
Convention on the Rights of the Child, 1989
Convention on the Rights of Persons with Disabilities and its Optional Protocol, 1975
Convention Relative to the Treatment of Prisoners of War, 1949
Convention on the Suppression of Unlawful Acts Relating to International Civil Aviation, 2010
Covenant of the League of Nations, 1919
Declaration on the Protection of All Persons from Being Subjected to Torture or Other Cruel, Inhuman or Degrading Treatment or Punishment, 1975
Declaration on the Protection of Women and Children in Emergency and Armed Conflict, 1974
Declaration on the Rights of Mentally Retarded Persons, 1971
Declaration of the Rights of the Child, 1965
Declaration on the Use of Scientific and Technological Progress in the Interests of Peace and for the Benefit of Mankind, 1975
Draft Comprehensive Convention on International Terrorism, 2006
European Convention for the Prevention of Torture and Inhuman or Degrading Treatment or Punishment, 1987
European Convention for the Protection of Human Rights and Fundamental Freedoms, 1950
European Convention on the Suppression of Terrorism (as amended by its Protocol), 1977
European Union Charter of Fundamental Rights, 2000
Fifth Conference for the Unification of Penal Law, 1933
First Conference for the Unification of Penal Law, 1927
Fourth Conference for the Unification of Penal Law, 1931
General Treaty for Renunciation of War as an Instrument of National Policy of 1928 (Kellogg-Briand Pact)
Geneva Conventions, 1949
Inter-American Convention Against Terrorism, 2002
International Convention Against the Taking of Hostages, 1979
International Covenant on Civil and Political Rights, 1966
International Convention on the Elimination of All Forms of Racial Discrimination, 1965
Inter-American Convention to Prevent and Punish Torture, 1985

Law of War Manuals

Mexico Army and Air Force Manual, 2009
New Zealand Military Manual, 1992
Peru International Humanitarian Law Manual, 2004
Sweden's International Humanitarian Law Manual, 1991
UK LOAC Manual, 2004

Abbreviations

ACHR	American Convention on Human Rights
ACHPR	African Commission on Human and Peoples' Rights
ADRDM	American Declaration of the Rights and Duties of Man
AHRLR	African Human Rights Law Reports
All ER	All England Reports
ASEAN	Association of South Asian Nations
AU	African Union
BCLR	Butterworths Constitutional Law Reports
CAT	Convention Against Torture and Other Cruel, Humiliating and Degrading Treatment or Punishment
CCT	Constitutional Court of South Africa
DDC	United States District Court, District of Columbia
DLR	Dominion Law Reports
D Mass	United States District Court. District of Massachusetts
EC	European Commission of Human Rights
ECHR	European Convention of Human Rights
ECtHR	European Court of Human Rights
eKLR	Kenya Law Reports
EWCA	Court of Appeal of England and Wales
EWHC	High Court of England and Wales
HCJ	High Court of Justice (Israel)
HRC	Human Rights Committee
IAm Comm of HR	Inter-American Commission of Human Rights
IACHR	Inter-American Court of Human Rights
ICAO	International Civil Aviation Authority
ICCPR	International Covenant on Civil and Political Rights
ICJ	International Court of Justice
ICTR	International Criminal Tribunal for Rwanda
ICTY	International Criminal Tribunal for the Former Yugoslavia
ILA	International Law Association
ILC	International Law Commission
ILM	International Legal Materials
ILR	International Law Reports
INSC	Supreme Court of India
ISIS	Islamic State of Iraq and Syria
LOAC	Law of Armed Conflict
NSWLR	New South Wales Law Reports

OAU	Organization of African Unity
OIC	Organization of Islamic Countries
PCIJ	Permanent Court of International Justice
QB	Queen's Bench Division
SAARC	South Asian Association for Regional Co-operation
SCR	Supreme Court Reports
SCSL	Special Court for Sierra Leone
SDNY	United States District Court for the Southern District of New York
STL	Special Tribunal for Lebanon
UKHL	United Kingdom, House of Lords
UN	United Nations
UNGA	United Nations General Assembly
UNSC	United Nations Security Council
WLR	Weekly Law Reports
ZASCA	Supreme Court of Appeal of South Africa
ZWHHC	High Court of Zimbabwe

Introduction

> Terrorism has achieved the status of almost universal condemnation, as have slavery, genocide, and piracy, and the terrorist is the modern era's *hosti humani generis* – an enemy of all mankind.[1]

Much like piracy, terrorism is a crime not against one state, but against humanity itself.[2] There is ample evidence of the wide condemnation of terrorism as undermining fundamental human rights as well as the stability of the state and political processes, and threatening international peace and security.[3] The United Nations General Assembly (UNGA) and the United Nations Security Council (UNSC) have both adopted specific resolutions dealing with terrorism.[4] Furthermore, at meetings of the 6th Committee, numerous delegations have in their general statements consistently reaffirmed their strong condemnation of terrorism in all its forms and manifestations.[5] The delegations

1 *Flatow v Islamic Republic of Iran* 999 F Supp 23 (DDC 1998). See further Douglas Burgess, '*Hostis Humani Generi*: Piracy, Terrorism and a New International Law' (2006) 13 University of Miami International and Comparative Law Review 298; Elimma Ezeani, 'The 21st Century Terrorist: *Hostis Humani Generis*?' (2012) 3 Beijing Law Review, 158–169.

2 See, eg, Alfred Rubin, 'The Law of Piracy (2nd edn, Transnational Publishers 1998) 1, 17; Lassa Oppenheim, *International Law: A Treatise*, Vol 1: Peace (2nd edn, Longman Green & Co 1912) 341. Piracy is an international crime: a crime not against one state, nor even all states, but against humanity itself.

3 See, eg, A/RES/60/288 (2006) (The United Nations Global Anti-Terrorism Strategy); S/RES 2249 (2015) (Threats to international peace and security caused by terrorist acts); S/RES 1368, 1373 and 1377 (2001); A/RES/69/127 (2014) and A/RES/69/17 (2014). See further 68th General Assembly Plenary, Reiterating Unequivocal Condemnation of Terrorism in all Forms, General Assembly Adopts Resolution Reaffirming Global Commitment to Combating Threat, 96th and 97th meetings, GA/11523, 13 June 2014 <http://www.un.org/press/en/2014/ga11523.doc.htm> accessed 13 March 2016.

4 See resolutions cited (n 3).

5 Summary Records of the Sixth Committee, 28th meeting *Official Records of the General Assembly*, 69th Session, A/C6/55/SR28, 7 October–14 November 2014, <https://papersmart.unmeetings.org/ga/69th-session/general-debate/statements/> accessed 8 August 2016. See, for example, the statements by Mr GH Dehghani of the Islamic Republic of Iran ('the Non-Aligned Movement condemns terrorism in all its forms and manifestations, wherever, by whoever and against whomsoever committed … which are unjustifiable whatever considera-tons or facts that may be invoked to justify them'); Mr E Zagaynov on behalf of the member states of the Shanghai Co-operation Organisation and the Russian Federation (reiterating the 'fundamental position of condemning terrorism in all its forms and manifestations, regardless of its motivation, whenever, wherever and by whomsoever committed'); Ms E Cujo on behalf of the European Union ('The international community must respond jointly by condemning terrorism in all its forms and manifestations'); Mr T Joyini on behalf of South

 | DOI:10.1163/9789004391543_002

described terrorism as a flagrant violation of international law and a grave threat to international peace and security and declared terrorist acts as being unjustifiable regardless of the reasons invoked by its perpetrators.[6]

The universal condemnation of terrorism gives rise to certain questions. First, has the prohibition of terrorism become a peremptory norm of general international law (*jus cogens*) – a norm accepted and recognized by the international community of states as a norm from which no derogation is permitted? Second, if the prohibition of terrorism has attained such status, what is the implication of this on counter-terrorism efforts by states in support of the prohibition of terrorism, where such measures infringe other *jus cogens* norms? These norms include the prohibition of torture, the right to a fair trial and the prohibition of the use of force under international law.

In the consideration of the questions above, it is noted that although a great deal has been written on both terrorism and *jus cogens* respectively, there is a paucity of literature that comprehensively addresses the role of *jus cogens* in the rules of international law relating to terrorism.[7] While writers have focused

Africa (speaking for the African Group) ('There is no justification for terrorism. African states strongly and unequivocally condemn terrorism in all its forms and manifestations, as well as all acts, methods and practices of terrorism wherever, by whomever, against whomever committed, including state terrorism. For no cause or grievance can terrorism be justified'); Mr A Heumann on behalf of Israel ('Israel wishes to reaffirm its strong commitment to counter terrorism and its uncompromising condemnation of terrorism in all its forms and manifestations, irrespective of its motivations'); See, further, 8th BRICS Summit – Goa Declaration, 16 January 2017, <https://brics2017.org/English/Documents/Summit/201701/t20170125_1410> accessed 26 October 2017, para 57: 'We strongly condemn terrorism in all its forms and manifestations and stress that there can be no justification whatsoever for any acts of terrorism, whether based upon ideological, religious, political, racial, ethnic or any other reasons'; David Pollock and Mohamed Abdelaziz, 'Arab states condemn "terrorist" Paris attacks' <http://english.alarabiya.net/en/News/middle-east/2015/11/14/Arab-states-denounce-Paris-attacks-as-violation-of-human-values-.html> accessed 1 December 2016; US Department of State 'United States Condemns Terrorist Attack on Istanbul's Ataturk Airport' 28 June 2016 <https://al.usembassy.gov/united-states-condemns-terrorist-attack-istanbuls-ataturk-airport/> accessed 7 August 2016; G20 Statement on the Fight Against Terrorism <https://www.consilium.europa.eu/en/press/press-releases/2015/11/16/g20-leaders-antalya-statement-terrorism> accessed 7 August 2016.

6 See statements by states in the sources cited (n 5).

7 Alfred Verdross, 'Forbidden Treaties in International Law: Comments on Professor Garner's Report on "The Law of Treaties"' (1937) 31 American Journal of International Law 571–77; Ulrich Scheuner, 'Conflict of Treaty Provisions with a Peremptory Norm of General International Law' (1969) 29 Zeitschrift für Ausländisches Öffentliches Recht und Völkerrecht 28–38; Gordon A Christenson, '*Jus Cogens*: Guarding Interests Fundamental to International Society' (1987–88) 28 Vanderbilt Journal of International Law 594–648; Stephen Marks, 'Branding the "War on Terrorism": Is there a "New Paradigm" of International Law?' (2006) 14 Michigan State Journal of International Law 71–119; Ben Saul, *Defining Terrorism in International*

on the threat posed by the 'war on terror' to civil liberties and human rights, very little attention has been paid to the idea of *jus cogens* in combating terrorism, including the question of whether the prohibition of terrorism has acquired the status of *jus cogens* and the effect of states' counter-terrorism efforts on other norms of international law which may also constitute *jus cogens* norms.[8]

This book will examine various aspects of international law relevant to terrorism and the relationship of these to the concept of *jus cogens* by means of an evaluation of treaty law, custom (through state practice and *opinio juris*), relevant literature and international jurisprudence.[9] State practice will be considered by analyzing court decisions, statutes, and the practice in connection with treaties and acts in connection with resolutions of organs of international organizations.[10] In respect of *opinio juris*, statements by states will be evaluated.[11] The evaluation will include a consideration of the universal

---

Law (Oxford University Press 2006); Ulf Linderfalk, 'The Effect of *Jus Cogens* Norms: Whoever Opened Pandora's Box, Did You Ever Think About the Consequences?' (2007) 18 European Journal of International Law 853–71; Rosa Pati, *Due Process and International Terrorism: an International Legal Analysis* (Martinus Nijhoff 2009); Thomas Weatherall, 'The Status of the Prohibition of Terrorism in International Law: Recent Developments' (2015) 46 Georgetown Journal of International Law 589–627; *Suresh v Canada* (Minister of Citizenship and Immigration) 1 SCR 3 (2002).

8 Rudolph Dolzer, 'Clouds on the Horizon of Humanitarian Law?' (2003) 28 Yale Journal of International Law 337–40; Joan Fitzpatrick, 'Speaking Law to Power: The War against Terrorism and Human Rights' (2003) 14 European Journal of International Law 241–64.

9 See the Statute of the International Court of Justice, 1946, art 38(1), which defines the sources of international law as follows: '(1) The Court, whose function is to decide in accordance with international law such disputes as are submitted to it, shall apply (a) international conventions, whether general or particular, establishing rules expressly recognized by the contesting states; (b) international custom, as evidence of a general practice accepted as law; (c) the general principles of law recognized by civilized nations; (d) subject to the provisions of Article 59, judicial decisions and the teachings of the most highly qualified publicists of the various nations, as subsidiary means for the determination of rules of law …'.

10 See the ILC Report on the work of the 66th session (2014) (5 May–6 June 2014 and 7 July–8 August 2014), A/69/10 Supplement No 10 240, draft conclusion 7, in terms of which state practice includes 'the conduct of states "on the ground", diplomatic acts and correspondence, legislative acts, judgments of national courts, official publications in the field of international law, statements on behalf of states concerning codification efforts, practice in connection with treaties and acts in connection with resolutions of organs of international organizations and conferences'.

11 See ILC Report (2014), A/69/10 (n 10), draft conclusion 11, noting that the forms of evidence of *opinio juris* (a general practice accepted as law) include, but are not limited to, 'statements by states which indicate what are or are not rules of customary international law, diplomatic correspondence, the jurisprudence of national courts, the opinions of

condemnation of terrorism, questions relating to the possible *jus cogens* status of the prohibition of terrorism and state responses to terrorism in the context of other rules of international law which may also constitute *jus cogens* norms.

This book will not elaborate on issues relating to the responsibility of states for internationally wrongful acts[12] or the consequences of *jus cogens* norms,[13] and will be limited to the prohibition of terrorism in peacetime. It will further exclude institutional aspects relating to the prohibition of terrorism, for example the responses by state military forces to terrorism, arrangements to counteract the financing of terrorism and the mandate and procedures of committees such as the Counter-Terrorism Committee.

This book will be divided into two parts. Part I, in chapters 2 and 3, will explore the prohibition of terrorism under international law, and consider the elements of a definition of terrorism which may have emerged under international law. It will then discuss whether there might be an accepted definition of terrorism under international law, notwithstanding the fact that the international treaty attempting to define terrorism remains unfinalized. Part II, in chapters 4, 5 and 6, will explore the issue of whether the prohibition of terrorism may have led to the limitation of other norms of international law – norms

government legal advisers, official publications in fields of international law, treaty practice and action in connection with resolutions of organs of international organizations and of international conferences. Inaction may also serve as evidence of acceptance as law'.

12 The Geneva Conventions and Protocols deal with international terrorism in conditions of armed conflict, but these fall outside the scope of this book which is limited to a consideration of international terrorism in peace time. See the Geneva Convention Relative to the Protection of Civilian Persons in Time of War, 1949 (Fourth Geneva Convention), arts 4 and 33, in terms of which all measures of intimidation or of terrorism are prohibited. See, also, the Protocol Additional to the Geneva Conventions of 12 August 1949 and Relating to the Protection of Victims of International Armed Conflicts, 1977 (Additional Protocol I) and the Protocol Additional to the Geneva Conventions of 12 August 1949 and Relating to the Protection of Victims of Non-International Armed Conflicts, 1977 (Additional Protocol II). Art 4(1) read with art 4(2)(d) of Additional Protocol II prohibits acts of terrorism against 'all persons who do not take a direct part in or who have ceased to take part in hostilities, whether or not their liberty has been restricted'. Furthermore, art 51(2) of Additional Protocol I and art 13(2) of Additional Protocol II state that '[t]he civilian population as such, as well as individual civilians, shall not be the object of attack. Acts or threats of violence the primary purpose of which is to spread terror among the civilian population are prohibited.' With regard to the application of the Geneva Conventions and Protocols in wartime, see the Fourth Geneva Convention, art 4; Additional Protocol I, arts 1(3) and (4); Additional Protocol II, art 1.

13 For a detailed analysis of the consequence of *jus cogens* norms, see eg Daniel Costelloe, *Legal Consequences of Peremptory Norms in International Law* (Cambridge University Press 2017).

which themselves may constitute norms of *jus cogens,* namely, the prohibition of torture, the right to a fair trial and the prohibition of the use of force. In other words, can states derogate from other norms of *jus cogens* in the fight against terrorism?

In Part I, chapter 2 will provide an overview of the prohibition of terrorism under international law from 50 AD, through the French Revolution, to acts of terrorism in the twentieth century. It will consider the various attempts to define terrorism through the ages, including at international conferences for the unification of penal law in the 1920s and 1930s and in the 1937 Convention for the Prevention and Punishment of the Crime of Terrorism, which never entered into force. It will furthermore consider how terrorism acquired an international element and discuss the continuing worldwide escalation in incidents of terrorism. Chapter 2 will further analyze the elements of terrorism having emerged under treaty law, UNSC resolutions and international jurisprudence as well as the yet-to-be-finalized draft Comprehensive Convention on International Terrorism. It will evaluate as state practice, national legislation and the approach of national courts in prohibiting and defining the offence of terrorism. On the basis of the analysis, this chapter will then consider whether a definition of international terrorism has emerged under customary international law notwithstanding the lack of an international treaty definition of terrorism. This analysis is important as, in terms of article 53 of the Vienna Convention on the Law of Treaties (Vienna Convention),[14] one of the criteria for a *jus cogens* norm is that, in the first instance, it is a norm of general international law, and general international law includes customary international law.

Chapter 3 will deal with the question of whether the prohibition of terrorism is a *jus cogens* norm. In order to address this question, this chapter will consider whether the prohibition of terrorism meets the criteria to enable a norm of general international law to be elevated to a norm of *jus cogens* as set out in article 53 of the Vienna Convention. Article 53 stipulates that a peremptory norm of general international law (*jus cogens*) is 'a norm accepted and recognized by the international community of states as a whole as a norm from which no derogation is permitted and which can be modified only by a subsequent norm of general international law having the same character'. In addition, it will consider whether the prohibition of terrorism meets the characteristics of *jus cogens* norms which may have emerged under international law, namely, that they protect the fundamental values of the international community, are hierarchically superior and are universally applicable.

14 The Vienna Convention on the Law of Treaties, 1969.

Part II will discuss whether counter-terrorism measures are consistent with certain other norms of international law which may be infringed during the fight against terrorism. In this regard, it will consider the effect of the prohibition of terrorism as a possible *jus cogens* norm on certain norms of international law which themselves may have attained *jus cogens* status. The analysis will evaluate whether the prohibition of terrorism as a *jus cogens* norm allows for any derogation by states from such norms, namely, the prohibition of torture, the right to a fair trial and the prohibition of the use of force during counter-terrorism measures.

Chapter 4 will discuss the prohibition of torture in the context of anti-terrorism measures. It will analyze the elements of torture under international law, as well as consider whether the prohibition of torture is a *jus cogens* norm. It will first consider which conduct constitutes torture in order to evaluate whether certain conduct, as part of counter-terrorism measures, amounts to torture. In this regard, the various elements of the definition of torture that have emerged under international law will be considered, including elements that have emerged from the widely-ratified UN Convention Against Torture and Other Cruel, Inhuman or Degrading Treatment or Punishment of 1984 (CAT) and customary international law. Additionally, this section will discuss whether torture in itself may constitute a *jus cogens* norm with reference to the criteria for *jus cogens* norms as discussed in chapter 3, as well as whether the prohibition of torture meets the characteristics of *jus cogens* norms as may have emerged under international law. Finally, it will consider the interaction between the prohibition of terrorism and the prohibition of torture and whether there can there be any balancing of the rights underlying these norms. In this regard, it will consider whether any limitation of the prohibition of torture can be justified during counter-terrorism measures.

Chapter 5 will analyze the right to a fair trial in the context of terrorism. Although the right to a fair trial consists of various elements, it will be argued that not all these elements are non-derogable and that there are certain core, non-derogable elements of the right to a fair trial. These core elements will be proposed as constituting core fair trial guarantees, namely, the right to a fair hearing, the presumption of innocence and the right to review. The chapter will then consider whether these rights may have attained *jus cogens* status under international law with reference to the criteria as set out in article 53 of the Vienna Convention. It will further be considered whether these norms exhibit the characteristics of *jus cogens* norms. Finally, the chapter will consider whether any limitation of core fair trial rights may be allowed in the context of counter-terrorism measures. This will be considered in light of the underlying values protected by the prohibition of terrorism as well as by the core fair trial rights under discussion.

Chapter 6 will contemplate the prohibition of the use of force in the context of anti-terrorism measures. It will provide a brief overview of the use of force as a *jus cogens* norm and, in particular, will consider which uses of force are *jus cogens* and whether the threat of the use of force and the right to self-defence are *jus cogens* norms. It will then discuss the requirements for the use of force in self-defence and consider issues such as what constitutes an armed attack;, when the acts of a non-state actor such as a terrorist are atrributable to a state; and the requirements for necessity and proportionality of the use of force under customary international law. Finally, it will consider whether the prohibition of terrorism as a *jus cogens* norm has led to a less restrictive interpretation of the requirements for using armed force in self-defence. In other words, it will debate whether the prohibition of terrorism as a *jus cogens* norm has resulted in a reduction in the scope of the prohibition of the use of force and a relaxation of the requirements of necessity and proportionality for the use of armed force in self-defence. It will further consider whether the prohibition of terrorism as a *jus cogens* norm has resulted in a reconsideration of the requirements for an act to constitute an armed attack and a possible lowering of the threshold to attribute the acts of non-state actors such as terrorists to a state.

In conclusion, this book will consider whether terrorism indeed has emerged as the *jus cogens* norm of our time and whether counter-terrorism measures may be imposed that limit other norms of international law, which may similarly enjoy *jus cogens* status, in support of the prohibition of terrorism. These questions are important in light of the escalating incidences of terrorism and the increasing efforts by the international community to eradicate them.

PART 1

CHAPTER 1

The Prohibition of Terrorism under International Law

1 Introduction

After the attacks of 11 September 2001 (9/11), the UNSC declared acts of international terrorism to be 'one of the most serious threats to international peace and security in the twenty-first century'.[1] The events of 9/11 arguably represented a 'Grotian moment'. In homage to Grotius as the father of international law, a Grotian moment is described by writers as a great leap forward in the field of international law or a paradigm-shifting development resulting in new rules of customary international law emerging with less state practice and with unusual rapidity and acceptance.[2] The events of 9/11 would indeed lead to fundamental changes in the response by the international community to international terrorism and the accelerated development of the rules of customary international law relating to the prohibition of international terrorism. In the years since 9/11, various UNGA and UNSC resolutions have supported the condemnation of terrorism. As an example, in 2014 numerous delegations reaffirmed their strong condemnation of terrorism and described terrorism as a flagrant violation of international law and a grave threat to international peace and security. Furthermore, acts of terrorism were declared unjustifiable regardless of the reasons invoked by their perpetrators.[3]

This book seeks to evaluate the role of *jus cogens* in the rules of international law relating to terrorism. This chapter discusses the prohibition of terrorism under international law. It will start with a brief history of the prohibition in section 2, followed by a study of how international terrorism is prohibited under treaties, UNSC resolutions and customary international law in section 3. On the basis of this analysis, section 4 will consider whether certain core elements of a definition of terrorism have emerged under international law. Discussions

---

1 S/RES 1377 (2001) (Threats to International Peace and Security Caused by Terrorist Acts).

2 Mathew Lyons, 'The Grotian Moment: Hugo Grotius and the Invention of International Law' <https://mathewlyons.wordpress.com/2011/10/12/the-grotian-moment-hugo-grotius-and-the-invention-of-international-law/> accessed 30 December 2016; Michael P Scharf, 'Seizing the "Grotian moment": Accelerated Formation of Customary International Law in Times of Fundamental Change' (2010) 43 Cornell International Law Journal 440.

3 See statements by states in the sources cited (Introduction, n 5).

 | DOI:10.1163/9789004391543_003

in the Sixth Committee and the *Ad Hoc* Committee on International Terrorism will further be considered. In conclusion, section 5 will attempt to determine whether in fact a substantive definition of international terrorism under international law has emerged.

2 A Brief History of the Prohibition of Terrorism under International Law

Terrorist activities have existed 'since the beginning of humanity'.[4] Perpetrators of the Jewish resistance to Roman rule in 50 AD, the so-called *sicariis*, have been described as the first terrorists.[5] The *sicariis* used short daggers to kill other Jews who were seen to be collaborating with Roman rule in crowded places before slipping away, causing terror among onlookers.[6] The English word 'terrorism' has its origins in state-perpetrated violence committed as part of the Reign of Terror during the French Revolution. When Robespierre ordered the public execution of 17 000 people who were considered a threat to the revolutionary government, his own supporters, in an attempt to identify the illegitimate use of terror, accused him of terrorism.[7] The word 'terrorism' made its first official appearance four years after the fall of Robespierre, in the *Dictionnaire de l'Académie Française* in 1798. It was defined as a system or regime of terror, and a terrorist was defined as an agent or supporter of the regime of terror.[8]

Although terrorism was initially associated with state-perpetrated violence, such as that committed during the Reign of Terror, the term was used in the mid-nineteenth century to include acts by non-state actors. This included

4 Arnold Amet, 'Terrorism and International Law: Cure the Underlying Problem, Not Just the Symptom' (2013) 19 Annual Survey of International and Comparative Law 17.

5 Richard Horsley, 'The Sicarii: Ancient Jewish "Terrorists"' (1979) 59 Journal of Religion 435–58; Morton Smith, 'Zealots and Sicarii: Their Origins and Relation' (1971) 64 Harvard Theologocal Review 1–19.

6 Ibid.

7 Alex Schmid, 'The Problems of Defining Terrorism' in Martha Crenshaw and John Pimlott (eds), *Encyclopedia of World Terrorism* (ME Sharpe 1997) vol 12, 13.

8 *Dictionnaire de l'Académie Française* online, (9th edn, 1798) <http://portail.atilf.fr/cgi-bin/getobject_?p.16:40./var/artfla/dicos/ACAD_1798/IMAGE/> accessed 1 January 2017. The dictionary contains the following definitions: '*terrorisme … [s]ystème, régime de la terreur. Voyez Terroriste*' (terrorism … system, regime of terror. See terrorist (own translation)); and '[*t*]*erroriste … [ag]ent ou partisan du régime de la Terreur qui avoit lieu par l'abus des mesures révolutionnaires*' (terrorist … agent or supporter of a regime of terror which has occurred by means of the abuse of revolutionary measures (own translation)).

the terrorist acts by French and Russian anarchists in their opposition to the existence of the state.[9] In the early twentieth century, acts of terrorism by non-state actors continued, including the Wall Street bombing of 1920.[10] Additional examples of terrorism as state-perpetrated violence were Stalin's ruling of Russia by terror, Germany's Nazi regime in the 1930s and 1940s, and the 'terror bombings' by German and Allied forces during World War II.[11]

Attempts were made to describe terrorism during various conferences in the early twentieth century, although what precisely constituted 'terrorism' could ultimately not be agreed upon. In particular, debates undertaken under the aegis of the International Conferences for the Unification of Penal Law and the League of Nations in the late 1920s and early 1930s situated terrorism in the vocabulary of international law, stating that it was an offence under international law.[12] The first international conference for the unification of criminal law was organized in Warsaw in 1927 by the Polish Commission for International Juridical Cooperation.[13] A number of topics in the field of international law were discussed at the conference.[14] In particular, the conference declared as a list of offences against the law of nations (offences *delicta juris gentium*), together with offences such as slavery and piracy, 'the intentional use of any instrument capable of producing a public danger' (*l'emploi intentionnel de tous moyens capables de faire courir un danger commun*) in respect of which the principle of universal jurisdiction applied.[15]

---

9 Ersel Aydinli, 'Before Jihadists There Were Anarchists: A Failed Case of Transnational Violence' (2008) 31 Studies in Conflict and Terrorism 903, 913.

10 Paul Avrich, *Anarchist Voices: An Oral History of Anarchism in America* (Princeton University Press 1996) 13–33.

11 See, further, Robert Conquest, *The Great Terror: Stalin's Purge of the Thirties* (MacMillan 1968) 3, 251. Note that this book will not deal with the prohibition of international terrorism in times of war, which is regulated by international humanitarian law, but only with the prohibition of international terrorism in peacetime. See Michael Walzer, *Just and Unjust Wars: A Moral Argument with Historical Illustrations* (3 edn, Basic Books 2000) 198; Igor Primoratz, 'Terrorism' in Edward Zalta (ed) *Stanford Encyclopedia of Philosophy* (2007) <https://plato.stanford.edu> accessed 16 November 2016.

12 Daniel Segesser and Myriam Gessler, 'Raphael Lemkin and the International Debate on the Punishment of War Crimes (1919–1948)' (2005) 7 Journal of Genocide Research 453–68. See, also, the First Conference for the Unification of Penal Law, 1927; the Third Conference for the Unification of Penal Law, 1930; the Fourth Conference for the Unification of Penal Law, 1931; the Fifth Conference for the Unification of Penal Law, 1933.

13 Segesser and Gessler (ibid.) 456.

14 Ibid., 457. See, further, 'Association Internationale de Droit Pénal' (1928) 5 Revue Internationale de Droit Pénal <http://gallica.bnf.fr/ark:12148/bpt6k12550937.textelimage> accessed 9 August 2017, 1.

15 Raphael Lemkin, 'Les Actes Constituant un Danger Général Interétatique Consideres Comme Delits du Droit des Gens' in Manuel López-Rey (ed), *Actes de la Vème Conférence*

The issue of the intentional use of instruments capable of producing public danger was again discussed at the international conferences for the unification of criminal law which followed the 1927 conference, held in Brussels in 1930 and in Paris in 1931.[16] During the Third Conference for the Unification of Criminal Law in Brussels in 1930, the word 'terrorism' was added in brackets after the reference to the use of an instrument capable of producing a public danger.[17] This was supported by some delegates from Eastern European countries, but it was opposed by Raphael Lemkin, who believed that the use of an instrument capable of producing a public danger should not be restricted to terrorism.[18] No agreement could be reached with regard to the wording.

Another attempt at the codification of the crime of terrorism was made in 1937 with the Convention for the Prevention and Punishment of the Crime of Terrorism, which did not enter into force owing to a lack of ratifications.[19] This Convention specifically referred to acts of terrorism as criminal acts directed against a state with the intent to create a state of terror in the minds of particular persons, a group of persons or the general public.[20] States were required to criminalize terrorist offences and encouraged to exclude these offences from any political offence exception in respect of extradition.[21]

More than a decade later, in 1949, following the horrors of World War II, the Geneva Conventions and their Additional Protocols specifically prohibited and criminalized terrorism and acts of terror against civilians committed in armed conflict, again without defining terrorism.[22] During the 1950s and 1960s,

Internationale pour l' Unification du Droit Pénal (Madrid 14–20 Octobre 1933) (A Pedone 1934) 48–56.

16 Segesser and Gessler (n 12) 457.

17 Amet (n 4) 29. Third Conference for the Codification of Penal Law, 1930.

18 Segesser and Gessler (n 12).

19 The Convention for the Prevention and Punishment of Terrorism 1937, art 1(2), League of Nations Official Journal (1934) 23–34.

20 Ibid.

21 Ibid., annex I 5.

22 The Geneva Conventions and Protocols deal with international terrorism in conditions of armed conflict. This falls outside the scope of this book, which is limited to a consideration of international terrorism in peacetime. See arts 4 and 33 of the Fourth Geneva Convention, 1949, in terms of which all measures of intimidation or of terrorism are prohibited. See also Additional Protocol I and Additional Protocol II to the Geneva Conventions. Art 4(1) read with art 4(2)(d) of Additional Protocol II prohibits acts of terrorism against 'all persons who do not take a direct part or who have ceased to take part in hostilities, whether or not their liberty has been restricted'. Further, art 51(2) of Additional Protocol I and art 13(2) of Additional Protocol II state that '[t]he civilian population as such, as well as individual civilians, shall not be the object of attack. Acts or threats of violence the primary purpose of which is to spread terror among the civilian population

terrorism began to acquire an international element. Terrorists took advantage of new technologies, and the hijacking of civilian aircraft by violent non-state actors became relatively common.[23] In addition to this, hijackings started to acquire the element of a specific political purpose which would come to characterize terrorist acts.[24] An example of this was in 1968 when gunmen from the Popular Front for the Liberation of Palestine hijacked an Israeli El Al passenger airliner on a flight from Rome to Tel-Aviv and demanded the release of hostages in exchange for their comrades imprisoned in Israel.[25]

Acts of terrorism continued to escalate with the 1988 bombing of Pan Am Flight 103 over Lockerbie, Scotland, which killed 270 persons, marking one of the most horrific acts of terrorism before 9/11.[26] In requiring Libya to comply with the requests for the extradition of the bombing suspects, the UNSC noted its deep concern with regard to international terrorism.[27] After the attacks of 9/11, it became evident that international terrorism had become 'a grave and growing global threat to international peace and security in the twenty-first century'.[28]

The rise of terrorism in Africa has seen the Islamist militant group Boko Haram carry out attacks on civilians as well as suicide bomb attacks in Nigeria.[29] There were further attacks in 2017 by the al Qaeda-affiliated al Shabaab terrorist group in Southern Somalia, including an attack on an African Union (AU) convoy in July 2017.[30] Al Shabaab also carried out terror attacks in Kenya, which

are prohibited.' With regard to the application of the Geneva Conventions and Protocols in wartime, see art 4 of the Fourth Geneva Convention; arts 1(3) and (4) of Additional Protocol I and art 1 of Additional Protocol II.

23 Alona Evans, 'Aircraft Hijacking: Its Cause and Cure' (1969) 63 American Journal of International Law 695, 697–98.

24 Jangir Arasly, 'Terrorism and Civil Aviation Security: Problems and Trends' (2005) The Quarterly Journal 75.

25 Agus Pramono, 'Aircraft Hijacking: A Legal Perspective (2014) 43 Masalah-Masalah Hukum <http://download.portalgaruda.org/article> accessed 9 August 2017, 487, 491.

26 Steve Emerson, 'The Lockerbie Terrorist Attack and Libya: A Retrospective Analysis' (2004) 36 Case Western Reserve Journal of International Law 487; 'Lockerbie: The 270 Victims' *Al Jazeera* <http://www.aljazeera.com/programmes/lockerbie/2014/03/lockerbie-270-victims-201431075240135389.html> accessed 9 August 2017.

27 S/RES/748 (1992) on Libya.

28 See S/RES/1377 (2001).

29 'At Least 11 Civilians Killed in Boko Haram Attack' *Al Jazeera* (1 October 2017) <http://www.aljazeera.com/news/2017/09/11-civilians-killed-boko-haram-attack-170902043943431.html> accessed 9 August 2017.

30 Ruchita Beri, *Rise of Terrorism in Africa* Institute for Defence Studies and Analyses <http://www.idsa.in/idsacomments/rise-of-terrorism-in-africa_rberi_130417> accessed 1 October 2017; 'Al-Shabab Fighters Attack African Union Convoy in Southern Somalia, Killing At Least 8' *Fox News* <http://www.foxnews.com/world/2017/07/30/

included the beheading of men in villages and the killing of policemen.[31] In Europe, terror attacks continued to increase with stabbing attacks and suicide bombings in 2016, perpetrated by assailants who had sworn allegiance to the Islamic State of Iraq and Syria (ISIS).[32] In March 2016, at least 34 people were killed and 190 wounded when three blasts shook Brussels, two at an airport and one on a subway. ISIS claimed responsibility.[33] In July 2016, two men stormed a French church in Normandy, France, took five people hostage and murdered an elderly priest by stabbing him in the chest and slitting his throat. This attack was carried out in the name of ISIS.[34] In addition, in July 2016, on Bastille Day, a truck deliberately plowed into a large crowd of people celebrating in Nice, France, killing 84 people and injuring hundreds. It was later claimed that the assailant had been radicalized by ISIS.[35]

In November 2016 a coordinated string of attacks (bombings and mass shootings) took place at a soccer stadium and a popular live music venue in Paris. Close to 130 people were killed and scores more injured. ISIS assumed responsibility.[36] In 2017, an attack in London left seven people dead and 48 injured when a van hit pedestrians on London Bridge before three men exited the vehicle and began stabbing people in a nearby market. Furthermore, an attack in Manchester left 22 people dead and 59 injured after a suicide bomber had targeted children and young adults at a concert by US singer Ariana Grande at the Manchester Arena.[37] Terrorism continues to be an issue of global concern.

3 The Status of the Prohibition of Terrorism

As discussed above, terrorism has faced widespread political condemnation. This section considers the prohibition of terrorism under international law as evidenced by various anti-terrorism treaties, UNSC resolutions and customary international law. It will further consider issues relating to the lack

al-shabab-fighters-attack-african-union-convoy-in-southern-somalia-killing-at-least-8.html> accessed 1 October 2017.

31 'Kenya: Nine Beheaded in Suspected Al-Shabab Attack' *Al Jazeera* <http://www.aljazeera.com/news/2017/07/kenya-attack-170708103555604.html> accessed 1 October 2017.

32 'A Timeline of Recent Terror Attacks in Europe' *Time Magazine* <http://time.com/4607481/europe-terrorism-timeline-berlin-paris-nice-brussels/> accessed 1 October 2017.

33 Ibid.

34 Ibid.

35 Ibid.

36 'London Bridge Attack: Timeline of British Terror Attacks' BBC NEWS <http://www.bbc.com/news/uk-40013040> accessed 1 October 2017.

37 Ibid.

of a universally agreed-upon definition of terrorism. Chapter 3 will consider whether the prohibition of terrorism has attained the status of *jus cogens*.

3.1 *Rules Prohibiting Terrorism Emanating from Treaty Law*

Various provisions in treaty law prohibit acts of terrorism and place obligations on states to prevent terrorism. In this regard, numerous international treaties and protocols were concluded during the period between 1963 and 2005 criminalizing certain terrorist conduct.[38] These treaties and protocols define offences relating to specific conduct, ranging from crimes against the person, civil aviation, shipping or continental platforms to crimes involving the use, possession or threatened use of bombs or nuclear materials and crimes concerning the financing of terrorism.[39] All these treaties and protocols follow a 'sectoral' approach. This means that they do not define international terrorism in general, but rather address particular acts of terrorism, such as acts of violence on board an aircraft and its unlawful seizure; unlawful acts against the safety of maritime navigation; the taking of hostages; terrorist bombings; the financing of terrorism; and nuclear terrorism.[40] Treaties adopted from the late 1990s include a specific intent, for example, the intent to cause death or serious bodily injury to a civilian or extensive destruction that is likely to result in major economic loss with the purpose of intimidating a population or compelling a government or an international organization to perform or to abstain from performing any act.[41]

Although the terrorist conduct in question differs in accordance with the treaty concerned, common prohibitions are contained in the various sectoral treaties. These prohibitions involve intentional acts of violence with an

---

38 The Convention on Offences and Certain Other Acts Committed on Board Aircraft, 1963 (Tokyo Convention); the International Convention Against the Taking of Hostages, 1979 (Hostages Convention); the Convention for the Suppression of Unlawful Acts Against the Safety of Maritime Navigation, 1988 (Maritime Safety Convention); the International Convention for the Suppression of Terrorist Bombings, 1997 (Terrorist Bombings Convention); the Convention for the Unification of Certain Rules for International Carriage by Air, 1999 (Montreal Convention); the International Convention for the Suppression of the Financing of Terrorism, 1999 (Terrorism Financing Convention); the International Convention for the Suppression of Acts of Nuclear Terrorism, 2005 (Nuclear Terrorism Convention). See further discussion in sec 3.1 of ch 2.

39 Ibid.

40 Ibid.; the Tokyo Convention; the Hostages Convention; the Maritime Safety Convention; the Terrorist Bombings Convention; the Montreal Convention; the Terrorism Financing Convention; the Nuclear Terrorism Convention.

41 Art 2 of the Nuclear Terrorism Convention (ibid.); art 2 of the Terrorism Financing Convention (ibid.); art 2 of the Terrorist Bombings Convention (ibid.).

international dimension that endanger or attempt to endanger the safety of an aircraft, ship or person, or attempt to do so.[42] The various anti-terrorism treaties further place an obligation on states to incorporate the proscribed crimes into their domestic criminal law and to make such crimes punishable

42 See, for example, art 3 of the Maritime Safety Convention (n 38): ('Any person commits an offence if that person unlawfully and intentionally (a) seizes or exercises control over a ship by force or threat thereof or any other form of intimidation; or (b) performs an act of violence against a person on board a ship if that act is likely to endanger the safe navigation of that ship; or (c) destroys a ship or causes damage to a ship or its cargo which is likely to endanger the safe navigation of that ship; or (d) places or causes to be placed, by any means whatsoever, a device or substance which is likely to destroy that ship, or cause damage to a ship or its cargo which endangers or is likely to endanger the safe navigation of that ship; or (e) destroys or seriously damages maritime navigational facilities or seriously interferes with their operation, if any such act is likely to endanger the safe navigation of that ship; or (f) communicates information which he knows to be false, thereby endangering the safe navigation of that ship; or (g) injures or kills any person, in connection with the commission or attempted commission of any of the offences set forth in subparagraphs (a) to (f)).' Art 4(1) of the Maritime Safety Convention (n 38) provides that '[t]his Convention applies if the ship is navigating or is scheduled to navigate into, through or from waters beyond the outer limit of the territorial limit of a single state, or the lateral limits of its territorial sea with adjacent states'. Art 1 of the Convention for the Suppression of Unlawful Seizure of Aircraft, 1970 (Hague Convention) provides that '[a]ny person who on board an aircraft in flight (a) unlawfully, by force or threat thereof, or by any other form of intimidation, seizes, or exercises control of, that aircraft, or attempts to perform any such act … commits an offence'; art 3 of the Hague Convention states that '[t]his Convention shall apply only if the place of take-off or the place of actual landing of the aircraft on board which the offence is committed is situated outside the territory of the state of registration of that aircraft'. Art 1 of the Montreal Convention (n 38) states that '[a]ny person commits an offence if he unlawfully and intentionally (a) performs an act of violence against a person on board an aircraft in flight if that act is likely to endanger the safety of that aircraft; or (b) destroys an aircraft in service or causes damage to such an aircraft which renders it incapable of flight or which is likely to endanger its safety in flight; or (c) places or causes to be placed on an aircraft in service, by any means whatsoever, a device or substance which is likely to destroy that aircraft, or to cause damage to it which renders it incapable of flight, or to cause damage to it which is likely to endanger its safety in flight; or (d) destroys or damages air navigation facilities or interferes with their operation, if any such act is likely to endanger the safety of aircraft in flight; or (e) communicates information which he knows to be false, thereby endangering the safety of an aircraft in flight'. Art 4(2) of the Montreal Convention provides that the Convention 'shall apply, irrespective of whether the aircraft is engaged in an international or domestic flight, only if (a) the place of take-off or landing, actual or intended, of the aircraft is situated outside the territory of the state of registration of that aircraft; or (b) the offence is committed in the territory of a state other than the state of registration of the aircraft'.

by penalties commensurate with the gravity of the offence.[43] In addition to this, the treaties provide for universal jurisdiction over the proscribed terrorist offences and oblige state parties to extradite or prosecute any suspected offenders found in their territory.[44] In its 2014 report on the obligation to extradite or prosecute, the International Law Commission (ILC) points out that the 'Hague formula' with regard to extradition or prosecution is a variation of similar provisions in the Geneva Conventions and 'has served as a model for several subsequent conventions aimed at the suppression of specific offences, principally in the fight against terrorism'.[45]

In addition, the sectoral anti-terrorist treaties provide that terrorism under no circumstances is justifiable by any political, philosophical, ideological, racial, ethnic, religious or other considerations.[46] The treaties further provide

43 See for example Conventions (n 38): art 3 of the Montreal Convention; art 4 of the Terrorist Bombings Convention; art 4 of the Terrorist Financing Convention; art 6 of the Nuclear Terrorism Convention; art 2 of the Hostages Convention. See further art 2 of the Hague Convention (n 42); art 2(2) of the Convention on the Prevention and Punishment of Crimes against Internationally Protected Persons including Diplomatic Agents, 1973.

44 See, for example, art 7 of the Hague Convention (n 42) and art 7 of the Montreal Convention (n 38), which contain the same wording, namely, '[t]he Contracting State in the territory of which the alleged offender is found shall, if it does not extradite him, be obliged, without exception whatsoever and whether or not the offence was committed in its territory, to submit the case to its competent authorities for the purpose of prosecution'. Art 8(1) of the Terrorist Bombings Convention (n 38) similarly states that '[t]he state party in the territory of which the alleged offender is present shall … if it does not extradite that person, be obliged, without exception whatsoever and whether or not the offence was committed in its territory, to submit the case without undue delay to its competent authorities for the purpose of prosecution, through proceedings in accordance with the laws of that state'. Art 10(1) of the Terrorist Financing Convention and art 11(1) of the Nuclear Terrorism Convention mirror the wording of art 8(1) of the Terrorist Bombings Convention. See further art 7 of the Convention on the Prevention and Punishment of Crimes against Internationally Protected Persons (n 43), art 8 of the Hostages Convention (n 38) and art 10 of the Maritime Safety Convention (n 38), which provide for the state in which the offender is found to extradite or proscute the offender.

45 The obligation to extradite or prosecute (*aut dedere aut judicare*) Final Report of the International Law Commission (2014) Yearbook of the International Law Commission vol II (part 2) 5.

46 See for example Preamble and art 6 of the Nuclear Terrorism Convention (n 38). The Preamble recalls 'the Declaration on Measures to Eliminate International Terrorism annexed to General Assembly Resolution 49/60 of 9 December 1994, in which, among others, the member states of the United Nations solemnly reaffirm their unequivocal condemnation of 'all acts, methods and practices of terrorism as criminal and unjustifiable, wherever and by whomever committed, including those which jeopardize the friendly relations among states and peoples and threaten the territorial integrity and security of states'. Art 6(1) states that '[e]ach state party shall adopt such measures as may be necessary, including, where appropriate, domestic legislation, to ensure that

that, in order to facilitate extradition, terrorist offences are not to be considered political offences (which are generally not extraditable under extradition treaties).[47] An analysis of the various sectoral anti-terrorism treaties illustrates how the development of prohibited offences evolved in response to increasingly sophisticated and diverse terrorist attacks. The Tokyo Convention was the first international treaty on aviation security and applied to acts that were already offences under penal law or acts that jeopardized the good order and discipline on board or the safety of the aircraft or of persons or property thereon.[48] The Tokyo Convention of 1963 was limited in application: It focused on 'unruly' passengers and did not expressly make the unlawful seizure of an aircraft an offence. The Hague Convention, however, adopted by the International Civil Aviation Organization (ICAO) seven years later, made the unlawful seizure or threat of seizure of an aircraft by threat or intimidation an offence.[49] This Convention also had its shortcomings, as it failed to address aircraft sabotage. Aircraft sabotage was subsequently criminalized in the Montreal Convention, which made it an offence to unlawfully and intentionally perform an act of violence which is likely to endanger the safety of the aircraft in flight, including causing damage to the aircraft and interfering with its operation.[50] The Hague and Montreal Conventions further required state parties to provide one another with the greatest measure of assistance with regard to criminal proceedings brought in respect of these offences.[51]

In 2010 the Convention on the Suppression of Unlawful Acts Relating to International Civil Aviation (Beijing Convention) and the Protocol Supplementary to the Convention for the Suppression of Unlawful Seizure of Aircraft (Beijing Protocol) were adopted.[52] The aforementioned conven-

---

criminal acts within the scope of this Convention, in particular where they are intended or calculated to provoke a state of terror in the general public or in a group of persons or particular persons, are under no circumstances justifiable by considerations of a political, philosophical, ideological, racial, ethnic, religious or other similar nature and are punished by penalties consistent with their grave nature'. Similar wording is contained in the Preamble and art 6 of the Terrorism Financing Convention (n 38) and the Preamble and art 5 of the Terrorist Bombings Convention (n 38).

47 See Conventions cited in n 38: arts 5 and 11 of the Terrorist Bombings Convention; arts 6 and 14 of the Terrorist Financing Convention; arts 6 and 15 of the Nuclear Terrorism Convention. See further arts 6 and 15 of the Draft Comprensive Convention against Terrorism, 2006.

48 Art 1 of the Tokyo Convention (n 38).

49 Art 1 of the Hague Convention (n 42).

50 Art 1 of the Montreal Convention (n 38).

51 Art 10 of the Hague Convention (n 42); art 11 of the Montreal Convention (n 38).

52 See the Convention on the Suppression of Unlawful Acts Relating to International Civil Aviation (Beijing Convention) 2010.

tion and protocol are not yet in force, and will not be discussed in detail. Nevertheless, these instruments are of interest in illustrating the progression in the proposed criminalization of new terrorist offences. For instance, the Beijing Convention criminalizes the use of devices, substances or weapons that endanger the safety of an airport; communicating false information which endangers the safety of an aircraft; using an aircraft to discharge biological, chemical or nuclear (BCN) weapons; releasing from an aircraft in service any BCN weapon or explosive, radioactive, or similar substance; or threats of or attempting, organizing or being an accomplice to any of the former.[53] It further criminalizes the use of an aircraft itself to cause death or serious injury (as was the case with 9/11).[54]

In 1996 the UNGA established an *Ad Hoc* Committee to draft international conventions for the suppression of terrorist bombings and acts of nuclear terrorism, to supplement related existing international instruments and to address means of further developing a comprehensive legal framework of conventions dealing with international terrorism.[55] The *Ad Hoc* Committee negotiated various texts which resulted in the adoption of three treaties: the International Convention for the Suppression of Terrorist Bombings (Terrorist Bombings Convention); the International Convention for the Suppression of Financing of Terrorism (Terrorist Financing Convention); and the International Convention for the Suppression of Acts of Nuclear Terrorism (Nuclear Terrorism Convention).[56]

Unlike the Tokyo, Hague and Montreal Conventions (Aviation Security Conventions), the Terrorist Bombings, Terrorist Financing and Nuclear Terrorism Conventions made explicit reference to the word 'terrorism', although none of the conventions defined the term. For instance, the treaties set out the aim of enhancing international cooperation among states to prevent certain acts of terrorism.[57] The Terrorist Bombings Convention makes it

53 Art 1 of the Beijing Convention (n 52).

54 Ibid.

55 A/RES/51/210 (1996) regarding *ad hoc* and special committees established on the Recommendation of the Sixth Committee <http://legal.un.org/committees/terrorism/> (accessed 6 January 2016). This was the second *ad hoc* committee established by the UNGA. The first *ad hoc* committee on international terrorism was established by the UNGA in 1972 (A/3034 (XXVII). This book will discuss the work of the second *ad hoc* committee responsible for the Draft Comprehensive Convention on Terrorism (1996).

56 See Conventions cited in n 38: The Terrorist Bombings Convention; the Terrorism Financing Convention; the Nuclear Terrorism Convention.

57 See the respective Preambles of the Terrorist Bombings Convention; the Terrorist Financing Convention; and the Nuclear Terrorism Convention. The preambles to these conventions contained similar wording, noting the deep concern of state parties over the

an offence for any person to unlawfully and intentionally place or detonate explosives in a public place, a state or government facility with the intent to cause death or serious bodily injury, or extensive destruction likely to result in major economic loss.[58] The Terrorism Financing Convention states that any person commits an offence who provides or collects funds with the intention that these should be used to carry out an act intended to cause death or serious bodily injury to a civilian.[59] The purpose of such an act is stipulated as being to intimidate a population or to compel a government or an international organization to do or to abstain from doing any act.[60] The Nuclear Terrorism Convention makes it an offence to possess nuclear material with the intent of causing death or serious bodily injury, causing substantial damage to property or to the environment or compelling a natural or legal person, an international organization or a state to do or refrain from doing any act.[61]

The Terrorist Bombings, Terrorism Financing and Nuclear Terrorism Conventions further require state parties to establish jurisdiction over, and make punishable under their domestic laws, the offences proscribed, and to extradite or prosecute persons accused of committing or aiding in the commission of these offences.[62] The conventions confirm that the political offence exception does not apply and that terrorism under no circumstances is justifiable.[63] The Terrorism Financing Convention contains the most specific obligations on states to take certain measures to combat terrorism. It requires state parties to take steps to prevent and counteract the financing of terrorists, to cooperate in preventing such financing, to hold legal persons and individuals who finance terrorism liable and to freeze assets and seize funds allocated for terrorist activities.[64]

---

worldwide escalation in acts of terrorism in all its forms and manifestations, and recalling all the UNGA resolutions on the matter in which the member states of the UN 'solemnly reaffirmed their unequivocal condemnation of all acts, methods and practices of terrorism as criminal and unjustifiable, wherever and by whomever committed'.

58 Art 2 of the Terrorist Bombings Convention (n 38).

59 Art 2(1)(b) of the Terrorist Financing Convention (n 38).

60 Ibid.

61 Art 2 of the Nuclear Terrorism Convention (n 38).

62 See Conventions cited in n 38: arts 3, 6 and 7 of the Terrorist Bombings Convention; arts 3, 7 and 10 of the Terrorism Financing Convention; arts 3, 9 and 11 of the Nuclear Terrorism Convention.

63 See Conventions cited in n 38: Arts 5 and 11 of the Terrorist Bombings Convention; arts 6 and 14 of the Terrorism Financing Convention; arts 6 and 15 of the Nuclear Terrorism Convention.

64 See the Terrorism Financing Convention (n 38).

A consideration of regional anti-terrorism treaties illustrates that some of these treaties include ordinary criminal offences as acts of terrorism, for example kidnapping, murder, and other assaults.[65] Others define terrorist offences as offences that are already criminalized under the various sectoral anti-terrorism treaties, including violence on board an aircraft, unlawful acts against the safety of maritime navigation, the taking of hostages, terrorist bombings, the financing of terrorism and nuclear terrorism.[66] In addition to referring to the aforementioned acts, certain treaties, such as the Arab Convention for the Suppression of Terrorism (Arab Convention), contain definitions of terrorism referring to violence causing harm to persons or property as well as acts intended to instil terror or fear.[67] The Convention of the Organization of the Islamic Conference on Combating International Terrorism (Islamic Convention) contains a definition similar to that in the Arab Convention and also refers to a motive or intention by the perpetrator to carry out 'an individual or collective criminal plan' or endangering international facilities.[68] The Shanghai Convention on Combating Terrorism, Separatism and Extremism (Shanghai Convention) and the Organization of African Unity Convention on the Prevention and Combating of Terrorism (OAU Convention) echo the elements of terrorism as an act causing serious injury to civilians or property with the purpose of coercing or intimidating 'any government, body, institution, the general public or any segment thereof' to do or abstain from doing any act.[69] The Commonwealth of Independent States Treaty on Cooperation

65 Art 8 of the Terrorism Financing Convention (n 38).

66 See art 2 of the Arab Convention for the Suppression of Terrorism 1998, which includes as terrorist acts the offences proscribed under the Aviation Security Conventions and other anti-terrorism treaties; see, further, art 1 of the European Convention on the Suppression of Terrorism (as amended by its Protocol) 1977; art 11 of the Inter-American Convention against Terrorism 2002; art 1 of the Additional Protocol to the South Asian Association for Regional Co-operation (SAARC) Regional Convention on Suppression of Terrorism 2004; art 1 of the Council of Europe Convention on the Prevention of Terrorism 2005; art II(1) of the ASEAN Convention on Counter-Terrorism 2007.

67 Art 2 of the Arab Convention for the Suppression of Terrorism (n 66) defines terrorism as 'any act or threat of violence, whatever its motives or purposes, that occurs for the advancement of an individual or collective criminal agenda, causing terror among people, causing fear by harming them, or placing their lives, liberty or security in danger, or aiming to cause damage to the environment or to public or private installations or property or to occupy or seize them, or aiming to jeopardize a national resource'.

68 Arts 2 and 3 of the Convention of the Organisation of the Islamic Conference (OIC) on Combating International Terrorism 1999; art 1 of the Convention of the Cooperation Council for the Arab States of the Gulf on Combating Terrorism, 2008.

69 Art 1(1) of the Shanghai Convention on Combating Terrorism, Separatism and Extremism 2001. Art 1 of the Organisation of African Unity (OAU) Convention on the Prevention and

in Combating Terrorism refers to a transnational element (attacking a representative of a foreign state or an internationally-protected staff member of an international organization) and includes biological terrorism.[70]

From what has been said above, it is evident that terrorism is prohibited as a treaty rule under various sectoral anti-terrorism conventions. Although these conventions do not define terrorism as such, they prohibit forms of conduct involving intentional, transnational acts of violence endangering the safety of aircraft and vessels or causing death or serious injury to civilians with a political purpose. As for regional treaties, the discussion above illustrates that several definitions of terrorism contain the elements of harm to a person or property, an intention to instil fear, a political purpose and a transnational element.

The international community has been making efforts towards developing a comprehensive legal framework in order to deal with international terrorism. The UNGA mandated an *Ad Hoc* Committee to elaborate on the drafting of a comprehensive convention against terrorism.[71] The work of the *Ad Hoc* Committee was continued by a Working Group of the Sixth Committee.[72] Both the *Ad Hoc* Committee and the Sixth Committee have made attempts to finalize

Combating of Terrorism 2002 defines a terrorist act as '(a) any act which is a violation of the criminal laws of a state party and which may endanger the life, physical integrity or freedom of, or cause serious injury or death to, any person, any number or groups of persons or causes or may cause damage to public or private property, natural resources, environmental or cultural heritage and is calculated or intended to (i) intimidate, put in fear, force, coerce or induce any government, body, institution, the general public or any segment thereof, to do or abstain from doing any act, or to adopt or abandon a particular standpoint, or to act according to certain principles; or (ii) disrupt any public service, the delivery of any essential service to the public or to create a public emergency; or (iii) create general insurrection in a state; (b) any promotion, sponsoring, contribution to, command, aid, incitement, encouragement, attempt, threat, conspiracy, organizing, or procurement of any person, with the intent to commit any act referred to in paragraphs (a)(i) to (iii)'.

70 Art 1 of the Commonwealth of Independent States Treaty on Cooperation in Combating Terrorism, 1999. 'Biological terrorism' means the use or threat of the use of nuclear, radiological, chemical or bacteriological (biological) weapons or their components, pathogenic micro-organisms, radioactive substances or other substances harmful to human health.

71 See A/RES/51/210 (1996). At its 51st session, the UNGA established an *ad hoc* committee to elaborate on the drafting of a comprehensive convention. At its first meeting, on 6 October 2008, the Sixth Committee established a Working Group to continue to carry out the mandate of the *ad hoc* committee. The Sixth Committee considered measures to eliminate international terrorism at its 2nd, 3rd, 4th, 14th and 26th meetings on 8, 9 and 24 October and on 14 November 2008. See 'Measures to eliminate international terrorism' (1972) in Summary of Work of the Sixth Committee A/63/100.

72 Ibid.

the Draft Comprehensive Convention on Terrorism (Draft Comprehensive Convention).[73] In this regard, many of the clauses in the anti-terrorism treaties drafted by the *Ad Hoc* Committee, such as provisions of the Terrorism Bombings and Terrorism Financing Conventions, are reflected in the Draft Comprehensive Convention. Unlike the sectoral treaties finalized by the *Ad Hoc* Committee, however, the Draft Comprehensive Convention contains a definition of terrorism. Although well over a decade has passed since the negotiations were commenced, the Draft Comprehensive Convention still has not been finalized owing to differences with regard to the definition of terrorism.[74] The next section will consider the prohibition of terrorism under UNSC resolutions.

3.2 *Rules Prohibiting Terrorism under United Nations Security Council Resolutions*

Terrorism has been widely condemned as undermining fundamental human rights as well as the welfare of the state and political processes and threatening international peace and security.[75] In terms of Chapter VII of the UN Charter, the UNSC is empowered to 'determine the existence of any threat to the peace, breach of the peace, or act of aggression'.[76] In order to bring such a threat to an end, the UNSC is further empowered to take measures that are legally binding on all states.[77] Before the adoption of UNSC Resolution 1373, UNSC resolutions

73 See the discussion on the Draft Comprehensive Convention 2006, para 4.3 below.

74 Stephen Marks, 'Branding the "War on Terrorism": Is there a "New Paradigm" of International Law?' (2006) 14 Michigan State University Journal of International Law 71, 75; Report of the *Ad Hoc* Committee Established by General Assembly Resolution 51/210 of 17 December 1996, 9th session (28 March–1 April 2005) A/60/37, Annex I 16–23.

75 See eg S/RES 1368, 1373 and 1377 (2001). S/RES/1377(2001), '[d]eclares that acts of international terrorism constitute one of the most serious threats to international peace and security in the twenty-first century, [f]urther declares that acts of international terrorism constitute a challenge to all states and to all of humanity'. See further S/RES/2249(2015) ('Reaffirming that terrorism in all forms and manifestations constitutes one of the most serious threats to international peace and security and that any acts of terrorism are criminal and unjustifiable regardless of their motivations, whenever and by whomsoever committed.').

76 Art 39 of the Charter of the United Nations, 1945; Christian Tomuschat, 'The Security Council and *Jus Cogens*' in Enzo Cannizzaro (ed), *The Present and Future of* Jus Cogens (5th edn, Cedam 2015) para 78. Tomuschat states that art 39 of the UN Charter contains 'a clear reference to action undertaken under Chapter VII of the Charter where the power of the SC to take enforcement action resides'.

77 See art 25 of the UN Charter, which states that all members of the United Nations 'agree to carry out and accept the decisions of the Security Council in accordance with the present Charter'. See further Ian Hurd, 'The UN Security Council and the International Rule of Law' (2014) Chinese Journal of International Politics 6: 'The Charter is a multilateral treaty

tended to focus on imposing obligations on states supporting targeted sanctions, such as the freezing of assets, a travel ban and a weapons embargo aimed at targeted individuals and groups. According to Strydom, the purpose of this and other resolutions was to force the Taliban to stop giving sanctuary and assistance to a network of terrorists, including al Qaeda.[78] These resolutions reaffirmed the suppression of international terrorism as essential for the maintenance of international peace and security.[79] It further recalled the relevant international counter-terrorism conventions and, in particular, the obligations of parties to those conventions to extradite or prosecute terrorists.[80]

Of the various UNSC resolutions, Resolution 1373 of 2001, which created the Counter-Terrorism Committee (CTC), had the most far-reaching effects to date.[81] It has a strong legislative nature, is binding on all states and, although it does not define terrorism, is global in nature and not time-bound.[82] This resolution provides for 12 obligatory obligations (states 'shall') and nine non-binding provisions in terms of which states are 'called upon' to act in a particular way.[83] Of the obligatory obligations, four require that all states take certain actions to prevent and suppress the financing of terrorist acts and four relate in general to states refraining from providing, preventing and denying safe havens to terrorists.[84] Three obligations deal with the administration of justice

that is binding on the states that sign it. It requires that they comply with its terms, and these terms include an extensive degree of deference to the Security Council.' See further Erika de Wet and Jure Vidmar (eds), *Hierarchy in International Law: The Place of Human Rights* (Oxford University Press 2012) 6.

78 See, for example, Resolutions 1267 (1999), 1989 (2011) and 2253 (2015) concerning ISIL (Da'esh), Al-Qaida, and associated individuals, groups, undertakings and entities). See Hennie Strydom, 'From Mandates to Economic Partnerships: The Return to Proper Statehood in Africa' (2007) 7 African Human Rights Law Journal 74–75. Strydom further argues that with regard to Afghanistan, 'the UN had to uphold the illusion of statehood in order to make it possible to deal with a situation in terms of the Charter and to hold the incumbent "government" responsible for enforcing UN resolutions'. He points out that 'some entity must be the addressee of even the weakest international response to a crisis' even if the entity in question is not a true sovereign state.

79 See the resolutions cited (n 78).

80 Ibid.

81 S/RES/1373 (2001).

82 Trevor Chimimba, 'United Nations Security Council Resolution 1373 (2001) as a Tool for Criminal Law Enforcement' in Tiyanjana Maluwa et al (eds), *The Pursuit of a Brave New World in International Law: Essays in Honour of John Dugard* (Brill Nijhoff 2017) 303.

83 Ibid., 308–9.

84 Ibid. See further S/RES 1373 (2001). Art 1 states: 'All states shall (a) prevent and suppress the financing of terrorist acts; (b) criminalize the wilful provision or collection, by any means, directly or indirectly, of funds by their nationals or in their territories with the intention that the funds should be used, or in the knowledge that they are to be used,

where states must take action to ensure that they have effective border control in place as well as measures to prevent counterfeiting, forgery or the fraudulent use of identity papers and travel documents.[85]

The nine non-binding provisions in terms of which states are 'called upon' to take certain actions are generally operational and aimed at improving domestic procedures and enhancing international cooperation in the suppression and prevention of terrorism.[86] In this regard, the various sets of provisions aim to improve investigations by the use of modern forms of information and communication technologies, and call upon states to become parties to relevant counter-terrorism instruments.[87] In addition, Resolution 1373 calls for

---

in order to carry out terrorist acts; (c) freeze without delay funds and other financial assets or economic resources of persons who commit, or attempt to commit, terrorist acts or participate in or facilitate the commission of terrorist acts; of entities owned or controlled directly or indirectly by such persons; and of persons and entities acting on behalf of, or at the direction of such persons and entities, including funds derived or generated from property owned or controlled directly or indirectly by such persons and associated persons and entities; (d) prohibit their nationals or any persons and entities within their territories from making any funds, financial assets or economic resources or financial or other related services available, directly or indirectly, for the benefit of persons who commit or attempt to commit or facilitate or participate in the commission of terrorist acts, of entities owned or controlled, directly or indirectly, by such persons and of persons and entities acting on behalf of or at the direction of such persons'. Art 2 'decides' that '[a]ll states shall (a) refrain from providing any form of support, active or passive, to entities or persons involved in terrorist acts, including by suppressing recruitment of members of terrorist groups and eliminating the supply of weapons to terrorists; (b) take the necessary steps to prevent the commission of terrorist acts, including by provision of early warning to other states by exchange of information; (c) deny safe haven to those who finance, plan, support, or commit terrorist acts, or provide safe havens; (d) prevent those who finance, plan, facilitate or commit terrorist acts from using their respective territories for those purposes against other states or their citizens'.

85 S/RES 1373 (2001). Art 2 further provides that '[a]ll states shall ... (e) ensure that any person who participates in the financing, planning, preparation or perpetration of terrorist acts or in supporting terrorist acts is brought to justice and ensure that, in addition to any other measures against them, such terrorist acts are established as serious criminal offences in domestic laws and regulations and that the punishment duly reflects the seriousness of such terrorist acts; (f) afford one another the greatest measure of assistance in connection with criminal investigations or criminal proceedings relating to the financing or support of terrorist acts, including assistance in obtaining evidence in their possession necessary for the proceedings'.

86 Chimimba (n 82) 310.

87 S/RES 1373 (2001) (n 3). Art 3 calls upon all states to '(a) find ways of intensifying and accelerating the exchange of operational information, especially regarding actions or movements of terrorist persons or networks; forged or falsified travel documents; traffic in arms, explosives or sensitive materials; use of communications technologies by terrorist groups; and the threat posed by the possession of weapons of mass destruction by

increased cooperation in respect of and full implementation of such instruments and UNSC Resolutions 1269 and 1368.[88] The requirement for states to report to the CTC has been noted as crucial by providing the CTC with powers of implementation and, thus, establishing a third party mechanism for engaging states in a consensual manner in order to discuss difficulties encountered in meeting their international counter-terrorism obligations.[89] Some of the resolutions, however, have been the subject of major controversy owing to their impact on the right to a fair trial.[90] This will be discussed in more detail in chapter 4.

In addition to Resolution 1373, various resolutions unequivocally condemned terrorism. Resolution 1377 of 2001 emphasized that 'acts of terrorism endanger innocent lives and the dignity and security of human beings everywhere, threaten the social and economic development of all states and undermine global stability and prosperity'.[91] Resolution 1390 of 2002 reiterated the support of the UNSC for international efforts to root out terrorism in accordance with the UN Charter; reaffirmed its unequivocal condemnation of the terrorist attacks of 9/11; expressed its determination to prevent all such acts; condemned the al-Qaeda network and other associated terrorist groups 'for the multiple criminal, terrorist acts, aimed at causing the deaths of numer-

---

terrorist groups; (b) exchange information in accordance with international and domestic law and cooperate on administrative and judicial matters to prevent the commission of terrorist acts; (c) cooperate, particularly through bilateral and multilateral arrangements and agreements, to prevent and suppress terrorist attacks and take action against perpetrators of such acts'. Art 4 notes with concern 'the close connection between international terrorism and transnational organized crime, illicit drugs, money-laundering, illegal arms-trafficking, and illegal movement of nuclear, chemical, biological and other potentially deadly materials, and in this regard emphasizes the need to enhance coordination of efforts on national, subregional, regional and international levels in order to strengthen a global response to this serious challenge and threat to international security'.

88 Chimimba (n 82) 310–11; S/RES 1373 (2001). Art 3 further calls upon all states to '(d) become parties as soon as possible to the relevant international conventions and protocols relating to terrorism, including the International Convention for the Suppression of the Financing of Terrorism of 9 December 1999; (e) increase cooperation and fully implement the relevant international conventions and protocols relating to terrorism and Security Council Resolutions 1269 (1999) and 1368 (2001)'.

89 Chimimba (n 82) 312; S/RES 1373 (2001). Para 6 of this resolution calls upon all states 'to report to the Committee, no later than 90 days from the date of adoption of this resolution and thereafter according to a timetable to be proposed by the Committee, on the steps they have taken to implement this resolution'.

90 See Dire Tladi and Gillian Taylor, 'On the Al Qaeda/Taliban Sanctions Regime: Due Process and Sunsetting' (2011) 10 Chinese Journal of International Law 771, paras 3–44; see S/RES/1267 (1999).

91 See the Preamble to S/RES 1377 (2001).

ous innocent civilians, and the destruction of property'; and reaffirmed that acts of international terrorism constituted a threat to international peace and security.[92] Paragraph 4 further recalled the obligation placed upon all member states to implement Resolution 1373 in full with regard to the Taliban, al-Qaeda and associated individuals and entities who have participated in or supported the financing, planning, facilitating and preparation or perpetration of terrorist acts.[93]

Resolution 1624 of 2005 confirmed the imperative to fight terrorism in all its forms and manifestations by all means in accordance with the UN Charter, condemned terrorism in all its forms and manifestations as unjustifiable and one of the most serious threats to peace and security, and affirmed that states must take all necessary and appropriate measures in accordance with international law to protect the right to life.[94] Further resolutions condemning specific terrorist attacks similarly confirmed that terrorism was a threat to international peace and security and expressed the determination of the UNSC to combat all forms of terrorism in accordance with its responsibilities under the UN Charter.[95] The Preamble of Resolution 2249 of 2015 provided for the freezing of assets of terrorists as well as a travel ban on terrorists.[96] The Preamble stated:

---

92 See the Preamble to S/RES 1390 (2002) on Afghanistan.

93 Note that the sanctions regime was extended to include ISIL in S/RES 2253 (2015).

94 See S/RES 1624 (2005) (Counter-Terrorism Implementation Task Force).

95 See S/RES 1438 (2002) (condemnation of bombings in Bali); S/RES 1440 (2002) (condemnation of hostage taking in Moscow); S/RES 1450 (2002) (condemnation of terrorist attacks in Kenya); S/RES 1465 (2003) (condemnation of bomb attacks in Bogota, Colombia); S/RES 1516 (2003) (condemnation of bombings in Istanbul); S/RES 1530 (2004) (condemnation of bomb attacks in Madrid); S/RES 1611 (2005) (condemnation of bomb attacks in London); S/RES 1618 (2005) (condemnation of terrorist attacks in Iraq).

96 See para 2 of S/RES/2249(2015), in terms of which the UNSC '[d]ecides that all States shall take the following measures with respect to Usama bin Laden, members of the Al-Qaida organization and the Taliban and other individuals, groups, undertakings and entities associated with them, as referred to in the list created pursuant to resolutions 1267 (1999) and 1333 (2000) to be updated regularly by the Committee established pursuant to Resolution 1267 (1999) hereinafter referred to as "the Committee"; (a) freeze without delay the funds and other financial assets or economic resources of these individuals, groups, undertakings and entities, including funds derived from property owned or controlled, directly or indirectly, by them or by persons acting on their behalf or at their direction, and ensure that neither these nor any other funds, financial assets or economic resources are made available, directly or indirectly, for such persons' benefit, by their nationals or by any persons within their territory; (b) prevent the entry into or the transit through their territories of these individuals, provided that nothing in this paragraph shall oblige any State to deny entry into or require the departure from its territories of its own nationals and this paragraph shall not apply where entry or transit is necessary for the fulfilment

> *Reaffirming* that terrorism in all forms and manifestations constitutes one of the most serious threats to international peace and security and that any acts of terrorism are criminal and unjustifiable regardless of their motivations, whenever and by whomsoever committed …

These UNSC resolutions support the unequivocal condemnation of terrorism irrespective of its justifications as well as the obligation on states to fight terrorism. The next section will consider the prohibition of terrorism under customary international law.

3.3 *Rules Prohibiting Terrorism under Customary International Law*

In exploring the prohibition of terrorism under customary international law, this section will first consider the elements constituting a terrorist act as set out in state practice, such as national legislation and the decisions of national courts. It will then consider evidence of *opinio juris* concerning the prohibition of terrorism in international law. Section 4.1 will then discuss whether certain core elements of a definition of terrorism have emerged under international law.

Both state practice and *opinio juris* are necessary components for the formation of a rule of customary international law.[97] In this regard, Koskenniemi re-

of a judicial process or the Committee determines on a case by case basis only that entry or transit is justified; (c) prevent the direct or indirect supply, sale and transfer, to these individuals, groups, undertakings and entities from their territories or by their nationals outside their territories, or using their flag vessels or aircraft, of arms and related material of all types including weapons and ammunition, military vehicles and equipment, paramilitary equipment, and spare parts for the aforementioned and technical advice, assistance, or training related to military activities'.

97 Constitution of the Maritime Safety Committee of the Inter-governmental Maritime Consultative Organisation Advisory Opinion (8 June 1960) (1960) ICJ Reports 150; *South West Africa* cases (*Ethiopia and Liberia v South Africa*) second phase (18 July 1966) (1966) ICJ Reports 6; *Nicaragua v US Merits* (27 June 1986) (1986) ICJ Reports 14; *Libya v Malta* (Continental Shelf) (3 June 1985) (1985) ICJ Reports 13; Delimitation of the Maritime Boundary in the Gulf of Maine Area (*Canada v United States*) (12 October 1984) (1984) ICJ Reports 246; Western Sahara Advisory Opinion (16 October 1975) (1975) ICJ Reports 12; Fisheries Jurisdiction (*UK v Iceland*) Merits (25 July 1974) (1974) ICJ Reports 3; BarcelonaTraction, Light and Power Company, Limited (*Belgium v Spain*) (Second Phase) ICJ (5 February 1970) (1970) ICJ Reports 3. See, further, ILC Report on the work of the 66th session (2014) (5 May–6 June 2014 and 7 July–8 August 2014), A/69/10 Supplement No 10 240, draft conclusion 7, in terms of which state practice includes 'the conduct of States "on the ground", diplomatic acts and correspondence, legislative acts, judgments of national courts, official publications in the field of international law, statements on behalf of states concerning codification efforts, practice in connection with treaties and acts in connection with resolutions of organs of international organizations and conferences'.

fers to the interplay between state practice and *opinio juris* as the two elements of international customary law.[98] State practice should be general (not necessarily universal) and consistent if it is to serve as evidence of custom.[99] If such practice is general and consistent, no prescribed duration is required.[100] Mere state conduct, however, is not sufficient to prove the creation of customary international law. It is necessary that states perform or abstain from conduct because of a belief that they are obliged to do so before international custom is created (*opinio juris*).[101] Writers have argued that unanimous resolutions can be evidence of *opinio juris*.[102] Furthermore, although UNGA resolutions are not formally binding, they can be evidence of *opinio juris* in instances when there is sufficient state practice to support the usage element.[103]

See further ibid., in terms of Draft Conclusion 11 the forms of evidence of *opinio juris* (a general practice accepted as law) includes, but are not limited to, 'statements by states which indicate what are or are not rules of customary international law, diplomatic correspondence, the jurisprudence of national courts, the opinions of government legal advisers, official publications in fields of international law, treaty practice and action in connection with resolutions of organs of international organizations and of international conferences. Inaction may also serve as evidence of acceptance as law.'

98 See Martti Koskenniemi, *From Apology to Utopia: The Structure of International Legal Argument* (Cambridge University Press 1989) 363, stating that '[b]ecause both elements [state practice and *opinio juris*] seek to delimit each other's distorting impact, the theory of custom needs to hold them independent from each other. But this it cannot do. Attempting to identify the presence of the psychological element, it draws inferences (presumptions) on the basis of material practice. To ascertain which acts of material practice are relevant for custom formation, it makes reference to the psychological element (ie those acts count which express the *opinio juris*) The psychological element is defined by the material and *vice versa*. This circularity prevents doctrine from developing a determinate method of custom-ascertainment. It has led to determining custom in terms of an equity which it can itself only regard as arbitrary.' See further Brian Lepard, 'The Necessity of *Opinio Juris* in the Formation of Customary International Law' (3 April 2015) <http://law.duke.edu/cicl/> accessed 9 August 2017. Lepard argues that where the majority of states have collectively decided that a certain norm ought to be law, this decision may be evidenced by state practice.

99 *North Sea Continental Shelf* cases (20 February 1969) (1969) ICJ Reports 3 para 42.

100 Ibid.

101 The *SS Lotus* case (*France v Turkey*) (7 September 1927) (1927) PCIJ Ser A No 10.

102 Bin Cheng, 'United Nations Resolutions on Outer Space: "Instant" International Customary Law?' (1965) 5 Indian Journal of International Law 23, 35–40; Julien Cantegreil, 'The audacity of the Texaco/Calasiatic Award: René-Jean Dupuy and the Internationalization of Foreign Investment Law' (2011) 22 European Journal of International Law 441, 449; Hugh Thirlway, *International Customary Law and Codification: An Examination of the Continuing Role of Custom in the Present Period of Codification of International Law* (Martinus Nijhoff 1972) 67.

103 Ibid.

Terrorism is criminalized in the domestic law of various states. In Africa the definitions of terrorism in relevant legislation tend to refer to certain common elements. These are a level of violence against persons or property, a political purpose and a transnational element.[104] Included as terrorist acts are acts disturbing the public order or interfering with public services and acts causing damage to the environment. There is also reference to bombings or explosions as well as certain criminal acts such as murder, hostage-taking and kidnapping. In South Africa, for instance, the Protection of Constitutional Democracy Against Terrorist and Related Activities Act contains an extensive definition of terrorism, which includes the elements of violence causing serious injury to a person or damage to property with the intent to cause fear in the civilian population or to compel a government to do or to abstain or refrain from doing any act. It further includes acts that are designed to cause disruption to essential facilities, banking and communications systems.[105]

---

104 See eg sec 1 of South Africa's Protection of Constitutional Democracy Against Terrorist and Related Activities Act 2004; secs 2(1)(a)–(m) of the Botswana Counter-Terrorism Act, 2014; sec 96 of the Lesotho Penal Code Act 2010; sec 7(2) of the Uganda Anti-Terrorism Act 2002; secs 1(1)(a)–(e) of the Ghana Anti-Terrorism Act 2008 (Act 762); secs 1(2) and (3) of the Nigeria Terrorism (Prevention) Act 2011.

105 Sec 1 of the Protection of Constitutional Democracy Against Terrorist and Related Activities (n 104) defines a terrorist activity as '(a) any act committed in or outside the Republic, which (i) involves the systematic, repeated or arbitrary use of violence by any means or method; (ii) involves the systematic, repeated or arbitrary release into the environment or any part of it or distributing or exposing the public or any part of it to (aa) any dangerous, hazardous, radioactive or harmful substance or organism; (bb) any toxic chemical; or (cc) any microbial or other biological agent or toxin; (iii) endangers the life, or violates the physical integrity or physical freedom of, or causes serious bodily injury to or the death of, any person, or any number of persons; (iv) causes serious risk to the health or safety of the public or any segment of the public; (v) causes the destruction of or substantial damage to any property, natural resource, or the environmental or cultural heritage, whether public or private; (vi) is designed or calculated to cause serious interference with or serious disruption of an essential service, facility or system, or the delivery of any such service, facility or system, whether public or private, including, but not limited to (aa) a system used for, or by, an electronic system, including an information system; (bb) a telecommunication service or system; (cc) a banking or financial service or financial system; (dd) a system used for the delivery of essential government services; (ee) a system used for, or by, an essential public utility or transport provider; (ff) an essential infrastructure facility; or (gg) any essential emergency services, such as police, medical or civil defence services; (vii) causes any major economic loss or extensive destabilisation of an economic system or substantial devastation of the national economy of a country; or (viii) creates a serious public emergency situation or a general insurrection in the Republic, whether the harm contemplated in paragraphs (a)(i) to (vii) is or may be suffered in or outside the Republic, and whether the activity referred to in subparagraphs (ii) to (viii) was committed by way of any means or method; and (b) which is intended, or by

The definition of terrorism in Botswana's Counter-Terrorism Act includes as terrorist acts those causing damage to a ship, aircraft or vehicle, crimes such as hostage-taking, hijacking, murdering and kidnapping as well as any incitement or conspiracy to commit terrorist acts.[106] It excludes any protest, dissent, demonstration or industrial action not intended to cause harm to any person or property and thus excludes peaceful demonstrations from the definition of a terrorist act.[107] The Lesotho and Ugandan Penal Codes include as terrorist acts violent acts causing damage to persons or property committed for a political purpose, and these states include criminal acts such as kidnapping and hostage-taking as examples of terrorist acts.[108] In Ghana, a terrorist act is defined as an act performed in furtherance of a political, ideological, religious, racial or ethnic cause which causes serious bodily harm to a person or to property and which may involve firearms or explosives.[109] In Nigeria, the Terrorism Prevention Act defines terrorism as an act that is deliberately done with malice or forethought and which causes serious harm to a person or property (including aircraft and ships), a country or an international organization, and which is intended to unduly compel a government or international organization to perform or abstain from performing any act or to intimidate a population. Similarly to Botswana's definition of terrorist acts, it excludes protests

its nature and context, can reasonably be regarded as being intended, in whole or in part, directly or indirectly, to (i) threaten the unity and territorial integrity of the Republic; (ii) intimidate, or to induce or cause feelings of insecurity within, the public, or a segment of the public, with regard to its security, including its economic security, or to induce, cause or spread feelings of terror, fear or panic in a civilian population; or (iii) unduly compel, intimidate, force, coerce, induce or cause a person, a government, the general public or a segment of the public, or a domestic or an international organisation or body or intergovernmental organisation or body, to do or to abstain or refrain from doing any act, or to adopt or abandon a particular standpoint, or to act in accordance with certain principles whether the public or the person, government, body, or organization or institution referred to in subparagraphs (ii) or (iii), as the case may be, is inside or outside the Republic; and (c) which is committed, directly or indirectly, in whole or in part, for the purpose of the advancement of an individual or collective political, religious, ideological or philosophical motive, objective, cause or undertaking'.

106 Secs 2(1)(a)–(m) of the Botswana Counter-Terrorism Act (n 104).

107 Ibid.

108 See sec 96 of the Lesotho Penal Code Act (n 104); sec 7(2) of the Uganda Anti-Terrorism Act (n 104).

109 Secs 1(1)(a)–(e) of the Ghana Anti-Terrorism Act (n 104). See further Katrin Kokott, 'The Impact of 9/11 on the South African Anti-Terrorism Legislation and the Constitutionality thereof' Unpublished LLM research paper, University of the Western Cape, 2005 <http://etd.uwc.ac.za/xmlui/bitstream/handle/11394/1673/Kokott_LLM_2005.pdf?sequence=1> accessed 13 July 2017, who notes that such clauses may be selectively used against opposition groups on the basis of political, cultural or religious considerations.

not intended to result in any harm.[110] In Cameroon, a terrorist act refers to the elements of harm (damage against the environment or cultural heritage), intimidation, a political purpose and the disruption of the national functioning of public or essential services.[111]

The definitions of terrorism in North Africa are broad in scope. In Algeria, the definition of a terrorist act includes acts targeting state security with the intent of spreading terror and causing harm to people or the environment, and lists actions such as desecrating graves; obstructing traffic or freedom of movement on roads; and gathering or sitting in in public spaces or interfering with public services.[112] This may lead to the unwarranted labelling of acts of peaceful demonstration or protest as terrorist acts. Egypt's Anti-Terrorism Law includes the elements of causing terror or causing harm to national unity; the environment; antiquities; money; buildings; and public or private properties. It further includes acts that impede public authorities, diplomatic and consular missions or regional and international organizations and bodies in Egypt from carrying out their work.[113] In Morocco, crimes constitute terrorist acts if they are intentionally related to an individual or collective enterprise with

---

110 Secs 1(2) and (3) of the Nigerian Terrorism (Prevention) Act (n 104).

111 Sec 2(1) of the Law on the Suppression of Acts of Terrorism in Cameroon, 2014 defines an act of terrorism as an act 'likely to cause death, endanger physical integrity, cause bodily injury or material damage, destroy natural resources, the environment or cultural heritage with intent to (a) intimidate the public, provoke a situation of terror or face the victim, the government and/or a national or international organization to carry out or refrain from carrying out an act, adopt or renounce a particular position; (b) disrupt the national functioning of public services, the delivery of essential services to the public to create a crisis situation among the public; (c) create widespread insurrection in the country'.

112 Sec 87*bis* of the Algerian Penal Code 1966 defines terrorism as 'any act targeting state security and national unity, territorial integrity, and the stability and normal functioning of institutions by any action whose objective is to spread terror among the population and create a climate of insecurity through moral or physical assault on people, through exposing their lives, freedom, or security to danger, or through damaging their properties; obstruct traffic or freedom of movement on the roads and gather or sit in public spaces; assault the symbols of the nation and the Republic and unearth or desecrate graves; assault the means of transportation and transport, the public and private properties, and possess or occupy them without legal justification; assault the environment or introduce into the atmosphere, into the earth or on its face, or into the waters, including territorial waters, a substance that would expose the health of humans or of animals, or the natural environment to danger; obstruct the work of public authorities, the freedom of worship, the exercise of public liberties, or the functioning of the establishments assisting public services; obstruct the functioning of public institutions, assault the lives or properties of their representatives, or impede the implementation of laws and regulations'.

113 Sec 1 of Egypt's Anti-Terrorism Law, 2015.

the objective of gravely undermining the public order through intimidation, terror or violence.[114] Tanzania's Prevention of Terrorism Act includes as terrorist acts those acts causing violence to a person or property, the environment, public services or essential infrastructure, committed for a political purpose and having a transnational element.[115]

In Ethiopia, the definition of terrorism contains a political purpose element as well as harm to a person or property.[116] The political purpose element is also reflected in Tunisia's Counter-Terrorism Law which defines a terrorist offence as a deliberate act aimed at spreading terror among the population or unduly compelling a state or an international organization 'to do what it is not obliged to do or refrain from doing what it is obliged to do'.[117] In Bhutan, a defendant is guilty of the offence of terrorism if the defendant, with intent to subvert the state, uses or trains another person to use a bomb or other lethal weapon against Bhutan or engages in a violent act or insurrection designed to generate fear in a community or a substantial section of society.[118]

In Bangladesh the definition of terrorism includes elements of intent to create panic as well as violence against persons and the destruction of property with a political purpose.[119] In Malaysia, the definition of terrorism includes acts causing serious bodily injury and acts of intimidation committed with a political purpose and which have a transnational element.[120] Timor Leste lists acts that destroy or prevent the operation of means of communication, public service facilities or international installations. It further specifically refers to acts maliciously causing collective danger through arson; nuclear energy; firearms; explosive substances or devices; booby-trapped packages or letters; as well as acts using biological or chemical weapons.[121] In Jamaica, the

114 Sec 218*bis* of the Moroccan Penal Code, 1962.

115 Sec 2 of the United Republic of Tanzania Prevention of Terrorism Act, 2002.

116 Sec 3 of the Ethiopian Anti-Terrorism Proclamation No 652/2009.

117 Sec 13 of the Tunisian Anti-Terrorism Law, 2015.

118 Sec 329 of the Penal Code of Bhutan, 2004 (as amended).

119 Sec 6 of the Bangladesh Anti-Terrorism Ordinance, 2008.

120 See sec 130B(2) of the Malaysian Penal Code 574 of 1936, as amended in which 'terrorist act' means an act or threat of action within or beyond Malaysia which involves serious bodily injury to a person and where '(b) the act is done or the threat is made with the intention of advancing a political, religious or ideological cause; and (c) the act or threat is intended or may reasonably be regarded as being intended to (i) intimidate the public or a section of the public; or (ii) influence or compel the Government of Malaysia or the Government of any State in Malaysia, any other government, or any international organization to do or refrain from doing any act'.

121 Sec 218 of the Penal Code of the Democratic Republic of Timor Leste Decree Law No 19/2009.

Terrorism Prevention Act defines terrorism as an act or omission intentionally causing death or serious bodily harm to a person or damage to property. It further includes a reference to the intent of the act of intimidating the public, a political purpose element and a transnational element.[122] Similarly, the Seychelles Prevention of Terrorism Act refers to terrorist conduct as an act causing death, serious bodily harm to a person or damage to property committed with political intent.[123] In Dominica and Vanuata the elements of terrorist acts are similar, namely, acts causing harm to persons or property, damage to the environment or the disruption of public services, with the intention of intimidating the public and with a political purpose.[124] The Prevention of Terrorism Act of Antigua and Barbuda includes violence to a person or property as elements of a terrorist act. It similarly requires a political purpose and includes any act causing mass destruction, as well as acts of assassination, kidnapping or hostage-taking.[125] In Trinidad and Tobago, a terrorist act includes the elements of loss of human life or serious bodily harm, damage to property or prejudice to national security or public services for a political purpose as well as a transnational element.[126]

In Spain, terrorism is defined as the commission of certain listed crimes (including injuring, kidnapping and murder) while acting as a member of, or collaborating with, armed bands or groups with the purpose of subverting

122 Sec 3(2) of the Jamaican Terrorism Prevention Act, 2005 states that '[a]ny person who commits an act, or omits to act, in the circumstances referred to in subsection (4) commits an offence if the act or omission intentionally (a) causes (i) death; or (ii) serious bodily harm, to a person; (b) endangers a person's life, or the health or safety of the public or any segment of the public; or (c) causes substantial property damage, whether to public or private property, if such damage is likely to result in the conduct or harm referred to in paragraph (a) or (b) … (4) The circumstances mentioned in subsection (2) are that the act or omission is committed in whole or in part for a political, religious or ideological purpose, objective or cause with the intention of (a) intimidating the public, or a segment of the public, with regard to its security, including its economic security; or (b) compelling a person, a government or a domestic or an international organization.'

123 Sec 2 of the Seychelles Prevention of Terrorism Act, 2004.

124 Sec 3(b) of the Dominican Suppression of the Financing of Terrorism (Amendment) Act, 2011; sec 73C of the Vanuatu Penal Code (Chapter 135), 1981.

125 Sec 1 of the Antigua and Barbuda Prevention of Terrorism Act 15 of 2001 defines a terrorist activity as an activity that '(a) involves a violent act or an act dangerous to human life, property or infrastructure; and (b) appears to be intended to (i) intimidate or coerce a civilian population; (ii) influence the policy of government by intimidation or coercion; or (iii) affect the conduct of a government by mass destruction, assassination, kidnapping or hostage taking'.

126 Sec 3(1) of the Trinidad and Tobago Anti-Terrorism Act, 2005 (as amended by Act 13 of 2018).

constitutional order or gravely disturbing public peace.[127] Belgium's Law on Intelligence and Security Services defines terrorism as the use of violence against persons or property for ideological or political motives in order to achieve one's goals through terror, intimidation or threats.[128] The Netherlands refers to terrorist offences as acts committed with the intention of causing fear among the population, unlawfully compelling 'a Dutch public authority or an institution or organization of the European Union based in The Netherlands to act or to refrain from certain acts or to tolerate certain acts' or seriously disrupting or destroying the fundamental political, constitutional, economic or social structures of the Netherlands or an institution or an organization of the European Union based in the Netherlands.[129] The Czech Republic's detailed definition of terrorism echoes the elements of acts of violence intended to spread fear and committed for a political purpose, and it lists as examples of terrorist acts crimes such as hostage-taking, kidnapping and hijacking as well as acts that cause the disruption of public services.[130] The Criminal Code of the Ukraine contains the elements of violence against a person for a political purpose.[131] The Albanian Penal Code similarly refers to terrorist acts as acts intended to spread panic and to destabilize a state, while the Andorran Penal Code includes acts aimed at the subversion of the constitutional order or a serious attack against peace and order through intimidation and terror.[132] In Saudi Arabia, the law defines a terrorist crime as any act undertaken in

---

127 Secs 571–580 of Spain's Penal Code, 1995; see, further, Richard Wilson, 'Prosecuting Pinoch: International Crimes in Spanish Domestic Law' (1999) 21 HRQ 927, 961–63.

128 Sec 8(1) para 2(b) of the Belgian Organic Law of the Intelligence and Security Services, 1998.

129 Sec 83 of The Netherlands Crimes of Terrorism Act, 2004 states that a terrorist aim means 'the aim to seriously intimidate the population or part of the population of a country, and/or to unlawfully force a government or international organization into acting, to refrain from acting or to tolerate, and/or to seriously destroy or disrupt the political, constitutional, economical or social structure of a country or international organization'.

130 Sec 311 of the Criminal Code of the Czech Republic, 2009.

131 Sec 258 of the Criminal Code of Ukraine, 2001 defines an act of terrorism as 'the use of weapons, explosions, fire or any other actions that exposed human life or health to danger or caused significant pecuniary damage or any other grave consequences, where such actions sought to violate public security, intimidate a population, provoke an armed conflict, or international tension, or to exert influence on decisions made or actions taken or not taken by government agencies or local government authorities, officials and officers of such bodies, associations of citizens, legal entities, or to attract attention of the public to certain political, religious or any other convictions of the culprit (terrorist), and also a threat to commit any such acts for the same purposes'.

132 Sec 330 of the Criminal Code of the Republic of Albania Law 7895, 1995; sec 421 of the Andorra New Penal Code, 2005 ('la subversion de l'ordre constitutionnel ou l'attentat grave de l'ordre et la paix public moyennant l'intimidation et la terreur').

pursuance of an individual or collective criminal enterprise for a political purpose. It does not stipulate violence as an element.[133] In Australia and New Zealand, terrorist acts include the elements of a political purpose and intimidation of the public.[134] The United States (US) federal law defines terrorism as any crime that appears to be intended to 'intimidate or coerce a civilian population, to influence the policy of a government by intimidation or coercion, or to affect the conduct of a government by mass destruction, assassination, or kidnapping'.[135] The Anti-Terrorism Act of the Bahamas and the Guatemalan Criminal Code refer to an act causing bodily harm or damage to property with a political purpose.[136] In Brazil, terrorism is defined as the practice by one or more individuals of certain acts for reasons of xenophobia, discrimination or prejudice with regard to race, colour, ethnicity or religion, when committed for the purpose of causing social or generalized terror and exposing persons, property, public peace, or public safety to danger.[137] The French Criminal Code lists terrorist offences as crimes committed with the goal of disturbing the public order through intimidation and terror, for example, violence against a person, kidnapping, hijacking, money laundering, offences using firearms and explosives and damage to property.[138] In Italy, the definition of terrorist acts reflects the requirement of inflicting serious harm as well as having a political purpose.[139]

It appears from the review of national legislation above that, while there are differences in the wording used, the elements common to the various definitions of terrorism and terrorist acts are that they are criminal acts or violence causing harm to persons or property, committed with the intent to spread fear, for a political purpose and with a transnational element. The question as to

133 The definitions clause of the Saudi Arabia Penal Law for Crimes of Terrorism and its Financing of 2013 defines terrorism broadly as 'any act carried out by an offender in furtherance of an individual or collective project, directly or indirectly, intended to disturb the public order of the state, or to shake the security of society, or the stability of the state, or to expose its national unity to danger, or to suspend the basic law of governance or some of its articles, or to insult the reputation of the state or its position, or to inflict damage upon one of its public utilities or its natural resources, or to attempt to force a governmental authority to carry out or prevent it from carrying out an action, or to threaten to carry out acts that lead to the named purposes or incite [these acts]'.

134 Sec 100(1) of the Australia Criminal Code Act 1995; secs 1 and 2 of the New Zealand Terrorism Suppression Act, 2002.

135 18 USC 2331 (2004).

136 Sec 3 of the Bahamas Anti-Terrorism Act of 2004; sec 391 of the Guatemala Criminal Code, Decree No 17–73, 1973.

137 Sec 2 of the Brazilian Anti-Terrorism Law, 2016.

138 Sec 421 of the French Penal Code, 1994, as amended by Law 2005–1550 of 2005.

139 Sec 270 *sexies* of the Italian Criminal Code, as amended by Law 155 of 2005.

whether these elements are supported in national jurisprudence will now be considered.

Initially terrorism was prosecuted as a sectoral or ordinary offence under existing anti-terrorism treaties. In the US, this was illustrated in the case of *Yousef*.[140] In *Yousef* the accused appealed a conviction for conspiracy to bomb a US aircraft in Asia as well as the bombing of the World Trade Centre in New York in 1993.[141] With regard to the conspiracy to bomb a US aircraft in Asia, Yousef argued that the bombing had occurred outside the US and that the US had had no jurisdiction under customary international or domestic law, as there was no internationally agreed-upon definition of terrorism and no universal jurisdiction over it.[142] The US District Court relied on the Montreal Convention which prohibited the destruction of aircraft, and upheld the conviction as being consistent with US treaty obligations, whether or not the bombing amounted to 'terrorism'.[143] Another example was the *Gaddafi* case in 2001.[144] The French Court of Cassation described the charge against Gaddafi as being one of complicity in the destruction of property (an aeroplane) by way of an explosion, which in turn resulted in the death of another, which the court generally referred to as being 'in connection with a terrorist enterprise'.[145] Even after 9/11, terrorist suspects, such as the British 'shoe bomber', Richard Reid, were more typically charged with ordinary offences such as attempted murder and the attempted use of a weapon of mass destruction, rather than with terrorism.[146] In the *Lockerbie* case, where a bomb destroyed an aircraft in flight, the accused faced charges of conspiracy and multiple murders, not terrorism.[147] Writers have offered various reasons for the approach by national

140 *United States v Yousef* 327 F 3d 56 (2d Cir 2003).

141 Ibid.

142 Ibid., 34 and 43.

143 Ibid., 34–38.

144 *The Prosecutor v Saif Al-Islam Gaddafi* (General Prosecutor at the Court of Appeal of Paris, Appeal Judgment, Appeal No 00-87215, Decision No 64, 2001) 125 ILR 490 (2001).

145 Ibid. The charge was described as 'complicité de destruction d'un bien par l'effet d'une substance explosive ayant entraîné la mort d'autrui, en relation avec une entreprise terroriste'.

146 *United States v Reid* 206 F Supp 2d 132 (D Mass 2002). See further Pam Belluck, 'Threats and Responses: The Bomb Plot; Unrepentant Shoe Bomber is Given a Life Sentence for Trying to Blow up Jet' *New York Times* (16 November 2016), <https://www.nytimes.com/2003/01/31/us/threats-responses-bomb-plot-unrepentant-shoe-bomber-given-life-sentence-for.html> accessed 16 November 2016; Ben Saul, *Defining Terrorism in International Law* (Oxford University Press 2006) 256.

147 'Lockerbie Suspects Ask for Reduced Charges: Two Libyans are Charged in Deaths of 270 People' (7 December 1999) <www.deseretnews.com/article/731811/Lockerbie-suspects-ask-for-reduced-charges.html?pg=all> accessed 5 September 2017.

courts to prosecute terrorism as an ordinary crime. In some instances, states may already have criminalized offences similar to terrorism while, in others, the fact that terrorism has political motives and that states often are the targets (or sponsors) of terrorism complicates the prosecution of terrorism.[148] In *Almog v Arab Bank*, while the US Federal Court did not use the term 'terrorism', it came close to referring to the elements of terrorism when it held that 'in light of the universal condemnation of organized and systematic suicide bombings and other murderous acts intended to intimidate or coerce a civilian population, this court finds that such conduct violates an established norm of international law'.[149]

State practice supporting the prohibition of terrorism is further evidenced by the widespread ratification of sectoral anti-terrorism treaties.[150] For example, of the 193 member states of the UN, the Tokyo Convention has been ratified by 186 member states, the Montreal Convention by 188 member states and the Hague Convention by 185 member states.[151] In addition to this, the Terrorism Bombings Convention has been ratified by 170 states and the Terrorist Financing Convention by 188 states.[152] Moreover, UNSC Resolution 1373 of 2001 required all member states to make terrorism a serious crime in domestic legislation.[153] This Resolution further established the CTC in order to follow up progress in the implementation of the resolution by member states.[154] Numerous states adopted national legislation prohibiting terrorism, as evidenced by mandatory state reports to the CTC.[155]

148 Madeline Morris, 'Terrorism: The Politics of Prosecution' (2005) 5(2) Chicago Journal of International Law 405–406; Christopher Walker, 'Irish Republic Prisoners, Political Detainees, Prisoners of War or Common Criminals?' (1984) 19 Irish Jurist 189.

149 *Almog v Arab Bank PLC* 471 F Supp 2d 257, 284 (EDNY 2007).

150 With regard to subsequent practice as a means of treaty interpretation, see ILC Second Report on Subsequent Agreements and Subsequent Practice in Relation to Treaty Interpretation UN Doc A/CN4/671 para 119 (26 March 2014); ILC First Report on Subsequent Agreements and Subsequent Practice in Relation to Treaty Interpretation UN Doc A/CN4/660 para 111 (19 March 2013).

151 For treaty ratifications, see <http://treaties.un.org/> accessed 6 January 2016.

152 Ibid. See further discussion in ch 2, sec 2.3.2.

153 Art 2(3) of S/RES/1373 (2001).

154 Ibid., arts 6 and 7.

155 See the following Acts listed in n 104: South Africa's Protection of Constitutional Democracy Against Terrorist and Related Activities Act; the Botswana Counter-Terrorism Act; the Lesotho Penal Code Act; the Uganda Anti-Terrorism Act; the Ghana Anti-Terrorism Act; the Nigerian Terrorism (Prevention) Act; the Cameroon Law on the Suppression of Acts of Terrorism 2014. See further sec 87*bis* of the Algerian Penal Code (n 112); the Egyptian Anti-Terrorism Law (n 113); the Tanzanian Prevention of Terrorism Act (n 115); the Ethiopian Anti-Terrorism Proclamation (n 116); the Tunisian

Moreover, UNGA resolutions that followed after 1980, the majority of which were adopted by consensus, are reflective of the *opinio juris* of states and unequivocally condemn terrorism 'wherever and by whomever committed' as

---

Anti-Terrorism Law (n 117); sec 329 of the Penal Code of Bhutan (n 118); the Bangladesh Anti-Terrorism Ordinance (n 119); sec 130B of the Malaysian Penal Code (n 120); sec 218*bis* of the Penal Code of the Democratic Republic of Timor Leste (n 121); the Jamaican Terrorism Prevention Act (n 122); the Seychelles Prevention of Terrorism Act (n 123); the Dominican Suppression of the Financing of Terrorism (Amendment) Act (n 124); sec 73C of the Vanuatu Penal Code (n 125); the Antigua and Barbuda Prevention of Terrorism Act (n 125); the Trinidad and Tobago Anti-Terrorism Act (n 126); arts 571–580 of the Penal Code of Spain (n 127); sec 8(1) para 2(b) of the Belgian Organic Law on the Intelligence and Security Services (n 128); the Netherlands Crimes of Terrorism Act (n 129); sec 311 of the Criminal Code of the Czech Republic (n 130); sec 258 of the Criminal Code of the Ukraine (n 131); sec 330 of the Criminal Code of the Republic of Albania (n 132); sec 230 of the Andorra New Penal Code, 2005; the Saudi Arabia Penal Law for Crimes of Terrorism and its Financing (n 133); sec 100(1) of the Australian Criminal Code Act (n 34); the New Zealand Terrorism Suppression Act (n 134); sec 1 of 18 USC 2331, 2004 (n 135); sec 3 of the Bahamas Anti-Terrorism Act (n 136); sec 391 of the Guatemalan Criminal Code (n 136); sec 2 of the Brazilian Anti-Terrorism Law (n 137); sec 421 of the French Penal Code (n 138). See further UNSC Counter-Terrorism Committee Country Reports: Resolution 1373 (2001) <http://www.un.org/en/sc/ctc/resources/countryreports.html> accessed 8 January 2017 where states, for example, reported on legislation and procedures that exist for freezing accounts and assets at banks and financial institutions. See letter dated 22 December 2001 from the Chargé d'Affaires of the Permanent Mission of the People's Republic of China to the United Nations addressed to the Chairman of the Security Council Committee established pursuant to Resolution 1373 (2001) (n 3) concerning counter-terrorism S/2001/1270 <https://www.refworld.org/pdfid.46d5712f8.pdf> accessed 23 October 2017, where China referred to its laws regarding the control of the sources of terrorist assets. See further Country Reports: East Asia and Pacific Overview <https://www.state.gov/j/ct/rls/crt/2015/257515.htm> accessed 25 October 2017, which included reports by Australia and China. Australia noted that its legal framework to counter terrorism included 'significant penalties for committing terrorist acts; recruiting for and supporting terrorist organizations; financing terrorism; urging violence and advocating terrorism; and travelling abroad to commit terrorist acts and recruitment offences'. China reported on a comprehensive counter-terrorism law approved in 2015 to 'provide legal support for counter-terrorism activities as well as collaboration with the international community'. See further letter dated 26 January 2006 from the Permanent Representative of the US to the United Nations addressed to the Chairman of the Counter-Terrorism Committee S2006/69 <https://www.refworld.org/docid/46dcleb5c.html> accessed 23 October 2017. The US reported that sec 806 of the US Patriot Act resulted in terrorist-related property being made subject to civil forfeiture. See further letter dated 17 March 2004 from the Permanent Representative of France to the United Nations addressed to the Chairman of the Counter-Terrorism Committee S/2004/226 <https://www.refworld.org/docid/46dcleb5c.html> accessed 23 October 2017, referring to regulations to control and prevent terrorists' access to weapons.

criminal and unjustifiable in all its forms and manifestations.[156] While earlier UNGA resolutions still referred to exceptions in the case of conduct of national liberation movements with regard to terrorist acts, later UNGA resolutions excluded these references and, while they acknowledged the right to self-determination, at the same time they unequivocally condemned terrorism.[157] The strongly-worded UNGA Declaration on Measures to Eliminate International Terrorism of 1994 states that criminal acts intended to provoke a state of terror among the general public for political purposes are in any circumstances unjustifiable, irrespective of any political, philosophical, ideological, racial, ethnic, religious or other reasons.[158] This resolution, as well as a further UNGA resolution on measures to eliminate international terrorism of 1996, which recalled the 1994 resolution, were adopted by consensus, and various binding UNSC resolutions confirmed the unequival condemnation of terrorism.[159] Although resolutions and statements by states did not define terrorism, they repeated the condemnation of terrorism in all its forms and

---

156 See Saul (n 146) 204. Earlier resolutions referred to measures to 'prevent' international terrorism; see A/RES/40/61 (1985) para 1 and A/RES 42/159 (1987) para 1: (153 votes to two (Israel and the US); one abstention (by consensus). Later resolutions used stronger wording to refer to measures to 'eliminate' international terrorism, such as A/RES 46/51 (1991) Preamble (by consensus); A/RES 50/53 (1995) para 1 (by consensus); A/RES 51/210 (1996) para 1 (by consensus); A/RES 52/165 (1997) para 1 (by consensus); A/RES 54/110 (2000) para 1 (by 149 votes to 0; two abstentions); A/RES 55/158 (2001) para 1 (by 151 votes to 0, two abstentions). Further resolutions, while supporting the view that terrorism must be eliminated, also focused on the violation of human rights in the context of terrorism: A/RES 48/122 (1993) para 1 (by consensus); A/RES 49/185 (1994) para 1; A/RES 50/186 (1995) para 2; A/RES/52/133 (1997) para 3; A/RES 54/164 (2000) (para 2); A/RES 57/219 (2003) Preamble; A/RES 58/81 (2004) para 1. See further A/RES 59/153 (2005) (strengthening international cooperation and technical assistance in promoting the implementation of the universal conventions and protocols related to terrorism within the framework of the activities of the United Nations Office on Drugs and Crime) (Preamble).

157 A/RES 44/29 (1989) 301–302 and A/RES/46/51 (1991)15. These resolutions reaffirm the right to self-determination, yet offer an unqualified condemnation of terrorism.

158 A/RES/49/60 (1994) (Measures to Eliminate International Terrorism).

159 See further A/RES/51/210 (1996); see para 1 of S/RES 1368 (2001). Para 1 '[u]nequivocally condemns in the strongest terms the horrifying terrorist attacks which took place on 11 September 2001 in New York, Washington DC and Pennsylvania and regards such acts, like any act of international terrorism, as a threat to international peace and security'; S/RES/1373 (2001) ('[r]eaffirming also its unequivocal condemnation of the terrorist attacks which took place in New York, Washington DC and Pennsylvania on 11 September 2001, and expressing its determination to prevent all such acts'); S/RES/1377 (2001) ('[r]eaffirms its unequivocal condemnation of all acts, methods and practices of terrorism as criminal and unjustifiable, regardless of their motivation, in all their forms and manifestations, wherever and by whomever committed'); S/RES/2249 (2015) ([r]eaffirming that terrorism in all forms and manifestations constitutes one of the most serious threats

manifestations and declared terrorist acts as being unjustifiable regardless of the reasons invoked by their perpetrators.[160] The consistent and repeated condemnation of specific acts of terrorism by states illustrates the *opinio juris* of states regarding the prohibition of terrorism.[161]

The 2016 massacre at an Orlando nightclub, perpetrated by a self-described adherent of the Islamic State ('ISIL/Daesh'), was denounced by world leaders. Afghanistan President Ashraf Ghani stated that nothing could justify the killing of civilians, while leaders of the Arab States (Saudi Arabia, the United Arab Emirates, Kuwait, Qatar and Egypt) called the attacks immoral and inhumane.[162] In its condemnation of the terrorist attacks on Paris and Istanbul's Ataturk Airport in 2016, the G20 stated: 'We condemn, in the strongest possible terms, the heinous terrorist attacks in Paris on 13 November and in Ankara on 10 October. They are an unacceptable affront to all humanity.'[163]

Terrorist attacks in 2017 were similarly condemned by states. After a bombing at a pop concert in Manchester in May 2017 which killed 22 people, UK Prime Minister Theresa May stated that '[a]ll acts of terrorism are cowardly attacks on innocent people but this attack stands out for its appalling, sickening cowardice, deliberately targeting innocent, defenceless children and young people'.[164] In response to the terror attack in August 2017 in Barcelona where a van rammed into a crowd of pedestrians, killing 13 people and injuring numerous others, Spanish Prime Minister Mariano Rajoy said that '[t]oday the fight against terrorism is the principal priority for free and open societies like ours. It is a global threat and the response has to be global.' President Vladimir Putin

to international peace and security and that any acts of terrorism are criminal and unjustifiable regardless of their motivations, whenever and by whomsoever committed').

160 Ibid.

161 Summary Records of the Sixth Committee, 28th meeting Official Records of the General Assembly' 69th Session, A/C6/55/SR28, 7 October–14 November 2014 <https://papersmart.unmeetings.org/ga/69th-session/general-debate/statements/> accessed 8 August 2017.

162 David Pollock and Mohamed Abdelaziz ('Arab states condemn "terrorist" Paris attacks') <http://english.alarabiya.net/en/News/middle-east/2015/11/14/Arab-statesdenounce-Paris-attacks-as-violation-of-human-values-.html> accessed 1 December 2016.

163 G20 Statement on the Fight Against Terrorism <https://www.consilium.europa.eu/en/press/press-releases/2015/11/16/g20-leaders-antalya-statement-terrorism> accessed 7 August 2016.

164 'Theresa May's Downing Street Statement on Manchester Terror Attack in Full' *The Telegraph* <http://www.telegraph.co.uk/news/2017/05/23/theresa-mays-downing-street-statement-manchester-terror-attack/> accessed 17 May 2017.

called for the world to unite in an 'uncompromising battle against the forces of terror' and condemned this 'cruel and cynical crime against civilians'.[165]

4 The Definition of Terrorism

Despite numerous attempts to define terrorism through the ages, to date there is no internationally agreed-upon definition of terrorism.[166] Nevertheless, definitions differ primarily with regard to semantics or emphasis rather than with regard to substance. The absence of a comprehensive definition of terrorism does not necessarily lead to the conclusion that the term 'terrorism' lacks a core meaning. The elements of terrorism that have emerged from treaties, state practice (including domestic jurisprudence), UN resolutions and international jurisprudence will be discussed below.

4.1 *Elements of Terrorism that Have Emerged from Treaty Law*

As discussed above, the various sectoral treaties and protocols between 1963 and 2005 have defined terrorism in a manner which specifically relates to the subject matter of the convention concerned. The wording of the Aviation Conventions illustrates a progression from merely criminalizing acts by 'unruly passengers' aboard an aircraft to adding as elements of criminalized acts the elements of unlawfulness, intent and a degree of violence. As discussed earlier, the Tokyo Convention only prohibited acts that jeopardized the safety of persons or property therein or good order on board.[167] The Hague Convention,

165 'How the World Reacted to the Barcelona Terror Attack' *The Telegraph* (18 August 2017) <http://www.telegraph.co.uk/news/2017/08/17/world-reacted-barcelona-terror-attack/> accessed 27 August 2017.

166 Alex Schmid and Albert Jongman, *Political Terrorism: A New Guide to Actors, Authors, Concepts, Data Bases, Theories, and Literature* (Transaction Publishers 1984) 75 (identifying 109 different academic definitions of terrorism); Saul (n 146) 57; League of Nations, Committee of Experts for the Progressive Codification of International Law, Replies of Governments League of Nations (1927) Doc C 196 M 70 1927 V 221. See further Geoffrey Levitt, 'Is "Terrorism" Worth Defining?' (1986) 13 Ohio Northern University law Review 97, who notes that '[t]he search for a legal definition of terrorism in some ways resembles the quest for the Holy Grail: Periodically, eager souls set out, full of purpose, energy and self-confidence, to succeed where so many others before have tried and failed' but that '[t]here is common ground amongst all of us on what constitutes terrorism'. See, also, the statement by Sir Jeremy Greenstock, Permanent Representative of the United Kingdom of Great Britain and Northern Ireland in the General Assembly debate on terrorism in UN General Assembly 56th session, 12th plenary meeting (1 October 2001) UN Doc A/56/PV12 18: 'What looks, smells and kills like terrorism is terrorism.'

167 Art 1 of the Tokyo Convention (n 42); art 4 of the Hague Convention (n 42).

on the other hand, stipulated that an offence is committed by any person who unlawfully, by force or intimidation, attempts to seize control, or seizes control, of an aircraft, or is an accomplice to any person committing such an offence.[168] The Montreal Convention required the unlawful act to be intentional, and it further included an act of violence against a person on board in addition to the destruction of the aircraft. It also criminalized any attempt to commit such an offence or acting as an accomplice to an offender.[169]

In treaties after 2000, it seemed that a higher degree of violence was required to constitute an act of terrorism. Furthermore, a political motive was included. In this regard, the Nuclear Terrorism Convention made it an offence for any person to unlawfully and intentionally possess or use radioactive material with the intent to cause death, serious bodily injury or substantial damage to property or to the environment.[170] It further criminalized the use of radioactive material '[w]ith the intent to compel a natural or legal person, an international organization or a State to do or refrain from doing an act'.[171] The Terrorist Bombings Convention mirrored the elements of unlawfulness and intent, and repeated the wording relating to the degree of violence as set out in the Nuclear Terrorism Treaty.[172] When referring to the intent to cause extensive destruction of a place, facility or system, this Convention added a reference to such destruction as being likely to result in, or resulting in, major economic loss.[173]

The Terrorism Financing Convention, in particular, expanded on the elements of terrorism. It has been argued that clause 2(1)(b) of this Convention constitutes an authoritative, workable and fair definition of international terrorism, and reflects the essence of what the world understands by the term 'terrorism'.[174] It defines an offence within the meaning of the Convention as any person providing or collecting funds with the intention of carrying out:

> any ... act intended to cause death or serious bodily injury to a civilian, or to any other person not taking an active part in the hostilities in a situation of armed conflict, when the purpose of such act, by its nature or

168 Art 4 of the Hague Convention (n 42).
169 Arts 1 and 1(3) of the Montreal Convention (n 38).
170 Arts 2(1)(a) and (b) of the Nuclear Terrorism Convention (n 38).
171 Ibid. See, also, art 2(1)(b)(iii) of the Nuclear Terrorism Convention.
172 Art 2(1) of the Nuclear Terrorism Convention (n 38).
173 Ibid.
174 See *Suresh v Canada* (Minister of Citizenship and Immigration) (2002) 1 SCR 3, para 93. See, further, Thomas Weatherall, 'The Status of the Prohibition of Terrorism in International Law: Recent Developments' (2015) 46 Georgetown Journal of International Law 586.

> context, is to intimidate a population, or to compel a government or an international organization to do or to abstain from doing any act.[175]

Although this article refers to the act being committed in the context of collecting funds with the intention of carrying out a terrorist act and is limited to terrorist acts during armed conflict, it is of importance as it includes not only the elements of intention and violence, but also specifically refers to harm to civilians and the political purpose of the act, as well as a transnational element. It further confirms that it is in all circumstances unjustifiable and impermissible to target civilians.[176] In addition to this, the elements of this definition are reflected in the Draft Comprehensive Convention on Terrorism of 2002, which will be discussed in detail below.

From the discussion above, it appears that certain common elements have emerged with regard to the definition of terrorism under international treaty law, namely, criminal acts intended to terrorize a population or to coerce an authority to do or abstain from doing any act. Similarly, under regional treaty law, definitions have in common a reference to violence causing harm to persons or property and an element of terror or fear. Treaties further refer to a transnational element. Additionally, while earlier treaties referred to a criminal enterprise, later sectoral treaties required the element of political purpose.

4.2 *Elements of Terrorism that Have Emerged from Customary International Law*

A review of national legislation reveals common elements in the definitions of several states with regard to the definition of terrorism. In Africa, legislation requires a level of violence against persons or property, a political purpose and a transnational element.[177] In Asian states, definitions of terrorism refer to an intention to create fear and panic as well as violence against persons and the

175 Art 2(1)(b) of the Terrorism Financing Convention (n 38).

176 Ibid.

177 Art 1 of South Africa's Protection of Constitutional Democracy Against Terrorist and Related Activities Act (n 104); secs 2(1)(a)–(m) of the Botswana Counter-Terrorism Act (n 106); sec 96 of the Lesotho Penal Code Act (n 104); sec 7(2) of the Uganda Anti-Terrorism Act (n 106); secs 1(1)(a)–(e) of the Ghana Anti-Terrorism Act (n 104); secs 1(2) and (3) of the Nigerian Terrorism (Prevention) Act (n 104); sec 2(1) of the Cameroon Law on the Suppression of Acts of Terrorism (n 155); sec 87*bis* of the Algerian Penal Code (n 112); sec 1 of the Egyptian Anti-Terrorism Law (n 113); sec 4 of the Tanzanian Prevention of Terrorism Act (n 115); sec 3 of the Ethiopian Anti-Terrorism Proclamation (n 116); sec 13 of the Tunisian Anti-Terrorism Law (n 117).

destruction of property with a political purpose.[178] Definitions further include references to serious bodily injury, intimidation and a transnational element.[179] In Dominica and Vanuatu, a terrorist act includes harm to persons or property; damage to the environment; the disruption of public services; an intent to intimidate the public; and a political purpose.[180] In Antigua and Barbuda, terrorism includes violence to a person or property, requires a political purpose and includes an act affecting the conduct of a government by mass destruction, assassination, kidnapping or hostage-taking.[181] In Trinidad and Tobago, terrorist acts include acts resulting in the loss of human life or serious bodily harm, causing damage to property or prejudice to national security or public services for a political purpose as well as a transnational element.[182] In Europe, acts of terrorism similarly include a political purpose element.[183] In this regard, the use of violence against persons or property for ideological or political motives in order to achieve one's goals through terror, intimidation or threats are referred to in European anti-terrorism legislation.[184]

In Saudi Arabia, a terrorist crime includes a political purpose element.[185] In Australia and New Zealand, terrorist acts similarly include the elements of a

178 Sec 329 of the Penal Code of Bhutan (n 118); sec 6 of the Bangladesh Anti-Terrorism Ordinance (n 119).

179 Sec 130B of the Malaysian Penal Code (n 120); sec 218*bis* of the Penal Code of the Democratic Republic of Timor Leste (n 121); sec 3(2) of the Jamaican Terrorism Prevention Act (n 122); sec 2 of the Seychelles Prevention of Terrorism Act (n 123). These acts also referred to the political purpose element.

180 Sec 3(b) of the Dominican Suppression of the Financing of Terrorism (Amendment) Act (n 124), sec 73C of the Vanuatu Penal Code (n 124).

181 Sec 1 of the Antiguau and Barbuda Prevention of Terrorism Act, 2001.

182 Sec 2 of the Trinidad and Tobago Anti-Terrorism Act (n 126).

183 See, for example, secs 571–580 of Spain's Penal Code (n 127).

184 Ibid. See further sec 8(1) para 2(b) of the Belgian Organic Law on the Intelligence and Security Services (n 128); sec 83 of the Dutch Crimes of Terrorism Act (n 129); sec 311 of the Criminal Code of the Czech Republic (n 130); sec 258 of the Criminal Code of Ukraine (n 131); sec 330 of the Criminal Code of the Republic of Albania (n 132); sec 230 of the Andorra Nouveau Code Pénal (n 132).

185 Sec 1(A) of the Saudi Arabia Penal Law for Crimes of Terrorism and its Financing (n 133) states: 'Terrorist crime: any act carried out by the perpetrator to commit a criminal activity either as an individual or as part of a group, whether directly or indirectly, towards the purpose of disrupting public order; harming the security of the community and the stability of the state; risking national unity; disabling the Basic Law or any of its articles; harming the reputation or status of the country; damaging public facilities and natural resources; or trying to coerce a branch of the authority into undertaking a certain course action or obstructing justice; or threatening or inciting the commission of any of the aforementioned acts.'

political purpose and the intimidation of the public.[186] US federal law defines terrorism as any crime that appears to be intended to 'intimidate or coerce a civilian population; to influence the policy of a government by intimidation or coercion; or to affect the conduct of a government by mass destruction, assassination, or kidnapping'.[187] The Bahamas Anti-Terrorism Act, as well as the Guatemala Criminal Code, refer to an act causing bodily harm or damage to property with a political purpose.[188] In Brazil, terrorism includes acts of xenophobia, discrimination or prejudice committed for the purpose of causing terror and exposing persons and property to danger.[189] In France, the definition of terrorist acts reflects the elements of violence and a transnational element.[190]

It has been argued that, although there are differences in national approaches to the prohibition of terrorism as appears from the discussion above, the common elements are harm to civilians; an intention to spread fear; a political purpose; and a transnational element.[191] Furthermore, in decisions after 9/11, national courts were willing to engage with the issue of a definition of terrorism. In the *Clavel* case, the Argentinean Supreme Court defined terrorism as a crime *juris gentium*, and pointed out that this involves the commission of cruelties upon the civilian population, subverts order and public security, has transnational effects and that its prosecution is in the interests of all civilized nations.[192] The elements of motive, violence and a political purpose were thus emphasized.

Moreover, in certain cases courts supported the prohibition of terrorism notwithstanding the absence of a definition. In the *Suresh* case, the appellant appealed against his denial of refugee status and deportation on the basis of his involvement in terrorism.[193] The Canadian Supreme Court noted that 'there is no single definition that is accepted internationally and one searches in vain for an authoritative definition'.[194] Nevertheless, the Court accepted

186 Sec 100(1) of the Australian Criminal Code Act (n 134); secs 1 and 2 of the New Zealand Terrorism Suppression Act (n 134).

187 Sec 1 of 18 USC 2331 (2004).

188 Sec 3 of the Bahamas Anti-Terrorism Act (n 136); sec 391 of the Guatemalan Criminal Code (n 136).

189 Sec 2 of the Brazilian Anti-Terrorism Law (n 137).

190 Sec 421 of the French Penal Code (n 138).

191 Annyssa Bellal, 'The 2009 Resolution of the Institute of International Law on Immunity and International Crimes: A Partial Codification of the Law?' (2011) 9 Journal of International Criminal Justice 227, 233, 263; S/RES 1373 (2001) para 2(e).

192 *Enrique Lautaro Arancibia Clavel* 259 (Arg Supreme Court) (2004).

193 *Suresh* case (n 174).

194 Ibid., 94, where the Court stated: 'We are not persuaded … that the term "terrorism" is so unsettled that it cannot set the proper boundaries of legal adjudication. The recently

that there was an agreed definition of international terrorism, though only for the purpose of applying Canadian immigration law. It further approved the definition in the Terrorism Financing Convention as a 'workable' definition.[195]

In *Madan Singh v State of Bihar*, decided by the Supreme Court of India, the appellants argued that they could not have been convicted of terrorism as the Indian anti-terrorism legislation concerned failed to specifically define terrorism.[196] The Court dismissed the appeal.[197] In arriving at its decision, the Court stated that the matter of finding a definition of terrorism 'has haunted countries for decades'.[198] It contemplated various definitions of terrorism, including a definition focusing on terrorism as violent actions for, *inter alia*, political reasons, and terrorism as a peacetime equivalent of a war crime.[199] The Court suggested that acts such as deliberate attacks on civilians, hostage-taking and the killing of prisoners in wartime could serve as the basis of an equivalent crime of terrorism in peacetime.[200] Finally, the Court was of the view that terrorism may be described in terms of the elements of violence (including death, injury or the destruction of property), an intent to cause fear, a political purpose and the result of the terrorist act being to cause a prolonged psychological effect on the victim and affecting society as a whole by terrorising and disturbing the harmony of society.[201]

---

negotiated International Convention for the Suppression on the Financing of Terrorism … approaches the definitional problem in two ways. First, it employs a functional definition in Art 2(a), defining "terrorism" as "[a]n act which constitutes an offence within the scope of and as defined in one of the treaties listed in the annex …" Second, the Convention supplements this offence-based list with a stipulative definition of terrorism. Art 2(1)(b) defines "terrorism" as "[a]ny act intended to cause death or serious bodily injury to a civilian, or to any other person not taking an active part in the hostilities in a situation of armed conflict, when the purpose of such act, by its nature or context, is to intimidate a population, or to compel a government or an international organization to do or to abstain from doing any act.' This definition encompasses the essence of what we understand by 'terrorism'.

195 Ibid., paras 96–98.

196 *Madan Singh v State of Bihar* (2004) INSC 225 (2 April 2004). See, also, sec 19 of the Indian Terrorist and Disruptive Activities (Prevention) Act, 1987 which does not define terrorism.

197 *Madan Singh* case (n 196).

198 Ibid.

199 Ibid. Judges Raju and Pasayat stated that '[i]f the core of war crimes – deliberate attacks on civilians, hostage-taking and the killing of prisoners – is extended to peacetime, we could simply define acts of terrorism veritably as "peacetime equivalents of war crimes"'.

200 Ibid.

201 Ibid. Judges Raju and Pasayat were of the view that '[i]t may be possible to describe it [terrorism] as use of violence when its most important result is not merely the physical and mental damage of the victim but the prolonged psychological effect it produces or has the potential of producing on the society as a whole. There may be death, injury, or

With regard to international jurisprudence, in the case of *Prosecutor v Galić* the International Criminal Tribunal for the Former Yugoslavia (ICTY) Trial Chamber stated that the prohibition against terror was a specific prohibition within the general prohibition of attacks on civilians.[202] Galić, as the commander of the Serbian forces, carried out a protracted sniping and bombing campaign on Sarajevo.[203] According to the Tribunal, these crimes were wilfully directed against the civilian population and resulted in serious injury or death with the primary purpose of spreading terror among the civilian population.[204] Furthermore, in the *Israeli Wall Advisory Opinion*, the International Court of Justice (ICJ) confirmed that

> deliberate and indiscriminate attacks against civilians with the intent to kill are the core element of terrorism which has been unconditionally condemned by the international community regardless of the motives which have inspired them.[205]

In addition to the above, the decision by the Appeals Chamber of the Special Tribunal for Lebanon (STL) in *Prosecutor v Ayyash*, involving the consideration

---

destruction of property or even deprivation of individual liberty in the process but the extent and reach of the intended terrorist activity travels beyond the effect of an ordinary crime capable of being punished under the ordinary penal law of the land and its main objective is to overawe the Government or disturb the harmony of the society or "terrorise" people and the society and not only those directly assaulted, with a view to disturb the even tempo, peace and tranquility of the society and create a sense of fear and insecurity.'

202 *Prosecutor v Galić* (Trial Judgment) ICTY 5 December 2003 IT-98-29-I paras 87, 114 and 120. The Court (para 114) referred to *Trial of Shigeki Motomura and 15 Others* 13 Law Reports of Trials of War Criminals (1947) 138–139, delivered by a court-martial sitting in Makassar in the Netherlands East-Indies, which was the first conviction for terror against a civilian population. The offences alleged in Motomura were described as 'systematic terrorism against persons suspected by the Japanese of punishable acts, taking the form of repeated, regular and lengthy torture and/or ill-treatment, the seizing of men and women on the grounds of wild rumours, repeatedly striking them … the aforesaid acts having led or at least contributed to the death, severe physical and mental suffering of many'. See, further, the Croatian case of *Prosecutor v Rajko Radulović & Others* K-15/95 (Judgment of 26 May 1997) where the Court convicted Radulović and other members of the army of 'Republika Srpska' in terms of, *inter alia*, art 33 of the Fourth Geneva Convention, 1949 as well as art 51 of Additional Protocol and art 13 of Additional Protocol II to the Conventions for their 'plan of terrorising and mistreating the civilians'.

203 *Galić* case (n 202) paras 61–251.

204 Ibid., para 87.

205 *Legal Consequences of the Construction of a Wall in the Occupied Palestinian Territory* 9 July 2004 (2004) ICJ Reports 136 paras 4–5.

of the crime of terrorism under Lebanese law as well as customary international law, is relevant.[206] The Appeals Chamber confirmed that under the Lebanese Criminal Code, acts of terrorism are acts intended to cause a state of terror and the use of a means liable to create a public danger (*un danger commun*).[207] The Appeals Chamber held that 'a customary rule of international law regarding the international crime of terrorism, at least in time of peace, has indeed emerged'.[208] It found the following elements for the crime of terrorism under customary international law: the threat of or the perpetration of a criminal act; the intent to spread fear among the population; directly or indirectly coercing a national or international authority to take some action or to refrain from taking such action; and a transnational element.[209] It further identified 'a belief of States that the punishment of terrorism responds to a social necessity (*opinio necessitatis*) and is hence rendered obligatory by the existence of a rule requiring it (*opinio juris*)' as evidenced by state practice'.[210] The Appeals Chamber stated that state practice evidencing *opinio juris sive necessitates* 'share[d] a core concept: Terrorism is a criminal action that aims at spreading terror or coercing governmental authorities and is a threat to the stability of society or the State', and the few States still insisting on an exception to the definition of terrorism can, at most, be considered persistent objectors.[211]

With regard to UN resolutions, until the 1990s these resolutions tended to treat terrorist acts within existing legal frameworks and did not attempt to define terrorism *per se*. For example, in cases of non-state aircraft hijacking and hostage-taking, the UNSC did not refer to 'terrorism' but treated these acts under the existing sectoral treaties on international civil aviation and the use of force.[212] In other instances the UNSC condemned specific acts such as hostage-taking, bombings, assassination attempts and abduction as manifestations of international terrorism without specifically linking these acts to a

206 *Prosecutor v Ayyash & Others* (STL-11-01/I), Interlocutory Decision on the Applicable Law: Terrorism, Conspiracy, Homicide, Perpetration, Cumulative Charging, Appeals Chamber, 16 February 2011 paras 42–62. See, also, S/RES 1757 (2007) para 1, in which the SC established the Special Tribunal for Lebanon (STL) in terms of ch VII in order to prosecute the persons responsible for the assassination of Rafic Hariri, the former Lebanese Prime Minister, and the deaths of 21 others on 14 February 2005.

207 Sec 314 of the Lebanese Penal Code, 1943; *Ayyash* case (n 206) para 48.

208 *Ayyash* (n 206) para 85.

209 Ibid.

210 Ibid., para 102.

211 Ibid., paras 102 and 110.

212 See eg S/RES/731 (1992) (on Libya, after the Lockerbie incident); S/RES 1044 and 1054 (1996) (condemnation of assassination attempt against President Mubarak of Egypt); S/RES/1440 (2002) (condemnation of hostage-taking in Moscow).

political motive.[213] Even Resolution 1373 with its strong legislative nature and binding obligations failed to define terrorism. It was only in 2004 that the UNSC adopted Resolution 1566 which, while not expressly stipulated as a definition of international terrorism, recalls that:

> criminal acts, including against civilians, committed with the intent to cause death or serious bodily injury, or taking of hostages, with the purpose to provoke a state of terror in the general public or in a group of persons or particular persons, intimidate a population or compel a government or an international organization to do or abstain from doing any act … constitute an offence within the scope of and as defined in the international conventions and protocols relating to terrorism.[214]

This wording encompasses the elements of a criminal act against civilians committed with the intent to cause serious harm and provoke terror, with the purpose of intimidation or a political purpose. It further refers to the transnational element. It is argued that, while to date there still is no internationally agreed-upon definition of terrorism, terrorism has obtained a core meaning under customary international law. The next section will consider how this core meaning is reflected in the definition of terrorism contained in the Draft Comprehensive Convention on International Terrorism (Draft Comprehensive Convention).

5 The Draft Comprehensive Convention on International Terrorism

In 1972, the UNGA decided to establish an *Ad Hoc* Committee on International Terrorism under UNGA Resolution 3034 (XXVII).[215] From the outset, there were complexities with regard to defining international terrorism, isolating its underlying causes and deciding on measures to prevent it.[216] Notwithstanding this, upon the completion of its work in 1979, the *Ad Hoc* Committee managed

213 See eg S/RES 1438 (2002) (condemnation of bombings in Bali); S/RES 1440 (2002) (condemnation of hostage-taking in Moscow); S/RES 1450 (2002) (condemnation of terrorist attacks in Kenya); S/RES 1465 (2003) (condemnation of bomb attacks in Bogota, Colombia); S/RES 1516 (2003) (condemnation of bombings in Istanbul); S/RES 1530 (2004) (condemnation of bomb attacks in Madrid); S/RES 1611 (2005) (condemnation of bomb attacks in London); S/RES 1618 (2005) (condemnation of terrorist attacks in Iraq).

214 S/RES 1566 (2004) para 3.

215 A/RES/3034 (XXVII) (1972).

216 *Suresh* case (n 174).

to agree on cooperative measures for the elimination of international terrorism, and the UNGA for the first time unequivocally condemned terrorism.[217] In 1996 the UNGA established the second *Ad Hoc* Committee on International Terrorism.[218] The purpose of this committee was to elaborate on international conventions for the suppression of terrorist bombings and acts of nuclear terrorism, to supplement related existing international instruments and to address a means of developing a comprehensive legal framework of conventions dealing with international terrorism.[219] The UNGA further allocated the item entitled 'Measures to eliminate international terrorism' to the Legal (Sixth) Committee.[220] The Sixth Committee considered the item at various meetings in 1997.[221]

During 2000, the Sixth Committee commenced its work on the elaboration of the Draft Comprehensive Convention on the basis of the working document submitted by India entitled the Draft Comprehensive Convention on International Terrorism.[222] The Draft Comprehensive Convention repeated many of the principles set out in the various sectoral treaties, such as the transnational element;, the principle that states must establish jurisdiction over the terrorist offence; make these offences punishable by appropriate penalties; and adopt measures to ensure that the offences concerned are not justifiable by political, philosophical, ideological, racial, ethnic, religious or similar considerations.[223] The Draft Comprehensive Convention further placed a duty on states to cooperate in the fight against terrorism and to extradite or prosecute offenders, and made it clear that no political exception defence was available.[224] At its 26th meeting, the *Ad Hoc* Committee recommended that the Sixth Committee (at the 57th session of the General Assembly) consider establishing a working group to be convened in October 2002 in order to urgently continue

217 A/RES/34/145 (1979), re-endorsed in A/RES/36/109 (1981) and A/RES/38/130 (1983).

218 *Ad Hoc* Committee established by A/RES/51/210 (1996).

219 Ibid.

220 Ibid.

221 See the 2nd, 27th to 30th and 32nd to 34th meetings of the Sixth Committee, respectively held on 27 September and 13, 14, 19 and 21 November 1997. The views of the representatives who spoke during the Committee's consideration of the item are reflected in the relevant summary records (A/C6/52/SR2 27–30 and 32–34). In the same year, the Sixth Committee adopted the text of the Terrorist Bombings Convention (n 38).

222 Working Document submitted by India on the Draft Comprehensive Convention on International Terrorism <http://www.satp.org/satporgtp/countries/india/document/papers/India_IntConv.htm> accessed 11 September 2017.

223 Ibid., arts 5 and 7.

224 Ibid., arts 10, 13, 15 and 16.

the elaboration of the Draft Comprehensive Convention.[225] At the 57th session of the UNGA, the Coordinator prepared the following text for discussion with regard to the definition of terrorism in the Draft Comprehensive Convention (article 2):

2(1) Any person commits an offence within the meaning of this Convention if that person, by any means, unlawfully and intentionally, causes:
(a) Death or serious bodily injury to any person; or
(b) Serious damage to public or private property, including a place of public use, a State or government facility, a public transportation system, an infrastructure facility or the environment; or
(c) Damage to property, places, facilities, or systems referred to in paragraph 1(b) of this article, resulting or likely to result in major economic loss,
when the purpose of the conduct, by its nature or context, is to intimidate a population, or to compel a Government or an international organization to do or abstain from doing any act.[226]

This is still the definition reflected in the Draft Comprehensive Convention today. The deadlock preventing the finalization of the Convention is not due to disagreement with regard to the substantive, inclusionary elements of the definition above, but rather with regard to the exclusionary elements. As will be discussed below, the disagreement revolves around whether acts prohibited under the Draft Comprehensive Convention should apply to the conduct of peoples struggling for self-determination and whether the activities of armed forces during an armed conflict and the activities undertaken by military forces of a state in the exercise of their official duties should be excluded from the definition of terrorism.

In this regard, the Coordinator, in draft article 18, proposed the text below with regard to the exceptions to the definition in articles 18(2) and (3):

(2) The activities of armed forces during an armed conflict, as those terms are understood under international humanitarian law, which are governed by that law, are not governed by this Convention.

---

225 Report of the Ad Hoc Committee established by General Assembly Resolution 51/210 (1996) sixth session (28 January–1 February 2002) A/57/37.

226 Ibid.; informal texts of arts 2 and 2*bis* of the Draft Comprehensive Convention, prepared by the Coordinator Annex II, 6.

(3) The activities undertaken by the military forces of a state in the exercise of their official duties, inasmuch as they are governed by other rules of international law, are not governed by this Convention.

Art 18(4) stated that '[n]othing in this article condones or makes lawful otherwise unlawful acts, nor precludes prosecution under other laws'.[227]

The members of the Organization of Islamic Countries (OIC) sought to amend subarticles (2) and (3) of the proposed text above as follows:

(2) The activities of the parties during an armed conflict, *including in situations of foreign occupation*, as those terms are understood under international humanitarian law, which are governed by that law, are not governed by this Convention (emphasis added).

(3) The activities undertaken by the military forces of a state in the exercise of their official duties, inasmuch as they are *in conformity with international law*, are not governed by this Convention[228] (emphasis added).

The only contentious areas, thus, were the exclusion of acts of people during a struggle for self-determination and the activities undertaken by the military forces of a state. It has been argued that, since both of these scenarios are regulated by other rules of international law, it was in fact unnecessary to repeat these controversial provisions in a convention designed to condemn and criminalize international terrorism.[229]

In 2007, another concerted effort was made in the *Ad Hoc* Committee to reach a compromise on the wording of the definition.[230] The coordinator, Maria Telalian, prepared informal summaries on the exchange of views in plenary meetings and during informal consultations on the Draft Comprehensive Convention. She then presented a text which attempted to capture the concerns of delegations in a way that would facilitate agreement on elements of an overall package.[231] The coordinator emphasized the fact that states needed

227 Ibid.; texts relating to art 18 of the Draft Comprehensive Convention Annex IV.

228 Ibid. See further art 2 of the Organisation of Islamic Cooperation (OIC) Convention, 1999; UN 'International Instruments Related to the Prevention and Suppression of International Terrorism' (2008) 190 <http://www.un-ilibrary.org/peacekeeping-and-security/international-instruments-related-to-the-prevention-and-suppression-of-international-terrorism_6866fb0e-en> accessed 26 October 2017.

229 Surya Subedi, 'The UN Response to International Terrorism in the Aftermath of the Terrorist Attacks in America and the Problem of the Definition of Terrorism in International Law' (2002) 4 International Law Forum du Droit International 159, 164–5.

230 Report of the Ad Hoc Committee established by General Assembly Resolution 51/210 of 17 December 1996 11th session (5, 6 and 15 February 2007) A/62/37 Annex to the Report.

231 Ibid., para 14.

to reflect upon the wording as an honest attempt to bridge a gap which had been insurmountable since 2000.[232]

In the proposed text, the preambular paragraphs from the Terrorist Bombings Convention and the Nuclear Terrorism Convention were duplicated in the Draft Comprehensive Convention. These paragraphs stipulated that the activities of military forces of states were governed by rules of international law outside the framework of the Convention, but that the exclusion of these actions from the coverage of the Convention did not condone or make lawful state terrorism and terrorist activities by military forces of states that otherwise would be unlawful.[233]

Furthermore, article 18(4) was amended slightly to add that an offence as defined in article 2 of the Convention remains punishable under other rules of international law.[234] This amendment sought to emphasize that there was no impunity intended and that a core of offences remained which should continue to be punishable irrespective of the regime that applies. In this regard, the new proposed article 18(5) stated that the Draft Comprehensive Convention was without prejudice to the rules of international law which are applicable during armed conflict, particularly the rules applicable to acts that are lawful under international humanitarian law.[235] This paragraph was intended to protect the continued applicability of international humanitarian law in relevant circumstances.[236] The text of article 18, however, was not agreed upon at the 2007 meeting of the *Ad Hoc* Committee.

Two years later, the Sixth Committee established a Working Group in order to further consider the issue of international terrorism.[237] At the third meeting of the Working Group, various delegations raised concerns with regard to the fact that the Draft Comprehensive Convention had not been finalized.[238]

232 Ibid., para 20.
233 Ibid., para 14.
234 Ibid.
235 Ibid.
236 Ibid., para 18.
237 See the report of the Sixth Committee 'Measures to Eliminate International Terrorism' (2008) 64th session A/64/37 Supplement No 37.
238 'Summary records of the Sixth Committee' (2009) 64th session, 3rd Meeting A/C6/64/SR3. See, for example, statement by Mr Al-Jarman (United Arab Emirates) para 9 ('delegations should make every effort to conclude work on the draft, urged delegations to seek common ground in finalizing the draft comprehensive convention'); Mr Mukongo Ngay (Democratic Republic of the Congo) para 20 ('urged delegations to pursue negotiations to conclude a draft comprehensive convention on international terrorism'); Mr Ayoob (Afghanistan) para 30 ('[c]oncluding the draft comprehensive convention on

At the 25th meeting of the Sixth Committee, it was resolved that the *Ad Hoc* Committee should meet on an expedited basis in 2010 and continue to elaborate the Draft Comprehensive Convention and discuss the question of convening a high-level conference under the auspices of the UN.[239] The *Ad Hoc* Committee duly met in 2010, and delegations expressed their willingness to work on the basis of the proposal presented by the Coordinator in 2007.[240] The Coordinator supported draft article 18 (including its inclusionary and exclusionary elements) as a suitable legal definition of acts of terrorism in a criminal law enforcement instrument such as the Convention.[241] Notwithstanding this, differences around the exclusion of acts of terrorism from the legitimate struggle of peoples in the exercise of their rights to self-determination as well as the exclusion of the acts of military forces of a state remained.[242]

During its subsequent meeting in 2013, there were further discussions by the *Ad Hoc* Committee with regard to the contentious article 18 of the Draft Comprehensive Convention (now draft article 3).[243] The similarities between the text of the contentious article 3 and language previously agreed upon in the Terrorist Bombings and Terrorist Financing Conventions, the texts of which had already been agreed upon, were further pointed out.[244] This applied in respect of articles 3(1) to 3(3) of the Draft Comprehensive Convention. Article 3(1) of the Draft Comprehensive Convention, which aimed at ensuring the integrity of international humanitarian law and argued that there was no impunity for acts committed by the military forces of the state, mirrored

international terrorism should be a top priority'); Mr Versón (Cuba) para 39 ('[i]t was important to conclude work on a draft comprehensive convention that would fill the gap in the existing United Nations counter-terrorism instruments'); Mr Badji (Senegal) para 48 (urged delegations to make every effort to reach agreement on a draft comprehensive convention); Mr Al-Adhami (Iraq) para 51 stressed ('the importance of completing the preparation of a draft comprehensive convention'); Mr Shapoval (Ukraine) para 52 (supported 'the early conclusion of the negotiations on a draft comprehensive convention on international terrorism'); Mr Yun Yong II (Democratic People's Republic of Korea) para 62 ('[i]t was essential to finalize without delay a draft comprehensive convention on international terrorism'); Ms Mwaipopo (United Republic of Tanzania) para 68 stated that '[w]ork on concluding a draft comprehensive convention on terrorism should be speeded up' and called on member states to 'muster the political will needed to reach agreement on the outstanding issues'.

239 Summary records of the Sixth Committee' (n 238) para 22.

240 Report of the Ad Hoc Committee (n 230) paras 12 and 14.

241 Ibid., para 16.

242 Ibid., para 11.

243 Ibid.

244 Ibid.

the wording of articles in the Terrorist Bombings and Terrorist Financing Conventions.[245] Article 3(2), which noted that armed activities in armed conflict were to be governed by international humanitarian law, corresponded in part to article 19(2) of the Terrorist Bombings Convention and article 4(2) of the Nuclear Terrorism Convention.

Article 3(3) corresponded to certain articles of the Terrorist Bombings and Terrorist Financing Conventions and stated that, if the activities of military forces of a state were governed by other rules of international law, they would not be governed by the Convention.[246] Article 3(4) ensured that acts amounting to an offence under article 2 would remain punishable under such other laws, while article 3(5) attempted to clarify the demarcation between acts covered by the Draft Comprehensive Convention and acts that were governed by international humanitarian law, and stressed the importance of preserving the integrity of international humanitarian law.[247]

However, no agreement could be reached on adopting the text of the 2007 proposal.[248] It was suggested that the lack of substantive progress would be noted and that the Committee would recommend that work continue in the context of a working group of the Sixth Committee during the 69th session of the General Assembly. It was envisaged that this would result in a pause in negotiations and provide an opportunity to convene a high-level conference on terrorism.[249] To date, however, there has been no agreement on draft article 3 of the Draft Comprehensive Convention, and it remains unfinalized.

Notwithstanding this, it is argued that discussions in the *Ad Hoc* Committee do not preclude a definition of international terrorism. The core elements of what states believe to constitute international terrorism is evident from the proposed definition in article 3 of the Draft Comprehensive Convention, with only the exclusionary elements in article 18 causing a deadlock. At the 2017 BRICS Summit, the BRICS leaders in their joint statement noted:

245 See art 19(1) of the International Convention for the Suppression of Terrorist Bombings (n 38) and art 4(1) of the International Convention for the Suppression of Acts of Nuclear Terrorism (n 38).

246 See para 3 of draft art 3, which corresponded to the latter part of art 19(2) of the Terrorist Bombings Convention (n 38) as well as art 4(2) of the Nuclear Terrorism Convention (n 38).

247 Ibid., paras 16, 17 and 32. Art 3(5) states that '[t]he present Convention is without prejudice to the rules of international law applicable in armed conflict, in particular those rules applicable to acts lawful under international humanitarian law'.

248 Ibid., para 32.

249 Ibid., paras 30–33.

> We strongly condemn terrorism in all its forms and manifestations and reiterate that there can be no justification for any act of terrorism anywhere or for whatever reasons. We note that the Draft Comprehensive Convention against International Terrorism is currently under the consideration of the UN General Assembly and call for its urgent adoption.[250]

6 Conclusion

A rule prohibiting terrorism is supported in both treaty law and state practice. Under treaty law, various forms of terrorist conduct are prohibited, and numerous UNSC resolutions have criminalized terrorist conduct. The UNSC has further unequivocally condemned all acts, methods and practices of terrorism as criminal and unjustifiable, regardless of their motivation, and certain UNSC resolutions, such as resolution 1373, have imposed binding, quasi-legislative obligations on member states against terrorism.

With regard to state practice, almost every nation in the world has adopted legislation prohibiting terrorism. Although approaches by states in definining terrorism differ in some respects, the common elements of what is understood under the term 'terrorism' are reflected in national legislation and jurisprudence, and it is argued that states are of the unanimous understanding that terrorism should be prohibited. Furthermore, numerous delegations have reaffirmed their condemnation of terrorism in all its forms and manifestations in statements before the UNGA. Additionally, the UNGA's 1994 Declaration on Measures against International Terrorism as well as UNSC Resolution 1566 have echoed the elements of terrorism as a criminal act with the intention of providing a state of terror among the general public for a political purpose. In addition to this, international tribunals have specifically addressed the elements of terrorism as including the elements of intentional crimes against civilians which result in serious harm or injury. Moreover, the ICTY has found that terrorism is a crime under customary international law with the following elements: a criminal act; the intent to spread fear among the population; a political motive; and a transnational element. All the evidence in this chapter thus supports the conclusion that the prohibition of terrorism is part of customary international law.

250 'Joint statement of the BRICS leaders' para 13 <https://brics2017.org/English/Documents/Summit/201701/t20170125_1403.html> accessed 29 August 2017.

Furthermore, although the definition of terrorism in the Draft Comprehensive Convention remains unfinalized, it is evident from the various discussions in the Sixth Committee and the *Ad Hoc* Committee that it is not the inclusionary elements (what constitutes acts of terrorism) that have held up the finalization of the Convention, but rather what ought to be excluded from the definition of international terrorism. The impasse relates to whether the use of armed forces by states against civilians should be included in the definition and whether there should be an exception for a right to resistance of peoples under foreign occupation. The failure to agree on the exclusionary elements, however, does not preclude the general understanding of what constitutes terrorism or that it is prohibited. In this regard, writers, including Cassese, have supported terrorism as a customary international law crime notwithstanding the absence of a definition and, in the *Ayyash* case, the Appeals Chamber of the STL similarly supported the prohibition of terrorism in peacetime.

Accordingly, it is argued that in international law terrorism has indeed attained a core, objectively determinable meaning. The common elements of international terrorism reflected in treaties, state practice and international jurisprudence are that it is an act of violence, committed with the intent to cause death or serious bodily injury to any person or to spread fear among civilians, for a political purpose with a transnational element, and the absence of an international treaty definition does not preclude the identification or prohibition of international terrorism.

CHAPTER 2

The Prohibition of Terrorism as a *Jus Cogens* Norm

1 Introduction

The previous chapter found support for both the prohibition of terrorism in international law and the emergence of a definition of terrorism under customary international law. This chapter will analyze whether the prohibition of terrorism as a rule of customary international law has acquired the status of *jus cogens*. To do this, it is necessary to analyze the criteria for the constitution of a *jus cogens* norm under the Vienna Convention on the Law of Treaties (Vienna Convention) as well as to consider whether the prohibition of terrorism possesses the core characteristics of *jus cogens* norms. This chapter will start with an historical overview of the evolution of *jus cogens* norms in section 2. This section is divided into sections 2.1 and 2.2. Section 2.1 briefly deals with the evolution of *jus cogens* norms under early international law, and section 2.2 discusses the evolution of *jus cogens* norms in the period after World War II up to the adoption of the Vienna Convention.[1]

Section 3 will consider the criteria for a *jus cogens* norm under the Vienna Convention, namely, a norm of general international law which is accepted and recognized by the international community of states as a whole as a norm from which no derogation is permitted. Section 4 will evaluate the core characteristics of *jus cogens* norms as these have emerged from international law by means of an analysis of state practice and international jurisprudence. Section 5 will consider whether the rules regarding the prohibition of terrorism discussed in chapter 2 meet the criteria for *jus cogens* norms as set out in article 53 of the Vienna Convention and whether the prohibition of terrorism displays the core characteristics of *jus cogens* norms as these have emerged in state practice and international jurisprudence.

2 An Historical Overview of *Jus Cogens*

The historical evolution of *jus cogens* will be discussed with reference to two periods – the period before the negotiation and conclusion of the Vienna Convention (roughly overlapping with the period before World War II) and the

1 The Vienna Convention on the Law of Treaties, 1969.

 | DOI:10.1163/9789004391543_004

period thereafter. While the discussion will provide a brief overview of the first period, the focus will be on the debates in the International Law Commission (ILC) leading to the adoption of the Vienna Convention. Although the concept of *jus cogens* was generally recognized before the adoption of the Vienna Convention, it was article 53 of the Vienna Convention that, for the first time, confirmed the concept of *jus cogens* as being part of international law.[2]

2.1 *The Period Preceding the Negotiation and Adoption of the Vienna Convention on the Law of Treaties*

Early international law writers of the seventeeth to nineteeth centuries were of the view that there are certain necessary principles of international law that are *jus scriptum* (obligatory law) and that bind all states regardless of consent.[3] These rules permitted no derogation as they were derived from a higher source, namely, natural law, and all treaties and customs that contravened this law were illegal.[4] The idea of a limit on state sovereignty and the existence of certain non-derogable obligations continued after World War I. In 1919 the principle of non-derogable obligations in the context of the law of treaties was referred to in the Covenant of the League of Nations. The Covenant provided for the abrogation of any obligations inconsistent with its terms, and stated that members of the League would not enter into such obligations.[5] Although this provision was applicable only between members of the League, and the provision itself was derogable, it illustrated the application of the concept of non-derogability, at least in treaty law.[6] It further illustrated that international law contemplated the possibility of limits to state consent.

Moreover, international case law and the writings of this period supported the invalidity of treaties on the basis of their inconsistency with another rule

2 Dire Tladi, '*Jus Cogens* in the Report of the International Law Commission 66th Session' (5 May–6 June and 7 July–8 August 2014) A/69/10 Annex 277; Arnold McNair, *The Law of Treaties* (Clarendon Press 1961) 215.

3 Hugo de Groot, *De Jure Belli Ac Pacis Libri Tres* (Clarendon Press 1625) book 1 ch 1; Emer de Vattel, *Le Droit des Gens, ou Principes de la Loi Naturelle, Appliqués à La Conduit et aux Affaires des Nations et des Souverains* (Neufchatel 1758) 1 Préliminaires secs 7, 21, 27 (distinguishing 'le droit des gens naturel, ou nécessaire' or obligatory law from 'le droit volontaire' or voluntary law; Christian Wolff, '*Jus Gentium Methodo Scientifica Pertractatum*' *in* James Scott (ed), *The Classics of International Law* (Clarendon Press 1764) 1 sec 5; Johan Bluntschli and James Scott (eds), *Le Droit International Codifié* (Librairie de Guillaumin et Cie 1874) 238–40.

4 De Groot (n 3) famously stated that principles of natural law were so immutable that not even God could change them.

5 Art 20 of the Covenant of the League of Nations, 1919.

6 Tladi (n 2) para 26.

of international law.[7] Although there was support for positivism and state sovereignty in the early twentieth century, various events after World War II seemed to indicate that international law imposed limits on state sovereignty.[8] These events included the creation of the United Nations (UN) in 1945, the Nuremberg trials of 1945–1946, and the adoption of the Universal Declaration of Human Rights (UDHR) of 1948.[9]

Despite being firmly rooted in natural law, the idea of certain peremptory, non-derogable norms eventually received a positivist slant with its formal inclusion in treaty law. In this regard, it was the work of the ILC in drafting the text which eventually became article 53 of the Vienna Convention that gave *jus cogens* its positivist flavour and established the criteria for *jus cogens.*[10] The various debates within the ILC, comments of states on the ILC text and discussions at the Vienna Conference will be evaluated below.

2.2 *The Negotiation and Conclusion of the Vienna Conference*

The UN was established after World War II. This was followed by the establishment of the ILC which had a mandate to promote progressive development

---

7 Paul Fauchille and Henry Bonfils, *Traité de Droit International Public* (Rousseau 1921) 1 (1); Alfred Verdross, 'Forbidden Treaties in International Law: Comments on Professor Garner's Report on "The Law of Treaties"' (1937) 31 American Journal of International Law 571 et seq; *Oscar Chinn* (*United Kingdom v Belgium*) Judgment, PCIJ Series A/B No 63ICGJ 313 (PCIJ 1932) (1934) (separate opinion of Judge Schücking) 149. See, further, *Pablo Nájera* (*France*) *v United Mexican States* Decision No 30-A (19 October 1928) UN Reports of International Arbitral Awards Vol 5 466, 470, where the French-Mexican Claims Commission interpreted a rule of the Covenant of the League of Nations requiring the registration of treaties as a *jus cogens* rule from which no derogation was permitted.

8 On support for state soveignty and positivism, see *The SS Lotus Case* (*France v Turkey*) (7 September 1927) (1927) PCIJ Ser A No 10 case 18 ('[i]nternational law governs relations between independent states. The rules of law binding upon states emanate from their own free will as expressed in conventions or by usages generally accepted as expressing the principles of law.'). See, further, Paul Guggenheim, *Traité de Droit International Public* (Georg & Co 1953) 57–8: 'Les règles de droit international n'ont pas un caractère imperatif. Le droit international admet en conséquence qu'un traité peut avoir n'importe quel contenu … L'appréciation de la moralité d'un traité conduit aisément à la reintroduction du droit naturel dans le droit des traités' (The rules of international law are not of a peremptory nature. International law accordingly recognises that a treaty may have any content … The assessment of the character of a treaty easily leads to the reintroduction of natural law into the law of treaties (own translation)). See further Hans Kelsen, *Principles of International Law* (Rinehart 1952) 344; Georg Schwarzenberger, 'International *Jus Cogens*?' (1965) 43 Texas Law Review 455, 467 (arguing that states cannot not be bound to any international norms without their consent).

9 Dire Tladi and Paulina Dlagnekova, 'The Will of the State, Consent and International Law: Piercing the Veil of Positivism' (2009) 21 South African Public Law 111, 116.

10 Ibid., 17–18.

and the codification of international law. At its first session in 1949, the ILC placed the law of treaties among the topics suitable for codification, and it appointed James Brierly as Special Rapporteur. Mr Brierly resigned in 1952 and was succeeded by Sir Hersch Lauterpacht, Sir Gerald Fitzmaurice and Sir Humphrey Waldock respectively.[11] Both Sir Hersch Lauterpacht and Sir Gerald Fitzmaurice in their respective reports dealt with the issue of the validity of treaties.[12] In his first report on the Law of Treaties, Sir Lauterpacht dealt with the legality of the object of a treaty.[13] Although his report did not explicitly use the term *jus cogens*, in his commentary Sir Lauterpacht expressed the view that the test for the legality of the object of a treaty is inconsistent with those overriding principles of international law 'which may be regarded as constituting principles of international public policy (*ordre international public*).'[14] He added that these principles need not necessarily have crystallized into a clearly accepted rule of law, but they may be expressive of rules of international morality that are so cogent that an international tribunal would regard them as forming part of the principles of law generally recognized by civilized nations (and which the ICJ is bound to apply by virtue of article 38(1)(c) of the ICJ Statute).[15]

It was in the third report on the law of treaties that Sir Fitzmaurice specifically used the term *jus cogens*.[16] He proposed that it was essential to the validity of a treaty that it should not contravene principles of international law that are *jus cogens*.[17] Furthermore, he recognized the non-derogable nature of *jus cogens* rules by suggesting that states could not contract out of these rules *inter se*.[18] In his commentary, he described *jus cogens* rules as rules of international law that are 'mandatory and imperative in any circumstances' and distinguished these rules from *jus dispositivum* in respect of which variation by states is possible.[19]

---

11 Karl Zemanek, 'The Vienna Convention on the Law of Treaties' United Nations Audiovisual Library of International Law 1 <http://legal.un.org/avl/ha/vclt/vclt.html> accessed 4 December 2016.

12 Report of the Special Rapporteur on the Law of Treaties, Sir Hersch Lauterpacht, Yearbook of the International Law Commission, 1953, Vol II, A/CN.4/63 93; and 1954, Vol II, A/CN.4/87 and Corr 1; Third Report by the Special Rapporteur on the Law of Treaties, Sir Gedald G Fitzmaurice, Yearbook of the International Law Commission (1958) II A/CN4/115 and Corr 1 26–27 under the title 'Legality of the object'.

13 Lauterpacht (n 12) 154 paras 1–3.

14 Lauterpacht (n 12) 155 para 4.

15 Ibid.

16 Fitzmaurice (n 12) 26 para 2.

17 Ibid.

18 Ibid., 27.

19 Ibid., 40 para 27.

The last Special Rapporteur on the Law of Treaties, Sir Humphrey Waldock, was appointed in 1961.[20] He prepared six reports and oriented the work towards the preparation of draft articles that would be capable of serving as the basis for an international convention.[21] Sir Waldock proposed a definition for *jus cogens* that was similar to the definition that would be adopted in article 53 of the Vienna Convention, namely

> a peremptory norm of general international law from which no derogation is permitted except upon a ground specifically sanctioned by general international law, and which may be modified or annulled only by a subsequent norm of general international law.[22]

Sir Waldock criticized as too broad Sir Lauterpacht's argument that a treaty is void if it its performance would involve an act illegal under international law, and supported Sir Fitzmaurice's assertion of limiting the cases of illegality to infringements of rules of the nature of *jus cogens*.[23] He noted that it was uncertain exactly which rules of international law constitute *jus cogens* and that the concept was comparatively recent in the midst of international law being at a stage of rapid development.[24] He thus recommended that it was sufficient to state in general terms that a treaty is void if it conflicts with a rule of *jus cogens*, but to leave the full content of this rule to be worked out in state practice and the jurisprudence of international tribunals.[25]

---

20 See Zemanek (n 11).

21 First Report on the Law of Treaties, by Sir Humphrey Waldock, Special Rapporteur A/CN.4/144 and Add.1 (26 March 1962); Second Report on the Law of Treaties, by Sir Humphrey Waldock, Special Rapporteur' A/CN.4/156 and Add.1–3 (20 March, 10 April, 30 April and 5 June 1963); Third Report on the Law of Treaties, by Sir Humphrey Waldock, Special Rapporteur, A/CN.4/167 and Add.1–3 (3 March, 9 June, 12 June and 7 July 1964); Fourth Report on the Law of Treaties, by Sir Humphrey Waldock, Special Rapporteur A/CN.4/177 and Add.1 and 2 (19 March, 25 March and 17 June 1965), Fifth Report on the Law of Treaties, by Sir Humphrey Waldock, Special Rapporteur A/CN.4/183 and Add.1–4 15 November 1965 (4 December 1965, 20 December 1965, 3 January 1966, and 18 January 1966) and Sixth Report on the Law of Treaties, by Sir Humphrey Waldock, Special Rapporteur A/CN.4/186 and Add.1–7 (11 March, 25 March, 12 April, 11 May, 17 May, 24 May, 1 June and 14 June 1966).

22 See Second Report on the Law of Treaties by Sir Humphrey Waldock (n 21) 39.

23 Ibid., 52 regarding the commentary on art 13. Sir Waldock suggested that 'a treaty is contrary to international law and void if its object or its execution involves the infringement of a general rule or principle of international law having the character of *jus cogens*'.

24 Ibid.

25 Ibid. See further 'Draft Articles on the Law of Treaties with Commentaries' Yearbook of the International Law Commission (1966) Vol II, para 3, where, in paragraph 3 of the commentary to Draft Article 50, the Commission stated: 'The emergence of rules having the character of *jus cogens* is comparatively recent, while international law is in the process

The ILC discussed the draft article proposed by Sir Waldock at various meetings, and generally supported his proposal that a treaty would be void if contrary to *jus cogens* was supported.[26] The discussions in the ILC led to draft article 37, which modified the text proposed by Sir Waldock and stated that a treaty is void if it conflicts with a peremptory norm of general international law from which no derogation is permitted and which can be modified only by a subsequent norm of general international law having the same character.[27] The ILC agreed to refer article 37 to the Drafting Committee.[28] When the wording was discussed again by the ILC in its 877th meeting in 1966 as draft article 50, the ILC stated in its commentary that the view that there 'is no rule from which states cannot of their own free will contract out [of] has become increasingly difficult to sustain' and that in codifying the law of treaties it must start from the basis that 'today there are certain rules which are non-derogable by states and may only be amended by another rule of the same character'.[29] States widely supported the concept of *jus cogens* during the meetings of the ILC.[30] The ILC ultimately adopted draft article 50 which stated:

---

of rapid development. The Commission considered the right course to be to provide in general terms that a treaty is void if it conflicts with a rule of *jus cogens* and to leave the full content of the rule to be worked out in state practice and in the jurisprudence of international tribunals.'

26 'Summary record of the 682nd meeting' A/CN4/SR682 Yearbook of the International Law Commission (1963) vol 1 53–60, especially paras 18 and 22 (see eg, Mr Rosenne's statement that this article is of utmost importance from a political and moral standpoint and that both Sir Humphrey and Sir Lauterpacht argued that the law in this regard is *lex lata*); 'Summary record of the 683rd meeting' A/CN4/SR683 Yearbook of the International Law Commission (1963) vol 1 62–67; 'Summary record of the 828th meeting' A/CN4/SR828 Yearbook of the International Law Commission (1966) vol 1 (part 1) 38 para 26 (see, eg, statement by Mr Yasseen that the 'concept of *jus cogens* in international law was unchallengeable').

27 Fitzmaurice (n 12) 34.

28 Ibid., 41 para 64.

29 Summary record of the 877th meeting A/CN/4/SR877 Yearbook of the International Law Commission (1966) vol 1 (part 2) 227 and 230–231 regarding draft art 50; Draft Articles on the Law of Treaties (n 25) 247–9 para 1 of the commentary to draft art 50. The same paragraph of the commentary also states that 'in codifying the law of treaties it must start from the basis that today there are certain rules from which states are not competent to derogate at all by a treaty arrangement, and which may be changed only by another rule of the same character'.

30 Tladi (n 2) 4–15. See, further, documents of the second part of the 17th session and of the 18th session including the reports of the Commission to the General Assembly Yearbook of the International Law Commission (1966) vol II 21 regarding statements by states, eg, statement by the US, 21 ('the concept embodied in this article would, if properly applied, substantially further the rule of law in international relations'); Algeria, 21 ('[t]he Algerian delegation endorses the approach of the Commission to the question of *jus cogens*');

> A treaty is void if it conflicts with a peremptory norm of general international law from which no derogation is permitted and which can be modified only by a subsequent norm of general international law having the same character.[31]

At the Vienna Conference, while a few states raised concerns that *jus cogens* was not well established and that it constituted an emerging or a new rule of international law,[32] there was also substantial support that *jus cogens* norms were already in existence.[33] France declared:

Brazil, 21 ('whatever doctrinal divergencies there may be, the evolution of international society since the Second World War shows that it is essential to recognize the peremptory nature of certain rules'); Czechoslovakia, 22 ('that provision is largely supported by state practice and international law and is endorsed by many authorities'); Ecuador, 22 ('endorses the initiative of the Commission in including a violation of *jus cogens* as a ground for invalidating a treaty'); France, 22 (the provision 'is one of the genuinely key provisions of the draft articles'); Ghana, 22 ('endorses the Commission's approach to the concept of *jus cogens*'); and the Philippines, 22 ('welcomes the Commission's decision to recognize the existence of peremptory norms of international law').

31 Draft Articles on the Law of Treaties with Commentaries (n 25) 247–9.

32 See United Nations Conference on the Law of Treaties, First Session, Vienna (26 March–24 May 1968) Summary records of the plenary meetings and of the meetings of the Committee of the Whole (A/CONF.39/11). Certain states were of the view that *jus cogens* was an emerging norm of international law. Mr Alvarez Tabio (Cuba) 52nd meeting, 296–7, para 34 ('article 50 represented an important contribution to the progressive development of international law and his delegation strongly supported it'); Mr Fattal (Lebanon), 52nd meeting, 297, para 42 ('[i]n spite of ideological difficulties, a shared philosophy of values was now emerging'); Mr Ratsimbazafy (Madagascar), 53rd meeting, 301, para 21 ('once the notion was established and recognized as such, it would become increasingly important in the law and life of the international community'). Only Turkey and Australia expressed reservations about the principle of *jus cogens* itself and did not support the inclusion of the *jus cogens* provision in the law of treaties. See Mr Miras (Turkey), 53rd meeting, 300, para 6. Turkey was of the view that the notion of *jus cogens* and the manner it had been articulated in the Commission's Draft Articles was 'not with a well-established rule, but with a new rule by means of which an attempt was being made to introduce into international law, through a treaty, the notion of "public policy" – *ordre public*'. See further Mr Harry (Australia) 55th meeting, 316, para 13. Australia was of the view that in the absence of any comprehensive list or any clear definition of what norms of general international law would have the character of *jus cogens*, it would be wrong to include the article in a convention on the law of treaties.

33 See United Nations Conference on the Law of Treaties (n 32). For example, see the statement by Mr Klestov (Union of Soviet Socialist Republics), 52nd meeting, 294, para 3 (arguing that the principle of *jus cogens* was recognized by the Commission and by many eminent jurists); Mr Suarez (Mexico), 52nd meeting, 294, paras 6–8 (stating that the existence of *jus cogens* is beyond doubt); Mr Yasseen (Iraq), 52nd meeting, 295, para 21 (stating the existence of *jus cogens* is beyond dispute); Mr Mwendwa (Kenya), 52nd meeting,

> The substance of *jus cogens* was what represented the undeniable expression of the universal conscience, the common denominator of what men of all nationalities regarded as sacrosanct, namely, respect for and protection of the rights of the human person.[34]

The Holy See noted that principles such as the prohibition of slavery and genocide had entered into positive law, but they had done so as rules of natural law ratified and sanctioned by positive law without losing their value as 'fundamental dictates of the universal conscience'.[35] Spain referred to international law as not being 'a creation of the will of states', but 'based on a natural law founded on the principles of *pacta sunt servanda* and *jus cogens*'.[36]

The Vienna Conference adopted a slightly modified version of the ILC's article 50 as article 53 of the Vienna Convention, adding a reference to the norm being accepted and recognized by the international community:

> A treaty is void if, at the time of its conclusion, it conflicts with a peremptory norm of general international law. For the purposes of the present Convention, a peremptory norm of general international law is a norm accepted and recognized by the international community of states as a whole as a norm from which no derogation is permitted and which can be modified only by a subsequent norm of general international law having the same character.[37]

296, para 28 (stating that *jus cogens* is a clearly existing fact); Mr Ogundere (Nigeria), 52nd meeting, 298, para 48 ('[i]nternational morality had become accepted as a vital element of international law, and eminent jurists had affirmed the principle of the existence of *jus cogens*, based on the universal recognition of an enduring international public policy deriving from the principle of a peremptory norm of general international law'); Mr Ruiz Varela (Colombia), 53rd meeting, 301, para 26 ('in principle the entire world recognized the existience of a public international order consisting of rules from which states could not derogate'. Mr Jacovides (Cyprus), 53rd meeting, 305, para 68 ([i]n recognizing the existence of a corresponding rule in public international law the International Law Commission had made a very great contribution both to the codification and to the progressive development of international law'). Mr de Castro (Spain), 55th meeting, 315, para 1 (the existence of *jus cogens* rules is obvious). See, however, the statement by Mr Miras (Turkey) made at the 53rd meeting, 300, paras 1 and 6, who argued against *jus cogens* as a well-established rule of international law.

34 United Nations Conference on the Law of Treaties (n 32) 54th meeting, para 32.

35 United Nations Conference on the Law of Treaties (n 32) 55th meeting, para 74.

36 United Nations Conference on the Law of Treaties (n 32) 4th Plenary Meeting, para 2 (Mr de Castro (Spain) referring o a statement made by late Spanish international lawyer Antonio de Luna).

37 Tladi (n 2) 18–19. The Commission also included art 64 (on the emergence of a new peremptory norm of general international law) and art 71 (consequences of the invalidity of a treaty which conflicts with the peremptory norm of general international law).

Today, the concept of *jus cogens* is widely recognized by international publicists.[38] It has further been discussed with approval by numerous international, regional and municipal courts.[39] Notwithstanding this, the precise nature of *jus cogens* norms, which norms qualify as *jus cogens*, and the consequences of *jus cogens* in international law remain subjects of debate.[40] In 2014, the ILC placed the topic '*Jus Cogens*' on its long-term programme of work.[41] In 2015, the ILC decided to place the topic on its current programme of work and to appoint a Special Rapporteur.[42] The criteria for *jus cogens* norms under section 53 of the Vienna Convention as well as its core characteristics in the light of relevant state practice and international jurisprudence will be explored below.

3 The Identification of *Jus Cogens* Norms in International Law

3.1 *The Criteria*

It is generally recognized that article 53 contains the criteria a norm must meet in order to be identified as a norm of *jus cogens*.[43] Linderfalk is of the view

---

38 Alexander Orakhelashvili, *Peremptory Norms in International Law* (Oxford University Press 2008); Robert Kolb, *Peremptory International Law* Jus Cogens – *A General Inventory* (Hart 2015); Tladi and Dlagnekova (n 9); Evan Criddle and Evan Fox-Decent, 'A Fiduciary Theory of *Jus Cogens*' (2009) 34 Yale Journal of International Law 331–87; CQ Christol, 'Judge Manfred Lachs and the Principle of *Jus Cogens*' (1994) 22 Journal of Space Law 33; John Dugard, *International Law: A South African Perspective* (4th edn, Juta 2001); Erika de Wet, '*Jus Cogens* and Obligations *Erga Omnes*' in Dinah Shelton (ed), *The Oxford Handbook of International Human Rights Law* (Oxford University Press 2013) 541–61; Jure Vidmar, 'Norm Conflicts and Hierarchy in International Law: Towards a Vertical International Legal System?' in Erika de Wet and Jure Vidmar (eds), *Hierarchy in International Law: The Place of Human Rights* (Oxford University Press 2012) 2, 11, 17.

39 *Siderman de Blake v Republic of Argentina* 965 F 2d 699 (9th Cir 1992); Armed Activities on the Territory of the Congo (*DRC v Rwanda*), Preliminary Objections 3 February 2006 (2006) ICJ Reports 6; *Nicaragua v US* (Jurisdiction and Admissibility) (27 November 1984) (1984) ICJ Reports 392; 38 and Criddle and Fox-Decent (n 38) 339.

40 Tladi (n 2) 274; See the ILC Report on the work of the 66th session (2014) (5 May–6 June 2014 and 7 July–8 August 2014), A/69/10 Supplement No 10 240. See, in particular, the statement by Austria, A/C6/69/SR19, 15, para 110; the statement by Finland (on behalf of the Nordic states), A/C6/69/SR19, 12, para 86; the statement by Japan, A/C6/69/SR20, 9, para 50; and the statement by the Slovak Republic, A/C6/69/SR20, 12, para 76.

41 ILC 'Report on the work of the 66th session' (n 40).

42 See Report of the International Law Commission on the work of its 67th session A/RES/70/236 (2015) para 7.

43 See Ulf Linderfalk, 'The Creation of *Jus Cogens* – Making Sense of Article 53 of the Vienna Convention' (2011) 71 Zeitschrift für Ausländisches Öffentliches Recht und Völkerrecht 359; Kamrul Hossain, 'The concept of *jus cogens* and the obligation under the UN Charter 3' (2005) Santa Clara Journal of International Law 75–6; Gennady Danilenko, 'International *Jus Cogens*: Issues of Law-Making' (1991) 2 European Journal of International Law 42–65.

that, while article 53 does not explain how *jus cogens* is created, it does provide the basis upon which a norm of *jus cogens* can be founded – in other words, the declaratory recognition by states of an existing rule of customary international law as a norm from which no derogation is permitted.[44]

The criteria or requirements for norms to qualify as *jus cogens* norms should not be confused with the characteristics of *jus cogens* norms. While article 53 reflects the formal requirements or criteria for a norm to be elevated to *jus cogens* status, the core characteristics speak to the typical features or qualities of *jus cogens* norms which flow from and are a necessary consequence of the criteria. In this regard, the Drafting Committee of the ILC has identified the characteristics of *jus cogens* norms.[45] These characteristics and their implications for identification of *jus cogens* norms are discussed separately in section 3.2 below.

In terms of article 53 of the Vienna Convention, for a norm to be elevated to *jus cogens* status, it must be a norm of general international law which is accepted and recognized by the international community as a whole as a norm from which no derogation is permitted and which can be modified only by a subsequent norm of general international law having the same character.[46] From that definition, the following criteria may be identified: First, a *jus cogens* norm must be a norm of general international law, and, second, it must be a norm that the international community of states as a whole recognizes and accepts as a norm from which no derogation is permitted. Each criterion will be discussed in turn below, and section 4 will consider whether the prohibition of terrorism meets these criteria.

3.1.1 A Norm of General International Law

For a norm to qualify as a norm of *jus cogens*, it must be a norm of general international law. The ILC Study Group on Fragmentation used the term 'general international law' to denote both rules of customary international law and general principles of law.[47] The International Law Association (ILA) similarly

44 Linderfalk (n 43) 361–4 explains that this is similar to art 38(1) of the ICJ Statute not being constitutive, but rather declaratory of customary international law.

45 See draft conclusion 2 on Peremptory Norms of International Law (*Jus Cogens*) provisionally adopted by the drafting committee of the International Law Commission at the 69th session of the International Law Commission (1 May–2 June and 3 July–4 August 2017), annexed to the statement of the Chairman of the Drafting Committee on Peremptory Norms of General International Law (*jus cogens*), Mr Aniruddha Rajput (26 July 2017), Annex http://legal.un.org/ilc/documentation/english/statements/2017_dc_chairman_statement_jc.pdf accessed 3 November 2017.

46 Art 53 of the Vienna Convention (n 1).

47 See Analytical Report of the Study Group of the International Law Commission finalized by Chairman Martti Koskenniemi 'Fragmentation of International Law: Difficulties

confirmed that general international law, as the law that applies to all states, is not limited to general custom and may include other forms of unwritten law such as 'fundamental' or 'constitutional' principles of international law.[48]

In practice, customary international law has been the most common basis for *jus cogens* norms.[49] In their various communications, states have expressed the view that norms of *jus cogens* arise from rules of customary international law.[50] Both domestic courts[51] and international courts[52] have based

---

Arising from the Diversification and Expansion of International Law' UN Doc A/CN4/L682 (13 April 2006) 92, 194.

48 ILA Committee on Formation of Customary (General) International Law, London Conference 'Final Report of the Committee: Statement of Principles Applicable to the Formation of General Customary International Law' (2000) 6, para 8 <http://www.ila-hq.org/index.php/committees> accessed 1 September 2017.

49 See Dire Tladi 'Second Report on Jus Cogens' in the Report of the International Law Commission 69th session (1 May–2 June and 3 July–4 August 2017) A/CN4/706, paras 43–47.

50 See, eg, statement by Pakistan, 34th session of the General Assembly, A/C.6/34/SR.22, 3, para 8: 'The principle of the non-use of force, and its corollary, were *jus cogens* not only by virtue of article 103 of the Charter but also because they had become norms of customary international law recognized by the international community'; see also United Kingdom, 34th session of the General Assembly, A/C.6/34/SR.61 11 para 46; Jamaica, 42nd session of the General Assembly, A/C.6/42/SR.29, 3, para 3: 'The right of peoples to self-determination and independence was a right under customary international law, and perhaps even a peremptory norm of general international law'.

51 See, eg, *Siderman de Blake v Argentina* (n 39) 715 citing *Committee of United States Citizens Living in Nicaragua v Reagan* 859 F.2d 929 (DC 1988) (United States) 940, where the US Court of Appeals described *jus cogens* norms as 'an elite subset of the norms recognized as customary international law'. The Court further noted that 'In contrast to ordinary rules of customary international law, *jus cogens* norms "embrace customary laws considered binding on all nations"'. In *Buell v Mitchell*, 274 F.3d 337 (6th Cir 1988) (United States) 373, the US Court of Appeals also noted with respect to *jus cogens* that '[s]ome customary norms of international law reach a "higher status" namely that of *jus cogens*'. In *Kazemi Estate v Iran* [2014] 3 SCR 176 (Canada) para 151, the Supreme Court of Canada described *jus cogens* norms as a 'higher form of customary international law'. In EXP No 0024-2010-PI/TC LIMA 25 *Del Número Legal de Congresistas Sentencia del Pleno Jurisdiccional Del Tribunal Constitucional del Perú del 21 de Marzo de 2011*, para 53, the Constitutional Tribunal of Peru stated that the *jus cogens* rules referred to 'customary international norms under the auspices of an *opinio juris seu necessitates*' ('Las normas de jus cogens parecen pues encontrarse referidas a normas internacionales consuentudinarias que bajo el auspicio de una opinio juris seu necessitatis').

52 See *Belgium v Senegal* (*Questions Relating to the Obligation to Prosecute or Extradite*) 2012 ICJ Reports 457, para 99. See also Military and Paramilitary Activities in and against Nicaragua (*Nicaragua v United States*) (Merits) (27 June 1986) (1986) ICJ Reports 14, para 274, where the International Court of Justice recognized the prohibition of torture as 'part of customary international law' that 'has become a peremptory norm (*jus cogens*)'. The Court referred to 'many of the rules of humanitarian law' as constituting 'intransgressible principles of international customary law', confirming the idea that *jus cogens*

their determination that a norm meets the criteria for *jus cogens* status on the fact that the relevant norm is already a norm of customary international law, and recognized that *jus cogens* norms emerge from rules of customary international law. The weight of academic literature similarly supports the idea that customary international law is the most obvious basis for the *jus cogens* status of international law rules.[53]

While the significance of customary international law in the identification of norms of *jus cogens* is hardly in dispute,[54] there are differences of view concerning the other sources.[55] In the writer's view, the view expressed in the second report of the Special Rapporteur that general principles of law can also serve

norms – referred to by the Court as 'intransgressible principles' – have a customary law basis. See also *Case Concerning Application of the Convention on the Prevention and Punishment of the Crime of Genocide* (*Bosnia and Herzegovina v Serbia and Montenegro*), Judgment of 26 February 2007, 2007 ICJ Reports 43, para 161. See, further, the separate opinion of Judge Simma in the *Case Concerning Oil Platforms* (*Islamic Republic of Iran v United States of America*), Judgment of 6 November 2003, 2003 ICJ Reports 161, para 6: 'I find it regrettable that the Court has not mustered the courage of restating, and thus reconfirming, more fully fundamental principles of the law of the United Nations as well as customary international law (principles that in my view are of the nature of *jus cogens*) on the use of force, or rather the prohibition on armed force.' See further Mucić et al (Čelebići) (IT-96-21-T), ICTY Trial Judgment of 16 November 1998, para 454, where the ICTY has noted that the prohibition against torture is a 'norm of customary international law' and it 'further constitutes a norm of *jus cogens*'. Similarly, in *Jelesić* (IT-95-10-T), ICTY Trial Judgment of 14 December 1999, para 60 the Court stated that 'there can be absolutely no doubt' that the prohibition against genocide in the Genocide Convention falls 'under customary international law' and is now 'at the level of *jus cogens*'.

53 Gérard Cahin, *La Coutume Internationale et les Organisations Internationales: L'incidence de la Dimension Institutionnelle sur le Processus Coutumier* (Pedone 2001) 615 ('voie normale et fréquente sinon exclusive'). See also Alphonse Rivier, *Droit International Public* (2nd edn, Pedone 2013) 566: 'Customary international law is at the forefront to give birth to rules designed to power the mandatory law.' See, additionally, Antonio Cassese, *International Law* (Oxford University Press 2005) 199: 'A special class of general rules made by custom has been endowed with a special legal force – they are peremptory in nature and make up the so-called *jus cogens*.' See, further, João Christófolo, *Peremptory Norms in Public International Law* (Schulthess 2016) 115: 'As the most likely source of general international law, customary norms would constitute *ipso facto* and *ipso iure* a privileged source of *jus cogens* norms.' For a contrary view, see Mark Janis, 'The Nature of *Jus Cogens*' (1987) 3 Connecticut Journal of International Law 359–63.

54 Statement of the Chairman of the Drafting Committee on Peremptory Norms of General International Law (*jus cogens*) (n 45) 6: 'Members agreed with the important position of the customary international law in the formation of peremptory norms of general international law.'

55 Ibid.

as the basis for *jus cogens* seems to be correct.[56] As in the case of customary international law, general principles are generally applicable.[57] Kelsen is of the view that the term 'general international law' designates 'norms of international law which are valid for all the states of the world'.[58] The ICJ has itself resorted to the use of the term 'general international law' in order to denote norms that are binding *erga omnes* and enforceable against all, as opposed to treaty (or other) norms that are binding *inter partes*.[59] General principles of law are, *per se*, part of general international law. Moreover, there is a particular correlation between *jus cogens* norms and general principles of law. Like *jus cogens*, 'general principles of law' as a source has been described as having a

56 'Second Report on *Jus Cogens*' (n 49) para 48.

57 See, eg, Sevrine Knuchel, *Jus Cogens: identification and Enforcement of Peremptory Norms* (Schultess 2015) 52: 'General principles [of law] may be elevated to *jus cogens* if the international community of states recognize and accept them as such.' See further Cançado Trindade, '*Jus Cogens*: The Material and the Gradual Expansion of its Material Content in Contemporary International Case Law' (2008) 35 Curso de Derecho International Organizado por el Comité Jurídico Interamericano 27. See also Thomas Weatherall, 'The Status of the Prohibition of Terrorism in International Law: Recent Developments' (2015) 46 Georgetown Journal of International Law 589–627; Thomas Kleinlein, '*Jus Cogens* as the "Highest Law"? Peremptory Norms and Legal Hierarchies' (2015) Netherlands Yearbook of International Law 195: 'A peremptory norm must first become general international law ie customary international law or general principles of law pursuant to article 38(1) of the ICJ Statute.' See also William Conklin, 'The Peremptory Norms of the International Community' (2012) 23 European Journal of International Law 840. Also compare Andrea Bianchi, 'Human Rights and the Magic of *Jus Cogens*' (2008) 3 European Journal of International Law 493: 'The possibility that *jus cogens* could be created by treaty stands in sharp contrast to the view that peremptory norms can emerge only from customary law'; Rafael Nieto-Navia 'International Peremptory Norms (*Jus Cogens*) and International Humanitarian Law' in Chand Vorah, Fausto Pocar, Yvonne Featherstone et al (eds), *Man's Inhumanity to Man: Essays on International Law in Honour of Antonio Cassese* (Kluwer Law International 2003) 613–15: 'One can state generally that norms of *jus cogens* can be drawn generally from the following identified sources of international law: (i) general treaties … and (ii) general principles of law recognized by civilized nations'; Orakhelashvili (n 38) 126; Elizabeth Vargas, 'In Quest of the Practical Value of *Jus Cogens* Norms' (2015) 46 Netherlands Yearbook of International Law 214: '*Jus cogens* derives from customary law and general principles of international law'.

58 Hans Kelsen, *Principles of International Law* (Rinehart 1952) 188.

59 *Barcelona Traction Light and Power Company Limited* (5 February 1970) 1970 ICJ Reports 32. See further statement by Mr Ago, Yearbook of the International Law Commission, vol I (Part One), 1966, Summary Record of the 828th Meeting (n 26) para 15: 'Even if a rule of *jus cogens* originated in a treaty, it was not from the treaty as such that it derived its character but from the fact that, even though derived from a treaty, it was already a rule of general international law.'

specific nature as 'moral commandments … considered by the conscience of mankind to be indispensable for the coexistence of man in organized society'.[60]

Dugard is of the opinion that there is a natural law basis to general principles of law, as evidenced by the way in which international courts have invoked, amongst others, considerations of humanity and principles of non-discrimination under the scope of general principles of law.[61] This seems to find support in the *Corfu Channel* case, where the United Kingdom argued that the obligations upon the Albanian authorities to notify and warn British warships of the existence of a minefield in Albanian territorial waters were based on certain general and well-recognized principles, namely, 'the elementary considerations of humanity', which are 'even more exacting in peace than in war'.[62]

Accordingly, an analysis of whether the prohibition of terrorism is a norm of general international law will consider that general international law consists of both customary international law and general principles of law. Treaty law does not constitute 'general international law' for the purposes of article 53 of the Vienna Convention.[63]

3.1.2 Accepted and Recognized

Not all norms of general international law are *jus cogens*. Thus, in addition to showing that a norm is one of general international law, for *jus cogens* status it is also necessary to show that the said norm is accepted and recognized as having a certain quality, namely, non-derogability. The language of article 53 of the Vienna Convention includes, in addition to non-derogability, the element that such a norm must be one that may be only modified by a subsequent norm having the same quality. The ILC Drafting Committee on *jus cogens* confirmed

---

60 Birgit Schlüter, *Developments in Customary International Law* (Martinus Nijhoff 2010) 74–9.

61 See *Corfu Channel Case* (*United Kingdom v Albania*) Merits ICJ (9 April 1949) 1949 ICJ Reports 6, 22; *Nicaragua v US* (n 52) para 114 (both cases invoking considerations of humanity); *South West Africa Cases* (*Ethiopia and Liberia v South Africa*) Second Phase (18 July 1966) (1966) ICJ Reports 6, 295–6 (referring to principles of non-discrimination). For views of writers that general principles in the sense of art 38(1)(c) have a natural law basis, see Malcolm Shaw, *International Law* (Cambridge University Press 2003) 92; Ian Brownlie, *Principles of Public International Law* (6 edn, Oxford University Press 2003) 15; Dugard (n 50) 36; Christopher Weeramantry, *Universalizing International Law* (Martinus Nijhoff 2004) 267–8.

62 *Corfu Channel* case (n 61) 22.

63 See, however, draft conclusion 5(2) adopted by the Drafting Committee of the International Law Commission (n 45) which states that '[t]reaty provisions and general principles of law may also serve as bases for peremptory norms of general international law (*jus cogens*)'.

that non-derogation and modification only by a subsequent norm of general international law are two aspects of the same criterion, namely, that of acceptance and recognition, and not two separate tests for a norm to fulfil the criteria for a *jus cogens* norm.[64] Accordingly, these aspects will not be discussed separately.

The wording 'accepted and recognized by international community of states as a whole as a norm from which no derogation is permitted' has been the topic of some debate.[65] Draft article 50 proposed by the ILC in its final Draft Articles on the Law of Treaties stated only that 'a treaty is void if it conflicts with a peremptory norm of general international law from which no derogation is permitted and which can be modified only by a subsequent norm of general international law having the same character'.[66] The Vienna Conference, however, adopted a slightly modified version of the ILC's article 50 as article 53 of the Vienna Convention, adding a reference to the norm being 'accepted and recognized by the international community of states as a whole' as a norm from which no derogation is permitted and which can be modified only by a subsequent norm of general international law having the same character.[67]

Positivists have argued that the above wording points to state consent as the words 'accepted' and 'recognized' imply consent to the peremptory character of the norm in question.[68] It has further been argued that *jus cogens* norms are subject to a double acceptance: A norm must first be recognized as a norm of general international law, whereafter the international community of states as

64 See draft conclusion 4 adopted by the Drafting Committee of the International Law Commission (n 45).

65 Criddle and Fox-Decent (n 38) 339; Grigorij Tunkin, '*Jus cogens* in contemporary international law' (1971) 1 & 2 University of Toledo Law Review 115.

66 Draft Articles on the Law of Treaties with Commentaries (n 25) 247–9.

67 Article 53 of the Vienna Convention (n 1): 'accepted and recognized by the international community of states as a whole' as a norm from which no derogation is permitted and which can be modified only by a subsequent norm of general international law having the same character'.

68 Mark Weisburd, 'The Emptiness of the Concept of *Jus Cogens* as Illustrated by the War in Bosnia-Herzegovina' (1995) 17 Michigan State Journal of International Law 1; Schwarzenberger (n 20) 471; Dinah Shelton, *Normative Hierarchy in International Law* (2006) 100 American Journal of International Law 298. See further De Wet, '*Jus Cogens* and Obligations *Erga Omnes*' (n 38) ch 23, 542, stating: 'Article 53 VCLT was thus negotiated so as to leave it to the "international community as a whole" to identify those international law norms belonging to the category of *jus cogens*. In essence, this implies that a particular norm is first recognized as customary international law, whereafter the international community of states as a whole further agrees that it is a norm from which no derogation is permitted. The international community of states as a whole would therefore subject a peremptory norm to "double acceptance"'.

a whole must further agree that such a norm is a norm from which no derogation is permitted.[69] The difficulty with any consent-based arguments in relation to *jus cogens* norms, however, is that non-derogability has been argued to lie at the core of these norms.[70] As such, *jus cogens* norms do not depend on, nor are they affected by, state consent, and embody principles of natural law common to all legal systems which do not require state consent.[71] *Jus cogens* norms confirm the high principles of international law which recognize the most important rights in international law, such as the right to be free from aggression, genocide, torture, slavery, and the right to self-determination, while at the same time giving legal form to the fundamental policies and goals of the international community in supporting these rights by way of the prohibition of aggression, genocide, torture, slavery and the advancement of self-determination.[72] It is hardly conceivable that, if states withhold their recognition of and acceptance that a rule is non-derogatory, that rule no longer enjoys *jus cogens* status (such as the prohibition of torture, slavery or genocide). The 'acceptance' or 'recognition' referred to in article 53 of the Vienna Convention, including the *opinio juris* of states discussed above, is not constitutive of *jus cogens* norms, but declaratory.[73] Article 53 does not purport to create a rule of *jus cogens*.[74] What article 53 requires is that states widely subscribe to the opinion that, on the basis of an authoritative set of rules existing in customary international law, no derogations from a certain rule are permitted and all modifications of the rule by means of ordinary international law are prohibited.[75] This recognition by states is based on a belief by the international

---

69 Shelton (n 38); De Wet (n 68).

70 Kolb (n 38) 2–9.

71 Orakhelashvili (n 38) 107; TS Rama Rao, 'International Custom' (1979) 19 Indian Joronal of International Law 520; Martti Koskenniemi, *From Apology to Utopia: The Structure of International Legal Argument* (Cambridge University Press 1989) 363; Janis (n 53) 361; Mary O'Connell, '*Jus Cogens*: International Law's Higher Ethical Norms' in Donald Childress (ed), *The Role of Ethics in International Law* (Cambridge University Press 2011) 94.

72 Dugard (n 38) 39.

73 Linderfalk (n 43) 359–373.

74 Ibid., 359.

75 Ibid., 362, 370. See further Summary Record of the 828th meeting (n 26) para 15 (statement by Mr Ago). Such an argument is consistent with arguments that *jus cogens* norms are *lex lata* and were already in existence at the time of the conclusion of the Vienna Convention. For example, during the debates, and in confirming the *lex lata* character of *jus cogens* rules, Mr Ago stated that it was not from the treaty itself that *jus cogens* rules derived their character, 'but from the fact that, even though derived from the treaty or when expressed in the treaty, it was already a rule of general international law'.

community that a norm is peremptory owing to the essential interests which that norm protects.[76]

Accordingly, an ordinary rule of customary international law becomes *jus cogens* due to the *opinio juris* of the international community of states as a whole that no derogation from such a rule is allowed (sometimes referred to as *opinio juris cogentis*). *Opinio juris cogentis* is different from *opinio juris sive necessitatis* in that, while the latter concerns the opinion of states that a particular norm is part of customary international law, the former relates to the opinion of states as to its non-derogability.

In connection with the requirement of 'acceptance and recognition', it is worth pointing out that it is the international community of states 'as a whole' that must accept and recognize the non-derogability of the norm in question. This has two implications. First, what must be sought is the acceptance by and recognition of states and not non-state entities.[77] Second, the phrase 'as a whole' itself is meant to indicate that it is not the view of individual states that is sought, and that it is not required that each state accepts and recognizes the quality of the norm.[78] In the words of the Chairman of the Drafting Committee, Mr Yaseen, when the Commission adopted the 1966 Draft Articles on the Law of Treaties, it would be sufficient 'if a very large majority did so.'[79]

3.2 *The Core Characteristics*

In addition to the criteria for the identification of *jus cogens* described in section 3.1 above, the Drafting Committee of the ILC has also identified certain characteristics of *jus cogens* norms.[80] These characteristics, however, are not

76 Orakhelashvili (n 38) 107.

77 See Draft Conclusion 7(3) adopted by the Drafting Committee of the International Law Commission (n 45) which provides that '[w]hile the attitude of other actors may be relevant in providing context and for assessing acceptance and recognition of the international community of states as a whole, these cannot, in and of themselves, form a part of such acceptance and recognition'.

78 See 'Second Report on *Jus Cogens*' (n 49) 34 para 67.

79 See the statement by Mr Yaseen, Chairman of the Drafting Committee, Official Records of the United Nations Conference on the Law of Treaties (n 32) 80th meeting, para 4. See also Draft Conclusion 7(2) adopted by the Drafting Committee of the International Law Commission (n 45) which provides: 'Acceptance and recognition by a very large majority of states is required for the identification of a norm as a peremptory norm of general international law (*jus cogens*); acceptance and recognition by all states is not required.' See also Vidmar (n 38) 543: 'This threshold for gaining peremptory status is high, for although it does not require consensus among all states ... it does require the acceptance of a large majority of states.'

80 See also Draft Conclusion 2 adopted by the Drafting Committee of the ILC (n 45); see also Tladi (n 21) 9 para 18.

additional elements or criteria of norms of *jus cogens*, but rather are descriptive elements.[81] The aforementioned characteristics, however, may be relevant in assessing the criteria for *jus cogens* norms of international law.[82]

In his First Report on *Jus Cogens*, the Special Rapporteur proposed that *jus cogens* norms reveal certain core characteristics: They protect the fundamental values of the international community; they are hierarchically superior; and they are universally applicable.[83] Some states disagreed with these characteristics.[84] However, the majority of states supported the characteristics.[85] At the 69th session of the ILC, the Drafting Committee on *jus cogens* adopted Draft Conclusion 2 setting out the general nature of *jus cogens* norms. The conclusion states that

> peremptory norms of general international law (*jus cogens*) reflect and protect fundamental values of the international community, are hierarchically superior to other rules of international law and are universally applicable.[86]

It is further argued that these characteristics are interconnected. It is the fact that *jus cogens* protects fundamental values that necessitates its hierarchical superiority above other norms of customary international law and treaty law

81 'First Report on *Jus Cogens* by Dire Tladi, Special Rapporteur' A/CN.4/693 (8 March 2016) 44 para 72: ('While these are core characteristics of *jus cogens*, they do not tell us how *jus cogens* are to be identified in contemporary international law.').

82 Tladi (n 49) 9 para 18.

83 Tladi (n 81) 45.

84 See Official Records of the General Assembly, 71st Session, Supplement No 10 (A/71/10). States that opposed the elements in Draft Conclusion 3 para 2 are China (A/C6/71/SR 24), para 89, noting that the elements 'are at variance with' art 53 of the Vienna Convention on the Law of Treaties; and the United States A/C.6/71/SR26 para 126.

85 States that supported the elements in para 2 of Draft Conclusion 3 are Brazil (A/C.6/71/SR 26), para 91; the Czech Republic (A/C.6/71/SR 24), para 72 ('[i]n our opinion *jus cogens* norms are exemptions to other rules of international law. They protect fundamental values of the international community and are universally applicable'); El Salvador (A/C.6/71/25), para 62; statement of Slovenia (on file with the author) ('notes the thorough consideration of the characteristics that are inherent in a *jus cogens* rule, and wishes to underline that it agrees with the enunciation of *jus cogens* as having a special and exceptional character, reflecting the common and overarching values … [and requiring] universal adherence'); and South Africa, A/C.6/71/SR. 26, para 87 ('We wish to express our disappointment and surprise that the Commission was not able to agree on what we believe are basic and uncontroversial characteristics. It is generally accepted that *jus cogens* norms are universally binding, reflect fundamental values and interests and are hierarchically superior').

86 See Draft Conclusion 2 of Peremptory Norms of General International Law (*jus cogens*) adopted by the ILC Drafting Committee (n 45) Annex.

and supports its universal applicability. Furthermore, *jus cogens* norms cannot be argued to be universally applicable if it can be set aside by conflicting norms of international law, and the reason that it cannot be so set aside again is a testament of its superiority. The characteristics of *jus cogens* norms will be further discussed below.

3.2.1 Fundamental Values

The ICJ has stated that 'the question whether a norm is part of *jus cogens* relates to the legal character of the norm'.[87] The ILC noted that 'it is not the form of a general rule of international law but the particular nature of the subject-matter with which it deals that may, in the opinion of the Commission, give it the character of *jus cogens*'.[88] As reflected in the statements by France and the Holy See at the Vienna Conference, *jus cogens* norms represent the universal conscience and safeguards human rights.[89] Furthermore, there is support in both international jurisprudence and state practice for the notion that *jus cogens* norms safeguard the fundamental values of the international community as a whole.[90]

In national case law, the Constitutional Court of Peru referred to the importance of the values underlying *jus cogens* norms.[91] South Africa's Constitutional Court has stated that *jus cogens* reflected the most fundamental norms of the international community.[92] Additionally, the Argentinian Supreme Court in the *Clavel* case defined terrorism as a 'crime *jus gentium*', the prosecution of which is not in the exclusive interests of the state injured by it, but 'benefits, ultimately, all civilized nations who are therefore obligated to co-operate in the global fight against terrorism'.[93] US case law has further noted the importance of the values underlying *jus cogens* obligations.[94]

---

87 Legality of the Threat or Use of Nuclear Weapons, (8 July 1996) (1996) ICJ Reports, 226, para 83.

88 Draft Articles on the Law of Treaties with Commentaries (n 25) 247.

89 See United Nations Conference on the Law of Treaties (n 32) 315 et seq; 55th meeting para 74.

90 Ibid. 158 (the prohibition of torture is part of customary international law and it has become a peremptory norm (*jus cogens*)).

91 *Sentencia del Pleno Jurisdiccional del Tribunal Constitucional del Perú Exp* n 0024-2010-PI/TC 53.

92 *Kaunda & Others v President of the Republic of South Africa & Others* (*Society for the Abolition of the Death Penalty in South Africa intervening as Amicus Curiae*) 2005 (4) SA 235 (CC).

93 *Enrique Lautaro Arancibia Clavel* 259 (Arg Supreme Court) (2004) 51–52.

94 Ibid.; *Siderman de Blake* (n 39); *Alvarez-Machain v United States* 331 F 3d 604 (2003, 9th Cir) 613; *Estate of Hernandez-Rojas v United States* US Dist LEXIS 136922 (SD Cal 2013) 14;

Additionally, in international jurisprudence the ICJ has used various terms to refer to the concept of fundamental values, ranging from 'fundamental rights' to fundamental 'interests' or 'values'.[95] In the *Application of the Convention on the Prevention and Punishment of the Crime of Genocide* case, the ICJ stated that *jus cogens* norms are peremptory because of the importance of the values they protect and, in this regard, it identified rules created for a humanitarian purpose as *jus cogens*.[96] The ICJ further referred to genocide as 'assuredly' being a norm of *jus cogens* in the *Democratic Republic of Congo v Rwanda* case.[97] Moreover, in *Reservations to the Convention on Genocide*, the Court expressed the view that genocide is contrary to moral law as it 'shocks the conscience of mankind'.[98] The prohibition of torture has further been named by the International Criminal Tribunal for the Former Yugoslavia (ICTY) as one of the most fundamental standards of the international community.[99] Furthermore, regional commissions such as the Inter-American Commission on Human Rights (IACHR) have confirmed that *jus cogens* norms derive their status from fundamental values held by the international community.[100]

In addition to this, various states have made statements before the UN General Assembly (UNGA) which support the view that *jus cogens* norms protect fundamental rights or fundamental humanitarian values.[101] Portugal was of the view that peremptory norms of international law were based on a common belief in certain fundamental values of international law and deserved

---

Doe v Reddy US Dist LEXIS 26120 (ND Cal 2003); *Al Rawi & Others, R (on the application of) v Secretary of State for Foreign and Commonwealth Affairs* & Another (2008) QB 289 153–4.

95 *Belgium v Senegal* (n 52) 1, 84, 182 (separate opinion of Judge Cançado Trindade).

96 *Application of the Convention on the Prevention and Punishment of the Crime of Genocide* (Bosnia and Herzegovina v Serbia and Montenegro) (26 February 2007) (2007) ICJ Reports 43.

97 DRC v Rwanda case (n 39) 6 para 64.

98 *Advisory Opinion Concerning Reservations to the Convention on the Prevention and Punishment of the Crime of Genocide* (28 May 1951) (1951) ICJ Reports 23. *Attorney General of Israel v Adolf Eichmann*, District Court of Jerusalem, 36 ILR 18, at 25, 26, 50 (Israel Dist Ct 1961). See also judgment of the Supreme Court sitting as Court of Criminal Appeals at 36 ILR 277, at 299, 304 (Israel Sup Ct 1962). In the *Eichmann* case, the Israeli District and Appeal Courts stated that Eichmann's crimes 'offended the whole of mankind and shocked the conscience of nations'.

99 Prosecutor v Furundžija (Trial chamber of ICTY, Judgment, 10 December 1998) IT-95-17/1-T10, 121 ILR para 153; *Al-Adsani v UK* (2001) 34 EHRR 273, 123 ILR 24 para 55.

100 *Michael Domingues v US* (Merits) (22 October 2000) Report No 62/02 case 12.285 para 49.

101 Germany, 55th session of the UN General Assembly, Sixth Committee, Agenda Item 159: 'Report on the work of the 52nd session (2000)' para 56; Finland, 52nd Meeting of the Committee of the Whole 'UN Conference on the Law of Treaties First Session Vienna' (26 March–24 May 1968).

to be 'better protected than others'.[102] South Africa, Yugoslavia and Costa Rica pointed out that *jus cogens* norms were essential for the protection of the fundamental interests or values of the international community, while Greece similarly referred to the protection of the fundamental interests of humanity. Mali and Morocco noted that *jus cogens* norms protect the fundamental interests of mankind.[103] The majority of statements (by Russia, Yugoslavia, France, Iran, South Africa, Costa Rica, Slovakia and Argentina), as well as the IACHR and regional case law, refer to the values that *jus cogens* seeks to protect as the values of the international community.[104]

Despite differences in terminology as discussed above, which includes references to fundamental 'interests', 'values', 'standards', 'fundamental interests of mankind' and 'values of the international community', it appears that there is ample reference in international jurisprudence and state practice to the fact that *jus cogens* reflects and safeguards fundamental, basic or higher interests

102 Portugal, 56th Session of the UN General Assembly, Sixth Committee, Agenda Item 162: 'Report of the International Law Commission on the Work of its 53rd session' (2001) para 66.

103 South Africa, 55th Session of the UN General Assembly, Sixth Committee Agenda Item 159: 'Report of the International Law Commission on the Work of its 52nd session' (2000) para 29; Yugoslavia, 31st Session of the UN General Assembly, Sixth Committee, Agenda Item 106: 'Report of the International Law Commission on the work of its 28th session' (1976) para 43; Costa Rica, 55th Session of the UN General Assembly, Sixth Committee, Agenda Item 159; Greece, 49th Session of the UN General Assembly, Sixth Committee, Agenda Item 137: 'Report of the International Law Commission the Work of its 46th session' (1994) para 90; 'Report of the International Law Commission on the Work of its 52nd session' (2000) para 63; Mali, 31st Session of the UN General Assembly, Sixth Committee, Agenda Item 106: 'Report of the International Law Commission on the work of its 28th session' (1976) para 69; Morocco, 40th Session of the UN General Assembly, Sixth Committee, Agenda Item 138: 'Report of the International Law Commission on the Work Fragmentation Report, para 374.

104 USSR, 31st Session of the UN General Assembly, Sixth Committee, Agenda Item 106: 'Report of the International Law Commission on the Work of its 28th Session' paras 24 and 43; Yugoslavia (n 103); France, 51st Session of the UN General Assembly, Sixth Committee Agenda Item 146: 'Report of the ILC on the Work of its 48th session' (6 May–26 July 1996) A/51/10 Supplement No 10 para 26; South Africa (n 103); Costa Rica (n 103); Argentina, 56th Session of the UN General Assembly, Sixth Committee, Agenda Item 162: 'Report of the International Law Commission on the Work of its 53rd session' para 52; Iran, 53rd Session of the UN General Assembly, Sixth Committee, Agenda Item 150: 'Report of the International Law Commission on the Work of its 50th session' para 12; *Siderman de Blake* (n 39) 717; *Alvarez-Machain v US* (n 94) 613; *Estate of Hernandez-Rojas v US* (n 94); *Doe v Reddy* (n 94).

or fundamental humanitarian values.[105] It is the fundamental nature of the values or interests that norms of *jus cogens* aim to protect which is significant.

Furthermore, writers have emphasized the essential community interests protected by *jus cogens* norms. De Wet argues that certain obligations are established for the protection of the international community as a whole (*erga omnes*), and that *jus cogens* norms, such as the prohibition of genocide and the prohibition of torture, have an *erga omnes* effect.[106] The ICJ has confirmed that peremptory norms exist on the basis of their relation to the international community.[107] In the *South-West Africa* cases, Judge Jessup, in a dissenting opinion, held that 'states may have a general interest – cognisable in the International Court – in the maintenance of an international regime adopted for the common benefit of the international society'.[108] In the *Barcelona Traction* case, the ICJ explained that the obligations of a state towards the international community as a whole are 'the concern of all states' in contrast to duties owed by one state to another state by virtue of a bilateral legal relationship *inter se*. It is this 'concern of all states' which results in the 'outlawing of acts of aggression, genocide, and ensures the rules concerning basic human rights, including protection from slavery and racial discrimination'.[109]

There further is a correlation between fundamental values and non-derogation. Hannikainen expresses the view that allowing derogations from a norm that protects an overriding value of the international community of states would seriously jeopardize such a value.[110] Byers adds that the non-derogable

---

105 USSR (n 104); Yugoslavia (n 103); France (n 104); Iran (n 104); South Africa (n 103) paras 18, 29, 56 and 63; Costa Rica (n 103); Slovakia, 56th Session of the UN General Assembly, Sixth Committee, Agenda Item 162: 'Report of the International Law Commission on the Work of its fifty-second session' para 18; Argentina (n 104) paras 13, 52 and 66; (ibid.) para 87; Spain, 27th Session of the UN General Assembly, Sixth Committee, Agenda Item 89; Greece (n 103) para 90; Al Rawi & Others, R (on the application of) v Secretary of State for Foreign and Commonwealth Affairs & Another (2006) ECWA 152–154; *Sentencia Del Pleno Jurisdiccional* case (n 91); *Michael Domingues* case (n 100) 49; *Siderman de Blake* (n 39); *Alvarez-Machain v US* (n 94); *Estate of Hernandez-Rojas* (n 94) 14; *Doe v Reddy* (n 94); *Kaunda* case (n 92) 169.

106 See De Wet (n 68) 554–558.

107 *United States Diplomatic and Consular Staff in Tehran* case (*US v Iran*), Provisional Measures (15 December 1979) (1979) ICJ Reports 7 19; *United States Diplomatic and Consular Staff in Tehran* (*Hostages* case) (*US v Iran*) Merits (24 May 1980) (1980) ICJ Reports 3 para 92; *Legal Consequences of the Construction of a Wall in the Occupied Palestinian Territory* 9 July 2004 (2004) ICJ Reports 136 paras 157 and 199; *Nicaragua* case (n 52) 100; *Furundžija* case (n 99) paras 151–157 and 260–262; East Timor (*Portugal v Australia*) (30 June 1995) (1995) ICJ Reports 90 214.

108 *South West Africa* cases (n 61) 373 (dissenting opinion of Judge Jessup).

109 *Barcelona Traction* case (n 59) paras 32–34.

110 Lauri Hannkainen, *Peremptory Norms* (*Jus Cogens*) *in International Law* (Finnish Lawyers' Publishing Company 1988) 207.

character of *jus cogens* norms results from the fact that states simply do not believe that it is possible to persistently object to, or contract out of, norms reflecting fundamental values of the international community.[111] *Jus cogens* rules limit the ability of states to create or change rules of international law and prevent states from violating fundamental rules of international public policy.

The prohibition of terrorism protects the fundamental right to human dignity. As early as 1988, the Preamble to the Maritime Safety Convention referred to the 'world-wide escalation of acts of terrorism in all its forms, which endanger or take innocent human lives, jeopardize fundamental freedoms and seriously impair the dignity of human beings'.[112]

3.2.2 Hierarchical Superiority

Authors have argued that *jus cogens* is a constitutive legal norm, allowing for the creation of norms that are hierarchically superior to other norms of international law.[113] This places *jus cogens* outside the formal sources of law as set out in article 38 of the ICJ Statute as higher norms derived from a non-consensual source.[114] As noted by Cassese, it is the fact that *jus cogens* norms have the power to invalidate conflicting rules of law with is a testament to, as well as a consequence of, its normative superiority.[115]

Dugard is of the opinion that the reason why *jus cogens* norms enjoy a hierarchically superior position to other norms in the international legal order is that they are 'a blend of principle and policy'.[116] It has been argued that *jus cogens* norms are 'super-norms' or 'super-laws' or 'supercustom' that hold the highest hierarchical position among all other norms and principles.[117] They hold this uppermost hierarchical point in international law regardless of

111 Michael Byers, 'Conceptualising the Relationship between *Jus Cogens* and *Erga Omnes* Rules' (1997) 66 Nordic Journal of International Law 211 212, 219–20.

112 Maritime Safety Convention (n 38).

113 Christol (n 38) 33; Alfred Verdross, '*Jus Dispositivum* and *Jus Cogens* in International Law' (1966) 60 American Journal of International Law 55.

114 Orakhelashvili (n 38) 37–38.

115 Antonio Cassese, '*Jus Cogens*' in Antonio Cassese (ed), *Realizing Utopia: The Future of International Law* (Oxford University Press 2012) 159.

116 Dugard (n 38) 39.

117 Carlo Focarelli, 'Promotional *jus cogens*: A critical appraisal of *jus cogens*' legal effects' (2008) 77 Nordic Journal of International Law 429–59; Michael Reisman, 'Unilateral Action and the Transformations of the World Constitutive Process: The Special Problem of Humanitarian Intervention' (2000) 11 European Journal of International Law 15; M Cherif Bassiouni, 'A functional approach to "general principles of international law"' (1990) 11 Michigan State Journal of International Law 801–9; Shaw (n 64) 117.

where they originate from and whether or not states have consented or agreed to them or their standing.[118]

Certain national courts specifically referred to the hierarchical position of *jus cogens* norms *vis-à-vis* other norms of international law. The Supreme Court of the Republic of the Philippines noted that a *jus cogens* norm holds 'the highest hierarchical position among all other customary norms and principles'.[119] The High Court of Zimbabwe confirmed that a *jus cogens* norm has primacy in the hierarchy of rules constituting the international normative order.[120] In *Siderman de Blake*, the US Court of Appeals similarly referred to the supremacy of *jus cogens* over all rules of international law.[121] Furthermore, the US District Court held that these norms enjoyed the highest status in international law and prevailed over both customary international law and treaties.[122] United Kingdom domestic courts referred to *jus cogens* as norms enjoying a higher rank than treaty law and customary rules, while the Supreme Court of Argentina stated that *jus cogens* norms are the highest source of international law, not only above treaty law, but over all of the sources of law.[123] Various other national court cases referred to *jus cogens* as having a higher rank than treaty law and customary rules.[124] Other cases referred to superior rules, or rules with the highest status or standing in international law.[125]

---

118 *Siderman de Blake* (n 39) 176.

119 *Bayan Muna v Alberto Romulo (in his capacity as Executive Secretary)* (2011) PHSC 112.

120 *Mann v Republic of Equatorial Guinea* (2008) 1 ZWHHC 12.

121 *Siderman de Blake* (n 39) 716. See also *Jones v Ministry of Interior for the Kingdom of Saudi Arabia & Others* (2007) 1 AC 270 (HL), 1 All ER 113 39.

122 See judgment by the US District Court for the District of Columbia in *Committee of US Citizens Living in Nicaragua v Reagan* (n 51) 935, applied in *Princz v Federal Republic of Germany* 26 F 3d 1166 (DC Cir 1994) 1173 and in *Sabbithi v Al Saleh* 623 F Supp 2d 93 (DDC 2009) 129; see further the US Court of Appeals, Second Circuit, in *United States v Yousef* 327 F 3d 56 (2d Cir 2003) 94; the US District Court for New York in *Garb v Republic of Poland* 207 F Supp 2d 16 (EDNY 2002) 129 and the US Court of Appeals for the Ninth Circuit in *Sarei v Rio Tinto* PLC 671 F.3d 736 (9th Cir 2010) 776 (Judge Schroeder, for the majority).

123 *Mazzeo Julio Lilo y otros* (Judgment of 13 July 2007) 2007-III-573 (Arg Supreme Court) para 53.

124 *R v Bow Street Metropolitan Stipendiary Magistrate, Ex parte Pinochet Ugarte* (No 3) (2000) 1 AC 147; *A & Others v Secretary of State for the Home Department* (No 2) (2005) (HL) 1 WLR 414 436; *Al Rawi* (n 105) 153; *A & Others v Secretary of State for the Home Department* (No 2) (2006) 2 AC 221 (HL), 1 All ER 575 33; *Al-Saadoon & Another, R (on the application of) v Secretary of State for Defence* (2008) EWHC 3098 85; *Youssef v Secretary of State for Foreign and Commonwealth Affairs* (2014) QB 728 53 and (2016) 2 WLR 509 17; *Al-Adsani v UK* (n 99) 30 (majority).

125 See eg judgments by the Court of First Instance of the European Communities in *Yusuf and Al Barakaat International Foundation v Council and Commission* (21 September 2005)

The notion of *jus cogens* norms as hierarchically superior has further been confirmed in international jurisprudence.[126] In his separate opinion in the *Application of the Genocide Convention* case, Judge Lauterpacht noted that '*jus cogens* is a concept which is superior to both customary international law and treaty'.[127] In the *Furundžija* case, the ICJ stated that the prohibition of torture as a norm of *jus cogens* relates to 'the hierarchy of rules in the international normative order', and that it has evolved into a *jus cogens* norm, which has a higher rank in the international hierarchy than treaty law and customary rules.[128] The IACHR has stated that *jus cogens* is a 'superior order of legal norms, which the laws of man or nations may not contravene'.[129] The European Court of Human Rights (ECtHR) similarly regarded *jus cogenzs* as a higher-ranking norm.[130]

Moreover, states have made statements referring to the higher status of *jus cogens* norms before the UNGA. Cuba referred to the higher principles of *jus cogens*, while Cyprus and Slovakia referred to hierarchically higher rules.[131] Portugal was of the view that *jus cogens* focused on the idea of a material hierarchy of norms, and that there are certain superior norms, which are non-derogable.[132] The Netherlands stated that *jus cogens* is 'hierarchically superior

---

ECR II-3533 282; *Kadi v Council and Commission* (21 September 2005) ECR II-3649 231 (referring to 'superior rules'). See further the judgments of US domestic courts in *Committee of US Citizens Living in Nicaragua v Reagan* (n 51) 935; *US v Yousef* (n 122); *Hwang Geum Joo v Japan* 172 F Supp 2d 52 (DC 2001) fn 4; *Garb v Republic of Poland* (n 122) 129; *Sabbithi v Al Saleh* (n 122) 12 (referring to 'higher status') and *Sarei v Rio Tinto* (n 122) 776 (Schroeder J, for the majority). See judgments of the US Court of Appeals in *United States v Matta Ballesteros* 71 F 3d 754 (10th Cir 1995) and *Siderman de Blake* (n 39); 715 and 717. In UK domestic courts, see further *Al-Adsani v UK* (n 99) 57; *Pinochet* (n 124) 147 (referring to rules with a 'higher standing').

126 Ibid.

127 *Application of Genocide* (Bosnia and Herzegovina v Serbia and Montenegro) Judgment (26 February 2007) (2007) ICJ Reports 2007) paras 325 and 440 (separate opinion of Judge Lauterpacht);

128 Prosecutor v Furundžija (n 99) 213, 260. See, further, DRC v Rwanda (n 51) para 10 regarding the separate opinion of Judge ad hoc Dugard. See, also, the dissenting opinion of Judge Al Khasawneh in Arrest Warrant of 11 April 2000 (DRC v Belgium) (14 February 2002) 2002 ICJ Reports 3; (2002) 41 ILM 536, para 7.

129 *Michael Domingues v US* (n 100) 49.

130 *Al-Dulimi and Montana Management Inc v Switzerland* Application No 5809/08 ECHR (21 June 2016) 576 para 34.

131 Mr Alvarez Tabio (Cuba), 22nd Session of the UN General Assembly, Sixth Committee, Agenda Item 86: 'Law of treaties' (1967) para 22; see further statements by Cyprus and Slovakia at the 54th Session of the UN General Assembly, Sixth Committee, Agenda Item 154: 'United Nations Decade of International Law' para 48.

132 See further statement by Portugal, 56th session of the General Assembly, Sixth Committee: 'The concepts of *jus cogens*, obligations *erga omnes* and international crimes of state or

within the international law system, irrespective of whether it took the form of written law or customary law'.[133] Finland was of the view that '*jus cogens* was the only instance of a real hierarchy in international law'.[134] The hierarchical superiority of *jus cogens* norms is necessary in light of the fact that conflicting Acts are of no force and effect and that no derogation from *jus cogens* norms is permitted.[135] The idea that a *jus cogens* norm can invalidate other norms necessarily implies the existence of a hierarchy of norms.

Authors have argued that *jus cogens* is a constitutive legal norm allowing for the creation of norms that are hierarchically superior to other norms of international law.[136] This places *jus cogens* outside the formal sources of law, as set out in article 38 of the ICJ Statute, as higher norms derived from a non-consensual source.[137] As noted by Cassese, it is a fact that *jus cogens* norms have the power to invalidate conflicting rules of law which is a testament to, as well as a consequence of, its normative superiority.[138]

3.2.3 Universal Application

The fact that no state may derogate from *jus cogens* norms may serve as a testament to the universal character of *jus cogens* norms. *Jus cogens* norms have been described as 'universally binding by their very nature'.[139] There is a close relationship between the universal application of *jus cogens* norms and the fact that *jus cogens* norms lead to *erga omnes* obligations.[140]

The idea that *jus cogens* norms are universally applicable and binding is also well-supported by state practice, including in the form of domestic court cases.[141] The United States, for example, argued that the *jus cogens* norm of

---

serious breaches of obligations under peremptory norms of general international law were based on a common belief in certain fundamental values of international law which, because of their importance to the international community as a whole, deserved to be better protected than others.'

133 The Netherlands, 68th Session of the UN General Assembly, Sixth Committee, A/C.6/68/SR.

134 Finland (on behalf of Denmark, Finland, Iceland, Norway and Sweden), 60th Session of the UN General Assembly, Sixth Committee, Agenda Item 80: 'Report of the ILC on the Work of its 57th session' (2 May–3 June and 11 July–5 August 2005) A/60/10.

135 Art 53 of the Vienna Convention (n 1).

136 Christol (n 38) 33; Verdross (n 113) 55.

137 Orakhelashvili (n 38) 37–38.

138 Cassese (n 115).

139 *Smith v Socialist People's Libyan Arab Jamahiriya* 101 F 3d 239 (2nd Cir 1996) 242.

140 De Wet (n 38).

141 In the US domestic courts, see *Tel-Oren v Libyan Arab Republic* (Judgment of 3 February 1984) 726 F2d 774, 233 (US App DC) 384; *Siderman de Blake* (n 39) 715; *Sampson v Federal Republic of Germany and Claims Conference* 250 F3d 1145 (7th Cir 2001) 1150; *Belhas v*

the prohibition of the use of force is a 'universal norm'.[142] Similarly, Bosnia and Herzegovina was of the view in the Application of the Convention on the Prevention and Punishment of the Crime of Genocide that *jus cogens* norms bind all states.[143] In a statement before the UNGA, Mongolia equated *jus cogens* norms to universally-recognized principles.[144] The ICJ itself has described the *jus cogens* norm of the prohibition of genocide as a norm with a 'universal character'.[145] In *Questions Relating to the Obligation to Extradite or Prosecute*, Judge Cançado Trindade stated that '*jus cogens* [is based] on the very foundations of a truly universal international law'.[146]

In addition to this, there are certain universally-condemned offences that clearly correspond to the violation of *jus cogens* human rights.[147] Although it is not the aim of this chapter to discuss issues of universal jurisdiction, this serves as further evidence of the 'universality' inherent in the *jus cogens* regime. Furthermore, due to the universal nature of a *jus cogens* norm, it does not seem plausible that there could be a different interpretation than the enforcement of such a norm being applicable against all states.[148]

4 Does the Prohibition of Terrorism Meet the Criteria and Characteristics of a *Jus Cogens* Norm?

There is as yet no authoritative statement by an international juridical organ which confirms the *jus cogens* status of the prohibition of terrorism.[149] However, the test for whether a norm is *jus cogens* is not whether international courts have determined that it is so. As stated in the introduction to

---

Moshe Ya'Alon, 515 F3d 1279 (DC Cir 2008) 1291–1292; *Abelesz v Magyar Nemzeti Bank*, 692 F 3d 661 (7th Cir 2012) 676. See further the judgment of the Federal Court of Australia in *Nulyarimma v Thompson* (1999) FCA 1192 (1 September 1999) 145 (Judge Merkel dissenting).

142 *Nicaragua* case (n 52) para 313.

143 *Case Concerning Application of the Convention on the Prevention and Punishment of the Crime of Genocide* (n 96).

144 See statement by Mongolia, 26th Session of the UN General Assembly, Sixth Committee, Agenda Item 89: 'Report of the Special Committee on the Question of Defining Aggression' para 34.

145 *Reservations to the Genocide Convention* case (n 105) 21.

146 *Belgium v Senegal* (n 52).

147 Predrag Zenović, 'Human Rights Enforcement Via Peremptory Norms: A Challenge to State Sovereignty' (2012) Riga Graduate School of Law Research Papers No 6 (13 September 2016) 44 <https://www.rgsl.edu.lv/uploads/files/RP_6_Zenovic_final.pdf> accessed 9 August 2017.

148 Ibid.

149 Weatherall (n 57) 616.

this article, the test is whether states accept and recognize such a norm as one from which no derogation is permitted. This requires an assessment not of international court decisions, but of actual state practice – although, of course international court decisions can assist as a subsidiary tool in determining whether the norm is recognized and accepted as non-derogable. This section will consider whether the prohibition of terrorism meets the criteria for *jus cogens*. It will do this by testing whether it meets the formal requirements as discussed in section 3.1. We will then assess whether the prohibition reflects the core characteristics described in section 3.2.

4.1 *The Prohibition of Terrorism and the Criteria for* Jus Cogens *Norms*

4.1.1 The Prohibition of Terrorism as a Norm of General International Law

As discussed, for a norm to qualify as a norm of *jus cogens*, it must first be shown to be a norm of general international law, which includes both rules of customary law and general principles of law. To determine whether the prohibition of terrorism is a norm of *jus cogens* thus requires an assessment of whether the prohibition is a norm of general international law, either in the form of customary international law or a general principle of law. As will be illustrated below, the prohibition of terrorism is widely reflected in practice and accepted as law.

State practice with regard to the prohibition of terrorism is evidenced by acts of states in connection with treaties as well as legislative Acts and national jurisprudence.[150] Numerous international treaties and protocols have been criminalizing certain terrorist conduct.[151] These treaties and protocols define

150 See, further, Draft Conclusion 7 of the ILC 'Report on the work of the 66th session' 241, in terms of which state practice includes 'the conduct of states "on the ground", diplomatic acts and correspondence, legislative acts, judgments of national courts, official publications in the field of international law, statements on behalf of states concerning codification efforts, practice in connection with treaties and acts in connection with resolutions of organs of international organizations and conferences'. In terms of Draft Conclusion 11, *opinio juris* includes 'statements by states which indicate what are or are not rules of customary international law, diplomatic correspondence, the jurisprudence of national courts, the opinions of government legal advisers, official publications in fields of international law, treaty practice and action in connection with resolutions of organs of international organizations and of international conferences. Inaction may also serve as evidence of acceptance as law.'

151 The 1963 Convention on Offences and Certain Other Acts Committed on Board Aircraft (Tokyo Convention); the 1979 International Convention against the Taking of Hostages (Hostages Convention); the 1988 Convention for the Suppression of Unlawful Acts against the Safety of Maritime Navigation (Maritime Safety Convention); the 1997 International Convention for the Suppression of Terrorist Bombings (Terrorist Bombings Convention);

offences relating to specific conduct, ranging from crimes against the person, civil aviation and shipping to crimes that involve the use, possession or threatened use of bombs or nuclear materials and crimes concerning the financing of terrorism.[152]

The aforementioned sectoral anti-terrorism treaties enjoy widespread ratification by states.[153] For example, out of the 193 member states of the UN, the Tokyo Convention has been ratified by 186 member states, the Montreal Convention by 188 member states and the Hague Convention by 185 member states.[154] In addition to this, the Terrorism Bombings Convention has been ratified by 170 states and the Terrorist Financing Convention by 188 states.[155] Moreover, UNSC Resolution 1373 of 2001 requires all member states to stipulate terrorism as a serious crime in domestic legislation.[156] Many states have adopted national legislation prohibiting terrorism.[157] The condemnation of

---

the 1999 Convention for the Unification of Certain Rules for International Carriage by Air (Montreal Convention); the 1999 International Convention for the Suppression of the Financing of Terrorism (Terrorism Financing Convention); the 2005 International Convention for the Suppression of Acts of Nuclear Terrorism (Nuclear Terrorism Convention').

152 Ibid.

153 With regard to subsequent practice as a means of treaty interpretation, see International Law Commission 'First report on subsequent agreements and subsequent practice in relation to treaty interpretation' (19 March 2013) UN Doc A/CN4/660 para 111; International Law Commission 'Second report on subsequent agreements and subsequent practice in relation to treaty interpretation' (26 March 2014) UN Doc A/CN4/671 para 119.

154 The following conventions cited in n 151: the Tokyo Convention; the Montreal Convention; the Convention for the Suppression of Unlawful Seizure of Aircraft, 1970 (Hague Convention). For treaty ratifications, see UN Growth in United Nations membership, 1945-present <www.un.org/en/sections/member-states/growth-united-nations-membership-1945 present/index.html> accessed 6 January 2016.

155 The following conventions cited in n 151: The Terrorist Bombings Convention; the Terrorism Financing Convention. For treaty ratifications, see further United States Treaty Collection <http://treaties.un.org/> accessed 6 January 2016.

156 Art 2(3) of S/RES 1373 (2001).

157 See South Africa's Protection of Constitutional Democracy Against Terrorist and Related Activities Act 2004; the Botswana Counter-Terrorism Act 2014; the Lesotho Penal Code Act, 2010; the Uganda Anti-Terrorism Act 2002; the Ghana Anti-Terrorism Act 2008; the Nigerian Terrorism (Prevention) Act 2011; the Cameroon Law on the Suppression of Acts of Terrorism, 2014; sec 87*bis* of the Algerian Penal Code, promulgated by Order No 66–156 of 18 Safar 1386 corresponding to 8 June 1966; the Egyptian Anti-Terrorism Law 2015; the Tanzanian Prevention of Terrorism Act 2002; the Ethiopian Anti-Terrorism Proclamation 2009; the Tunisian Anti-Terrorism Law 2015; sec 329 of the Penal Code of Bhutan 2004; the Bangladesh Anti-Terrorism Ordinance, 2008; sec 130B of the Malaysian Penal Code 374 of 1936 as amended; sec 218*bis* of the Penal Code of the Democratic Republic of Timor Leste 2009; the Jamaican Terrorism Prevention Act 2005; the Seychelles Prevention of Terrorism

terrorism is further supported in national jurisprudence and statements at the ILC.[158]

With regard to *opinio juris*, writers have argued that unanimous resolutions can be evidence of *opinio juris*, and UNGA resolutions, although not formally binding, can be evidence of *opinio juris* in instances when there is sufficient state practice to support the usage element.[159] The *opinio juris* of states are reflected in numerous UNGA resolutions, which unequivocally condemn terrorism.[160] Furthermore, the customary nature of the prohibition on terrorising the

---

Act 2004; the Dominican Suppression of the Financing of Terrorism (Amendment) Act 2011; sec 73C of the Vanuatu Penal Code [Cap 135] 1981; the Antigua and Barbados Prevention of Terrorism Act 2001; the Trinidad and Tobago Anti-Terrorism Act 2005 as amended by Act 13 of 2018; arts 571–580 of the Penal Code of Spain 1995 (as amended by Organic Law 5/2010); sec 8(1) para 2(b) of the Belgian Organic Law on the Intelligence and Security Services 1998; the Netherlands Crimes of Terrorism Act 2004; sec 311 of the Criminal Code of the Czech Republic 2009; sec 258 of the Criminal Code of Ukraine 2001; sec 330 of the Criminal Code of the Republic of Albania, Law No 7895 of 1995; sec 230 of the Andorra New Penal Code 2005; the Saudi Arabia Penal Law for Crimes of Terrorism and its Financing 2013; sec 100(1) of the Australian Criminal Code Act 1995; the New Zealand Terrorism Suppression Act 2002; sec 1 of 18 USC 2331 2004; sec 3 of the Bahamas Anti-Terrorism Act, 2004; sec 391 of the Guatemalan Criminal Code, 1973; sec 2 of the Brazilian Anti-Terrorism Law 2016; sec 421 of the French Penal Code of 1994, as amended by Law 2005-1550 of 2005.

158 *Barcelona Traction Light and Power Company Limited* (n 59) 32. See further statement by Mr Ago, Yearbook of the International Law Commission, vol I (Part One), 1966, Summary Record of the 828th Meeting (n 26) para 15: 'Even if a rule of *jus cogens* originated in a treaty, it was not from the treaty as such that it derived its character but from the fact that, even though derived from a treaty, it was already a rule of general international law.'

159 Bin Cheng, 'United Nations Resolutions on Outer Space: "Instant" International Customary Law?' (1965) 5 Indian Journal of International Law 35–40; Julien Cantegreil, 'The audacity of the Texaco/Calasiatic Award: René-Jean Dupuy and the Internationalization of Foreign Investment Law' (2011) 22 European Journal of International Law 449; Hugh Thirlway, *International Customary Law and Codification: An Examination of the Continuing Role of Custom in the Present Period of Codification of International Law* (Martinus Nijhoff 1972) 67.

160 Earlier resolutions referred to measures to 'prevent' international terrorism; see A/RES/40/61 (1985) para 1 and A/RES 42/159 (1987) para 1 (153 votes to two (Israel and the US), one abstention (by consensus)). Later resolutions used stronger wording to refer to measures to 'eliminate' international terrorism, such as A/RES 46/51 (1991) Preamble (by consensus); A/RES 50/53 (1995) para 1 (by consensus); A/RES 51/210 (1996) para 1 (by consensus); A/RES 52/165 (1997) para 1 (by consensus); A/RES 54/110 (2000) para 1 by 149 votes to 0; two abstentions); A/RES 55/158 (2001) para 1 (by 151 votes to 0, two abstentions). Further resolutions, while supporting the view that terrorism must be eliminated, also focused on the violation of human rights in the context of terrorism: A/RES 48/122 (1993) para 1 (by consensus); A/RES 49/185 (1994) para 1; A/RES 50/186 (1995) para 2; A/RES/52/133 (1997) para 3; A/RES 54/164 (2000) (para 2); A/RES 57/219 (2003) Preamble; A/RES 58/81 (2004) para 1. See further A/RES 59/153 (2005).

civilian population is further indicated in article 51(2) of Additional Protocol I to the Geneva Convention and article 13 of Additional Protocol II, both of which prohibit acts or threats of violence with the primary purpose of spreading terror among civilians, and both of which articles enjoy widespread support. Article 51(2) was adopted with 77 votes in favour, one against and 16 abstentions, and no concerns or reservations were expressed by states,[161] while article 13 was adopted by consensus.[162] Furthermore, state practice, such as declarations by government officials and military manuals, confirms that the prohibition of terrorism is part of customary international law.[163]

---

161 Art 51(2) of Additional Protocol I to the Geneva Conventions, 1949 states that '[t]he civilian population as such, as well as individual civilians, shall not be the object of attack. Acts or threats of violence the primary purpose of which is to spread terror among the civilian population are prohibited.'

162 Art 13 of Additional Protocol I to the Geneva Conventions, 1949 provides: '1. The civilian population and individual civilians shall enjoy general protection against the dangers arising from military operations. To give effect to this protection, the following rules shall be observed in all circumstances. 2. The civilian population as such, as well as individual civilians, shall not be the object of attack. Acts or threats of violence the primary purpose of which is to spread terror among the civilian population are prohibited. 3. Civilians shall enjoy the protection afforded by this Part, unless and for such time as they take a direct part in hostilities.' See further *Prosecutor v Stanislav Galić*, Case No IT-98-29-A, Appeals Chamber, Judgment, 30 November 2006, para 87. See further L Paredi, 'The War Crime of Terror: An Analysis of International Jurisprudence' 4 <www.internationalcrimesdatabase.org/upload/documents/20150610T161544-Laura20%Paredi20%Brief_final.pdf> accessed 11 November 2017.

163 See Islamic Statement against Terrorism: 'The undersigned, leaders of Islamic movements, are horrified by the events of Tuesday 11 September 2001 in the United States which resulted in massive killing, destruction and attack on innocent lives. We express our deepest sympathies and sorrow. We condemn, in the strongest terms, the incidents, which are against all human and Islamic norms. This is grounded in the Noble Laws of Islam which forbid all forms of attacks on innocents … (Surah al-Isra 17:15)' *MSA News* (14 September 2001) <www.mafhoum.com/press5/147529.htm> accessed 11 November 2017. See Ecuador's Naval Manual (1989): 'The civilian population as such, as well as individual civilians, may not be the object of attack or of threats or acts of intentional terrorization'; Germany's Military Manual (1992): 'Measures of intimidation or of terrorism' are prohibited use of acts or threats of violence in order to spread terror among the civilian population; Ireland's Basic LOAC Guide (2005): 'Attacks or threats of violence intended to terrorise the civilian population are also prohibited'; Kenya's LOAC Manual (1997): It is forbidden 'to spread terror among the civilian population through acts or threats of violence'; Nigeria's Manual on the Laws of War: 'Terror attacks directed mainly against the civilian population are forbidden'; the UK LOAC Manual (2004): 'Acts or threats of violence, the primary purpose of which is to spread terror among the civilian population are prohibited'; Sweden's IHL Manual (1991): 'Attacks deliberately aimed at causing heavy losses and creating fear among the civilian population' are prohibited; the US Naval Handbook (1995): 'The civilian population as such, as well as individual civilians, may not be the object of attack or of threats or acts of intentional terrorization'; the US Air Force

With regard to international jurisprudence, in *Prosecutor v Galić*, Stanislav Galić, Commander of the Bosnian Serb forces, was accused of having conducted a protracted campaign of sniping and shelling against the civilian population in Sarajevo in contravention of articles 51(2) and 13 of Additional Protocols I and II to the Geneva Convention, respectively.[164] The ICTY Trial Chamber found Galić guilty of the war crime of terrorism.[165] Galić appealed the judgment on the basis that the Trial Chamber could only exercise jurisdiction over customary law-based crimes.[166] On appeal, the Appeals Chamber had to determine whether terrorism had emerged in customary international law as an international crime.[167] It found that the prohibition of terrorism enshrined in the Additional Protocols to the Geneva Conventions indeed belonged to customary international law.[168] Furthermore, in the Israeli Wall Advisory Opinion, the ICJ confirmed that 'deliberate and indiscriminate attacks against civilians with the intent to kill are the core element of terrorism which has been unconditionally condemned by the international community regardless of the motives which have inspired them'.[169]

In addition to the above, the decision by the Appeals Chamber of the Special Tribunal for Lebanon (STL) in *Prosecutor v Ayyash*, involving the consideration of the crime of terrorism under Lebanese law as well as customary

Pamphlet (1976): 'Acts or threats of violence which have the primary object of spreading terror among the civilian population are prohibited.'

164 See Count 1: Infliction of terror, *Prosecutor v Stanislav Galić* Case No IT-98-29-I, Indictment, 26 March 1999. The accusation in count 1 reads as follows: 'Violations of the Laws or Customs of War (unlawfully inflicting terror upon civilians as set forth in Article 51 of Additional Protocol I and Article 13 of Additional Protocol II to the Geneva Conventions of 1949) punishable under article 3 of the Statute of the Tribunal. From about 10 September 1992 to about 10 August 1994, Stanislav Galić, as Commander of Bosnian Serbs forces comprising or attached to the Sarajevo Romanija Corps, conducted a protracted campaign of shelling and sniping upon civilian areas of Sarajevo and upon the civilian population, thereby inflicting terror and mental suffering upon its civilian population.' See further Paredi (n 162) 2.

165 See *Prosecutor v Stanislav Galić*, Case No IT-98-29-T, Trial Chamber, Judgment, 5 December 2003, 769 (5 December 2003) (Count 1). Galić was convicted of unlawfully inflicting terror upon civilians as set out in art 51 of Additional Protocol I and art 13 of Additional Protocol II to the Geneva Conventions of 1949.

166 *Prosecutor v Stanislav Galić*, Case No IT-98-29-A, Appeals Chamber, Judgment, 30 November 2006, paras 69–98. See further Paredi (n 162) 2.

167 Paredi (n 162).

168 Ibid., 90: 'The prohibition of terror against the civilian population as enshrined in Article 51(2) of Additional Protocol I and Article 13(2) of Additional Protocol II clearly belonged to customary international law from at least the time of its inclusion in those treaties.'

169 *Legal Consequences of the Construction of a Wall in the Occupied Palestinian Territory* (n 107), paras 4–5.

international law, is relevant.[170] The Appeals Chamber held that 'a customary rule of international law regarding the international crime of terrorism, at least in time of peace, has indeed emerged'.[171] It further identified 'a belief of states that the punishment of terrorism responds to a social necessity (*opinio necessitatis*) and is hence rendered obligatory by the existence of a rule requiring it (*opinio juris*)' as evidenced by state practice.[172] The Appeals Chamber stated that state practice evidencing *opinio juris sive necessitatis* 'share[s] a core concept: Terrorism is a criminal action that aims at spreading terror or coercing governmental authorities and is a threat to the stability of society or the State', and the few states still insisting on an exception to the definition of terrorism can, at most, be considered persistent objectors.[173]

It is argued that the prohibition of terrorism protects an overriding value of the international community – the right to human dignity – which supports its unequivocal condemnation by states. In light of what is set out above, it is a norm of customary international law. As customary international law forms part of general international law, it follows that the prohibition of terrorism is a norm of general international law.

4.1.2 Acceptance and Recognition of the Prohibition of Terrorism as Non-Derogable

As discussed in this section, terrorism is prohibited under various anti-terrorism treaties[174] and United Nations Security Council (UNSC) and UNGA

---

170 *Prosecutor v Ayyash* et al (STL-11-01/I), Interlocutory Decision on the Applicable Law: Terrorism, Conspiracy, Homicide, Perpetration, Cumulative Charging, Appeals Chamber, 16 February 2011 paras 42–62.

171 Ibid., para 85.

172 Ibid., para 102.

173 Ibid., paras 102 and 110.

174 See, eg, art 2(1) of the Terrorism Financing Convention (n 151) which provides that '[a]ny person commits an offence within the meaning of this Convention if that person by any means, directly or indirectly, unlawfully and wilfully, provides or collects funds with the intention that they should be used or in the knowledge that they are to be used, in full or in part, in order to carry out (a) an act which constitutes an offence within the scope of and as defined in one of the treaties listed in the annex; or (b) any other act intended to cause death or serious bodily injury to a civilian, or to any other person not taking an active part in the hostilities in a situation of armed conflict, when the purpose of such act, by its nature or context, is to intimidate a population, or to compel a government or an international organization to do or to abstain from doing any act'. Art 18(1) further provides that 'state parties shall cooperate in the prevention of these offences by taking all practicable measures, including by adapting their domestic legislation, if necessary, to prevent and counter preparations in their respective territories for the commission of such offences, including (a) measures to *prohibit* illegal activities of persons and organizations

resolutions. These treaties make it clear that the prohibition of terrorism is non-derogable: Terrorism under no circumstances is justifiable by political, philosophical, ideological, racial, ethnic, religious or other considerations. For example, the Terrorist Bombings, Terrorism Financing and Nuclear Terrorism Conventions confirm that the political offence exception does not apply and that terrorism is under no circumstances justifiable.[175]

The Draft Comprehensive Convention on International Terrorism further requires that states must establish jurisdiction over terrorist offences, make these offences punishable by appropriate penalties and adopt measures to ensure that these offences are not justifiable by political, philosophical, ideological, racial, ethnic, religious or similar considerations.[176] Terrorism is prohibited in the national legislation of numerous states and states' support of this prohibition is evidenced by mandatory state reports to the Counter-Terrorism Committee.[177] In national jurisprudence, the prohibition of terrorism has simi-

---

that knowingly encourage, instigate, organize or engage in the commission of such offences' (emphasis added). See further art 15 of the Terrorist Bombing Convention (n 150) which contains similar wording in respect of offences under this Convention as well as art 7 of the Nuclear Terrorism Convention (n 151).

175 The following conventions cited in n 151: arts 5 and 11 of the Terrorist Bombings Convention; arts 6 and 14 of the Terrorism Financing Convention; arts 6 and 15 of the Nuclear Terrorism Convention.

176 Ars 5 and 7 of the Draft Comprehensive Convention on International Terrorism, 2006.

177 See n 156. See further UNSC Counter-Terrorism Committee Country reports: Resolution 1373 (2001) <http://www.un.org/en/sc/ctc/resources/countryreports.html> accessed 8 January 2017, where states, for example, reported on legislation and procedures that exist for freezing accounts and assets at banks and financial institutions. See letter dated 22 December 2001 from the Charge d'Affaires of the Permanent Mission of the People's Republic of China to the United Nations addressed to the Chairman of the Security Council Committee established pursuant to Resolution 1373 (2001) concerning counter-terrorism S/2001/1270 (27 December 2001) <www.refworld.org/pdfid46d5712f8.pdf> accessed 23 October 2017, where China referred to its laws relating to the control of the sources of terrorist assets. See further Country Reports: East Asia and Pacific Overview (2015) <www.state.gov/j/ct/rls/crt/2015/257515.htm> accessed 23 October 2017, which included reports by Australia and China. Australia noted that its legal framework to counter terrorism included 'significant penalties for committing terrorist acts; recruiting for and supporting terrorist organizations; financing terrorism; urging violence and advocating terrorism; and travelling abroad to commit terrorist acts and recruitment offences'. China reported on comprehensive counter-terrorism law approved in 2015 to 'provide legal support for counter-terrorism activities as well as collaboration with the international community'. See further letter dated 26 January 2006 from the Permanent Representative of the United States of America to the United Nations addressed to the Chairman of the Counter-Terrorism Committee S2006/69 (3 February 2006) <https://www.refworld.org/docid/46de6022d.html> accessed 23 October 2017. The US reported that sec 806 of the

larly been supported. In the *Clavel* case, for example, the Argentinian Supreme Court defined terrorism as a crime *juris gentium* and stated that its prosecution is in the interests of all civilized nations.[178]

Furthermore, UNGA resolutions that followed 1980, the majority of which were adopted by consensus, are reflective of the *opinio juris* of states and unequivocally condemned terrorism 'wherever and by whomever committed' as criminal and unjustifiable in all its forms and manifestations.[179] While earlier UNGA resolutions still referred to exceptions for the conduct of national liberation movements with regard to terrorist acts, later UNGA resolutions excluded these references and, while acknowledging the right to self-determination, at the same time they unequivocally condemned terrorism.[180] The strongly-worded UNGA Declaration on Measures to Eliminate International Terrorism of 1994 states that criminal acts intended to provoke a state of terror in the general public for political purposes are in any circumstances unjustifiable, irrespective of any justification of a political, philosophical, ideological, racial, ethnic, religious or any other nature.[181] This resolution as well as a further UNGA Resolution on measures to eliminate international terrorism of 1996, which recalled the 1994 resolution, was adopted by consensus and various binding UNSC resolutions confirmed the unequivocal condemnation of terrorism.[182] These resolutions reiterated the condemnation of terrorism in all its

US Patriot Act resulted in terrorist-related property being made subject to civil forfeiture. See further letter dated 17 March 2004 from the Permanent Representative of France to the United Nations addressed to the Chairman of the Counter-Terrorism Committee S/2004/226 (29 March 2004) <https://documents-dds-ny.un.org/doc/UNDOC/GEN/N04/288/37/PDF/N0428837.pdf?OpenElement>accessed 23 October 2017, referring to regulations to control and prevent terrorist access to weapons.

178 *Enrique Lautaro Arancibia Clavel* (n 93). See further *Suresh v Canada (Minister of Citizenship and Immigration)* (2002) 1 SCR 3) para 93.

179 See Ben Saul, *Defining Terrorism in International Law* (Oxford University Press 2006) 204.

180 A/RES 44/29 (1989) 301–302 and A/RES/46/51 (1991) 15. These resolutions reaffirm the right to self-determination yet offer an unqualified condemnation of terrorism.

181 A/RES/49/60 (1994) (Measures to eliminate international terrorism).

182 A/RES/51/210 (1996); S/RES 1368 (2001). Para 1 'unequivocally condemns in the strongest terms the horrifying terrorist attacks which took place on 11 September 2001 in New York, Washington, DC and Pennsylvania and regards such acts, like any act of international terrorism, as a threat to international peace and security'; S/RES/1373 (2001) '[r]eaffirming also its unequivocal condemnation of the terrorist attacks which took place in New York, Washington, DC and Pennsylvania on 11 September 2001, and expressing its determination to prevent all such acts'; S/RES/1377 (2001) '[r]eaffirms its unequivocal condemnation of all acts, methods and practices of terrorism as criminal and unjustifiable, regardless of their motivation, in all their forms and manifestations, wherever and by whomever committed'; S/RES/2249 (2015) '[r]eaffirming that terrorism in all forms and manifestations

forms and manifestations and declared terrorist acts unjustifiable regardless of the reasons invoked by its perpetrators.[183]

The consistent and repeated condemnation of acts of terrorism by states and the reiteration that nothing can ever justify terrorism further illustrate the *opinio juris* of states regarding the prohibition of terrorism.[184] World leaders

---

constitutes one of the most serious threats to international peace and security and that any acts of terrorism are criminal and unjustifiable regardless of their motivations, whenever and by whomsoever committed'.

183 Ibid.

184 Summary Records of the Sixth Committee, 28th meeting Official Records of the General Assembly, 69th Session, A/C6/55/SR28 (7 October–14 November 2014) <https://papersmart.unmeetings.org/ga/69th-session/general-debate/statements> (accessed 8 August 2017). See, eg, the statements by Mr GH Dehghani of the Islamic Republic of Iran: 'The Non-Aligned Movement condemns terrorism in all its forms and manifestations, wherever, by whoever and against whomsoever committed … which are unjustifiable whatever consideratons or facts that may be invoked to justify them.' Mr E Zagaynov on behalf of the member states of the Shanghai Co-operation Organisation and the Russian Federation reiterated the 'fundamental position of condemning terrorism in all its forms and manifestations, regardless of its motivation, whenever, wherever and by whomsoever committed'; Ms E Cujo on behalf of the European Union: 'The international community must respond jointly by condemning terrorism in all its forms and manifestations'; Mr T Joyini on behalf of South Africa (speaking for the African Group): 'There is no justification for terrorism. African states strongly and unequivocally condemn terrorism in all its forms and manifestations, as well as all acts, methods and practices of terrorism wherever, by whomever, against whomever committed, including state terrorism. For no cause or grievance can terrorism be justified'; Dr AM Khan on behalf of Pakistan: 'Pakistan denounces terrorism in all its forms and manifestations and condemns killings by terrorists anywhere in the world, committed for whatever purpose. Nothing – no ideology, no religion, no creed, no cause – can justify or sanction the dastardly acts and heinous crimes committed under the banner of terrorism'; Mr H Haniff on behalf of Malaysia: 'Malaysia would like to express in the strongest terms our condemnation of terrorism in all its forms and manifestations, as well as all acts, methods and practices of terrorism irrespective of where, when or whomever commits it and the reason behind it. No matter how feasible it might be, any hideous act of terrorism could not be justifiable'; Mr O Hilale on behalf of Morocco: 'Le Royaume du Maroc tient à cette occasion à réitérer sa condamnation ferme du terrorisme dans toutes ses formes, en oulignant que rien ne peut justifier un acte terroriste' (translated as: The Kingdom of Morocco wishes at this occasion to reiterate its firm condemnation of terrorism in all its forms, while emphasizing that nothing can justify a terrorist act); Mr A Heumann on behalf of Israel: 'Israel wishes to reaffirm its strong commitment to counter terrorism and its uncompromising condemnation of terrorism in all its forms and manifestations, irrespective of its motivations'; Mr DM Laki on behalf of Uganda: 'Uganda condemns terrorism in all its forms and manifestations, for whatever purpose and by whomsoever. Terrorism can never be justified under any pretext'; Mr LA Ajawin on behalf of South Sudan: 'My government strongly rejects and condemns terrorism in all its forms and manifestations, committed by whomever, whatever, for whatever objective'; Mr F Metrev on behalf of Algeria: 'Algeria would like to reiterate its strong and unequivocal condemnation of all forms of terrorism,

denounced the 2016 massacre at an Orlando nightclub, perpetrated by a self-described adherent of the Islamic State (ISIL/Daesh). Afghanistan President Ashraf Ghani stated that nothing could justify the killing of civilians, while leaders of the Arab States (Saudi Arabia, the United Arab Emirates, Kuwait, Qatar and Egypt) called the attacks immoral and inhumane.[185] In its condemnation of the terrorist attacks on Paris and Istanbul's Ataturk Airport in 2016, the G20 stated: 'We condemn, in the strongest possible terms, the heinous terrorist attacks in Paris on 13 November and in Ankara on 10 October. They are an unacceptable affront to all humanity.'[186]

States similarly condemned terrorist attacks in 2017. Following the bombing at a pop concert in Manchester in May 2017 that killed 22 people, United Kingdom Prime Minister Theresa May stated: 'All acts of terrorism are cowardly attacks on innocent people but this attack stands out for its appalling, sickening cowardice, deliberately targeting innocent, defenceless children and young people.'[187] In response to the terror attack in August 2017 in Barcelona, where a van rammed into a crowd of pedestrians, killing 13 people and injuring

regardless of its motivation, wherever, whenever and by whomsoever committed.' See, further, 8th BRICS Summit – Goa Declaration (16 January 2017) <https://brics2017.org/English/Documents/Summit/201701/t20170125_1410.html> accessed 26 October 2017 para 57: 'We strongly condemn terrorism in all its forms and manifestations and stressed that there can be no justification whatsoever for any acts of terrorism, whether based upon ideological, religious, political, racial, ethnic or any other reasons' and the Declaration on preventing and countering terrorism and violent extremism (Jakarta, Indonesia, March 2017), where the governments of the member states of the Indian Ocean Rim Association, Australia, Bangladesh, Comoros, India, Indonesia, Iran, Kenya, Madagascar, Malaysia, Mauritius, Mozambique, Oman, Seychelles, Singapore, Somalia, South Africa, Sri Lanka, Tanzania, Thailand, United Arab Emirates and Yemen stated that they 'unequivocally condemn all acts of terrorism'. See further D Burke, 'Muslim leaders: 'We will not allow the extremists to define us' <https://pressroom/2006/pages> accessed 3 September 2017; David Pollock and Mohamed Abdelaziz, 'Arab states condemn "terrorist" Paris attacks' <http://english.alarabiya.net/en/News/middle-east/2015/11/14/Arab-states-denounce-Paris-attacks-as-violation-of-human-values-.html> accessed 1 December 2016; 'Arab Government and Media Reactions to the Orlando Attack 15 June 2016' <http://www.washingtoninstitute.org/policy-analysis/view/arab-government-and-media-reactions-to-the-orlando-attack> accessed 7 August 2016; US Department of State 'United States Condemns Terrorist Attack on Istanbul's Ataturk Airport' 28 June 2016, <http://www.state.gov/r/pa/prs/ps/2016/06/259153.htm> accessed 7 August 2016; G20 Statement on the Fight Against Terrorism <http://www.consilium.europa.eu/en/meetings/international-summit/2015/11/g20-statement-on-the-fight-against-terrorism_pdf/> accessed 7 August 2016.

185 Ibid.

186 G20 Statement (n 184).

187 'Theresa May's Downing Street Statement on Manchester Terror Attack in Full' *The Telegraph* (17 May 2017) <http://www.telegraph.co.uk/news/2017/05/23/theresa-mays-downing-street-statement-manchester-terror-attack/> accessed 27 August 2017.

numerous others, Spanish Prime Minister Mariano Rajoy said: 'Today the fight against terrorism is the principal priority for free and open societies like ours. It is a global threat and the response has to be global.' President Vladimir Putin called for the world to unite in an 'uncompromising battle against the forces of terror' and condemned this 'cruel and cynical crime against civilians'.[188] Already in 1998, it had been suggested that '[t]errorism has achieved the status of almost universal condemnation, as have slavery, genocide, and piracy, and the terrorist is the modern era's *hosti humani generis* – an enemy of all mankind'.[189]

5 The Core Characteristics and the Prohibition of Terrorism as a *Jus Cogens* Norm

Based on the analysis above it may be concluded that the prohibition of terrorism is a norm of *jus cogens*. While the characteristics described in section 3.2 themselves are not requirements, they may bolster and confirm the *jus cogens* character of a norm and may be relevant in assessing the criteria for *jus cogens* norms of international law.[190] Therefore, it is useful to inquire whether the prohibition of terrorism reflects the core characteristics.

First, *jus cogens* norms seek to protect fundamental, basic or higher interests or fundamental humanitarian values.[191] These fundamental values include human rights and the right to human dignity, which are fundamental and belong to all people.[192] It seems clear that the prohibition of terrorism safeguards the fundamental values of humanity and human dignity. Terrorism constitutes a threat to the basic human dignity and its prohibition reflects 'the general will of the international community'.[193] Acts of terrorism are committed with the intent to spread fear among innocent civilians.[194] This infringes on the basic

188 'How the World Reacted to the Barcelona Terror Attack' *The Telegraph* (18 August 2017) <http://www.telegraph.co.uk/news/2017/08/17/world-reacted-barcelona-terror-attack/> accessed 27 August 2017.

189 *Flatow v Islamic Republic of Iran* 999 F Supp 23 (DDC 1998).

190 Second Report on *Jus Cogens* (n 49) 18.

191 *Germany v Italy (Jurisdictional Immunities of the State)* (3 February 2012) 2012 ICJ Reports 99, para 92.

192 Bruno Simma and Philip Alston, 'The Sources of Human Rights Law: Custom, *Jus Cogens*, and General Principles' (1995) 6 European Journal of International Law 43.

193 Weatherall (n 57) 626; Jurisdictional Immunities of the state (n 95) para 92.

194 Para 3 of S/RES/1566 (2004) (threats to international peace and security); *Prosecutor v Ayyash & Others* (STL-11-01/I) Interlocutory Decision on the Applicable Law: Terrorism, Conspiracy, Homicide, Perpetration, Cumulative Charging, Appeals Chamber, 16

right to human dignity and the right of human beings not to be used as instruments for the furtherance of a political or ideological goal.

In the *Madan* case, the Indian Supreme Court was of the view that terrorist violence 'affects society as a whole by terrorising and disturbing the harmony of society'.[195] Similarly, the Argentinian Supreme Court in the *Clavel* case defined terrorism as a 'crime *jus gentium*', the prosecution of which is not in the exclusive interest of the state injured by it, but 'benefits, ultimately, all civilized nations who are therefore obligated to cooperate in the global fight against terrorism'.[196] Further, as stated by the ICJ in the *Reservations to the Convention on Genocide* case and as evidenced by near-universal condemnation by states, terrorism can be said to 'shock the conscience of mankind'.[197] These cases confirm the obvious fact that the prohibition of terrorism reflects and protects the fundamental values of the international community.

Second, it is argued that if the prohibition of terrorism has the power to nullify competing norms, it suggests a form of hierarchy *vis-à-vis* other norms of international law. By way of analogy, there can be no valid treaty or UNSC resolution sanctioning terrorist acts. The condemnation of terrorism under treaty law, custom, UNGA and UNSC resolutions and international jurisprudence, irrespective of its justification, as well as the acceptance and recognition by the international community of states as a whole that no derogation from this prohibition is permitted, may indicate support for the hierarchical superiority of the prohibition of terrorism *vis-à-vis* other norms of international law. For example, UN Resolution 1624 of 2005 confirmed the imperative to fight terrorism in all its forms and manifestations by all means in accordance with the UN Charter. This resolution condemned terrorism in all its forms and manifestations as unjustifiable and one of the most serious threats to peace and security and affirmed that states must take all necessary and appropriate measures in accordance with international law to protect the right to life.[198] This strong condemnation supports the position of this norm as hierarchically superior to 'ordinary' norms of customary international law or treaty law.

Lastly, the hierarchical superiority of *jus cogens* norms ties in with its universal applicability. Although sectoral treaties are enforceable only between the parties to the treaty, anti-terrorism treaties have been widely ratified and

---

February 2011; *Prosecutor v Galić* (Trial Judgment) ICTY 5 December 2003 IT-98–29-I para 41; *Advisory Opinion Concerning Legal Consequences of the Construction of a Wall* (n 169) paras 4–5.

195 *Madan Singh v State of Bihar* (2004) INSC 225 (2 April 2004).

196 *Clavel* (n 93) 51–52.

197 See n 105.

198 See S/RES 1624 (2005) (Counter-Terrorism Implementation Task Force).

many of the later anti-terrorism treaties made provision for universal jurisdiction over the proscribed terrorist offences and oblige state parties to extradite or prosecute any suspected offenders found in their territory.[199] This may further support the universal applicability of the prohibition of terrorism. In *United States v Yousef* the United States Court of Appeals noted that certain *jus cogens* crimes, such as piracy and crimes against humanity, are not only universally condemned, but occur outside of a zone in which an adequate judicial system operates and thus necessitates universal jurisdiction.[200] Although there is more case law supporting fundamental values protected by the prohibition of *jus cogens*, the various UNSC resolutions condemning terrorism that are binding on all states and impose quasi-legislative obligations on states as well as various sectoral conventions which provides for universal jurisdiction, could possibly be an indication of the universal applicability of the prohibition of terrorism. For example, in 1987 the Restatement (Third) of Foreign Relations Law suggested that certain acts of terrorism could possibly be counted among

199 See eg arts 3, 6, 7 and 8 of the Terrorist Bombings Convention (n 151). Art 8(1) states: 'The state party in the territory of which the alleged offender is present shall, in cases to which art 6 applies, if it does not extradite that person, be obliged, without exception whatsoever and whether or not the offence was committed in its territory, to submit the case without undue delay to its competent authorities for the purpose of prosecution, through proceedings in accordance with the laws of that state. Those authorities shall take their decision in the same manner as in the case of any other offence of a grave nature under the law of that state.' See further arts 3, 7 and 10 of the Terrorist Financing Convention (n 151). Art 10(1) of the Terrorist Financing Convention mirrors the wording of art 8(1) of the Terrorist Bombings Convention. See further arts 3, 9 and 11 of the Nuclear Terrorism Convention (n 151) and arts 4 and 7 of the Hague Convention (n 154). Art 11(1) of the Nuclear Terrorism Convention mirrors the wording of art 8(1) of the Terrorist Bombings Convention. Art 7 of the Hague Convention states: 'The Contracting State in the territory of which the alleged offender is found shall, if it does not extradite him, be obliged, without exception whatsoever and whether or not the offence was committed in its territory, to submit the case to its competent authorities for the purpose of prosecution. Those authorities shall take their decision in the same manner as in the case of any ordinary offence of a serious nature under the law of that state'; and arts 5 and 7 of the Montreal Convention (n 151). Art 7 states: 'The Contracting State in the territory of which the alleged offender is found shall, if it does not extradite him, be obliged, without exception whatsoever and whether or not the offence was committed in its territory, to submit the case to its competent authorities for the purpose of prosecution. Those authorities shall take their decision in the same manner as in the case of any ordinary offence of a serious nature under the law of that state.' See further arts 3 and 7 of the Convention on the Prevention and Punishment of Crimes against Internationally Protected Persons, Including Diplomatic Agents (n 43); arts 5 and 8 of the Hostages Convention (n 151). The wording of art 8 of the Hostages Convention is similar to that in art 8(1) of the Terrorist Bombings Convention and art 10(1) of the Terrorist Financing Convention. See further arts 6, 7 and 11 of the Maritime Safety Convention (n 151).

200 See *Yousef* case (n 122).

'offences recognized by the community of nations as of universal concern', which supports universal jurisdiction to define and punish such acts.[201]

The universal applicability of the prohibition of terrorism is necessary in light of its hierarchical superiority and the fact that the prohibition of terrorism is an issue of global concern. As discussed, the Terrorist Bombings, Terrorism Financing and Nuclear Terrorism Conventions require that state parties establish jurisdiction over and make punishable under their domestic laws the offences proscribed, and extradite or prosecute persons accused of committing or aiding in the commission of these offences.[202] Furthermore, the UNSC has taken measures, which are legally binding on all states, to address terrorism as a threat to global peace and security.[203] For example, Resolution 1373 of 1999 is binding on all states and requires all member states to make terrorism a serious crime in domestic legislation.[204]

6 Conclusion

This chapter set out to establish whether the prohibition of terrorism has attained *jus cogens* status. In order to understand why *jus cogens* norms have binding power, the evolution of the concept through the ages was discussed. Although steeped in the natural law tradition, it was illustrated that *jus cogens* attained a positivist flavour in the nineteenth and twentieth centuries when the ideas of nationalism and state sovereignty were paramount. Even in these times, though, positivism still clung to a certain ethical notion of justice founded in natural law.

---

201 Restatement (Third) of Foreign Relations Law of the United States (1987) para 404.

202 Arts 3, 6 and 7 of the Terrorist Bombings Convention (n 151); arts 3, 7 and 10 of the Terrorist Financing Convention (n 151); arts 3, 9 and 11 of the Nuclear Terrorism Convention (n 151).

203 See art 25 of the UN Charter, which states that all members of the United Nations 'agree to carry out and accept the decisions of the Security Council in accordance with the present Charter'. See further Ian Hurd, 'The UN Security Council and the International Rule of Law' (2014) The Chinese Journal of International Politics 6: 'The Charter is a multilateral treaty that is binding on the states that sign it. It requires that they comply with its terms, and these terms include an extensive degree of deference to the Security Council.' See further Erika de Wet and Jure Vidmar (eds), *Hierarchy in International Law: The Place of Human Rights* (Oxford University Press 2012) 6.

204 Trevor Chimimba, 'United Nations Security Council Resolution 1373 (2001) as a tool for criminal law enforcement' in Tiyanjana Maluwa and others (eds), *The Pursuit of a Brave New World in International Law: Essays in Honour of John Dugard* (Brill Nijhoff 2017) 535–6; art 2(3) of S/RES 1373 (2001).

Article 53 of the Vienna Convention gave *jus cogens* norms an objective and concrete form by identifying the criteria for these norms to be elevated to *jus cogens* status. The prohibition of terrorism is not only a rule of customary international law, but there is also ample evidence that it has been accepted and recognized by the international community of states as a norm from which no derogation is permitted. Moreover, the prohibition of terrorism reflects the core characteristics of *jus cogens* norms. The prohibition protects the fundamental values of the international community, is hierarchically superior to other norms of international law and is universally applicable.

The prohibition of terrorism as a *jus cogens* norm demonstrates that *jus cogens* norms can emerge, and thus are not immutable. They often emerge in response to contemporary challenges. It is doubtful that 20 years ago the argument that the prohibition of terrorism was *jus cogens* could have been undisputed. Twenty years ago there was very little practice in support of the existence of a general norm of international law prohibiting terrorism, and even less practice supporting the idea that such prohibition was non-derogable. Yet, the rise in incidences of terrorism and the solidarity of the world against terrorism have led to the emergence of the prohibition, not only as a general rule of international law, but as a norm of *jus cogens.* Weatherall aptly describes the emergence of the prohibition of terrorism as the most recent *jus cogens* norm to emerge in response to historical exigencies by making the following observation:

> Peremptory norms emerge as legal responses to the needs of international society to prohibit conduct that shocks the conscience of humanity. Historically, terrorism has been condemned as an affront to the dignity of the human person: human beings cannot be reduced to instruments of political gain through violence and incitement of fear.[205]

205 Weatherall (n 57) 627.

PART 2

CHAPTER 3

The Prohibition of Terrorism and the Prohibition of Torture

1 Introduction

In evaluating the role of *jus cogens* in the rules of international law relating to terrorism, Part I considered the prohibition of terrorism under international law and found that this prohibition had acquired the status of *jus cogens*.[1] The current part of the book (Part II) considers whether the importance of the fight against terrorism and the universal condemnation of terrorism might permit states to use all necessary means, without limitation, to fight the scourge of terrorism, even if these means infringe upon other norms that protect fundamental human rights and values of the international community.

The particular question considered in this chapter is whether a state can decide to authorize particular types of punishment, such as torture, if it would serve the fight against terrorism. Certain states have advanced arguments in favour of derogating from the prohibition of torture in the fight against terrorism, and the argument has found some support from scholars.[2] Nevertheless,

1 See ch 2.

2 Richard Posner, 'Torture, Terrorism, and Interrogation' in Stanley Levinson (ed), *Torture: A Collection* (Oxford University Press 2004) 294 (arguing that 'there is such a thing as a lesser wrong committed to avoid a greater one'); Alan Dershowitz, 'Tortured Reasoning' in Stanley Levinson (above) 266 (arguing that torture is being used in the war on terrorism and that it is better for the rule of law to have such practices inside rather than outside the legal system); Alan Dershowitz, 'The Torture Warrant: A Response to Professor Strauss' (2003) 48 New York Law School Law Review 275; Bernard Gert, 'Justifying Violence' (1969) 66 The Journal of Philosophy 623 (expressing the view that, while all killing and torturing for pleasure or profit is clearly immoral, 'killing and torturing to prevent greater killing and torturing may sometimes be allowed by public reason'). See further 'Torture Techniques Endorsed by the Bush Administration *The Guardian* (17 April 2009) <www.theguardian.com/world/2009/apr/17/torture-methods-interrogation-george-bush-approved> accessed 12 August 2017, stating that torture and coercion were openly sanctioned as tools of interrogation at the highest levels of the Bush administration; 'Donald Trump May be Seeking to Reinstate Torture Methods for Detained Terrorist Suspects' *The New York Times* (26 January 2017) <www.news.com.au/finance/work/leaders/donald-trump-may-be-seeking-to-reinstate-torture-methods-for-detained-terrorist-suspects/news-story/7d265cf92958ef86c9258391c60e6116> accessed 12 August 2017; 'Israel Admits Torture' *BBC News* (2000) <http://news.bbc.co.uk/2/hi/middle_east/637293.stm> accessed 12 August 2017.

 DOI:10.1163/9789004391543_005

there has been a strong call for counter-terrorism measures to comply with states' obligations under international law, including the prohibition of torture. For example, Oehmichen is of the view that the preservation of human rights is vital to prevent terrorism and that diminishing the rights of civilians ultimately destroys the faith of the people in the state. This, in turn, undermines the power of the state, and exacerbates, rather than diminishes, terrorism.[3] Other authors have raised concerns regarding the use of torture in the fight against terrorism.[4]

It is recognized that the relationship between the prohibition of torture and counter-terrorism measures could be approached from a normative perspective, that is, whether states *should* be free to commit acts of torture to prevent acts of terrorism in the protection of the greater good and potentially saving countless lives. The question could also be addressed from an empirical perspective by considering, for example, whether permitting acts of torture could prevent the loss of life; in other words, whether torturing suspects could produce evidence that could be used to prevent terrorist attacks. This book, and hence this chapter, adopts a purely doctrinal approach and considers the relationship between the two sets of rules, namely, the prohibition of torture and the prohibition of terrorism, from the perspective of the rules of international law as they stand.

In section 2, this chapter will begin with a discussion of the status of the prohibition of torture under international law. It will consider which acts constitute torture in order to evaluate whether certain conduct, as part of

---

3 Anna Oechmichen, 'Terrorism and Anti-Terrorism Legislation: The Terrorised Legislator?' PhD thesis, Leiden University (2009) 338–42 <http://hdl.handle.net/1887/13852> accessed 1 July 2017; Amnesty International 'Torture in 2014: 30 Years of Broken Promises' <https://www.amnestyusa.org/sites/default/files/act400042014en.pdf> accessed 12 April 2016. See further Vittorio Bufacchi and Jean Maria Arrigo, 'Torture, Terrorism and the State: A Refutation of the Ticking-Bomb Argument' (2006) 23 Journal of Applied Philosophy 355 (arguing for 'the unconditional refutation of any attempt to justify torture, without exceptions'); Neil MacMaster, 'Torture: From Algiers to Abu Ghraib' (2004) 46 Race and Class 12 ('historically, whenever states started on the slippery slope of enabling a restricted or "controlled" use of duress, this inevitably deteriorated into a monstrous system of brutality'). See also Report of the Special Rapporteur on Torture and Other Cruel, Inhuman or Degrading Treatment or Punishment, Nils Melzer, appointed by UNHRC Resolution 1985/33, A/HRC/34/54 (14 February 2017) Yearbook of the International Law Commission II para 14: 'The Special Rapporteur observes with alarm that, since the turn of the century, the rise of transnational terrorism, organized crime and other actual or perceived threats has given way to an increasing tolerance of violent political narratives and popular beliefs that not only trivialize torture and other cruel, inhuman or degrading treatment or punishment, but even promote and incite their use in the name of national security and the fight against terrorism.'

4 Bufacchi and Arrigo (n 3); MacMaster (n 3).

counter-terrorism measures, amounts to torture. In this regard, various elements of the definition of torture that have emerged from regional and international treaty law, including the widely-ratified UN Convention Against Torture and Other Cruel, Inhuman or Degrading Treatment or Punishment of 1984 (CAT), will be considered. The prohibition of torture by states contained in various regional conventions and national legislation will further be analyzed as evidence of state practice for the purposes of the formation of customary international law.[5] In this regard, article 31(3)(b) of the Vienna Convention on the Law of Treaties provides that 'any subsequent practice in the application of the treaty which establishes the agreement of the parties regarding its interpretation' can be taken into account for the purposes of treaty interpretation.[6] Accordingly, regional and national practice occurring 'in the application of the treaty' is relevant for purposes of the interpretation of the treaty concerned. Furthermore, in its 2014 report on subsequent agreements and subsequent practice in relation to treaty interpretation, the ILC stated that '[s]tates and courts should make every effort to conceive an agreed subsequent practice of the parties as an effort to interpret the treaty in a particular way'.[7] This includes the enactment of domestic legislation or the conclusion of new international agreements for the purpose of implementing a treaty.[8]

In addition, this section will discuss the elements of the definition of torture that have emerged under customary international law by having regard to state practice, including national case law, legislation and *opinio juris*. It will further be evaluated how the prohibition of torture is supported in international jurisprudence as a subsidiary source of international law. Following an analysis of the prohibition of torture under international law, section 3 will evaluate whether the prohibition of the use of torture, as defined in the CAT, or components of the definition, has obtained *jus cogens* status. The prohibition of torture will be evaluated in terms of the criteria for a norm to be elevated to

5 Philip de Man, *State Practice, Domestic Legislation and the Interpretation of Fundamental Principles of International Space Law* (Leuven Centre for Global Governance Studies Working Paper No 181, 2017) <https://ghum.kuleuven.be/ggs/publications/working_papers/new_series/wp-171-180/wp181deman.pdf> accessed 2 October 2017. See further Sir Humphrey Waldock 'Sixth Report on the Law of Treaties' (1966) II Yearbook of the International Law Commission 221, who is of the view that subsequent practice by states is an authentic means of interpretation, as 'it constitutes objective evidence of the understanding of the parties as to the meaning of the treaty'.

6 Ibid.

7 ILC 'Second Report on Subsequent Agreements and Subsequent Practice in Relation to Treaty Interpretation' (26 March 2014) UN Doc A/CN4/671 para 119.

8 ILC 'First Report on Subsequent Agreements and Subsequent Practice in Relation to Treaty Interpretation' (19 March 2013) UN Doc A/CN4/660 para 111.

jus cogens status as set out article 53 of the Vienna Convention. Furthermore, it will be considered whether the prohibition of torture meets the characteristics of *jus cogens* norms as discussed in chapter 3, namely, that it protects the fundamental interests of the international community, is hierarchically superior and is universally applicable. Whether the prohibition of torture has been elevated to a *jus cogens* norm will then be discussed.

Finally, section 4 will contemplate the interaction between the prohibition of torture and the prohibition of terrorism. It will evaluate whether a normative weighing between these two prohibitions or, alternatively, a limitation of the prohibition of torture, is possible, having regard to the fundamental norms that both the prohibition of torture and the prohibition of terrorism seek to protect.

2 The Prohibition of Torture under International Law

Before the CAT entered into force in 1987, there was no treaty definition of torture and cruel, inhuman or degrading treatment or punishment, although this conduct was prohibited in a number of regional and international treaties.[9] For example, the European Convention of Human Rights (ECHR) provided that 'no-one shall be subjected to torture or to inhuman or degrading treatment or punishment'.[10] In dealing with permissible derogations in times of public emergencies, it provided that no derogation from the prohibition of torture is allowed.[11] In terms of article 7 of the International Covenant on Civil and Political Rights (ICCPR), '[n]o one shall be subjected to torture or to cruel, inhuman or degrading treatment or punishment. In particular, no one shall be subjected without his/[her] free consent to medical or scientific experimentation.'[12] Article 4(2) of the ICCPR provided that no derogation from the prohibition of torture is permitted.[13] This applies even '[i]n time of public emergency which threatens the life of the nation'.[14]

---

9 See, for example, the European Convention for the Protection of Human Rights and Fundamental Freedoms, 1950 (ECHR); the International Covenant on Civil and Political Rights, 1966 (ICCPR); the American Convention of Human Rights, 1969 (ACHR); and the African Charter on Human and Peoples' Rights, 1981 (Banjul Charter).

10 Art 3 of the ECHR (n 9).

11 Art 15(2) of the ECHR (n 9).

12 Art 7 of the ICCPR (n 9).

13 Ibid., art 4(2).

14 Karima Bennoune, 'Terror/Torture' (2008) (26) Berkeley Journal of International Law 11.

In terms of the American Convention of Human Rights (ACHR), torture and cruel, inhuman, or degrading punishment or treatment were prohibited.[15] It did not allow any derogation from the prohibition of torture, even 'in time of war, public danger, or other emergency that threatens the independence or security'.[16] The African Charter on Human and Peoples' Rights (Banjul Charter) guaranteed the right of every individual to human dignity, and listed torture and cruel, inhuman or degrading punishment and treatment as examples of a form of exploitation and degradation.[17] This illustrated a strong link between torture and the infringement upon human dignity (for instance, by using the word 'degradation'), and it seemed to imply that torture and cruel, inhuman or degrading punishment are regarded as particularly severe forms of exploitation and degradation, in the same category as slavery.

The Inter-American Convention to Prevent and Punish Torture (IACPPT) of 1985 stated that '[n]o one shall be subjected to torture or to cruel, inhuman, or degrading punishment or treatment. All persons deprived of their liberty shall be treated with respect for the inherent dignity of the human person.'[18] It further confirmed that no derogation is allowed in times of public emergency, and added that '[n]either the dangerous character of the detainee or prisoner, nor the lack of security of the prison establishment or penitentiary shall justify torture'.[19]

The first attempt to define torture in an international instrument was in 1975, when the UN General Assembly (UNGA) adopted the Declaration on the Protection of All Persons from Being Subjected to Torture or Other

15 Art 5(2) of the ACHR (n 9).

16 Ibid., arts 27(1) and (2).

17 Art 5 of the Banjul Charter (n 9) states that '[e]very individual shall have the right to the respect of the dignity inherent in a human being and to the recognition of his legal status. All forms of exploitation and degradation of man, particularly slavery, slave trade, torture, cruel, inhuman or degrading punishment and treatment shall be prohibited.'

18 See the Preamble to the Inter-American Convention to Prevent and Punish Torture, 1985 (IACPPT), which states: 'Aware of the provision of the American Convention on Human Rights that no one shall be subjected to torture or to cruel, inhuman, or degrading punishment or treatment; [r]eaffirming that all acts of torture or any other cruel, inhuman, or degrading treatment or punishment constitute an offense against human dignity and a denial of the principles set forth in the Charter of the Organization of American States and in the Charter of the United Nations and are violations of the fundamental human rights and freedoms proclaimed in the American Declaration of the Rights and Duties of Man and the Universal Declaration of Human Rights.'

19 Ibid., art 5.

Cruel, Inhuman or Degrading Treatment or Punishment (Declaration against Torture).[20] In terms of the Declaration:

1 Torture means any act by which severe pain or suffering, whether physical or mental, is intentionally inflicted by or at the instigation of a public official on a person for such purposes as obtaining from him or a third person information or confession, punishing him for an act he has committed or is suspected of having committed, or intimidating him or other persons. It does not include pain or suffering arising only from, inherent in or incidental to, lawful sanctions to the extent consistent with Standard Minimum Rules for the Treatment of Prisoners.

2 Torture constitutes an aggravated or deliberate form of cruel, inhuman or degrading treatment or punishment.[21]

As the Declaration was a non-binding instrument, the UNGA in 1977 agreed that work on a binding treaty prohibiting torture should commence. The CAT was adopted by the UNGA in 1984 and entered into force in 1987.[22] The definition of torture in the CAT adopted many elements of the Declaration and, as at June 2017, it had been ratified or acceded to by 161 states.[23] It defines torture for the purposes of the CAT as:

---

20 Arts 1 and 2 of the Declaration on the Protection of All Persons from Being Subjected to Torture or Other Cruel, Inhuman or Degrading Treatment or Punishment, 1975.

21 Ibid.

22 Convention against Torture and Other Cruel, Inhuman or Degrading Treatment or Punishment, 1984 (CAT).

23 United Nations Treaty Ratifications <http://treaties.un.org/> accessed 6 January 2016. The Convention has been ratified or acceeded to by the following states: Afghanistan, Albania, Algeria, Antigua and Barbuda, Argentina, Armenia, Australia, Austria, Azerbaijan, Bahrain, Bangladesh, Belarus, Belgium, Belize, Benin, Bolivia, Bosnia and Herzegovina, Botswana, Brazil, Bulgaria, Burkina Faso, Burundi, Cambodia, Cameroon, Canada, Cape Verde, Chad, Chile, China, Colombia, Congo, Costa Rica, Côte d'Ivoire, Croatia, Cuba, Cyprus, Czech Republic, Democratic Republic of the Congo, Denmark, Djibouti, Ecuador, Egypt, Equatorial Guinea, El Salvador, Estonia, Ethiopia, Finland, France, Gabon, Georgia, Germany, Ghana, Greece, Guatemala, Guinea, Guyana, The Holy See, Honduras, Hungary, Iceland, Indonesia, Ireland, Israel, Italy, Japan, Jordan, Kazakhstan, Kenya, Kuwait, Kyrgyzstan, Latvia, Lebanon, Lesotho, Liberia, Libya, Liechtenstein, Lithuania, Luxembourg, Malawi, Maldives, Mali, Malta, Mauritius, Mauritania, Mexico, Moldova, Monaco, Mongolia, Morocco, Mozambique, Namibia, Nepal, The Netherlands, New Zealand, Niger, Nigeria, Norway, Panama, Paraguay, Peru, Philippines, Poland, Portugal, Qatar, Republic of Korea, Romania, Russian Federation, Saint Vincent and the Grenadines, Saudi Arabia, Senegal, Serbia and Montenegro, Seychelles, Sierra Leone, Slovak Republic, Slovenia, Somalia, South Africa, Spain, Sri Lanka, Swaziland, Sweden, Switzerland, Syrian Arab Republic, Tajikistan, Timor Leste, the former Yugoslav Republic of Macedonia, Togo,

> any act by which severe pain or suffering, whether physical or mental, is intentionally inflicted by or at the instigation of a public official on a person for such purposes as obtaining from him or a third person information or confession, punishing him for an act he or a third person has committed or is suspected of having committed, or intimidating or coercing him or a third person or for any reason based on discrimination of any kind, when such pain or suffering is inflicted by or at the instigation of or with the consent or acquiescence of a public official or other person acting in an official capacity. It does not include pain or suffering arising only from, inherent in or incidental to lawful sanctions.

The definition of torture in the CAT differed in various respects from the definition of torture contained in the Declaration against Torture. In terms of the CAT, torture also applies to an act intentionally inflicting severe pain or suffering for the purpose of punishing a person for an act that not only such a person, but a third person, has committed or is suspected of having committed. Furthermore, a torturous act can be committed by coercing a person, and the purpose of the torture includes torture for any reason based on discrimination of any kind.[24]

The CAT definition further excluded pain or suffering arising only from, inherent in or incidental to lawful sanctions to the extent consistent with Standard Minimum Rules for the Treatment of Prisoners, from the definition of torture. It was argued that the aforementioned rules are limited in scope and lack legally-enforceable status in international law.[25] The omission further appears to indicate that pain or suffering resulting from any lawful sanction, not just sanctions imposed upon detainees and prisoners, are excluded from the definition of torture.[26] The CAT also omitted the notion that torture constitutes an aggravated or deliberate form of cruel, inhuman or degrading treatment or punishment.[27] This possibly signalled a move away from the focus on

Tunisia, Turkey, Turkmenistan, Uganda, Ukraine, the United Kingdom, the United States, Uruguay, Uzbekistan, Venezuela, Yemen and Zambia.

24 Art 1 of the CAT (n 22).

25 Report of the Working Group on a Draft Convention against Torture and Other Cruel, Inhuman or Degrading Treatment or Punishment E/CN4/L1470 (12 March 1979) E/CN4/L1470 Agenda item 10(a) para 21.

26 Mathew Lippman, 'The Development and Drafting of the United Nations Convention Against Torture and Other Cruel Inhuman or Degrading Treatment or Punishment' (1994) 17 Boston College International and Comparative Law Review 314–15.

27 Ibid.

the degree of torture constituting either torture or cruel, inhuman or degrading treatment or punishment. The CAT did not attempt to define cruel, inhuman or degrading treatment or punishment and left it to signatory states to prevent acts of cruel, inhuman or degrading treatment or punishment in their territories.[28]

In terms of the definition of torture in the CAT, the four elements of torture are severe pain or suffering; intent; purpose; and state involvement.[29] These elements are important in the later evaluation of conduct which may constitute torture as part of anti-terrorism measures, and also in considering whether a derogation from the prohibition of torture is allowed. The CAT further provides that torture is to be designated and defined as a specific crime by states in their domestic legislation and that any definition of torture in legislation must be consistent with the definition set out in article 1 of the CAT and should incorporate the offences of cruel, inhuman or degrading treatment or punishment.[30] In this regard, torture is widely prohibited in the domestic legislation of states.[31]

---

28 Signatory states are obligated to report every four years to the Committee on their activities under the Convention.

29 Interim report of the Special Rapporteur on Torture and Other Cruel, Inhuman or Degrading Treatment or Punishment, Manfred Nowak (28 July 2008), A63/175 para 46.

30 Art 16 of the CAT (n 22).

31 Art 46 of the Constitution of the Bolivarian Republic of Venezuela, 1999 ('Everyone is entitled to respect for his or her physical, mental and moral integrity, therefore: (1) No person shall be subjected to penalties, torture, cruelty, inhuman or degrading treatment. Every victim of torture or cruel, inhumane or degrading treatment effected or tolerated by agents of the state has the right to rehabilitation'); art 182 of the Venezuela Criminal Code, 2000; art 23 of the Constitution of Tunisia, 2014 ('The state protects human dignity and physical integrity, and prohibits all types of moral and physical torture'; art 12 of the Constitution of Cameroon, 1972; arts 12(1)(d) and (e) of the Constitution of the Republic of South Africa, 1996; arts 16 and 61(2) of the Constitution of the DRC, 2005; art 101*bis* of the Criminal Code of the DRC, 2011; arts 25(a) and 29 of the Constitution of Kenya, 2010; arts 8(2)(b) of the Constitution of Namibia, 1990; arts 24 and 44 of the Constitution of the Republic of Uganda, 1995; arts 2, 3 and 4 of the Uganda Prevention and Prohibition of Torture Act, 2012; art 132(a) of the Sudan Constitution, 2005; art 2 of the Kenya National Police Service Act, 2011; art 51 of the Kenya National Intelligence Service Act, 2012; arts 94–95 of the Turkish Criminal Code, 2004; art 2(24)(h) of the Constitution of Peru, 1993; art 12 of the Constitution of Colombia, 1991; art 178 of the Columbia Penal Code Law, 2000; art 209-A of the Honduras Criminal Code (approved by decree 144–83), 1983; art 14(2) of the Constitution of the Islamic Republic of Pakistan, 1973 ('No person shall be subjected to torture for the purpose of extracting evidence'); art 53(2) of the Constitution of Syrian Arabic Republic, 2012; sec 269.1 of the Canadian Criminal Code, 1985; art 40 of the Constitution of the Republic of Poland, 1997 ('No one may be subjected to torture or cruel, inhuman, or degrading treatment or punishment'); art 7(2) of the Constitution of Greece, 1975 (as amended); art 21(2) of the Constitution of the Russian Federation, 1993; art 117 of the Criminal Code of the Russian Federation No 63-Fz of 13 June 1996; art 9(2) of

The discussion below will analyze the elements of torture under treaty law and will also discuss the prohibition under customary international law in order to determine whether there are some elements of the definition of torture that are common to these sources of law. International jurisprudence will be considered as a subsidiary source. With regard to the elements of torture as they appear in the CAT, the first discussion will focus on whether the degree or 'severity' of pain and suffering is a requirement for an act to constitute torture. This will include a consideration of the difference between torture, on the one hand, and cruel, inhuman or degrading treatment or punishment on the other, and whether this difference is applied in practice. It will further be evaluated whether intent, purpose and the commission of torture by a public official as requirements for an act to constitute torture are supported in state practice. These issues will be explored with reference to the use of torture as a counter-terrorism measure. After this analysis, the question of whether elements of the definition have attained *jus cogens* status will be considered.

2.1 *The Elements of Torture*

2.1.1 Severe Pain and Suffering

The first element in the definition of torture that features in both the Declaration Against Torture and the CAT is that of 'severe pain and suffering'. The Declaration contains an added element referring to the degree of the torture involved, stating that torture is an aggravated or deliberate form of cruel, inhuman or degrading treatment or punishment. As mentioned above, this reference to torture being an aggravated form of cruel, inhuman or degrading treatment or punishment was omitted from the CAT. The question therefore arises as to whether severity is a requirement for pain and suffering to constitute torture and, closely related to this, whether there is an element of 'aggravation' or 'deliberation' required to elevate cruel, inhuman or degrading treatment or punishment to torture. This is important as it may be argued that certain conduct, as part of counter-terrorism measures, is not 'severe' enough to constitute torture.

With regard to domestic legislation, although pain and suffering in some form are included in all national legislation reviewed, legislation differs with regard to the element of severity. Some national legislation refers to the severity element. In South Africa, Kenya and Uganda, national legislation requires

the Criminal Procedure Code of the Russian Federation No 174-Fz of 18 December 2001; art 126 of the Constitution of Sri Lanka, 1978; art 2 of the Saudi Arabia Law of Criminal Procedure of 16 October 2001; art 3 of the South African Prevention of Combating and Torture of Persons Act, 2013.

severe pain and suffering to constitute torture.[32] In Cameroon, the Criminal Code requires pain or severe suffering for an act to constitute torture (thus restricting severity to the suffering but not the pain).[33] The Democratic Republic of the Congo's Law Criminalising Torture requires intent and severe pain or suffering, whether physical or mental.[34] Canadian legislation refers to the

32 In South Africa, art 3 of the Prevention of Combating and Torture of Persons Act 2013 defines torture as 'any act or omission, by which severe pain or suffering, whether physical or mental, is intentionally inflicted on a person (a) for such purposes as to (i) obtain information or a confession from him or her or any other person; (ii) punish him or her for an act he or she has committed, is suspected of having committed or of planning to commit; or (iii) intimidate him or her or any other person to do, or to refrain from doing, anything; or (iv) for any reason based on discrimination of any kind, when such pain or suffering is reflected by or at the instigation of, or with the consent or acquiescence of a public official or other person acting in an official capacity, but does not include pain or suffering arising only from, inherent in or incidental to lawful sanctions'. In Kenya, sec 51(4) of the National Intelligence Service Act (n 31) defines torture as any act by which severe pain or suffering, whether physical or mental, is intentionally inflicted on a person for the purpose of (i) obtaining information or a confession from the person or from a third person; (ii) punishing the person for an act which that person or a third person has committed or is suspected of having committed; (iii) intimidating or coercing that person or a third person; or (iv) for any reason based on discrimination of any kind, when such pain or suffering is inflicted by or at the instigation of or with the consent or acquiescence of a public official or other person acting in an official capacity. Further, in Kenya, sec 2 of the National Police Service Act and sec 51 of the National Intelligence Service Act provide that '[c]ruel, inhuman and degrading treatment or punishment means a deliberate and aggravated treatment or punishment not amounting to torture, inflicted by a person in authority or the agent of the person in authority against a person under his custody, causing suffering, gross humiliation or debasement to the person'. In Uganda, art 2(1) of the Prevention and Prohibition of Torture Act defines torture as 'any act or omission, by which severe pain or suffering whether physical or mental, is intentionally inflicted on a person by or at the instigation of or with the consent or acquiescence of any person whether a public official or other person acting in an official or private capacity for such purposes as (a) obtaining information or a confession from the person or any other person; (b) punishing that person for an act he or she or any other person has committed, or is suspected of having committed or of planning to commit; or (c) intimidating or coercing the person or any other person to do, or to refrain from doing, any act'.

33 Art 132(5) of the Cameroon Penal Code, 1967 (as amended by Act 97/009) defines torture to mean '[a]ny act by which severe pain or suffering, whether physical or mental, is intentionally inflicted by or at the investigation of a public official or with his express or tacit consent on a person for such purposes as obtaining from him or a third person information or confession, punishing him for an act he or a third person has committed or is suspected of having committed, or intimidating or putting pressure on him or a third person, or for any other motive based on any form of discrimination whatsoever. Torture shall not include pain or suffering arising only from, inherent in or incidental to lawful sanctions.'

34 Art 48*bis* of Law No 11/008 of 9 July 2011.

severity of the pain and suffering, defining torture as 'any act or omission by which severe pain or suffering' occurs.[35] Latvia requires that the acts must cause 'particular' pain or suffering to victims, while Greece and Luxembourg use the word 'acute' instead of 'severe'.[36] In Uganda, severe pain and suffering includes the intentional or threatened infliction of physical pain or suffering; the administration or threatened application of mind-altering substances 'or other procedures calculated to disrupt profoundly the senses or the personality'; as well as the threat of imminent death.[37] Further, the definition includes not only such threats to the victim, but also the threat that another person will suffer this fate. Accordingly, the definition is wide and does not seem to require actual physical pain and suffering.

In Algeria, the definition of torture requires severe pain and suffering.[38] In Armenia, the Criminal Code defines torture as causing strong pain or physical or mental suffering and distinguishes between degrees of torture.[39] In Sri Lanka, an act which causes severe pain, whether physical or mental, constitutes torture, but the reference to suffering is omitted.[40] In the Philippines, torture refers to an act by which severe pain and suffering, whether physical or

35 See art 269(1)(2) of the Canada Criminal Code C-46, 1985.

36 Consideration of Reports Submitted by State Parties under Article 19 of the Convention, Latvia, UN Doc CAT/C/21/Add.4 6, <docstore.ohcr.org.SelfServices/FilesHandler.ashx .enc.> accessed 12 August 2017; Consideration of Reports Submitted by State Parties under Article 19 of the Convention, Greece, UN Doc CAT/C/61/Add.2 230 <docstore.ohcr.org .SelfServices/FilesHandler.ashx.enc.> accessed 6 May 2017; Consideration of Reports Submitted by State Parties under Article 19 of the Convention, Luxembourg, UN Doc CAT/C/SR.517, 7 (May 1, 2017) <docstore.ohcr.org.SelfServices/FilesHandler.ashx.enc.> accessed 6 May 2017.

37 Art 2(1) of the Prevention and Prohibition of Torture Act (n 32).

38 Art 263*bis* of the Penal Code of Algeria, 1966: 'Est entendu par torture tout acte par lequel une douleur ou des souffrances aiguës, physiques ou mentales sont intentionnellement infligées à une personne quelqu'en soit le mobile.' (Torture is understood to mean any act by which severe pain or suffering, whether physical or mental, is intentionally inflicted on any person, whatever the motive) (own translation).

39 Art 119 of the Armenia Criminal Code, 2003. See, e.g., art 119(6) which refers to torture inflicted "with particular cruelty."

40 Art 12 of the Sri Lanka Convention against Torture and other Cruel, Inhuman or Degrading Treatment or Punishment Act, 1994 defines torture as 'any act which causes severe pain, whether physical or mental, to any other person, being an act which is done for any of the following purposes: (i) obtaining from such other person or a third person, any information or confession; or (ii) punishing such other person for any act which he or a third person has committee, or is suspected of having committed; or (iii) intimidating or coercing such other person or a third person; or (b) done for any reason based on discrimination, and being in every case, an act which is done by, or at the initiation of, or with the consent or acquiescence of, a public officer or other person acting in an official capacity'.

mental, is intentionally inflicted.[41] As a precondition to ratifying the CAT, the United States (US) submitted formal understandings including a more precise definition of mental torture, and argued that only extreme forms of pain or suffering amounted to torture.[42]

In Mexico, the definition of torture refers to severe pain and suffering, whether physical or mental.[43] In the UK, torture is prohibited in the Criminal Justice Act which refers to severe pain and suffering.[44] In France, the Ministry of Justice circular of 14 May 1993 on the Criminal Code that entered into force on 1 March 1994 supports the definition in article 1 of the CAT as well as the requirement of severity.[45] Croatia requires physical or mental pain or severe

41 Sec 3(a) of the Phillipines Anti-Torture Act, 2009 prohibits '[o]ther forms of cruel, inhuman and degrading treatment or punishment' and this is defined as 'a deliberate and aggravated treatment or punishment not set out under acts of torture, inflicted by a person in authority or his or her agent against a person under his/her custody 'which attains a level of severity causing suffering, gross humiliation or debasement to the latter'. Sec 3(b) further prohibits '[o]ther forms of cruel, inhuman and degrading treatment or punishment is defined as a deliberate and aggravated treatment or punishment not set out under acts of torture, inflicted by a person in authority or his or her agent against a person under his/her custody which attains a level of severity causing suffering, gross humiliation or debasement to the latter'.

42 See 18 US Code sec 2340 (2004). See further Convention against Torture and Other Cruel, Inhuman or Degrading Treatment or Punishment, Reservations, Understandings and Declarations Made by the United States of America <https://www.unhchr.state.gov/documents/organization/100296.pdf> accessed 12 August 2017. The US ratified the CAT with reservations. It stated that mental pain or suffering refers to prolonged mental harm caused by or resulting from (1) the intentional infliction or threatened infliction of severe physical pain or suffering; (2) the administration or application, or threatened administration or application, of mind altering substances or other procedures calculated to disrupt profoundly the senses or the personality; (3) the threat of imminent death; or (4) the threat that another person will imminently be subjected to death, severe physical pain or suffering, or the administration or application of mind altering substances or other procedures calculated to disrupt profoundly the senses or personality'.

43 See Mexico's Federal Act on the Prevention and Punishment of Torture, 1991.

44 See art 134 of the UK Criminal Justice Act, 1988.

45 See Committee Against Torture Consideration of Reports Submitted by States Parties Under Article 19 of the Convention, Third Periodic Reports of States Parties due in 1996, CAT/C/34/add.19, report by France (10 January 2005) para 9, referring to the wording of the circular that '[g]enerally speaking, there may be qualified as torture within the meaning of article 1 of the Convention against Torture and Other Cruel, Inhuman or Degrading Treatment or Punishment, adopted at New York on 10 December 1984, any act whereby severe pain or suffering, whether physical or mental, is intentionally inflicted on a person'. See further France's Law of Armed Conflict Manual, 2001, 122. This manual refers to the 1984 Convention against Torture and defines torture as any act by which severe pain or suffering, whether physical or mental, is intentionally inflicted on a person for such purposes as obtaining from him or a third person information or a confession, punishing

physical or mental suffering to constitute torture.[46] Egyptian law imposes no requirements with regard to the degree or extent of pain or suffering.[47] The Greek Penal Code refers to 'acute' instead of 'severe', and torture is broadly defined to include any systematic infliction of acute physical pain or physical exhaustion endangering the health of a person, mental suffering and any illegal use of chemicals, drugs or other natural or artificial means aimed at bending the victim's will.[48] Under the Iraqi Penal Code, torture includes the use of force or menaces, but is not defined in terms of pain and suffering.[49]

The Turkish Penal Code contains a comprehensive reference to torture. It devotes part 3 of its legislation to 'Torture and torment'.[50] While it does not

---

him for an act he or a third person has committed or is suspected of having committed, or intimidating or coercing him or a third person, or for any reason based on discrimination of any kind.

46 Art 176 of the Criminal Code of Croatia 111 of 15 July 2003 states that '[a]n official or another person who, acting upon the instigation or with the explicit or implicit consent of a public official, inflicts on a person physical or mental pain or severe physical or mental suffering for such purposes as to obtain from him or a third person information or a confession, or punishes him for a criminal offence he or a third person has committed or is suspected of having committed or who intimidates or coerces him for any other reason based on discrimination of any kind shall be punished by imprisonment for one to eight years'. See further Consideration of Reports Submitted by State Parties Under Article 19 of the Convention, Croatia, UN Doc CAT/C/54/Add3 12, <docstore.ohcr.org.SelfServices/FilesHandler.ashx.enc.> accessed 1 May 2017.

47 Consideration of Reports Submitted by State Parties Under Article 19 of the Convention, Egypt, UN Doc CAT/C/34/Add.11 49, <docstore.ohcr.org.SelfServices/FilesHandler.ashx.enc.> accessed 1 May 2017. Egypt states that '[t]he provisions of Egyptian law are broader and more general than those of the Convention, since article 1 of the latter defines torture as any act by which severe pain or suffering is inflicted, whereas Egyptian law imposes no prerequisites concerning the degree or extent of pain or suffering'.

48 Consideration of Reports Submitted by State Parties Under Article 19 of the Convention, Greece (n 36).

49 Iraq Penal Code, 1969.

50 Art 94(1) of the Turkish Penal Code, 2004 provides that '[a] public officer who performs any act towards a person that is incompatible with human dignity, and which causes that person to suffer physically or mentally, or affects the person's capacity to perceive or his ability to act of his own will or insults them shall be sentenced to a penalty of imprisonment for a term of three to twelve years. (2) If the offence is committed against (a) a child, a person who is physically or mentally incapable of defending himself or a pregnant woman; or (b) a public officer or an advocate on account of the performance of his duty, a penalty of imprisonment for a term of eight to fifteen years shall be imposed. (3) If the act is conducted in the manner of sexual harassment, the offender shall be sentenced to a penalty of imprisonment for a term of ten to fifteen years. (4) Any other person who participates in the commission of this offence shall be sentenced in a manner equivalent to the public officer.' Further, art 95(1) states that '[w]here the act of torture causes (of the victim) (a) a permanent impairment of the functioning of any one of the senses or an

require the severity of an act to constitute torture, it provides for a range of acts ranging from torture to torment, implying separation by degree.[51] It criminalizes any act incompatible with human dignity which causes a person to suffer physically or mentally or affects the person's ability to act of his own will.[52] The element of severity appears from a section that specifically provides for aggravated torture on account of its consequences, namely, where the torture causes permanent physical or mental impairment, death or the loss of a child where the victim is a pregnant woman.[53] It further prohibits 'torment' with harsher penalties should such torment be inflicted on a child, a person who is physically or mentally incapable of defending himself, a pregnant woman or the family of the perpetrator. 'Torment', however, is not defined.[54]

Kazakhstan's Penal Code does not contain the severity requirement although it refers to torture as the infliction of physical and mental suffering by means of systematic harassment or other violent actions.[55] The Russian Criminal Code does not require the pain or suffering to be severe.[56] That said, its Criminal Code further refers to the infliction of physical or mental suffering by means of systematic beating or by any other violent actions in the section

organ; (b) a permanent speech defect; (c) a distinct and permanent scar on the face; (d) a situation which endangers a person's life; or (e) the premature birth of a child, where the victim is a pregnant woman, the penalty determined in accordance with the above article shall be increased by one half. (2) Where the act of torture causes (of the victim) (a) an incurable illness or if it has caused the victim to enter a vegetative state, (b) the complete loss of functioning of one of the senses or organs; (c) the loss of the ability to speak or loss of fertility; (d) a permanent disfigurement of the face; or (e) the loss of an unborn child, where the victim is a pregnant woman, the penalty determined in accordance with the article above shall be doubled. (3) Where an act of torture results in the breaking of a bone, the offender shall be sentenced to a penalty of imprisonment for a term one to six years according to the effect of the broken bone on his ability to function in life. (4) Where an act of torture causes the death of the victim, the penalty to be imposed shall be aggravated life imprisonment.' Art 96(1) provides that '[a]ny person who performs any act which results in the torment of another person shall be sentenced to a penalty of imprisonment for a term of two to five years. (2) Where the acts falling under the above paragraph are committed against inter alia a child who cannot protect himself due to corporal or spiritual disability or a pregnant woman, a penalty of imprisonment for a term of three to eight years shall be imposed.'

51 Ibid.

52 Ibid., art 94(1).

53 Ibid.

54 Ibid.

55 Art 347–1 of the Kazakstan Criminal Code, Law No 167 of 16 July 1997 refers to torture as the '[d]eliberate causation of physical or psychic suffering'.

56 Art 117(1) of the Criminal Code of the Russian Federation (n 31).

dealing with torture, which does seem to refer to a degree of severity.[57] The German Constitution provides that a detained person 'may not be subjected to mental or physical ill-treatment'.[58] Accordingly, the national legislation of various states is inconsistent with regard to the severity element, but consistent in relation to the inclusion of a form of pain and suffering in the definition of torture.[59]

In national case law, in the 1995 case of *Xuncax v Gramajo*, a US federal district court deemed a combination of blindfolding, repeated acts of rape, burning with cigarettes, beating, and lowering into a foul-smelling pit during interrogation by the Guatemalan military to constitute torture.[60] This is consistent with the US view discussed above that severity is a requirement for torture. As regards matters before the African Commission on Human and Peoples' Rights (African Commission), the Commission found in the *Abdel Hadi Radi* case that the treatment of persons with the aim of extracting confessions from the victims and as punishment for the killing of policemen which ranged from 'severe beating with whips and sticks, doing the *Arannabb Nut* (rabbit jump); heavy beating with water hoses on all parts of their bodies; death threats; forcing them to kneel with their feet facing backwards in order to be beaten on their feet and asked to jump up immediately after; as well as other forms of ill-treatment' which resulted in serious physical injuries and psychological trauma, amounted to torture.[61]

The case law of regional treaty bodies placed less emphasis on the requirement of severity and seemed to illustrate a move towards the prohibition of torture in the absence of physical violence (including the threat of violence and mental torture). In this regard, the practice of the Human Rights Committee (HRC) in deciding torture cases under the Optional Protocol to the ICCPR illustrates that the HRC did not clearly distinguish between torture and cruel, inhuman and degrading treatment or punishment or clarify when a torturous act would be regarded as severe.[62] In the *Estrella* case, for example, the complainant, a pianist, was subjected to severe physical and psychological torture,

57 Ibid.
58 Sec 104(1) of the Basic Law for the Federal Republic of Germany, 1949.
59 For example, South Africa, Kenya, Uganda, Cameroon, the DRC, Canada, Latvia, Greece, Luxemburg, Bahrain, Sri Lanka, Philippines, Algeria, Mexico, the US and the UK require a degree of severity for an act to constitute torture. No severity is required in the definitions of torture in Egypt, Spain, Turkey, Kazakhstan, Bangladesh, Iraq, Brazil, Russia and Croatia.
60 *Xuncax v Gramajo* 886 FSupp (D Mass 1995) 162, 174, 178.
61 *African Commission, Abdel Hadi, Ali Radi & Others v Republic of Sudan*, Communication 368/09 (5 November 2013) para 71.
62 See art 7 of the ICCPR (n 9).

including a threat that his hands would be cut off by an electric saw in an effort to force him to admit subversive activities.[63] The HRC found a contravention of the prohibition of torture and cruel, inhuman and degrading treatment or punishment under the ICCPR, as well as a contravention of the complainant's right to human dignity as the complainant was detained under inhuman prison conditions during the first days of his detention.[64] In the *Cabreira* case, on the other hand, despite detailed allegations of torture (including beatings, near-drownings and a lack of food), the HRC found only a contravention of the complainant's right to human dignity.[65] In the *Bequio* case the HRC found a violation of the prohibition of torture and cruel, inhuman and degrading treatment or punishment in the ICCPR, as well as a contravention of the complainant's right to human dignity, not on the basis of torture but on the basis that the complainant had 'not been treated in prison with humanity and with respect for the inherent dignity of the human person'.[66]

Later decisions took into account the personal circumstances of the relevant victim. For example, it would appear that in cases where there was evidence of severe torture or the victim was elderly and suffered from a medical condition, the HRC was more likely to refer to 'torture' in its decisions. In the *Peñarrieta* case the victim was in poor health and had a skull fracture which for some time had not received medical attention. He was also subjected to severe torture, including physical beatings, electric shocks and immersion in water, and the torture was proven by medical certificates.[67] The HRC stated in its decision that the victim had been subjected to 'torture and inhuman treatment'.[68]

Furthermore, the decisions of the CAT Committee, established to monitor the application of the CAT, similarly have not dealt with the difference between torture and other forms of cruel, inhuman or degrading conduct or treatment,

---

63 *Miguel Angel Estrella v Uruguay* Communication 74/1980 UNHR Committee (17 July 1980) UN Doc Supp No 40 (A/38/40) 150 (1983) para 1.6.

64 Ibid., para 10.

65 *Cabreira v Uruguay* Communication 105/1981 UNHR Committee (7 August 1981) UN Doc CCPR/C/OP/2 (1990) para 11. The HRC only dealt with the torture allegations after the date on which the Covenant and the Optional Protocol entered into force for Uruguay.

66 *Bequio v Uruguay* Communication 88/1981 UNHR Committee (14 March 1981) UN Doc CCPR/C/OP/2 (1990) para 12.

67 *Lafuente Peñarrieta & Others v Bolivia* Communication 176/1984 UNHR Committee (2 November 1987) UN Doc CCPR/C/OP/2 201 (1990) paras 1.3, 10.4.

68 Ibid., para 16. See further *Acosta v Uruguay* Communication 110/1981 UNHR Committee (12 August 1981) UN Doc Supp No 40 (A/39/40) 1984 para 14. In the *Acosta* matter, allegations were similarly of severe torture but, to a large extent, were unsubstantiated, and the HRC found that the complainant had been subjected to inhuman treatment but did not refer to torture in its finding.

and the definitional threshold between the two forms of conduct remains as unclear as it was when the CAT was adopted.[69] However, the Committee has indicated support for a broad interpretation of what constitutes torture. In this regard it noted that, as mental torture is included in the definition of torture in the CAT, the threat of torture or mock executions themselves may amount to psychological torture.[70] With regard to pscychological torture, instances where captured Taliban and al Qaeda operatives were allegedly subjected to physical and psychological 'stress and duress' techniques, including being deprived of sleep for long periods, held blindfolded or hooded or bound in awkward painful positions, arguably would constitute such torture.[71]

Early case law of the European Commission (EC) in deciding contraventions under the ECHR points to a tendency to distinguish torture from cruel, inhuman and degrading treatment or punishment by the degree of suffering involved. For example, in the *Greek* case in 1969 the EC considered the concept of torture and its relationship to the concept of inhuman treatment and degrading treatment.[72] Subsequent to a military *coup* in Greece in 1967 and the imposition of martial law, Denmark, Norway and Sweden brought an inter-state case against Greece with regard to allegations of torture of political opponents to the Greek regime.[73] In its report the EC described torture as 'an aggravated form of inhuman treatment'.[74] The EC, therefore, distinguished between torture and inhuman treatment on the basis of aggravation.

69 See UN Committee Against Torture General Comment No 2: Implementation of Article 2 by States Parties, 24 January 2008 CAT/C/GC/2 para 3 which states that '[t]he obligations to prevent torture and other cruel, inhuman or degrading treatment or punishment (hereinafter "ill-treatment") … are indivisible, interdependent and interrelated. The obligation to prevent ill-treatment in practice overlaps with and is largely congruent with the obligation to prevent torture.'

70 Committee against Torture Report on Argentina UN Doc A/45/44 1990 para 154.

71 'US Decries Abuse but Defends Interrogations' *Washington Post* (26 December 2000) <https://www.washingtonpost.com/> accessed 3 October 2017.

72 *The Greek Case* Report of the Commission: Application No 3321/67, *Denmark v Greece*, Application No 3322/67; *Norway v Greece*, Application No 3323/67; *Sweden v Greece*, Application No 3344/67; *Netherlands v Greece* (1970) EC 1 1; H Danelius, 'Torture and Cruel, Inhuman or Degrading Treatment or Punishment' (1989) 58 Nordic Journal of International Law 180.

73 James Beckett, 'The Greek Case before the European Rights Commission' (1970) 1 Human Rights 98.

74 Ibid., para 186. The Court stated that 'the word "torture" is often used to describe inhuman treatment, which has a purpose, such as the obtaining of information or confessions, or the infliction of punishment, and it is generally an aggravated form of inhuman treatment. Treatment or punishment of an individual may further be said to be degrading if it grossly humiliates a person before others or drives him to act against his will or conscience.'

Furthermore, in dealing with the deplorable conditions in Greek detention facilities where political prisoners were kept, the EC held that degrading treatment or punishment constituted a category by itself involving severe humiliation or coercion of a person to act against his or her own will or conscience.[75]

In other instances, the EC and the European Court of Human Rights (ECtHR) have characterized the same conduct as constituting either torture or cruel, inhuman and degrading treatment or punishment. In the case of *Ireland v United Kingdom*, suspected terrorists were subjected to wall-standing, hooding, subjection to noise, deprivation of sleep and deprivation of food and drink. The EC was of the view that the combined use of these five techniques of interrogation constituted torture.[76] The ECtHR, on the other hand, determined that while the use of these techniques constituted inhuman and degrading treatment, the techniques 'did not occasion suffering of the particular intensity and cruelty implied by the word torture as so understood'.[77] The ECtHR, thus, seemed to follow the same line of thinking as the EC in the *Greek* case, distinguishing between torture and inhuman and degrading treatment on the basis of the degree of suffering involved.[78]

Selmouni v France marked a departure from the previous thinking of the ECtHR discussed above. The complainant, arrested for drug trafficking, alleged that he had been subjected to ill-treatment while in police custody, which included assault, indecent assault and threats of violence.[79] In order to determine whether a particular form of ill-treatment should be qualified as torture,

---

75 Ibid.

76 *Ireland v the United Kingdom* EC 512 Yearbook of European Convention on Human Rights 489–491 (1976).

77 *Ireland v the United Kingdom* Application No 5310/71 ECHR (1978) 602 Yearbook of European Convention on Human Rights (Judgment) para 57: 'Although the five techniques, as applied in combination, undoubtedly amounted to inhuman and degrading treatment, although their object was the extraction of confessions, the naming of others and/or information and, although they were used systematically, they did not occasion suffering of the particular intensity and cruelty implied by the word torture as so understood.' According to the Court, the notion of torture was characterised by "a special stigma" attaching to "deliberate inhuman treatment causing very serious and cruel suffering".'

78 *Ireland* case (ibid.) 84. In the Separate Opinion of Judge Zekia (dissenting), he did not share the view that extreme intensity of physical or mental suffering is a requisite for a case of ill-treatment to amount to 'torture' as contemplated in art 3 of the ECHR and that all the relevant circumstances should be considered. He advocated a more subjective definition taking into account 'the nature of ill-treatment inflicted, the means and methods employed, the repetition and duration of such treatment, the age, sex and health condition of the person exposed to it, the likelihood that such treatment might injure the physical, mental and psychological condition of the person exposed'.

79 *Selmouni v France* Application No 25803(94) ECHR (1 December 1977) paras 20, 24.

the court was of the view that it must have regard to the distinction between torture and inhuman or degrading treatment as set out in article 3 of the ECHR. It noted that it remained to be established whether the pain or suffering inflicted on Mr Selmouni could be defined as 'severe' within the meaning of article 1 of the CAT. The Court, however, was of the view that this 'severity' was relative, and it depended on all the circumstances of the case, including the duration of the treatment, its physical or mental effects, and the sex, age and state of health of the victim.[80] The Court stated that the CAT was a 'living instrument which must be interpreted in the light of present-day conditions'.[81] Accordingly, certain acts, which had in the past been classified as inhuman and degrading treatment and not torture, could be classified differently in future.[82] It noted that the increasingly high standard being required in the area of the protection of human rights and fundamental liberties 'inevitably requires greater firmness in assessing breaches of the fundamental values of democratic societies'.[83] It has been argued that the Court was indicating that it regarded as torture the mixed physical and psychological pressures involved in the five interrogation techniques to which terrorist suspects were subjected in the *Northern Ireland* case.[84] Furthermore, in response to Israel's country report in 1997, the Concluding Observation of the CAT Committee stated that the following methods of interrogation constituted torture: restraining in very painful conditions; hooding; sounding of loud music or sleep deprivation for prolonged periods; threats, including death threats; violent shaking; and 'using cold air to chill'.[85] In *Aksoy v Turkey* the applicant complained that he had been tortured during his detention in 1992 on suspicion of aiding and abetting the Workers' Party of Kurdistan, listed by Turkey as a terrorist organization. This involved the applicant being stripped naked, with arms tied together behind his back, and being suspended by his arms. The ECtHR found a violation of the

80 Ibid., para 100.

81 Ibid., para 101. With respect to the view that the CAT is a living instrument, the ECtHR referred to *Tyrer v the United Kingdom* (25 April 1978) Series A No 26, 15 para 31; *Soering v United Kingdom Application* 14038/88 ECHR (7 July 1989), 40 para 91 sec 102; and *Loizidou v Turkey* (23 March 1995) Series A No 310, 26 sec 71.

82 *Selmouni v France* (n 79) para 101.

83 Ibid.

84 *A & Others v Secretary of State for the Home Department* (No 2) (2005) (HL) 1 WLR 53 where Lord Bingham of Cornwall indicated that the techniques used in *Ireland v UK* might now be held to constitute torture under art 3 of the ECHR.

85 Committee against Torture, Consideration of Reports Submitted by States Parties under Article 19 of the Convention: Conclusions and Recommendations of the Committee Against Torture, 257 UN Doc A/52/44 (5 September 1997).

prohibition of torture.[86] The Inter-American Commission of Human Rights (IACHR) has similarly supported a broad interpretation of the prohibition of torture and the right to humane treatment during anti-terrorist initiatives.[87] This included a consideration of detention conditions of suspected terrorists and the treatment of persons in situations of particular vulnerability, including women, children and non-nationals, especially when considering conduct during interrogations of such persons by state agents.[88] In various cases before the IACHR, it made no reference to severity or aggravation being a requirement to constitute torture.[89]

From the evaluation above, it appears that the severity requirement may no longer be regarded by regional commissions and courts as an integral requirement for conduct complained of to constitute torture. Furthermore, the practice of the EC and the ECtHR illustrates that the distinction between torture and cruel, inhuman or degrading treatment or punishment is disappearing, as conduct which used to constitute inhuman treatment may now constitute torture. The requirements of intent and purpose as set out in the CAT will be discussed below.

2.1.2 Intent and Purpose

Under the CAT, torture is defined as any act by which severe pain or suffering is intentionally inflicted on a person for certain purposes, namely, for obtaining information or a confession, for punishment, intimidation or coercion or for any reason based on discrimination of any kind.[90] It has been argued that torture is most likely to occur in the quest for information in the context of

86 *Aksoy v Turkey* Application No 21987/93 (18 December 1996) para 14, sec III.

87 Report of the Inter-American Commission on Human Rights, Right to Humane Treatment OEA/Ser.L/V/11/116 para 164 <http://cidh.oas.org/Terrorism/Eng/exe.htm> accessed 3 October 2017.

88 *Loayza-Tamayo v Peru* IACtHR (17 September 1997) Series C No 33, para 57.

89 See, eg, *Martin de Mejía v Peru* Inter-American Commission on Human Rights IAm Comm of HR (1 March 1996) case 10.970, Report 5/96. Mejía was a victim of torture where her rape involved physical and mental pain, was committed for the purpose of punishing and intimidating her and was perpetrated by a public official (a member of the security forces). The IACHR, however, made no reference to severity nor to aggravation as being requirements for constituting torture. See further *Morales v Guatemala* Inter-American Commission of Human Rights, (8 March 1998) Ser C No 37 134. The IACtHR held that torture included the use of methods upon a person intended to obliterate the personality of the victim or to diminish his or her physical or mental capabilities, even if the methods do not cause physical pain or torture (tying, beating, etc).

90 See art 1 of the CAT (n 22).

security.[91] This is especially relevant in the event of interrogation of suspected terrorists. Torturous acts inflicted for private purposes which do not include the aforementioned listed purposes, therefore, do not constitute torture in terms of the CAT.

Furthermore, it is argued that the intentional infliction of pain and suffering should not be separated from the prohibited purpose requirement. The requirement of specific intent is thus met where there has been an intentional infliction of pain or suffering for a prohibited purpose.[92] With the exception of the Rome Statute, all international instruments defining torture, such as the Declaration against Torture, the Inter-American Torture Convention and the International Criminal Court Elements of Crimes Concerning the War Crime of Torture under the ICC Statute in Respect of International and Non-International Armed Conflict, contain a purposive element.[93] The absence of the purposive element (as well as the absence of a reference to the public status of the perpetrator) in the definition of torture in the Rome Statute may reflect the fact that the Rome Statute is restricted to individual criminal responsibility, while the other instruments attempt to codify international human rights law which, in principle, involves the establishment of state responsibility.[94]

91 Aditi Bagchi, 'Intention, Torture, and the Concept of State Crime' (2009) 114(1) Pennsylvania State Law Review 41.

92 Oona Hathaway, Aileen Nolan and Julia Spiegel, 'Tortured Reasoning: The Intention to Torture under International Law' (2012) 52 Virginia Jorunal of International Law 802, 836. See further Hermann Burgers and Hans Danelius, *The United Nations Convention Against Torture: A Handbook on The Convention Against Torture And Other Cruel, Inhuman or Degrading Treatment Or Punishment* (Martinus Nijhoff 2008) 41. Burgers and Danelius, the Swedish representatives who presented the first draft of the CAT to the UN, are of the view that 'where pain or suffering is the result of an accident or mere negligence, the criteria for regarding the act as torture are not fulfilled'. See further Special Rapporteur on Torture and Other Cruel, Inhuman or Degrading Treatment or Punishment, Report on Torture and Other Cruel, Inhuman or Degrading Treatment or Punishment, Manfred Nowak, Human Rights Council, UN Doc A/HRC/13/39/Add5 (5 February 2010) 188, who argued that by way of contrast, cruel, inhuman or degrading treatment or punishment has been argued to be a general intent crime. This is so because, where torture requires the deliberate infliction of severe pain or suffering for a specific purpose, such as extracting a confession or information from the victim, cruel, inhuman or degrading treatment or punishment entails the infliction of pain or suffering without a specific purpose or intent.

93 Nigel Rodley, 'The Definition(s) of Torture in International Law' (2002) 55 Current Legal Problems 467–8. See art 1 of the Declaration on the Protection of All Persons from Being Subjected to Torture or Other Cruel, Inhuman or Degrading Treatment or Punishment, 1975; art 2 of the IACPPT (n 18); art 8(2)(a)(ii).1 and art 8(2)(c)(i).4 of the ICC Elements of Crimes Official Records of the Assembly of States Parties to the Rome Statute of the International Criminal Court, First session, New York, 3–10 September 2002, part II.B.

94 Rodley (n 93) 487. See art 7(2)(e) of the Rome Statute of the ICC, 1998.

In domestic legislation, individual states have differed in implementing the intent and purpose requirements. The definitions of some states mirror the definition in the CAT. The intentional infliction of pain and suffering for the purpose of obtaining information or a confession, for punishment, intimidation, coercion, or for any reason based on discrimination of any kind is referred to in the national legislation of South Africa, Uganda and Kenya.[95] South Africa's definition mirrors that of the CAT in respect of the intent requirement. The required intent relates to the pain and suffering inflicted (which cannot be inflicted negligently/accidently) and not tothe purpose of the act of torture.[96] The Turkish Penal Code does not require intent and refers to torture as any act incompatible with human dignity, which causes a person to suffer physically or mentally or affects the person's capacity to perceive or his ability to act of

95 See art 3 of the Prevention of Combating and Torture of Persons Act (n 32) which defines torture as 'any act or omission, by which severe pain or suffering, whether physical or mental, is intentionally inflicted on a person (a) for such purposes as to (i) obtain information or a confession from him or her or any other person; (ii) punish him or her for an act he or she has committed, is suspected of having committed or of planning to commit; or (iii) intimidate him or her or any other person to do, or to refrain from doing, anything; or (iv) for any reason based on discrimination of any kind, when such pain or suffering is reflected by or at the instigation of, or with the consent or acquiescence of a public official or other person acting in an official capacity, but does not include pain or suffering arising only from, inherent in or incidental to lawful sanctions'. Art 132(5) of the Cameroon Penal Code, 1967 (as amended by Act 97/009) defines torture to mean '[a]ny act by which severe pain or suffering, whether physical or mental, is intentionally inflicted by or at the investigation of a public official or with his express or tacit consent on a person for such purposes as obtaining from him or a third person information or confession, punishing him for an act he or a third person has committed or is suspected of having committed, or intimidating or putting pressure on him or a third person, or for any other motive based on any form of discrimination whatsoever. Torture shall not include pain or suffering arising only from, inherent in or incidental to lawful sanctions.' See further art 2 of the Kenya National Intelligence Service Act 28 of 2012 ('"torture" means any act by which severe pain or suffering, whether physical or mental, is intentionally inflicted on a person for such purposes of (i) obtaining information or a confession from the person or from a third person; (ii) punishing the person for an act which that person or a third person has committed or is suspected of having committed; (iii) intimidating or coercing the person or a third person; or (iv) for any reason based on discrimination of any kind'). Art 2 further defines cruel, inhuman and degrading treatment or punishment as a deliberate and aggravated treatment not amounting to torture. In South Africa, the Prevention of Combating and Torture of Persons Act, 2013 (n 32) similarly defines torture as an intentional act inflicting severe pain and suffering on a person for the purposes of obtaining information or a confession, intimidation, coercion or for any reason based on discrimination of any kind.

96 Act 3 of the South African Prevention of Combating and Torture of Persons Act 2013 (n 32).

his own will.[97] Latvia defines torture as multiple or prolonged acts, causing particular pain or suffering, which are 'committed by the guilty person, being fully aware of it'.[98] The nature of this 'awareness' is not clear but seems to indicate something similar to (although admittedly not the same as) intent.[99] The Constitution of the Islamic Republic of Pakistan of 1973 prohibits torture for the purpose of extracting evidence.[100]

Under the definitions of certain states, the purposes of the perpetrator of torture are not mentioned at all.[101] This has the effect of broadening the definition of torture. For example, in the US the federal anti-torture statute does not include the list of purposes necessary for the action to be considered torture.[102] It defines torture as an act committed by a person acting 'under the colour of law' specifically intended to inflict severe physical or mental pain or suffering (other than pain or suffering incidental to lawful sanctions) upon another person within his/her custody or physical control.[103] It therefore requires specific intent but makes no reference to purpose.[104] The US, as a precondition to ratifying the CAT, also submitted formal understandings which limited its understanding of torture to acts performed with a specific intent to cause pain and suffering.[105] This is similar to the situation in Uganda, where 'torture' means

97 Art 94(1) of the Turkish Penal Code (n 50).

98 Consideration of Reports Submitted by State Parties under Article 19 of the Convention, Latvia, (n 36).

99 Gail Miller, 'Defining Torture' *Floersheimer Center Occasional Papers* (2006) 13–14 <https://cardozo.yu.edu/sites/default/files/Defining%20Torture.pdf> accessed 23 October 2017.

100 Constitution of the Islamic Republic of Pakistan (n 31).

101 See 18 US Code 2340(1) (2004) ('torture means an act committed by a person acting under the color of law specifically intended to inflict severe physical or mental pain or suffering (other than pain or suffering incidental to lawful sanctions) upon another person within his custody or physical control').

102 Title 18, Part I, Ch 113C of the US Code (n 101). The law consists of three sections (2340, 2340A and 2340B).

103 Ibid.

104 See Miller (n 99) 14, who argues that the US Department of Justice says that the specific intent standard would be met if an act was performed with the conscious desire to inflict severe physical or mental pain or suffering. On the other hand, the standard would likely not be met if an individual acted in good faith and performed a reasonable investigation establishing that his conduct would not inflict severe physical or mental pain or suffering.

105 The US ratified the CAT with reservations, understandings and declarations (see n 42). The US stated that mental pain or suffering refers to 'prolonged mental harm caused by or resulting from (1) the intentional infliction or threatened infliction of severe physical pain or suffering; (2) the administration or application, or threatened administration or application, of mind altering substances or other procedures calculated to disrupt profoundly the senses or the personality; (3) the threat of imminent death; or (4) the threat

'an act committed by a person specifically intended to inflict severe physical or mental pain or suffering', but there is no reference to the purpose of the act.[106] In Algeria, torture is understood to mean any act by which severe pain or suffering, whether physical or mental, is intentionally inflicted on any person whatever the motive.[107] The focus is the intentional infliction of pain and suffering.

Certain states include in the definition of torture the condition that the victim must be a detainee. This has the effect of limiting the definition of torture. For example, in Mexico the Federal Act does not refer to torture committed for any reason based on discrimination of any kind but requires that, when an individual commits the crime, the person tortured must be a detainee.[108] In Bahrain, the Penal Code refers to the torture of a detained person by or under the control of a public employee or public servant in order to obtain information, extract a confession or punish, intimidate or coerce that person or another person.[109] In Sri Lanka there is no intent requirement, but the purposes of the torture are aligned with those in the CAT, although severity applies only to pain and not suffering.[110] The definition of torture in the Armenian Criminal

---

that another person will imminently be subjected to death, severe physical pain or suffering, or the administration or application of mind altering substances or other procedures calculated to disrupt profoundly the senses or personality'.

106 Art 2 of the Uganda Prevention and Prohibition of Torture Act (n 31) ('[t] orture' means an act committed by a person acting under colour of law specifically intended to inflict severe physical or mental pain or suffering [other than pain or suffering incidental to lawful sanctions] upon another person within his/her custody or physical control').

107 Art 263*bis* of the Penal Code of Algeria (n 38).

108 Report of the Special Rapporteur on Torture and Other Cruel, Inhuman or Degrading Treatment or Punishment, Juan Méndez, on his mission to Mexico (21 April to 2 May 2014) A/HRC/28/68/Add para 13–14.

109 See Consideration of Reports Submitted by States Parties under Article 19 of the Convention Pursuant to the Optional Reporting Procedure, Bahrain (16 June 2016) para 93 CAT/C/BHR/3 <http://www.refworld.org/publisher/CAT.html> accessed 23 October 2017. The government of the Kingdom promulgated Act No 52 (2012) on 9 October 2012, amending the definition of torture in art 208 of the Penal Code. Art 208 of the Bahrain Penal Code, 1976 (as amended) criminalizes the infliction of severe pain or suffering, whether physical or mental, on a detained person by or under the control of a public employee or public servant in order to obtain information, extract a confession or punish, intimidate or coerce that person or another person.

110 The Sri Lanka Convention Against Torture and Other Cruel, Inhuman or Degrading Treatment or Punishment, 1994 provides that '[t]orture means any act which causes severe pain, whether physical or mental, to any other person, being an act which is (a) done for any of the following purposes, that is to say (i) obtaining from such other person or a third person, any information or confession; or (ii) punishing such other person for any act which he or a third person has committed, or is suspected of having committed;

Code fails to recognize the purpose element and the state official element.[111] In Indonesia the definition excludes torture for purposes of punishment.[112]

Moreover, national legislation differs with regard to including torture for discriminatory reasons as is required under the CAT. Spain's definition states that the act of torture must be for the purpose of obtaining a confession, information or for punishment.[113] It excludes torture for discriminatory reasons. The definitions of torture in Peru, Guatemala and Honduras similarly do not include discrimination of any kind as one of the elements of the crime of torture.[114] Tunisia's definition of torture limits the discrimination in question to racial discrimination.[115] In Brazil, the purpose of the torturous act includes torture as a way of enforcing personal punishment or a preventive measure, and the types of discrimination are specified as racial or religious, which has a limiting effect.[116] Uganda's definition of torture largely follows the CAT definition

---

or (iii) intimidating or coercing such other person or a third person; or (b) done for any reason based on discrimination, and being, in every case, an act which is done by, or at the initiation of, or with the consent or acquiescence of, a public officer or other person acting in an official capacity'.

111 Art 119 of the Armenia Criminal Code, 2003.

112 Consideration of Reports Submitted by State Parties under Article 19 of the Convention, Indonesia, UN Doc CAT/C/47/Add.3 66, <docstore.ohcr.org.SelfServices/FilesHandler.ashx.enc.> accessed 10 August 2017.

113 Consideration of Reports Submitted by State Parties under Article 19 of the Convention, Spain, UN Doc CAT/C/55/Add.5 16, <docstore.ohcr.org.SelfServices/FilesHandler.ashx.enc.> accessed 10 August 2017, citing art 174 of the Spanish Penal Code.

114 Art 321 of the Penal Code of Peru Legislative Decree No 635 (8 April 1991) <www.refworld.org/docid/3e5365d84.html> accessed 6 May 2017; art 209-A of the Penal Code of Honduras; art 201*bis* of the Penal Code of Guatemala, 1973.

115 Art 101*bis* of the Tunisian Criminal Code, 1968, as amended by Law No 89 of 2 August 1999 and Decree 2011-106 of 22 October 2011. The amended Code provides that any public 'official or similar person who orders, encourages, endorses or keeps silent about torture' could be considered a perpetrator. See also Report of the Special Rapporteur on Torture and Other Cruel, Inhuman or Degrading Treatment or Punishment, Mr Juan E Méndez, Addendum: Follow up report: Missions to the Republic of Tajikistan and Tunisia, A/HRC/28/68/Add2 (27 February 2015) para 64, noting that Tunisia's reference to racial discrimination rather than to 'discrimination of any kind' as a reason for torture is overly narrow and, thus, excludes an array of other possible forms of discrimination.

116 Art 1 of Brazil's Law No 9.455 1997 states as the purpose of torture 'to obtain information, a statement or confession from the victim or a third person; to induce action or inaction of a criminal nature, on grounds of racial or religious discrimination; or to submit someone, under one's custody, power or authority, with the use of violence or serious threat, to intense physical or mental suffering, as a way to enforce personal punishment or a preventive measure'.

but includes the fact that torture can be by way of an omission, and excludes a reference to discrimination of any kind as the purpose of torture.[117]

The 1936 case of *Brown v Mississippi* was significant as it illustrated the danger of false confessions obtained as a result of torture. In this case, the police physically tortured suspects until they confessed to a murder they had not committed.[118] In various later cases, the US Federal courts excluded statements as a result of coercion and torture.[119] The US Third Circuit Court of Appeals in *Zubeda v Ashcroft* decided that the purpose of torture as intimidation or coercion had been met where the appellant was gang-raped by soldiers in the Democratic Republic of the Congo (DRC), who tied up her father and brother and forced them to watch the rape, after which the soldiers decapitated her father and brother with machetes and set fire to the family home while Zubeda's mother and sister were still inside.[120] It found that 'the conduct described in the DRC was for the purpose of coercing and intimidating Zubeda and/or members of her family' given the gang rape, and that family members were forced to watch. The rape was thought to be to intimidate the appellant from reporting her mother's rape by soldiers to the authorities, and the court stated that it was difficult to imagine conduct that is more intimidating.[121] Similarly, the IACHR has concluded that intention was satisfied by a showing that the act – in this case, rape – inflicted pain or suffering for a prohibited purpose, including 'personal punishment and intimidation'.[122] In South Africa in *S v Mthembu*, the Supreme Court of Appeal referred to torture as:

117 Act 3 of Uganda's Prevention and Prohibition of Torture Act (n 31) defines torture as any act or omission, by which severe pain or suffering, whether physical or mental, is intentionally inflicted on a person by or at the instigation of or with the consent or acquiescence of any person whether a public official or other person acting in an official or private capacity for such purposes as (a) obtaining information or a confession from the person or any other person; (b) punishing that person for an act he or she or any other person has committed, or is suspected of having committed or of planning to commit; or (c) intimidating or coercing the person or any other person to do, or to refrain from doing, any act' (emphasis added).

118 *Brown v Mississippi* 297 US Reports (1936) 278.

119 *United States v Ghailani* 2010 US Dist LEXIS 107830 (SDNY) (6 October 2010) (excluding statements as the product of coercion); *Mohammed v Obama*, 704 F Supp 2d 1, 28–29 (DDC 2009) (excluding statements as tainted by the physical and psychological effects of prior torture).

120 *Zubeda v Ashcroft* 333 F3d (3rd Cir 2003) para IIA.

121 Ibid.

122 *Martin de Mejia v Peru* (n 89).

> [a]ny act by which severe pain or suffering, whether physical or mental, is intentionally inflicted on a person for such purposes as obtaining from him or a third person information or a confession … when such pain and suffering is inflicted by or at the instigation of or with the consent or acquiescence of a public official or any other person acting in an official capacity.

The Supreme Court of Appeal stated that '[i]t is important to emphasize that the definition requires the act to be performed for the purpose of obtaining "information or a confession"'. This is the mischief at which the CAT is aimed.[123]

The ECtHR has found that intent is satisfied when the 'treatment' administered to an accused, that is, being hung naked by his arms with his arms tied behind his back, 'could only have been deliberately inflicted' and where it was 'administered with the aim of obtaining admissions or information from the applicant'.[124] The ICTY has taken the position that, for an act to constitute torture, one of the enumerated purposes must exist, although it stated that 'there is no requirement that the conduct must be *solely* perpetrated for a prohibited purpose'. The prohibited purpose must simply be part of the motivation behind the conduct.[125] The International Criminal Tribunal for the Former Yugoslavia (ICTY) has supported the view that an act of torture occurs when it is shown that an accused inflicted pain and suffering for the purpose of obtaining information or a confession.[126] Similarly, the International Criminal Tribunal for Rwanda (ICTR) has determined that torture has occurred when severe harm has been inflicted for a prohibited purpose, such as discrimination.[127]

In the context of terrorism, in the case of *Durant and Ugarte v Peru* decided by the IACtHR in 2000, the complainants were both arbitrarily arrested and incarcerated (without arrest warrants or their being found guilty of felonies) on suspicion of participation in terrorist acts, and both were killed during a

123 *S v Mthembu* (379/07) (2008) ZASCA 51 para 30.

124 Prosecutor v Furundžija (Trial chamber of ICTY, Judgment, 10 December 1998) IT-95-17/1-T10, 121 ILR 213, 260.

125 *The Prosecutor v Zejnil Delalic & Others* ICTY Case No IT-96-21-T (16 November 1998) para 454.

126 *Prosecutor v Furundžija* (n 124) 118. The ICTY combined the intent and purpose requirements and stated that the accused 'must participate in an integral part of the torture and partake of the purpose behind the torture, that is the intent to obtain information or a confession, to punish or intimidate, humiliate, coerce or discriminate against the victim or a third person'.

127 *Prosecutor v Akayesu* Case No ICTR-96-4-T (2 September 1998) 682–83; *Semanza v Prosecutor* Case No ICTR-97-20-T (15 May 2003) 545.

prison riot by the use of excessive force by Peruvian armed forces.[128] The majority ruling found against a violation of article 5(2) of the IACHR (prohibition of torture, and cruel, inhumane or degrading treatment) on the basis of a lack of sufficient evidence that Riveira and Ugarte suffered these acts by the state while detained in prison.[129] The Court was of the view that forced disappearance and disproportionate and unjustified use of force alone are insufficient for a finding of torture, cruel, inhumane, or degrading treatment.[130] In his dissenting opinion, however, Judge De Roux Rengifo asserted that it may be concluded that the victims suffered severe mental and physical anguish between the time of the riot suppression efforts and the time of their deaths so as to amount to cruel, inhumane, or degrading treatment.[131] In *Aksoy v Turkey*, which involved the torture of a suspected terrorist, the ECtHR confirmed the requirements of both intensity of the suffering as well as the aim of obtaining information or admissions from the applicant.[132] In *Aydin v Turkey*, a young woman was held in detention by police for questioning on suspicion of being involved in a group considered as terrorists by the state. While in detention she was stripped, beaten, sprayed with cold water, blindfolded and raped. The European Court held that rape was constitutive of torture.[133] Accordingly, it appears from the discussion in this section that torture requires the intentional infliction of some form of pain and suffering for a prohibited purpose. The following section will consider the requirement that torture must be committed by a public official.

2.1.3 Public Official

There further is a relationship between the torturous conduct and the person by whom it is committed. The CAT definition of torture provides that to constitute torture an act must be 'inflicted by or at the instigation of or with the consent or acquiescence of a public official or other person acting in an official capacity'.[134] It has been argued that the CAT in fact is primarily concerned with

---

128 *Durand and Ugarte v Peru* IACHR (16 August 2000) Ser C No 68 59.

129 Ibid., 79.

130 Ibid.

131 *Durand and Ugarte* case (n 128) 191; see partially Dissenting Opinion of Judge De Roux Rengifo.

132 *Aksoy* case (n 86) 64.

133 European Court of Human Rights, *Aydin v Turkey*, Communication 23178/94, 25 September 1997.

134 Art 1 of the CAT (n 22).

torture that is the result of state policy; cruelty inflicted by private individuals unrelated to state activity does not qualify as torture.[135]

It may be argued that the relationship between the purpose for which an act is committed and state interests or policies is illustrated by the reference to a public official.[136] This satisfies a link with state involvement and excludes acts by an official for private reasons.[137] Possibly because private torture is generally regarded as criminal conduct under national laws, the drafters of the CAT considered an international convention for private torture unnecessary.[138] Moreover, the wording 'acquiesced in or instigated' widens the scope with regard to state involvement as it covers private acts consented to by a public official, and it may include state inaction in the face of private violence.[139] One of the UN Special Rapporteurs on Torture, Nigel S Rodley, interpreted the state action requirement to be met when public officials are 'unable or unwilling to provide effective protection from ill-treatment, including ill-treatment by non-state actors'.[140]

In domestic legislation, a number of countries include some reference to the public official requirement in their definitions of torture. In ratifying the CAT, the US presented the following understanding concerning the public official requirement: 'The definition of torture in article 1 is intended to apply only to acts directed against persons in the offender's custody or physical control' and 'with reference to article 1 of the Convention, the US understands that the term "acquiescence" requires that the public official, prior to the activity constituting torture, has awareness of such activity and thereafter breaches his legal responsibility to intervene to prevent such activity'.[141] United Kingdom (UK) legislation makes it an offence for any public official to 'intentionally inflict

135 See Louis Henkin, 'Remarks on Draft Restatement of the Foreign Relations Law of the United States (Revised)' (1982) 76 American Society of International Law Procedure 184, 190. Henkin argues that a policeman who tortures in violation of a national constitution and on his own authority would not be violating international customary law.

136 Miller (n 99) 17–18.

137 Ibid.

138 Question of the Human Rights of All Persons Subjected to Any Form of Detention or Imprisonment, Summary Prepared by the Secretary-General in Accordance with Commission Resolution E/CN4/l314/Add.2 (31 January 1979) 6, 29.

139 Miller (n 99) 18.

140 See Office of the United Nations High Commissioner for Human Rights, Human Rights Fact Sheet No 4 Combating Torture 34 (May 2002) <http://www.un-documents.net/ohchr/factsheet04rev.1en.pdf> accessed 26 October 2017.

141 US Reservations, Declarations and Understandings (n 42). See *Khouzam v Ashcroft* 361 F 3d 161 (24 February 2004) para 40, where the US Court of Appeals noted that the first draft of understandings required the public official to have 'knowledge' of such activity. However, the knowledge requirement was changed to mere 'awareness' after the Senate

severe pain or suffering on another in the performance … of his official duties'.[142] In France, article 222–3 of the Criminal Code, which enumerates aggravating circumstances relevant to torture and acts of barbarity, expressly refers to the commission of such acts by public officials.[143]

The public official requirement is further reflected in the legislation of various countries. Cameroon requires that the act of torture be committed by a public official or any other person acting in an official capacity or at his instigation or with his consent, whether explicitly or implicitly.[144] In Guatemala, an act of torture must have been conducted 'with the authorization, support or acquiescence of the state authorities'.[145] For an act to constitute torture in Croatia, such an act must be performed by 'an official or any other person … acting with the encouragement or the express or tacit approval of an official person'.[146] In Sudan, a public services official who tortures an accused for the purpose of obtaining a confession or issues an order to this effect, faces imprisonment.[147] The Penal Code of Spain specifically refers to the public official requirement.[148] In Bangladesh, the Torture and Custodial Death (Prevention) Act passed in 2013, aimed at curbing the torture of people in custody, confirms the public official requirement and refers to an act done by dint of the power

Foreign Relations Committee expressed concern that the conditions 'created the impression that the United States was not serious in its commitment to end torture worldwide'.

142 Art 134(2) of the UK Criminal Justice Act, 2003.

143 ICRC 'Customary IHL' France: Practice Relating to Rule 90; arts 222–3 of the Criminal Code, 1992 <https://ihl-databases.icrc.org/customary-ihl/eng/docs/v2_cou_fr_rule90_sectionb> accessed 9 August 2017.

144 Sec 132(5) of the Cameroon Penal Code (n 95).

145 Consideration of Reports Submitted by State Parties under Article 19 of the Convention, Guatemala, UN Doc CAT/C/49/Add.2, 9, <docstore.ohcr.org.SelfServices/FilesHandler.ashx.enc.> accessed 13 August 2017.

146 Consideration of Reports Submitted by State Parties under Article 19 of the convention, Croatia 12 (n 46).

147 Art 115(2) of Sudan's Criminal Code, 1991, states that '[e]very person who, having public authority entices, or threatens, or tortures any witness, or accused, or opponent to give, or refrain from giving any information in any action, shall be punished, with imprisonment, for a term, not exceeding three months, or with fine, or with both'.

148 Art 174 of Spain's Penal Code, 1995 states that '[t]orture is committed by the public authority or officer who, abusing his office, and in order to obtain a confession or information from any person, or to punish him for any act he may have committed, or is suspected to have committed, or for any reason based on any kind of discrimination, subjects that person to conditions or procedures that, due to their nature, duration or other circumstances, cause him physical or mental suffering, suppression or decrease in his powers of cognizance, discernment or decision, or that in any other way attack his moral integrity. Those found guilty of torture shall be punished with a sentence of imprisonment from two to six years if the offence is serious, and of imprisonment from one to three years if it is not.'

of any government officer or government power.[149] In Algeria, the Criminal Justice Act of 1988 makes it an offence for any public official to 'intentionally inflict severe pain or suffering on another in the performance ... of his official duties'.[150]

In the Philippines, torture means an act 'inflicted by or at the instigation of or with the consent or acquiescence of a person in authority or agent of a person in authority'.[151] Under the Iraqi Penal Code, any public official or agent who tortures or orders the torture of an accused, witness or informant in order to compel him to confess to the commission of an offence or provide information about such an offence is punishable by imprisonment or by penal servitude.[152]

In Iceland, however, there is no state actor requirement, and torture may occur in all situations regardless of whether or not the act was performed by a public official.[153] In Indonesia, torture does not have to be committed by a public official.[154] In Russia, Belgium, and the Dominican Republic the involvement of a public official is similarly not required.[155]

149 Art 2(1) of the Bangladesh Torture and Custodial Death (Prevention) Act, 2013.

150 Algeria Code of Criminal Procedure, 1966.

151 The Philippines Anti-Torture Act (n 41) defines torture as '[a]n act by which severe pain or suffering, whether physical or mental, is intentionally inflicted on a person for such purposes as obtaining from him/her or a third person information or a confession; punishing him/her for an act he/she or a third person has committed or is suspected of having committed; or intimidating or coercing him/her or a third person; or for any reason based on discrimination of any kind, when such pain or suffering is inflicted by or at the instigation of or with the consent or acquiescence of a person in authority or agent of a person in authority. It does not include pain or suffering arising only from, inherent in or incidental to lawful sanctions'.

152 Art 333 of the Iraqi Penal Code, 1969 provides that '[a]ny public official or agent who tortures or orders the torture of an accused, witness or informant in order to compel him to confess to the commission of an offence or to make a statement or provide information about such offence or to withhold information or to give a particular opinion in respect of it is punishable by imprisonment or by detention'.

153 Consideration of Reports Submitted by State Parties under Article 19 of the Convention, Iceland, UN Doc CAT/C/59/Add.2 58 <docstore.ohcr.org.SelfServices/FilesHandler.ashx .enc.> accessed 13 August 2017.

154 See art 33(1) of Indonesia's Law no 39 of 1999: 'Everyone has the right to freedom from torture, or cruel, inhuman and degrading punishment or treatment.' Art 4 of this Law lists the right not to be tortured as a 'human right that cannot be diminished under any circumstances whatsoever'. See further Consideration of Reports Submitted by State Parties under Article 19 of the Convention, Addendum, UN Doc CAT/C/Add.1, Indonesia (n 112).

155 Art 117 of the Criminal Code of the Russian Federation (n 31) and art 417*bis* of the Criminal Code of the Kingdom of Belgium, 2003; art 42(1) of the Constitution of the Dominican Republic, 2015.

In *Tachiona v Mugabe* the complainants alleged that the ZANU-PF party, led by President Mugabe, together with other individual defendants acting in their personal capacities and as senior officers of ZANU-PF, had planned and executed a campaign of violence including murder, torture, terrorism, rape, beatings and the destruction of property. The applicants invoked the Alien Tort Claims Act, the Torture Victim Protection Act, the general federal jurisdictional statute and fundamental norms of international human rights law.[156] The US District Court for the Southern District of New York stated that the legislative history of the Torture Victims Protection Act confirmed that the state action condition was intended to make it clear that a plaintiff must establish some governmental involvement in the torture or killing to prove a claim, and that the statute does not attempt to deal with torture or killing by purely private groups.[157] The state action requirement was further confirmed by the US Court of Appeals (Second Circuit) in *Kadic v Karadzic*, where the Court stated that torture and summary execution 'are proscribed by international law only when committed by state officials or under color of law'.[158]

Acquiescence has further been liberally interpreted by the US Ninth Circuit. In *Zheng v Ashcroft*, where the petitioner sought relief from deportation on the basis that he was likely to be tortured if returned to China, the petitioner claimed that the Chinese government acquiesced in his torture by third-party smugglers.[159] The Court adopted a liberal interpretation of the term 'acquiescence', holding that torture does not require that the acts be 'willfully accepted' by government officials.[160] It found a sufficient nexus between the public officials and those who inflicted the harm because the officials were 'aware' of the torturous acts.[161] The test is whether the government 'would turn a blind eye to torture'.[162] In South Africa, the Supreme Court of Appeal found evidence of an accomplice extracted through torture by police inadmissible, even where the accomplice testified years after the torture had been inflicted.[163]

---

156 *Tachiona v Mugabe*, 169 F Supp 2d 259 (SDNY 2001) 264. See the Alien Torts Claims Act 28 USC § 1350 (1948); Torture Victim Protection Act Pub L 102-256, 106 Stat 73 (12 March 1992).

157 Ibid., 316.

158 See further *Kadic v Karadzic*, 70 F3d 232, 239–40, 243 (2d Cir 1995) (citing the Convention Against Torture, pt I, art 1) (defining torture as 'inflicted by or at the instigation of or with the consent or acquiescence of a public official or other person acting in an official capacity').

159 *Zheng v Ashcroft* 332 F3d 1186, 1194 (9th Cir 2003).

160 Ibid., 1196–97.

161 Ibid., 1189.

162 Ibid., 1194.

163 *S v Mthembu* (n 123) para 30.

The case law of the ECtHR further supported this expanded view of state involvement. Torture may include actions taken by private individuals if the state has an obligation to protect the victims and such an obligation may arise under domestic law, as was the case in *Z v The United Kingdom*.[164] Holding the government responsible for the inhuman and degrading treatment inflicted on four children by their parents, the ECtHR found that states must take measures designed to ensure that individuals within their jurisdiction are not subjected to torture or inhuman or degrading treatment, including such ill-treatment administered by private individuals.[165] The Court ruled that, as the state knew or should have known that these children were at risk of severe abuse by their parents, the state had an affirmative obligation to prevent torture or inhuman or degrading treatment.[166]

In *Dimitrov v Serbia and Montenegro* before the UN Committee against Torture, Dimitrov was arrested and taken to a police station without explanation. During his interrogation the police 'struck [Dimitrov] repeatedly with a baseball bat and a steel cable, and kicked and punched him all over his body' for 13 hours.[167] The Committee determined that Serbia and Montenegro had committed torture, based in part on the 'severe pain or suffering intentionally inflicted [on Dimitrov] by public officials in the context of the investigation of a crime'.[168] *In Martin de Mejia v Peru* the IACHR summarized the definition of torture in the IACPPT as encompassing three elements: an intentional act through which physical and mental pain and suffering is inflicted on a person; committed with a purpose; and committed by a public official or by a private person acting at the instigation of the former.[169] The ICTY Appeal Chamber, as well as the ICTR, however, have taken the view that the presence of a state official or of any other authority-wielding person in the torture process is not necessary for the offence to be regarded as torture under international humanitarian law.[170] This may be because the International Criminal Tribunals are concerned with individual criminal responsibility. Arguably, such actions

164 *Z & Others v United Kingdom* (Application No 29392/95) (31 May 2001) ECHR.

165 Ibid., 69–75.

166 Ibid., 74.

167 UN Committee against Torture *Jovica Dimitrov v Serbia and Montenegro* UN Doc CAT/C/34/D/171/2000 (3 May 2005).

168 Ibid., 2.1.

169 *Martin de Mejia v Peru* (n 89).

170 *Prosecutor v Kunarac, Kovac & Vukovic & Others* (Trial Chamber of ICTY, Judgment, 22 February 2001) IT-96-23 and 23/1 para 148; *Prosecutor v Semanza* ICTR Case No ICTR-97-20 (15 May 2003) paras 342–3.

would then constitute private acts of torture without a nexus or imputation of the conduct to the state.

In the context of terrorism, public officials (such as officials working for the US Central Intelligence Agency) are often accused of being the perpetrators of torture. According to reports of the International Red Cross, interrogation sessions of detainees in Abu Ghraib and Guantanamo Bay included ill-treatment, including deprivation of sleep, food and water, exposure to extreme levels of heat and cold, stress and standing positions, waterboarding, sexual degradation and other cruel treatment which amounted to torture.[171] Furthermore, it has been argued that the widespread use of torture in the war against terrorism and the consistency of methods used indicate that incidents of torture were not merely rare exceptions committed by certain individuals, but an actual strategic element in the interrogations of detained terrorists and terrorist suspects.[172] Arguably, this points to some form of state involvement.

From the discussion above it appears that there is support for the elements of torture as the intentional infliction of pain and suffering with the purpose of obtaining information or a confession, or for intimidation or coercion, in treaty law and state practice. Although state practice differs with regard to the elements of intent, purpose and the public official requirement, 161 state parties have ratified or acceded to the CAT and, therefore, are bound by the definition of torture under the CAT.

Furthermore, with regard to the purpose of torture, it often occurs in situations such as detention and during interrogation, and it involves the extraction of information as well as state involvement. With regard to severity, however, there seems to be a shift towards a wider definition of what constitutes torture, such as threats of torture. Moreover, it is recognized that torture is relative to the personal circumstances of the victim concerned. The core elements of the definition of torture, therefore, are argued to be a form of pain and suffering, intent, involvement of a public official and a purpose to obtain information, a confession, or for intimidation or coercion.

---

171 ICRC 'Report on the Treatment of Fourteen "High Value Detainees" in CIA Custody' (2007) <https://assets.nybooks.com/media/doc/2010/04/22/icrc-report.pdf> accessed 7 October 2017, 12; ICRC (2004) 'Report of the International Committee of the Red Cross (ICRC) on the Treatment by the Coalition Forces of Prisoners of War and Other Protected Persons by the Geneva Conventions in Iraq During Arrest, Internment and Interrogation' 8 <www.derechos.org/nizkor/us/doc/icrc-prisoner-report-feb-2004.pdf> accessed 7 October 2012.

172 Alex Bellamy, 'No pain, no gain? Torture and Ethics in the War on Terror' (2006) 82(1) International Affairs 121–48.

3 Is the Prohibition of Torture a *Jus Cogens* Norm?

In chapter 3 it was proposed that there are certain criteria for a norm to constitute a *jus cogens* norm. A *jus cogens* norm is a norm of general international law, which is accepted and recognized by the international community of states as a whole as a norm from which no derogation is permitted and which can be modified only by a subsequent norm of general international law having the same character.[173]

3.1 *The Criteria under the Vienna Convention on the Law of Treaties*

3.1.1 A Norm of General International Law

The first criterion for a *jus cogens* norm is that the norm in question must be a norm of general international law. As discussed in chapter 2, general international law includes general principles of law as well as customary international law.[174] It is argued that, based on widespread state practice supporting the prohibition of torture, it is a norm of customary international law and, therefore, a norm of general international law. This is further supported in jurisprudence. For example, the Kenyan Court of Appeal has noted that, even if Kenya had not ratified the CAT, it would 'still have been bound to proscribe torture within its territory under customary international law'.[175] The ICTY has found that the definition of torture contained in article 1 of the UNCAT represents customary international law.[176]

3.1.2 Accepted and Recognized

In order to meet the criteria set out in article 53 of the Vienna Convention for a norm to qualify as a *jus cogens* norm, the prohibition of torture must be

173 Art 53 of the Vienna Convention on the Law of Treaties 1969.

174 Analytical Report of the Study Group of the International Law Commission finalized by Chairman Martti Koskenniemi 'Fragmentation of International Law: Difficulties Arising from the Diversification and Expansion of International Law' UN Doc A/CN4/L682 (13 April 2006) 92, 194.

175 *Koigi Wamwere v the Attorney-General* (2015) eKLR 6.

176 See *Prosecutor v Furundžija* (n 124); *Prosecutor v Delacic & Others* (16 November 1998) Case No IT-96-21-T, para 454 and *Prosecutor v Kunarac & Others* (n 170), para 466. See further art 5 of the Statute of the International Criminal Tribunal for the Former Yugoslavia, 1993. Under the Statutes of the ICTY and the ICTR, the crime of torture is considered both a war crime and a crime against humanity. In *Prosecutor v Duško Tadić* (27 February 2001) ICTY Case No IT-94-1-A-AR77 3249, the ICTY Appeals Chamber abandoned the armed conflict requirement and held that '[i]t is now a settled rule of customary international law that crimes against humanity do not require a connection to international armed conflict'.

accepted and recognized by the international community of states as a whole as a norm from which no derogation is permitted. Evidence of such acceptance and recognition includes public statements on behalf of states; official publications; governmental legal opinions; diplomatic correspondence; and decisions of national courts.[177]

In *Ashcraft v Tennessee*, the US Supreme Court stated:

> There have been, and are now, certain foreign nations ... which convict individuals with testimony obtained by police organizations possessed of unrestrained power to seize persons ... hold them in secret custody and wring from them confessions by physical or mental torture. So long as the Constitution remains the basic law of this Republic, America will not have that kind of government.[178]

In the Supreme Court of Canada, in *Kazemi Estate v Iran*, Judge LeBel (for the majority) confirmed the acceptance of the prohibition of torture by states as non-derogable:

> In the same manner that principles of fundamental justice are principles 'upon which there is some consensus that they are vital or fundamental to our societal notion of justice' ... *jus cogens* norms are customs accepted and recognized by the international community of states from which no derogation is permitted.[179]

In *Tachiona v Mugabe* the US District Court for New York noted that 'torture is among the practices defined in the world's nations, through treaties, conventions and declarations' as being a violation of customary international

177 See eg Prosecutor v Furundžija (n 124) para 156 where the ICTY referred to, amongst others, the following domestic court cases: Siderman de Blake v Republic of Argentina 965 F 2d 699 (9th Cir 1992) ; Committee of US Citizens Living in Nicaragua v Reagan (n 51); Calibri v Assasie-Gyimah 921 F Supp 1189, 1196 (SDNY 1996); In re Estate Ferdinand E Marcos 978 F2d 493 (9th Cir), Marcos Manto v Thajane, 508 US 972, 125L Ed 2d 661, 113 S Ct. 2960.

178 Ashcraft v Tennessee 322 US 143, 155 (1944).

179 *Kazemi Estate v Islamic Republic of Iran* 2014 SCC 151–152: 'I am prepared to accept that *jus cogens* norms can generally be equated with principles of fundamental justice and that they are particularly helpful to look to in the context of issues pertaining to international law, just as principles of fundamental justice are the "basic tenets of our legal system"'. See further *Re BC Motor Vehicle Act* (1985) 2 SCR 486, 503, noting that *jus cogens* norms are a higher form of customary international law.

law, non-derogable in all situations and a *jus cogens* norm.[180] The Special Rapporteur on Torture and Other Cruel, Inhuman or Degrading Treatment or Punishment, Mr P Kooijmans, in his report concluded that if there were some disagreement in the UNGA with respect to CAT, it had to do with the methods of control and implementation – there was no disagreement whatsoever about the fact that torture is absolutely forbidden.[181] In *Mendoza & Others v Argentina*, the IACHR, as a basis for its *jus cogens* status, advanced the nature of the prohibition of torture in 'universal and regional treaties' which 'establish this prohibition and the non-derogable right not to be subjected to torture' as well as 'numerous international instruments [that] establish that right and reiterate the same prohibition, even under international humanitarian law'.[182] In *Belgium v Senegal*, in justifying its conclusion that the prohibition against torture is a norm of *jus cogens*, the ICJ noted that the prohibition was grounded on 'widespread international practice and the *opinio juris* of states', that it appears in 'numerous international instruments of universal application and the domestic law of almost all states and that acts of torture are regularly denounced within national and international fora'.[183]

180 See *Tachiona v Mugabe* (n 156) 259, 279, where the US District Court for the Southern District of New York noted that '[t]he world's nations, through treaties, conventions and declarations, have established standards defining as violations of customary international law, practices such as genocide, crimes against humanity, torture, forced disappearance, extra-judicial killings and terrorism'. See further *Siderman de Blake* (n 177) 717: 'The right to be free from torture is fundamental and universal, a right deserving of the highest stature under international law, a norm of *jus cogens*.'

181 Torture and Other Cruel, Inhuman or Degrading Treatment or Punishment, report by Special Rapporteur, Mr P Kooijmans, UN Doc E/CN4/1986/15 (1986) 1 para 3.

182 *Mendoza & Others v Argentina Inter-American Commission for Human Rights*, IAm Comm of HR (14 May 2013) Ser C No 260 para 199.

183 *Belgium v Senegal* (*Questions Relating to the Obligation to Prosecute or Extradite*) 2012 ICJ Reports para 99. This wording was repeated in the Report of the United Nations Working Group on Arbitrary Detention – Basic Principles and Guidelines on the Right of Anyone Deprived of their Liberty to Bring Proceedings Before a Court A/HRC/30/37 (6 July 2016) para 11 ('[t]he prohibition of arbitrary detention is supported by the widespread international practice and on the *opinio juris* of states. It appears in numerous international instruments of universal application and has been introduced into the domestic law of almost all States'). In *Belgium v Senegal*, para 99, Judge Trindade stated that '[i]t has, at last, been recognized that conscience refers to superior values which stand above the "will", and that law emanates from the common conscience of what is juridically necessary (*opinio juris communis necessitatis*). Distinctly from the formal "sources" of international law, which are nothing more than the means or vehicles of formation of its norms, conscience (expressed in the *opinio juris communis*) appears distinctly, in my understanding, as its material "source" par excellence, affirming the binding character of such norms.

Various UN policy statements and resolutions have further confirmed the absolute and universally-recognized prohibition against torture.[184] The Declaration against Torture was adopted without dissent and is widely considered to be part of customary international law.[185] In terms of the Declaration, no derogation from the prohibition of torture is allowed. In addition, the absence of objections to the absolute prohibition of torture during the drafting of the CAT arguably signifies an unconditional acceptance of this prohibition.[186] In addition to this, states have made statements before the UN that they reject torture. In a statement before the UN, Israel declared that it categorically prohibits torture, including the torture of persons under interrogation, and recognizes the prohibition of torture as absolute. Israel stated that

> [e]ven if there were no statutory provisions prohibiting it, the state of Israel would honor the universal prohibition on the use of torture, for the state of Israel is founded on the values of the biblical prophets whose legacy to mankind is the basis of moral law, central to which is the need to respect all men, and to refrain from causing harm to any man's dignity, life or person.[187]

It is therefrom, ie, from the universal juridical conscience, that the peremptory norms of international law (*jus cogens*) ultimately emanate.'

184 Declaration Against Torture (n 93) 91; Principles of Medical Ethics Relevant to the Role of Health Personnel, Particularly Physicians, in the Protection of Prisoners and Detainees against Torture and Other Cruel, Inhuman or Degrading Treatment or Punishment, A/RES/37/194 (1982) annex, 37 UN GAOR Supp No 51 211, art 5 of Supplementary Convention on the Abolition of Slavery, the Slave Trade, and Institutions and Practices Similar to Slavery (1956) (act of mutilating, branding or marking a slave); art 2 of the Convention on the Prevention and Punishment of the Crime of Genocide, 1948 (serious bodily or mental harm to members of the group); art II of the International Convention on the Suppression and Punishment of the Crime of Apartheid, 1974 (serious bodily or mental harm by subjecting them to torture); para 5 of the Declaration on the Protection of Women and Children in Emergency and Armed Conflict, 1974; art 5 of the International Convention on the Elimination of All Forms of Racial Discrimination; principle 9 of the Declaration of the Rights of the Child, 1965; para 6 of the Declaration on the Use of Scientific and Technological Progress in the Interests of Peace and for the Benefit of Mankind, 1975; para 6 of the Declaration on the Rights of Mentally Retarded Persons, 1971; para 10 of the Convention on the Rights of Persons with Disabilities and its Optional Protocol, 1975; rule 31 of the Standard Minimum Rules for the Treatment of Prisoners, 1957 and 1977); art 5 of Code of Conduct for Law Enforcement Officials, 1979.

185 *Filartiga v Pena-Irala* 630 F 2d 876 (2d Cir 1980) 882–3.

186 Iveta Chenerva, 'The Drafting History of Article 2 of the Convention Against Torture' (2012) 9(1) Essex Human Rights Review 1.

187 Statement by Israeli representative at 18th session of United Nations Committee against Torture, Geneva, Switzerland (7 May 1997) <http://mfa.gov.il/mfa/internatlorgs/speeches/

It further stated that 'despite the current predicament of the state and the pressing need to fight terrorism, investigators are never, and never have been, authorized to use torture, even if its use might possibly prevent some terrible attacks and save human lives'.[188] The UK has similarly condemned torture. On her first visit to the US as Prime Minister of the UK, Theresa May firmly rejected the US President's suggestion that torture might be acceptable.[189] In the US, the Department of State submitted its initial report on the compliance of the US with the CAT in 1999. Both this report and the Second Report submitted in 2005 by the Bush administration denounced torture and stated that it was unjustifiable under any circumstance. The First Report included the following statement:

> Torture is prohibited by law throughout the United States. It is categorically denounced as a matter of policy and as a tool of state authority. Every act constituting torture constitutes a criminal offense under the law of the United States. No official of the government, federal, state or local, civilian or military, is authorized to commit or to instruct anyone else to commit torture. Nor may any official condone or tolerate torture in any form. No exceptional circumstances may be invoked as a justification for torture. United States law contains no provision permitting otherwise prohibited acts of torture or other cruel, inhuman or degrading treatment or punishment to be employed on grounds of exigent circumstances (for example, during a 'state of public emergency') or on orders from a superior officer or public authority.[190]

---

pages/statement%20by%20israeli%20representative%20to%20un%20committe.aspx> accessed 4 September 2017.

188 Ibid. Israel further stated that it 'categorically deplores and prohibits the practice of torture, including, of course, that against persons under interrogation' and that moral law, central to which is the right to human dignity, are historic Jewish values which are 'enshrined today in the Israeli Constitution and include a prohibition on the use of torture'. It stated that '[t]his prohibition on torture is absolute. As a result, and despite the current predicament of the state and the pressing need to fight terrorism, investigators are never, and never have been, authorized to use torture, even if its use might possibly prevent some terrible attacks and save human lives'.

189 'Theresa May "Absolutely" Condemns Torture Ahead of Trump Visit' *Toronto Sun*, <www.Torontosun.Com/2017/01/26/Theresa-May-Absolutely-Condemns-Torture-Ahead-Of-Trump-Visit> accessed 13 August 2017; 'Trump Claims Torture Works but Experts Warn of its "Potentially Existential" Costs *The Guardian* <www.theguardian.com/us-news/2017/jan/26/donald-trump-torture-absolutely-works-says-us-president-in-first-television-interview> accessed 13 August 2017.

190 US Department of State Initial Report of the United States of America to the UN Committee against Torture (1999) 6.

In its Second Periodic Report, the US stated:

> The United States stands against and will not tolerate torture under any circumstances: [N]o circumstance whatsoever, including war, the threat of war, internal political instability, public emergency, or an order from a superior officer or public authority, may be invoked as a justification for or defense to committing torture. The Second Periodic Report admits that, with the attacks against the United States of September 11, 2001, global terrorism has fundamentally altered our world and that in fighting terrorism, the US remains committed to respecting the rule of law, including the US Constitution, federal statutes, and international treaty obligations, including the Torture Convention.[191]

The ICJ in *Belgium v Senegal* stated that the prohibition on torture is part of customary international law and had become a peremptory norm (*jus cogens*).[192] It stated that the prohibition against torture

> is grounded in a widespread international practice and on the *opinio juris* of states. It appears in numerous international instruments of universal application (in particular the Universal Declaration of Human Rights of 1948, the 1949 Geneva Conventions for the protection of war victims; the International Covenant on Civil and Political Rights of 1966; General Assembly Resolution 3452/30 of 9 December 1975 on the Protection of All Persons from Being Subjected to Torture and Other Cruel, Inhuman or Degrading Treatment or Punishment), and it has been introduced into the domestic law of almost all states; finally, acts of torture are regularly denounced within national and international fora.[193]

Furthermore, the ICJ in *Questions Relating to the Obligation to Prosecute or Extradite* identifies the prohibition of torture as 'part of customary international law' which 'has become a peremptory norm (*jus cogens*)'.[194] The Kenyan Court of Appeal further noted that the prohibition of torture 'is a principle of *jus cogens* and is a peremptory norm of international law'.[195] Further, the Restatement on Foreign Relations of the US defines *jus cogens* to include

---

191 US Department of State Second Periodic Report of the United States of America to the UN Committee against Torture 6 (2005) 4, 17.

192 *Belgium v Senegal* (n 183) para 99.

193 Ibid.

194 Ibid.

195 *Koigi Wamwere v the Attorney-General* (2015) eKLR 6.

torture or other cruel, inhuman or degrading treatment or punishment.[196] Although adherence to the criteria in article 53 of the Vienna Convention is sufficient to constitute a *jus cogens* norm, as discussed earlier, the characteristics, however, may be relevant in assessing the criteria for *jus cogens* norms.[197] The aforementioned characteristics are discussed below.

3.2 *Core Characteristics*

This section will consider whether the prohibition of torture meets the characteristics of a *jus cogens* norm: It must protect certain fundamental values, form part of a superior hierarchy of norms and be universally applicable.[198] First, with regard to fundamental values, the prohibition against torture protects the right to human dignity.[199] In *S v Makwanyane* the South African Constitutional Court stated that '[r]ecognising a right to dignity is an acknowledgment of the intrinsic worth of human beings: Human beings are entitled to be treated as worthy of respect and concern.'[200] Human dignity is considered to be what gives a person his or her intrinsic worth and respect and the value for life. Manifested in the all-embracing concepts of humanity and *menswaardigheid*, it is highly priced.[201] In *Filartiga v Pena-Irala* the US Court of Appeals for the Second Circuit stated that there at present there was 'no dissent from the view that human rights and fundamental freedoms guaranteed in the UN Charter include, at a bare minimum, the right to be free from torture'.[202]

In the *Pinochet* case the House of Lords referred to the US Court of Appeals case of *Siderman v Argentina* in stating that *jus cogens* is derived from values taken to be fundamental by the international law community.[203] In the UK,

---

196 The American Law Institute 'Restatement of the Law, Third, Foreign Relations Law of the United States' (1987) para 7.

197 Tladi, D 'Second Report on Jus Cogens' in the Report of the International Law Commission 69th session (1 May–2 June and 3 July–4 August 2017) A/CN4/706 'Second Report' para 18.

198 See discussion in ch 3, sec 4.

199 See for example *Belgium v Senegal* (n 183). The value of the right to human dignity was shaped by the reaction against Nazi ideology and events during World War II. See, for example, James Whitman, *On Nazi 'Honour' and the New European 'Dignity' in Darker Legacies of Law in Europe: The Shadow of National Socialism and Fascism over Europe and its Legal Traditions* (Hart Publishing 2003) 243; *East Timor (Portugal v Australia)* (30 June 1995) ICJ Reports 90; *Prosecutor v Kunarac* (n 170); *Prosecutor v Delalic* (n 125).

200 *S v Makwanyane* 1995 (6) BCLR 665 (CC) para 328. See further Hardy Jones, *Kant's Principle of Personality* (University of Wisconsin Press 1971) 127; *Belgium v Senegal* (n 183).

201 *Makwanyane* case (n 200) para 307.

202 Ibid., 882.

203 *R v Bartle and Commissioner of Police, Ex Parte Pinochet* (1999) UKHL 17; *A & Others v Secretary of State for the Home Department* (No 2) (2005) (HL) 1 WLR 414 436 citing *Siderman* (n 177). In the *Siderman* case, an action was brought in the US against Argentina

the Queen's Bench Division of the England and the Wales High Court of Justice in *R (Mohamed) v Secretary of State for Foreign and Commonwealth Affairs* emphasized the prohibition of torture as a fundamental standard of the international community: 'Clearly, the *jus cogens* nature of the prohibition against torture articulates the notion that the prohibition has now become one of the most fundamental standards of the international community.'[204] In *Kazemi Estate v Iran* before the Canadian Supreme Court, Judge LeBel (for the majority) observed: 'Our Court cannot entertain any doubt that the prohibition of torture has reached the level of a peremptory norm.'[205]

Moreover, the IACtHR and the ICTY have confirmed the fundamental values underlying the prohibition of torture. The IACtHR has stated that all persons have attributes inherent to their human dignity that make them possessors of fundamental rights that may not be disregarded and which are superior to the power of the state.[206] The ICTY in the *Furundžija* case stated that it was the importance of the values that are protected by the prohibition against torture which makes it a norm that enjoys a higher rank in the international hierarchy than treaty law and even 'ordinary' customary rules.[207] In the *Mukoko* case the Supreme Court of Zimbabwe seemed to equate the prohibition of torture itself with a fundamental right and excluded evidence obtained in contravention of the prohibition of torture, inhuman and degrading treatment.[208]

---

for torture committed in Argentina by Argentinian military personnel. The appellants argued, among other things, that state immunity was trumped or superseded by the *jus cogens* norm of prohibition of torture. The Circuit Court agreed that the prohibition of official torture had attained the status of *jus cogens* and that any state engaged in official torture violated *jus cogens*.

204 *R (Mohamed) v Secretary of State for Foreign and Commonwealth Affairs* (2009) 1 WLR 2579; *Al Rawi & Others v Secretary of State for Foreign and Commonwealth Affairs & Another* (2008) QB 289 154.

205 *Kazemi Estate v Iran* (n 179) 209 47.

206 Advisory Opinion OC-18/03 of 17 September 2003, requested by the United Mexican States Juridical Condition and Rights of Undocumented Migrants, para 100.

207 *Furundžija* case (n 124) para 151, reognizing that the *jus cogens* nature of the prohibition against torture has become one of the most fundamental standards of the international community.

208 *Mukokov Attorney-General* (2012) JOL 29664 (ZS). Art 15(1) of the Lancaster Constitution of Zimbabwe provided that '[n]o person shall be subjected to torture or to inhuman or degrading punishment or other such treatment'. The same prohibition has been enshrined in art 53 of the Constitution of Zimbabwe, 2013. Art 53 provides that '[n]o person may be subjected to physical or psychological torture or to cruel, inhuman or degrading treatment or punishment'. See further Jamil D Mujuzi, 'Evidence Obtained through Violating the Right to Freedom from Torture and Other Cruel, Inhuman or Degrading Treatment in South Africa' (2015) 15 African Human Rights Law Journal 89–109.

Second, the prohibition of torture is hierachically superior. This is linked to the importance of the fundamental values protected by this norm. In domestic case law, in *R v Bow Street Metropolitan Stipendiary Magistrate & Others; Ex Parte Pinochet* (*No 3*) (*Pinochet* (*No 3*)), the House of Lords considered the government of Spain's request to extradite Senator Pinochet to stand trial for crimes committed while he was head of state in Chile.[209] Lord Browne-Wilkinson stated that '[b]ecause of the importance of the values it protects, this principle has evolved into a peremptory norm or *jus cogens*, that is a norm that enjoys a higher rank in the international hierarchy than treaty law and even "ordinary" customary rules'.[210] In the judgment of the England and Wales Court of Appeal in *A & Others v Secretary of State for the Home Department* (*No 2*), Lord Justice Neuberger relied upon Lord Browne-Wilkinson's opinion in *Pinochet* (*No 3*) and the judgment of the majority of the ECtHR in *Al-Adsani v United Kingdom* to conclude that the prohibition of torture has a higher rank than ordinary customary rules and is a *jus cogens* norm.[211] The Courts of First Instance of Levadia, Greece and the District Court of Columbia similarly were of the view that the stronger normative quality of the *jus cogens* prohibition of torture should prevail above conflicting non-peremptory norms.[212]

With regard to the jurisprudence of the ECtHR, in *Al-Adsani v UK* the plaintiff filed a claim for compensation in the UK against the government of Kuwait for alleged torture by members of the Kuwaiti intelligence services.[213] The minority judgment found that the nature of *jus cogens* norms means that a state violating such rules cannot invoke hierarchically lower rules to avoid the consequences of its illegal actions.[214] The ECtHR has similarly referred to 'the peremptory effect of the higher-ranking norm of *jus cogens* prohibiting and punishing torture'.[215]

Finally, and, it is argued, linked to its superior status, the prohibition of torture is universally applicable. Norms that have attained the status of *jus*

---

209 *Ex Parte Pinochet* (No 3) (n 203), see *further A & Others v Secretary of State for the Home Department* (No 2) (2006) 2 AC 22, 33, citing *Prosecutor v Furundžija* (n 124) para 153.

210 *Prosecutor v Furundžija* (n 124).

211 *A & Others v Secretary of State for the Home Department* (No 2) (2005) 1 WLR 414, citing *Ex Parte Pinochet* (n 203) and *Al-Adsani v United Kingdom* Application No 35763/97 ECHR (21 November 2001) 761, 30.

212 See *Distomo v Prefecture of Voiotia* 137/1997 (1998) and *Princz v Federal Republic of Germany* 813 F Supp 22 (DDC 1992). See further Erika de Wet, 'The Prohibition of Torture as an International Norm of *Jus Cogens* and its Implications for National and Customary Law' (2004) 15 European Journal of International Law 97–121, 106.

213 *Al-Adsani v UK* (n 211).

214 Ibid., 106; dissenting opinion of Judge Rozaklis and Caflisch, *Al-Adsani v UK* (n 211) para 3.

215 *Al-Dulimi and Montana Management Inc v Switzerland* (n 154) para 34.

cogens 'prevail over and invalidate international agreements and other rules of international law in conflict with them'.[216] In *Siderman v De Blake* the US Court of Appeals recognized the prohibition of torture as 'specific, universal and obligatory'.[217] In *Mann v Republic of Equatorial Guinea* the High Court of Zimbabwe considered an appeal by a foreign national serving a sentence in Zimbabwe who was the subject of an extradition request by Equatorial Guinea.[218] The Court of First Instance granted the extradition request. The appellant argued, *inter alia*, that the Court had erred in failing to address its mind specifically as to whether Zimbabwe would be violating any of its international obligations should it extradite the appellant. In a concurring judgment, Judge Patel considered the issue of whether the fact that Zimbabwe is not a party to the CAT entitles it to disregard the requirements of article 3 and extradite an alleged offender to a state where he would be in danger of being subjected to torture. After stating that '[i]t is ... incontrovertible that torture is universally prohibited' at the international level, Judge Patel held:

> The first corollary of the universal proscription of torture is that it imposes upon every state obligations which are applicable *erga omnes*, that is to say, towards all other states, which are then endowed with correlative rights. The second corollary is that the principle against torture has evolved into a peremptory norm or *jus cogens*, viz a principle endowed with primacy in the hierarchy of rules that constitute the international normativeorder.[219]

In *Prosecutor v Furundžija* the ICJ's conclusion that the prohibition of torture was a norm of *jus cogens* was based, *inter alia*, on the extensiveness of the prohibition, including the fact that states are 'prohibited from expelling, returning or extraditing' a person to a place where they may be subject to torture.[220] This further supports the universality principle which assumes that every state has an interest in exercising jurisdiction to combat egregious offences that states have condemned universally.[221]

---

216 *Siderman de Blake* (n 177) 716, quoting Third Restatement of the Foreign Relations Law of the US, 1987 para 102.

217 *Siderman de Blake* case (n 177). See further *Hilao v Marcos*, 25 F3d 1467, 1475 (9th Cir 1994); *Kadic v Karadzic* (n 158); *Abebe-Jira v Negewo*, 72 F3d 844, 847 (11th Cir 1996).

218 *Mann v Republic of Equatorial Guinea* (2008) ZWHHC 1.

219 Ibid., 12.

220 Ibid., 152.

221 Stephanie Williams, 'Your Honor, I am Here Today Requesting the Court's Permission yo Torture Mr Doe: The Legality of Torture as a Means to an End v The Illegality of Torture as

In light of the above, it is argued that the prohibition of torture has obtained *jus cogens* status.[222] In the *Furundžija* case the ICTY explicitly noted that the prohibition of torture, as contained in human rights treaties, is an absolute right that may never be derogated from, not even in a state of emergency.[223] The IACtHR in *Tibi v Ecuador* stated that '[t]here is an international legal system that absolutely forbids all forms of torture … and this system is now part of *jus cogens*'.[224] In addition, the IACtHR, the ECtHR and various UN committees, including the UN Committee on Civil and Political Rights and the UN Committee on Torture, have upheld the prohibition of torture.[225] Moreover, the ICTY has held that the prohibition against torture both in times of peace and during armed conflict constitutes a norm of *jus cogens* which is non-derogable.[226]

4 The Prohibition of Torture and the *Jus Cogens* Prohibition of Terrorism

The prohibition of torture and the prohibition of terrorism are both *jus cogens* norms from which no derogation is permitted. As discussed in chapter 3 of this book, terrorism denotes specific types of killings which are prohibited and from which no derogation is allowed – the terrorist killing of innocent

---

a Violation of *Jus Cogens* Norms under Customary International Law' (2004) 12 University of Miami International and Comparative Law Review 325.

222 *Filartiga v Pena-Irala* 630 F 2d 876 (2d Cir 1980) 882–83 and *Ex parte Pinochet* (No 3) (n 203).

223 *Prosecutor v Furundžija* (n 124) para 144.

224 *Tibi v Ecuador* Inter-American Commission for Human Rights, IAm Comm of HR (7 September 2004) Ser C No 114, IHRL 1497 para 143. See further *Durand and Ugarte v Peru* (n 128) 68 59.

225 *Maritza Urrutia v Guatemala* Inter-American Commission for Human Rights, IAm Comm of HR (27 November 2003) Ser C No 103, para 85; *Ireland v the UK* (n 77) para 167; *Opuz v Turkey* Application No 33401/02 ECHR (9 June 2009) para 176; *Soering v United Kingdom* (n 81) para 91; *Selmouni v France* (n 79) para 24; *Kurt v Turkey*, Application No 24276/94, ECHR (25 May 1998); Concluding Observations on Yugoslavia, Committee against Torture (1999) UN Doc A/54/44, para 47; Committee against Torture, Communication 207/02; *Dragan Dimitrijevic v Serbia and Montenegro* (24 November 2004) paras 2.1 and 5.3; Communication 28/1978 *Weinberger v Uruguay*, Committee on Civil and Political Rights, (29 October 1980) paras 2 and 16; Communication 973/01; *Khalilova v Tadjikistan*, Committee on Civil and Political Rights (18 October 2005) para 6.2; Communication 124/82; *Muteba v Zaire* Committee on Civil and Political Rights (24 March 1983) para 8.2.

226 *Prosecutor v Kunarac & Others* (n 170); *The Prosecutor v Delalic* (n 125); T Meron, 'International Criminalization of Internal Atrocities' (2005) 89 American Journal of International Law 571.

civilians.[227] This prohibition is supported by widely-ratified anti-terrorism treaties and near-universal condemnation by states.[228] The prohibition of torture enjoys similar support. The question arises as to how to address the prohibition of torture in the context of the prohibition of terrorism.[229]

The argument that torture could in exceptional cases be permissible has been increasingly present in the rhetoric of politicians.[230] After 9/11, it was alleged that the protection of human rights compromises the ability of states to respond to terrorism. Torturing suspected terrorists was suggested to be a legitimate tool which should be allowed in extreme cases to extrapolate important information from terrorist suspects, which might save hundreds of lives.[231] It was argued that there are 'very unpleasant but very real cases in which we are morally permitted – indeed morally compelled – to do terrible things'.[232] Related to this is the argument that leaders may violate morality in order to secure the good of the communities they protect and that it would be difficult to prove that valuable information has never been extracted under torture.[233] The converse of this argument is that terrorism continues despite the torture of terrorist suspects. US Senator John McCain, a former detainee and victim of torture during the Vietnam War, argued that, under torture, one admits to anything.[234] Both Israel and the US have infamously used questionable

227 See discussion in ch 1.

228 *Flatow v Islamic Republic of Iran* 999 F Supp 23 (DDC 1998).

229 See discussion in ch 2.

230 See, eg, Transcript of US Joint Congressional hearing 'Extraordinary Rendition in US Counterterrorism Policy: The Impact on Transatlantic Relations' of Subcommittee on International Organizations, Human Rights and Oversight and Subcommittee on Europe, and in particular the arguments of Republican Congressman Rohrabacher: <http://fas.org/irp/cpngress/2007_hr/rendition.pdf> accessed 16 April 2017.

231 See further Nigel Rodley, 'The Prohibition of Torture: Absolute Means Absolute' (2006) 34 Denver Journal of International law and Policy 145–60; 'Article 15–6 Investigation of the 800th Military Police Brigade – The Taguba Report: A Report Prepared by Major General AM Taguba on Alleged Abuse of Prisoners by Members of the 800th Military Police Brigade at the Abu Ghraib Prison, Baghdad' <https://fas.org/irp/agency/dod/taguba.pdf> accessed 16 April 2017.

232 Charles Krauthammer, 'The Truth about Torture' in Levinson (n 2).

233 See Michael Walzer, 'Political Action: The Problem of Dirty Hands' and Jean Elshtain 'Reflection on the Problem of Dirty Hands' in Levinson (n 2); see further Helen Fine, *Human Rights and Wrongs: Slavery, Terror, Genocide* (Paradigm Publishers 2007) 63–76, noting that the French authorities have argued at length that employing torture in Algeria has led to successful counter-terrorism efforts.

234 See John McCain, 'Torture's Terrible Toll' *Newsweek* (21 November 2005) <http://www.newsweek.com/tortures-terrible-toll-115193> accessed 16 April 2017. 34, where he stated that abusive treatment of detainees 'often produces bad intelligence because under torture a person will say anything he thinks his captors want to hear – whether it is true

interrogation methods in their wars on terror.[235] These, however, are normative questions. This section will consider the doctrinal relationship between the prohibition of torture and the prohibition of terrorism in light of their respective *jus cogens* characters.

Can there be a balancing of rights between the prohibition of torture and the prohibition of terrorism? In order to determine this, it must be considered which underlying values are protected by these prohibitions. Both prohibitions protect the right to human dignity. With regard to the prohibition of terrorism, the killing of innocent civilians uses people as a means to an end and infringes their basic dignity as human beings. With regard to torture, according to a report by Amnesty International, '[e]very time a helpless individual is being tortured, our own dignity and humanity is being diminished and degraded', and there is no act which is 'more a contradiction of our humanity than the deliberate infliction of pain by one human being on another, the deliberate attempt over a period of time to kill a man without his dying'.[236] Accordingly, it does not seem that a weighing of the two norms with reference to their underlying values is possible.

The next question is whether in fact there is any legal antinomy between the prohibition of torture and the prohibition of terrorism as *jus cogens* norms. A legal antinomy arises where two contrary legal commandments cannot be applied in their entirety to the same situation, and the normative conflict must be solved by either harmonising the competing norms or applying one to the detriment of the other.[237] It has been argued that justice is the fundamental value underlying the goal of solving legal antinomies.[238] In situations of antinomy, solving the conflict may involve the invalidity or the limitation of

or false – if he believes it will relieve his suffering ... the terrorists we interrogate under less than humane standards of treatment are also likely to resort to deceptive answers' (28 October 2017) <http://www.newsweek.com/tortures-terrible-toll-115193> accessed 16 April 2017.

235 Miriam Gur-Arye, 'Can the War Against Terror Justify the Use of Force in Interrogations? Reflection in Light of the Israeli Experience' in Levinson (n 2).

236 Amnesty International *Torture in 2014: 30 Years of Broken Promises* <www.amnestyusa.org/sites/default/files/act400042014en.pdf.> accessed 2 April 2016, 11, 25. See further *Attorney-General of Israel v Adolf Eichmann*, District Court of Jerusalem, 36 ILR 18, 25, 26, 50 (Israel Dist Ct 1961). See also judgment of the Supreme Court sitting as Court of Criminal Appeals at 36 ILR 299, 304 (Israel Sup Ct 1962).

237 Chaïm Perelman, 'Les Antinomies en Droit, Essay de synthèse' in Chaïm Perelman (ed), *Les Antonomies en Droit* (Bruylant 1965) 393.

238 Robert Kolb, 'Conflits Entre Norms de *Jus Cogens*' in Jean Salmon (ed) *Droit de Puvoir, Pouvoir de Droit, Mélanges offerts à Jean Salmon* (Bruylant 2007) 484; Christófolo *Solving Antinomies between Peremptory Norms in Public International Law* (Schulthess 2016) 7.

one of the norms or the maintenance of both as valid after the antinomy has been solved.[239] It may further involve a weighing of the norms concerned. The weighing rule means specifying the interests protected by the competing norms and assigning relative weights to each interest.[240] This is particularly apposite to *jus cogens* norms, where the ILC, in its Commentary to article 50 (now article 53) of the Draft on the Law of Treaties, stated that 'it is not the form of a general rule of international law, but the particular nature of the subject matter with which it deals that may, in the opinion of the ILC, give it the character of *jus cogens*'.[241] There may be instances, however, where it is simply impossible to justify the notion that one competing norm should prevail over another, for example, where norms embody equally important underlying values.

In the context of the prohibition of terrorism as a *jus cogens* norm, the ticking time-bomb scenario will be used as an example of the difficulties that arise when considering whether the prohibition of torture can be limited in the context of anti-terrorism measures. In this scenario, a terrorist has placed a bomb in a large city that will cause a catastrophic loss of life.[242] The terrorist is the only person who knows where the bomb is and how to defuse it. Can the prohibition of torture be limited in order to torture the terrorist to extract the information? Authors have argued that this is the kind of situation in which torture 'is not merely permissible but morally mandatory' and that, in this scenario, there is no reason not to torture the terrorist.[243] Indeed, Dershowitz notes that, in this situation, where it concerns the violation of the rights of a single criminal individual to save the lives of thousands of innocent people, most people would agree that torture is allowed.[244] 'Coercive' techniques of

239 Christófolo (n 238) 24.

240 Robert Alexy, *A Theory of Constitutional Rights* (Oxford University Press 2010) 64–8.

241 Draft Articles on the Law of Treaties with Commentaries' Yearbook of the International Law Commission (1966) Vol II 247.

242 Fatima Kola, 'Torture and Terrorism – A Case Study' (2007) 85 Supplement UCL Jurisprudence Review 97.

243 Michael Levin, 'The Case for Torture' <http://people.brandeis.edu/~teuber/torture.html> accessed 5 September 2017. Levin states that 'if the only way to save those lives is to subject the terrorist to the most excruciating … pain, what grounds can there be for not doing so? None.'

244 Dershowitz 'Tortured Reasoning' (n 2). See further Marcy Strauss, 'Torture' (2003–2004) 48 New York Law School Law Review 48, who argues that 'torturing a suspect as a last resort, when there is no alternative and when hundreds, thousands, potentially hundreds of thousands of lives hang in the balance, is not morally bankrupt – it is the only conclusion that makes sense.'

interrogation that would normally not be considered should, thus, be pursued in the war on terrorism.[245]

There are many difficulties with the ticking time-bomb scenario. First, it is entirely hypothetical and rests on numerous untested assumptions.[246] What is assumed is the certainty of guilt; the proportionality of the crime to the consequence (that there will be a major loss of life); necessity (that there are no other options available); the efficacy of torture (that a response will be elicited and that the response will be truthful); and control (the torture itself must be applied in a controlled manner so that it meets its objective and nothing more).[247] The likelihood of such a clear-cut situation occurring is minimal.[248] Any limitation of the prohibition of torture is a slippery slope and opens the door to government abuse. For example, after the Landau Commission of Inquiry of 1987 permitted 'moderate physical pressure' in the interrogation of detainees suspected of hostile terrorist activities, the Israeli human rights group B'Tselem estimates that security services used torture against 85 per cent of Palestinian detainees under interrogation.[249]

In domestic jurisprudence, the Spanish Supreme Court similarly condemned the use of torture and ill-treatment, including physical abuse and threats, against terrorist suspects during incommunicado detention.[250] In *Public Committee Against Torture in Israel v the State of Israel* the Supreme Court of Israel rejected the government's arguments on possible justifications for the use of physical means during the interrogation of individuals suspected

245 Alan Dershowitz, *Why Terrorism Works: Understanding the Threat, Responding to the Challenge* (Yale University Press 2002) 131–4.

246 See Kola (n 242) 99–109.

247 Ibid.

248 Ibid., 98.

249 'Israeli Government Report Admits Systematic Torture of Palestinians' *The Guardian* (13 August 2017) <www.theguardian.com/world/2000/feb/11/israel> accessed 13 August 2017. See further Commission of Inquiry into the Methods of Investigation of the General Security Service Regarding Hostile Terrorist Activity <http://www.cambridge.org/core/journals/israel-law-review/article/commission-of-inquiry-into-the-methods-of-investigation-of-the-general-security-service-regarding-hostile-terrorist-activity/2feeb59b40b66a41e9ff-3633c0d3bf69> accessed 13 August 2017. The Landau Commission was appointed by the Israeli government to review the interrogation methods used against terrorist suspects. The Commission's recommendations were struck down by the Supreme Court – see *Public Committee Against Torture v State of Israel* HCJ 5100/94 (1999) 817.

250 *Case of Igor Portu and Mattin Sarasola* Spanish Supreme Court (2 November 2011). See further Amnesty International 'Spain: Civil Guards Convicted of Torture' (10 January 2011) <www.amnesty.org/en/library/asset/EUR41/002/2011/en/60b24c89-1115-4124-aa36-68f3705efc84/eur410022011en.html> accessed 1 May 2017.

of hostile terrorist activities.[251] Israel's High Court of Justice found that 'lighter forms' of torture, such as shaking, are not allowed during the interrogation of suspects of terrorism, even if they were going to prevent foreseeable attacks planned in the near future.[252]

In *Mohamed v President of the RSA & Others* the South African Constitutional Court heard an application for leave to appeal against a judgment in the Cape of Good Hope High Court.[253] The appellant was identified by the FBI as a suspect for whom an international arrest warrant had been issued in connection with the bombing of the US embassy in Tanzania in August 1998.[254] He was apprehended by South African immigration authorities and handed over to the FBI for the purpose of being taken to the US to be put on trial for the bombing of the embassy.[255] On his arrival in the US, he was charged with various offences relating to the bombing and informed by the court that the death sentence could be imposed on him if he were convicted.[256] The court stated that, in terms of the South African Constitution, everyone has the right to freedom and security of the person, which includes the right not to be subjected to torture and cruel, inhuman or degrading treatment.[257] South African law considers the death sentence to be cruel, inhuman and degrading punishment.[258]

In *Saadi v Italy* the ECtHR dealt with a case where the applicant, a Tunisian national living in Italy, was arrested in Italy on suspicion of involvement in international terrorism.[259] The applicant challenged the decision by the Italian Minister of the Interior to deport him to Tunisia on the basis that this would expose him to the risk of being subjected to torture and cruel, inhuman or degrading treatment or punishment contrary to article 3 of the European Convention.[260] The UK exercised its right to intervene as a third party.[261] The UK government advanced the argument that, if a respondent state adduced evidence that there was a threat to national security, stronger evidence had to be adduced by the applicant to prove that he would be at risk of ill-treatment in

251 Public Committee Against Torture in Israel (n 249).
252 Ibid., 24.
253 *Mohamed & Another v President of the Republic of South Africa & Others* CCT 17/01 (28 May 2001) 2–18.
254 Ibid.
255 Ibid.
256 Ibid.
257 *Mohamed* case (n 253) 23; secs 12(1)(d) and (e) of the South African Constitution, 2006.
258 See *S v Makwanyane* 1995 (3) SA (CC) 391.
259 *Saadi v Italy* Application No 37201/06, Council of Europe: ECtHR (28 February 2008).
260 Ibid.
261 Ibid., para 7.

the receiving country.[262] The court considered that 'the argument based on the balancing of the risk of harm if the person is sent back against the dangerousness he or she represents to the community if not sent back is misconceived'.[263] The prospect that a person may pose a serious threat to the community if not returned does not in any way reduce the degree of risk of ill-treatment that the person may be subjected to on return.[264] The ECtHR held that the deportation of the applicant to Tunisia would constitute a violation of article 3 of the European Convention.[265] In *Hilal v United Kingdom* the ECtHR held that the deportation of a Tanzanian citizen from the UK to Tanzania would be in breach of article 3 of the Convention as the deportee would face the serious risk of being subjected to torture or inhuman and degrading treatment in Tanzania.[266]

In other cases, the ECtHR has confirmed that even in the most difficult circumstances, such as in the fight against terrorism, torture and inhuman or degrading treatment or punishment are prohibited in absolute terms irrespective of the conduct of the person concerned.[267] In *Al-Adsani v United Kingdom* the ECtHR noted that Article 3 of the European Convention prohibiting torture was an absolute right and that no exceptions were permitted under any circumstances.[268] In *Chahal v United Kingdom* the ECtHR held that, even in the fight against terrorism, torture is prohibited in absolute terms.[269]

In *Soering v United Kingdom* the ECtHR held that:

262 *Saadi* case (n 259) para 122.

263 Ibid.

264 Ibid., paras 140–1.

265 Ibid., para 160.

266 *Hilal v The United Kingdom*, Application No 45276/99 ECHR (6 June 2001) para 28.

267 *Labita v Italy* Application No 26772/95 ECHR (6 April 2000) para 119; see further *Gäfgen v Germany* Application No 22978/05 (1 June 2010) 87; *Ramirez Sanchez v France* Application No 59450/00 (4 July 2006) para 116.

268 *Al Adsani v UK* (n 211) para 59.

269 *Chahal v United Kingdom* Application No 22414/93 ECHR (5 November 1996) para 79. The Court noted that it is 'well aware of the immense difficulties faced by states in modern times in protecting their communities from terrorist violence. However, even in these circumstances, the Convention prohibits in absolute terms torture or inhuman or degrading treatment or punishment, irrespective of the victim's conduct. The prohibition provided by article 3 against ill-treatment is equally absolute in expulsion cases. Thus, whenever substantial grounds have been shown for believing that an individual would face a real risk of being subjected to treatment contrary to article 3 if removed to another state, the responsibility of the contracting state to safeguard him or her against such treatment is engaged in the event of expulsion. In these circumstances, the activities of the individual in question, however undesirable or dangerous, cannot be a material consideration.'

> [i]t would hardly be compatible with the underlying values of the Convention … were a contracting state knowingly to surrender a fugitive to another state where there were substantial grounds for believing that he would be in danger of being subjected to torture, however heinous the crime allegedly committed. Extradition in such circumstances, while not explicitly referred to in the brief and general wording of article 3, would plainly be contrary to the spirit and intendment of the article, and in the Court's view this inherent obligation not to extradite also extends to cases in which the fugitive would be faced in the receiving state by a real risk of exposure to inhuman or degrading treatment or punishment proscribed by that article.[270]

In the case of *Al-Asad* before the African Commission, Al-Asad, a citizen of Yemen who lived and worked in Tanzania, brought a complaint against the Republic of Djibouti. He claimed that he had been apprehended by who he believed were two Tanzanian men and flown to a destination which he believed was in the territory of the Republic of Djibouti. He was detained in isolation for two weeks, interrogated regarding terrorist-related activities and subjected to various forms of torture and ill-treatment. He was then put onto a plane and flown to three detention facilities allegedly operated by the US, two of which were in Afghanistan, where he claimed he was tortured. He alleged the breach of, *inter alia*, the prohibition of torture under the African Charter. The African Commission held that given that the alleged violation related to the *jus cogens* prohibition of torture, the fact that the receiving state (the US, that would execute the torture) was not party to the African Charter did not absolve a sending state from its obligations under the Charter relating to the act of sending the victim to the third state.[271]

The case law above has illustrated that there is no tolerance for a limitation of the absolute prohibition of torture, even in the context of terrorism. There can be no balancing of rights or limitation of values in order to arrive at any type of normative hierarchy, as both the prohibition of terrorism and the prohibition of torture protect the same fundamental value, namely, the right to human dignity. Both prohibitions are norms of *jus cogens* which permit of no deviation. In light of this, torture cannot be allowed in any form as a part of counter-terrorism measures.

---

270 *Soering v The United Kingdom* (n 81) 88.

271 *Mohammed Abdullah Saleh Al-Asad v The Republic of Djibouti* Communication 383/10, ACHPR (12 May 2014).

5 Conclusion

This chapter has illustrated that the prohibition of torture is absolute. A definition of torture was agreed upon in the CAT and no exceptions are allowed in respect of this prohibition. Section 2 analyzed the prohibition of torture under treaty, custom and international jurisprudence. In addition to various treaties prohibiting torture, as well as support for the prohibition in international jurisprudence, it was found that the prohibition of torture is a rule of customary international law and is supported by various UN resolutions, national legislation and case law.

Having established that the prohibition of torture is both a rule of treaty and custom, section 3 evaluated which elements of torture appear from the sources of international law. The elements of intent, severe pain and suffering, purpose and the commission of the act of torture by a public official appeared as elements. With regard to the severity of the pain involved, only the infliction of some form of pain and suffering was a consistent element, as opposed to specific references to the severity of the treatment involved. International jurisprudence illustrated that whether an act amounts to torture often turns on the facts of the case and the victim involved. Section 4 considered whether the prohibition of torture is a *jus cogens* in light of the criteria and characteristics of *jus cogens* norms as set out in chapter 3. It found that the prohibition of torture met both criteria, and exhibited the characteristics of *jus cogens* norms. Section 5 considered whether the prohibition of torture could be limited in the context of anti-terrorism measures. It was found that both the prohibition of terrorism and the prohibition of torture protect the underlying value of human dignity which cannot be limited. There is no legal antinomy between the two norms and both can be applied without any need for limitation. The prohibition of torture, thus, remains absolute even in the context of terrorism.

Accordingly, it is submitted that no limitation of the prohibition of torture can be allowed without affecting the essence of this prohibition, including in the context of the prohibition of terrorism. This is supported by the non-derogability of the prohibition of torture as a *jus cogens* norm and support for this non-derogability in treaty law, custom and international jurisprudence. Any exception is a slippery slope and dilutes the protection intended by this prohibition.

CHAPTER 4

The Prohibition of Terrorism and the Right to a Fair Trial

1 Introduction

The previous chapter considered the effect of the prohibition of terrorism as a *jus cogens* norm on the prohibition of torture, and found that the prohibition of torture itself is a *jus cogens* norm, an absolute prohibition that is not subject to limitation, even in the context of another *jus cogens* norm such as the prohibition of terrorism. The question addressed in this chapter is whether the right to a fair trial and due process considerations can serve to limit the ability of states to take measures in order to address terrorism.

Various international instruments guarantee the right to a fair trial. The Universal Declaration of Human Rights (UDHR) of 1948 provides:

> Everyone is entitled in full equality to a fair and public hearing by an independent and impartial tribunal, in the determination of his rights and obligations and of any criminal charge against him.[1]

Other conventions, such as the European Convention of Human Rights (ECHR) and the International Covenant of Civil and Political Rights (ICCPR), expanded on the fair trial rights contained in the UDHR and provided for extensive due process guarantees.[2] In fact, it has been argued that there is 'no aspect

---

1 Art 10 of the Universal Declaration of Human Rights 1948.

2 Art 6 the European Convention for the Protection of Human Rights and Fundamental Freedoms, 1950 (ECHR) provides: '1 In the determination of his civil rights and obligations or of any criminal charge against him, everyone is entitled to a fair and public hearing within a reasonable time by an independent and impartial tribunal established by law. Judgment shall be pronounced publicly but the press and public may be excluded from all or part of the trial in the interests of morals, public order or national security in a democratic society, where the interests of juveniles or the protection of the private life of the parties so require, or to the extent strictly necessary in the opinion of the court in special circumstances where publicity would prejudice the interests of justice. 2 Everyone charged with a criminal offence shall be presumed innocent until proved guilty according to law. 3 Everyone charged with a criminal offence has the following minimum rights: (a) to be informed promptly, in a language which he understands and in detail, of the nature and cause of the accusation against him; (b) to have adequate time and facilities for the preparation of his defence; (c) to defend himself in person or through legal assistance of his own choosing or, if he has not sufficient

 DOI:10.1163/9789004391543_006

of preparation for **trial** or of criminal procedure which is not touched by, or indeed determined by, the principle of a fair trial'.[3] Given the practical scope of this chapter which aims to evaluate whether the right to fair trial can be restricted during counter-terrorism measures, all the elements that make up

---

means to pay for legal assistance, to be given it free when the interests of justice so require; (d) to examine or have examined witnesses against him and to obtain the attendance and examination of witnesses on his behalf under the same conditions as witnesses against him; (e) to have the free assistance of an interpreter if he cannot understand or speak the language used in court.' In terms of article 14(1) of the International Covenant on Civil and Political Rights, 1966 (ICCPR), '[a]ll persons shall be equal before the courts and tribunals. In the determination of any criminal charge against him, or of his rights and obligations in a suit at law, everyone shall be entitled to a fair and public hearing by a competent, independent and impartial tribunal established by law.' Art 14(2) provides that '[e]veryone charged with a criminal offence shall have the right to be presumed innocent until proved guilty according to law'. Art 14 further provides: '3 In the determination of any criminal charge against him, everyone shall be entitled to the following minimum guarantees, in full equality (a) to be informed promptly and in detail in a language which he understands of the nature and cause of the charge against him; (b) to have adequate time and facilities for the preparation of his defence and to communicate with counsel of his own choosing; (c) to be tried without undue delay; (d) to be tried in his presence, and to defend himself in person or through legal assistance of his own choosing; to be informed, if he does not have legal assistance, of this right; and to have legal assistance assigned to him, in any case where the interests of justice so require, and without payment by him in any such case if he does not have sufficient means to pay for it; (e) to examine, or have examined, the witnesses against him and to obtain the attendance and examination of witnesses on his behalf under the same conditions as witnesses against him; (f) to have the free assistance of an interpreter if he cannot understand or speak the language used in court; (g) not to be compelled to testify against himself or to confess guilt. 4 In the case of juvenile persons, the procedure shall be such as will take account of their age and the desirability of promoting their rehabilitation. 5 Everyone convicted of a crime shall have the right to his conviction and sentence being reviewed by a higher tribunal according to law. 6 When a person has by a final decision been convicted of a criminal offence and when subsequently his conviction has been reversed or he has been pardoned on the ground that a new or newly discovered fact shows conclusively that there has been a miscarriage of justice, the person who has suffered punishment as a result of such conviction shall be compensated according to law, unless it is proved that the non-disclosure of the unknown fact in time is wholly or partly attributable to him. 7 No one shall be liable to be tried or punished again for an offence for which he has already been finally convicted or acquitted in accordance with the law and penal procedure of each country.' Art 6(3) of the ECHR provides that '[e]veryone charged with a criminal offence has the following minimum rights: (a) to be informed promptly, in a language which he understands and in detail, of the nature and cause of the accusation against him; (b) to have adequate time and facilities for the preparation of his defence; (c) to defend himself in person or through legal assistance of his own choosing or, if he has not sufficient means to pay for legal assistance, to be given it free when the interests of justice so require; (d) to examine or have examined witnesses against him and to obtain the attendance and examination of witnesses on his behalf under the same conditions as witnesses against him; (e) to have the free assistance of an interpreter if he cannot understand or speak the language used in court'.

3 *John Fairfax Publications Pty Ltd v Hitchcock* (2004) 61 NSWLR 344 paras 22–23.

the right to a fair trial will not be discussed here. Accordingly, certain core elements will be identified which are thought to be most relevant and which may constitute core fair trial guarantees in the context of anti-terrorism measures. These elements are the presumption of innocence, the right to a hearing before a fair and impartial tribunal and the right to review. Section 2 will motivate why these are proposed as core elements of the right to a fair trial, with specific reference to treaty law, custom and international jurisprudence.

Section 3 will evaluate whether the core elements of the right to a fair trial discussed in section 2 have obtained *jus cogens* status with reference to the criteria for a norm to be elevated to *jus cogens* status in terms of article 53 of the Vienna Convention on the Law of Treaties (Vienna Convention) as discussed in chapter 3 above. Furthermore, it will be considered whether the suggested core elements of the right to a fair trial exhibit the characteristics of *jus cogens* norms.[4] Finally, section 4 will discuss the interaction between the right to a fair trial and the prohibition of terrorism, and consider whether certain core rights that form part of the right to a fair trial are capable of limitation in the context of anti-terrorism measures.

2 Core Fair Trial Rights

When establishing which fair trial rights may be 'core' rights, it will be considered whether certain fair trial rights may be regarded as non-derogable. Article 4(1) of the ICCPR allows for derogations from states' obligations under the ICCPR in a time of public emergency which threatens the life of the nation.[5] Although the ICCPR contains a list of rights from which no derogation is allowed, even in times of public emergency, this list does not include the right to a fair trial.[6] Accordingly, it appears that limitations to certain fair trial rights are allowed.

---

4 See ch 3.

5 Art 4(1) of the ICCPR (n 2) states that '[i]n time of public emergency which threatens the life of the nation and the existence of which is officially proclaimed, the States Parties to the present Covenant may take measures derogating from their obligations under the present Covenant to the extent strictly required by the exigencies of the situation, provided that such measures are not inconsistent with their other obligations under international law and do not involve discrimination solely on the ground of race, colour, sex, language, religion or social origin'.

6 Art 4(2) of the ICCPR (n 2). Similarly, the ECHR does not list the right to a fair trial as non-derogable and provides for derogation on similar terms as article 14(1) of the ICCPR.

While chapter IX(2) of the Guidelines on Human Rights and the Fight against Terrorism adopted by the Committee of Ministers of the Council of Europe in 2002 states that '[a] person accused of terrorist activities has the right to a fair hearing, within a reasonable time, by an independent, impartial tribunal established by law', it also provides that:

> [t]he imperatives of the fight against terrorism may nevertheless justify certain restrictions to the right of defence, in particular with regard to (i) the arrangements for access to and contacts with counsel; (ii) the arrangements for access to the case-file; (iii) the use of anonymous testimony.[7]

The European Court of Human Rights (ECtHR) has allowed limitations on certain fair trial rights, such as the right to a public (as opposed to a closed) hearing where it is necessary and proportionate to ensure the efficacy of a secret surveillance regime to support the fight against terrorism and other serious crimes.[8] Furthermore, in *Ibrahim & Others v the United Kingdom*, the ECtHR allowed a temporary delay in providing some of the applicants with access to a lawyer. The applicants had been arrested on suspicion of having detonated bombs planted on the underground system, which ultimately failed to explode.[9] At the time of their initial police questioning, there had been an urgent need to prevent serious adverse consequences for the public, namely, further suicide attacks. Accordingly, there had been compelling reasons for the temporary restrictions on the applicants' right to legal advice. The Court held that there had been no violation of the applicants' rights to a fair trial and legal assistance. The Court was further satisfied that the proceedings as a whole, in respect of each of the three applicants, had been fair.[10] Additionally, national security concerns arising in the context of terrorism have justified the use of

7 See Council of Europe Committee of Ministers 'Guidelines on Human Rights and the Fight against Terrorism' 11 July 2002 <http://www.refworld.org/docid/47fdfb220.html> (accessed 21 October 2017). Ch IX(2) further provides that '[s]uch restrictions to the right of defence must be strictly proportionate to their purpose, and compensatory measures to protect the interests of the accused must be taken so as to maintain the fairness of the proceedings and to ensure that procedural rights are not drained of their substance'.

8 *Kennedy v United Kingdom* Application No 26839/05 ECHR (18 May 2010) paraa 184–91.

9 *Case of Ibrahim & Others v The United Kingdom* Applications No 50541/08, 50571/08, 50573/08 and 40351/09) (13 September 2016).

10 *Ibrahim & Another v Secretary of State for the Home Department* (2010) EWHC 764 (Admin), United Kingdom: High Court (England and Wales) (13 April 2010) <www.refworld.org/cases,GBR_HC_QB,4bc6d6a02.html> accessed 26 March 2017 para 235.

anonymous witnesses or the provision of a redacted summary of information to a criminally accused.[11]

Notwithstanding the above, the HRC has interpreted certain 'fundamental principles of a fair trial' as being non-derogable.[12] In General Comment 29, dealing with derogations from provisions of the ICCPR during a state of emergency (provided for in article 4(1) of the ICCPR), the HRC stated that only a court of law may try and convict a person for a criminal offence, that the presumption of innocence must be respected, and that where a state party deviates from the fair trial rights in the ICCPR, and in order to protect non-derogable rights, 'the right to take proceedings before a court to enable the court to decide without delay on the lawfulness of detention, must not be diminished'.[13] State parties may in no circumstances invoke article 4(1) of the ICCPR 'as justification for acting in violation of humanitarian law or peremptory norms of international law', for example 'through arbitrary deprivations of liberty or by deviating from fundamental principles of fair trial, including the presumption of innocence'.[14] The first Special Rapporteur on the Promotion and Protection of Human Rights and Fundamental Freedoms while Countering Terrorism, Martin Scheinin, affirmed that the fundamental principles of the right to a fair trial may not be subject to derogation and that any derogation

---

11 Report of the United Nations High Commissioner for Human Rights on the Protection of Human Rights and Fundamental Freedoms While Countering Terrorism (A/HRC/22/26) para 38. Human Rights Committee, Communication No 1051/2002, *Ahani v Canada*, UN Doc CCPR/C/80/D/1051/2002 (2004) para 10.4.

12 General Comment No 29: Derogations from provisions of the Covenant during a state of emergency, General Comment on article 4, UNHR Committee, CCPR/C/21/Rev1/Add11 (31 August 2001) para 11.

13 Ibid., para 16. The HRC states that '[s]afeguards related to derogation, as embodied in article 4 of the Covenant, are based on the principles of legality and the rule of law inherent in the Covenant as a whole. As certain elements of the right to a fair trial are explicitly guaranteed under international humanitarian law during armed conflict, the Committee finds no justification for derogation from these guarantees during other emergency situations. The Committee is of the opinion that the principles of legality and the rule of law require that fundamental requirements of fair trial must be respected during a state of emergency. Only a court of law may try and convict a person for a criminal offence. The presumption of innocence must be respected. In order to protect non-derogable rights, the right to take proceedings before a court to enable the court to decide without delay on the lawfulness of detention, must not be diminished by a State party's decision to derogate from the Covenant.' See further General Comment No 29 (n 12) para 6: 'The fact that some of the provisions of the Covenant have been listed in article 4 (para 2), as not being subject to derogation does not mean that other articles in the Covenant may be subjected to derogations at will, even where a threat to the life of the nation exists.'

14 Ibid.

must not circumvent the protection of non-derogable rights.[15] Even during a state of emergency, therefore, the principles of legality and the rule of law require that the fundamental requirements of fair trial must be respected.[16]

With regard to the right to review, the Human Rights Committee (HRC) has further stated that state parties may not derogate from the requirement of effective judicial review of detention.[17] The HRC was of the view that the right of anyone arrested or detained on a criminal charge to be brought promptly before a judge and be entitled to either a trial within a reasonable time or to release and the right to review, are inherent to the ICCPR as a whole.[18] Moreover, the HRC stated in General Comment 29 that in light thereof that certain elements of the right to a fair trial are explicitly guaranteed under international humanitarian law during armed conflict, there is no justification for derogation from these guarantees during other emergency situations.[19] The HRC argued that those aspects of a fair trial that are common to the legal regimes dealing with both types of armed conflict – international and non-international – are part of customary international law and provide the minimum yardstick from which no derogation is permissible.[20] Moreover, international criminal tribunals, such as the ICTY, have held that the right to a fair hearing is essential.[21] Furthermore, the Statute and Rules of Procedure of the ICTY and ICTR incorporated the right to a competent hearing before an independent and impartial tribunal.[22]

---

15 Report of the Special Rapporteur, Martin Scheinin, on the Promotion and Protection of Human Rights and Fundamental Freedoms while Countering Terrorism (6 August 2008) A/63/223 p 2 and section B, para 12.

16 Ibid.

17 See Official Records of the General Assembly, 49th session, Supplement No 40 (A/49/40) vol I annex XI para 2; the Committee's Concluding Observations on Israel (1998) (CCPR/C/79/Add93) para 21.

18 Ibid.

19 Ibid.

20 General Comment No 29 (n 12) para 16. Under international humanitarian law, Common Article 3 of the Geneva Conventions, 1949 guarantees the core elements of the right to a fair trial. It prohibits the 'passing of sentences and the carrying out of executions without previous judgment pronounced by a regularly constituted court' and affords 'all the judicial guarantees which are recognized as indispensable by civilized peoples'.

21 *Prosecutor v Tadić* Opinion and Judgment, IT-94-1-T (7 May 1997) 38; Common article 3(d) of the Geneva Conventions, 1949.

22 See art 21 of the Statute of the International Tribunal for the Prosecution of Persons Responsible for Serious Violations of International Humanitarian Law Committed in the Territory of the Former Yugoslavia Since 1991, UN Doc S/25704 (1993) (as amended) which reflects the due process standards set forth in art 14 of the ICCPR. See further International Tribunal for the Prosecution of Persons Responsible for Serious Violations of International Humanitarian Law Committed in the Territory of the Former Yugoslavia

In light of the above it will be argued that the core non-derogable fair trial rights to be discussed in the context of the prohibition of terrorism are the right to a hearing before a fair and impartial tribunal, the presumption of innocence and the right to review. Fair trial rights that have been subject to limitation, such as the right to a public hearing, the right to witnesses and the right to counsel, will accordingly not be included in the discussion. The proposed core fair trial rights will be considered in the light of treaty law, state practice and international jurisprudence.

2.1 *The Right to a Hearing before a Fair and Impartial Tribunal*

As discussed above, the right to a fair trial is contained in numerous international and regional treaties and United Nations General Assembly (UNGA) declarations.[23] The right to 'a fair and public hearing by an independent and impartial tribunal' is guaranteed by the UDHR.[24] The wording of article 10, guaranteeing a person's right to a public hearing in the determination of his/her rights and obligations *and* any criminal charge against him/her confirms that this basic right applies in both civil and criminal proceedings. The ECHR similarly guarantees the right of an accused to a fair and public hearing within a reasonable time by an independent and impartial tribunal established by law 'in the determination of his civil rights and obligations or of any criminal charge against him'.[25] The ICCPR was adopted in 1966, and it expanded upon the fair trial rights in the UDHR. The ICCPR has been widely ratified and has 169 state parties.[26]

Article 14(1) of the ICCPR provides:

Since 1991, Rules of Procedure and Evidence, UN Doc IT/32/Rev.11 (1997); Statute of the International Criminal Tribunal for Rwanda (as amended) UN Doc S/RES/955 (1994); International Criminal Tribunal for Rwanda, Rules of Procedure and Evidence UN Doc ITR/3/REV.1 (1995).

23 Art 5 of the ECHR (n 2); arts 3(a), 9(1) and 14 of the ICCPR (n 5); art 8 of the Banjul Charter, 1981; art XVIII of the ADRDM, 1949; art 5 of the International Convention on the Elimination of All Forms of Racial Discrimination, 1965.

24 See art 10 of the UDHR (n 1).

25 Art 6(1) of the ECHR (n 2) provides that '[i]n the determination of his civil rights and obligations or of any criminal charge against him, everyone is entitled to a fair and public hearing within a reasonable time by an independent and impartial tribunal established by law. Judgment shall be pronounced publicly but the press and public may be excluded from all or part of the trial in the interests of morals, public order or national security in a democratic society, where the interests of juveniles or the protection of the private life of the parties so require, or to the extent strictly necessary in the opinion of the court in special circumstances where publicity would prejudice the interests of justice.'

26 For treaty ratifications, see <http://treaties.un.org/> accessed 6 January 2016.

> All persons shall be equal before the courts and tribunals. In the determination of any criminal charge against him, or of his rights and obligations in a suit at law, everyone shall be entitled to a fair and public hearing by a competent, independent and impartial tribunal established by law.[27]

Similarly to article 10 of the UDHR, the protection afforded by article 14(1) extends to the entire judicial process and all suits at law, and not only criminal proceedings.[28] Although it contains an exception to the right that the hearing itself must be held in public, it requires that the findings of a criminal hearing must be made public.[29] The American Convention of Human Rights (ACHR) guarantees similar fair trial rights. Art 8(1) of the ACHR states that

> [e]very person has the right to a hearing, with due guarantees and within a reasonable time, by a competent, independent, and impartial tribunal, previously established by law, in the substantiation of any accusation of

---

27 Art 14(1) of the ICCPR (n 2).

28 General Comment No 32, Right to Equality before Courts and Tribunals and to a Fair Trial, UNHR Committee 19th session, Geneva (9 to 27 July 2007), UN Doc CCPR/C/GC/32 (2007); See further David Weissbrodt and Mattias Hallendorff, '*Travaux Préparatoires* of the Fair Trial Provisions – Articles 8 to 11 – of the Universal Declaration of Human Rights' (1999) 21 Human Rights Quarterly 26; Ian Brownlie (editor's preface), in D McGoldrick (ed), 'The Human Rights Committee: Its Role in the Development of the International Covenant on Civil and Political Rights' (1994) 415 <https://global.oup.com/academic/product/the-human-rights-committee-9780198258940?cc=za&lang=en&> accessed 15 May 2017, stating that the term 'suit at law' refers to various types of court proceedings, including administrative proceedings, because the concept of a suit at law depends on the nature of the right involved rather than the status of one of the parties. See further Guide on Article 6 of the European Convention on Human Rights Rights to a Fair Trial (civil limb) <www.echr.coe.int/Documents/Guide_Art_6_ENG.pdf> accessed 20 August 2017, sec 1A, paras 1–22. Sec 6(1) applies to criminal and civil proceedings, although certain minimum rights are guaranteed in criminal trials in terms of arts 6(3)(a)–(e) of the ICCPR (n 2).

29 Art 14(1) of the ICCPR (n 2) provides that '[a]ll persons shall be equal before the courts and tribunals. In the determination of any criminal charge against him, or of his rights and obligations in a suit at law, everyone shall be entitled to a fair and public hearing by a competent, independent and impartial tribunal established by law. The press and the public may be excluded from all or part of a trial for reasons of morals, public order (ordre public) or national security in a democratic society, or when the interests of the private lives of the parties so requires, or to the extent strictly necessary in the opinion of the court in special circumstances where publicity would prejudice the interests of justice; but any judgment rendered in a criminal case or in a suit at law shall be made public except where the interest of juvenile persons otherwise requires or the proceedings concern matrimonial disputes or the guardianship of children.'

> a criminal nature made against him or for the determination of his rights and obligations of a civil, labor, fiscal, or any other nature.[30]

The Association of South Asian Nations (ASEAN) Human Rights Declaration similarly provides for the right to a fair and public trial.[31] In Africa, fair trial rights are contained in the African **Charter** on Human and Peoples' Rights (Banjul Charter).[32] Additionally, the Arab Charter on Human Rights (Arab Charter) guarantees every person the right to a fair trial that affords adequate guarantees before a competent, independent and impartial court.[33]

In addition to the above, state practice illustrates that states have reflected in their constitutions the fair trial guarantees set out in international conventions. For example, the right to a hearing before a fair and impartial tribunal is set out in section 35(3) of the South African Constitution, which provides that

> [e]veryone has the right to have any dispute that can be resolved by the application of law decided in a fair public hearing before a court or, where appropriate, another independent and impartial tribunal or forum.[34]

30 Art 8(1) of the ACHR (n 9). See further art 8(5) which provides that '[c]riminal proceedings shall be public, except insofar as may be necessary to protect the interests of justice'.

31 Art 20 of the ASEAN Human Rights Declaration 2012.

32 Art 7(1)(d) of the Banjul Charter (n 23) provides that '[e]very individual shall have the right to have his cause heard. This comprises … (d) the right to be tried within a reasonable time by an impartial court or tribunal.'

33 Art 13(1) of the Arab Charter on Human Rights 2004 states that '[e]verybody has the right to a fair trial in which sufficient guarantees are ensured, conducted by a competent, independent and impartial tribunal established by law, in judging the grounds of criminal charges brought against him or in determining his rights and obligations. State Parties shall ensure financial aid to those without the necessary means to pay for legal assistance to enable them to defend their rights.' Art 13(2) provides that '[t]he hearing shall be public other than (except) in exceptional cases where the interests of justice so require in a democratic society which respects freedom and human rights'. 'The accused shall be presumed innocent until proved guilty at a lawful trial in which he has enjoyed the guarantees necessary for his defence.'

34 Art 35 of the South African Constitution, 1996. See in general Pamela Schwikkard, 'A Constitutional Revolution in South African Criminal Procedure?' (2015) <https://lawexplores.com/a-constitutional-revolution-in-south-african-criminal-procedure> accessed 26 August 2017 regarding the evolution in fair trial provisions since the apartheid era. Schwikkard notes that the fair trial provisions in the South African Constitution are extensive, arguably owing to the procedural excesses and abuses of the right to a fair trial of the apartheid rule, including detention without trial.

In Ghana, the Constitution guarantees a person charged with a criminal offence a fair hearing within a reasonable time by a court.[35] The Constitution of Cameroon provides for the right to a fair and public hearing before an impartial tribunal.[36] The Constitution of the Democratic Republic of the Congo (DRC) guarantees that all persons have the right to have their case heard by a competent judge within a reasonable time.[37] In Greece, the Constitution guarantees legal protection by the courts.[38] Hungary's Constitution states that

> [e]very person shall have the right to have any charge against him or her, or any right and duty in litigation, adjudicated by a legally established, independent and impartial court in a fair public trial within a reasonable period of time.[39]

Similar provisions are contained in the Constitution of Germany.[40] In terms of the Constitution of Portugal everyone is guaranteed access to the law and the courts in order to defend rights and interests that are protected by law and justice shall not be denied to anyone owing to a lack of financial means.[41] The Constitution of the Russian Federation provides everyone with the protection of their rights and freedoms in court.[42] In the US, the Sixth Amendment guarantees various fair trial rights, including the right of the accused to a speedy

35 See art 19(1) of the Constitution of Ghana 1992 (as amended): 'A person charged with a criminal offence shall be given a fair hearing within a reasonable time by a court.'

36 Art 3 of the Constitution of Cameroon, 1972 (as amended) states that '[e]veryone has the right to life, liberty and security of person'. Sec 10 provides that '[e]veryone is entitled in full equality to a fair and public hearing by an independent and impartial tribunal, in the determination of his rights and obligations and of any criminal charge against him'.

37 See art 10 of the Constitution of the DRC, 2005.

38 Art 20 of the Constitution of Greece, 1975 states that '1 Every person shall be entitled to receive legal protection by the courts and may plead before them his views concerning his rights or interests, as specified by law ...'

39 Art XXVIII(1) of the Fundamental Law of Hungary, 2011.

40 See art 103(1) of the Basic Law for the Federal Republic of Germany, 1949, which provides that '[i]n the courts everyone shall be entitled to a fair hearing in accordance with the law'. Art 104(3) states that '[a]ny person provisionally detained on suspicion of having committed a criminal offence shall be brought before a judge no later than the day following his arrest; the judge shall inform him of the reasons for the arrest, examine him, and give him an opportunity to raise objections. The judge shall, without delay, either issue a written arrest warrant setting forth the reasons therefor or order his release.'

41 Art 20(1) of the Constitution of Portugal, 1967 states that '[e]veryone shall have the right to a fair and public hearing of his case, without undue delay, before a competent, impartial and independent court'.

42 Art 46(1) of the Constitution of the Russian Federation, 1993 provides that '[e]veryone shall be guaranteed judicial protection of his (her) rights and freedoms'. Art 47(1) states

and public trial.[43] Access to the law and courts is guaranteed in France and Lithuania.[44] The Italian, Spanish and Israeli Constitutions guarantee the right to a fair trial.[45] Zimbabwe's Constitution provides that '[e]very person accused of an offence has the right to a fair and public trial within a reasonable time before an independent and impartial court'.[46]

In addition to the above, national jurisprudence has supported minimum fair trial rights such as the right to hearing. In the 2004 case of *Rasul v Bush* two Australian and 12 Kuwaiti citizens designated as enemy combatants by the government alleged that they had been held at Guantanamo Bay since early 2002, were not allowed access to counsel or knowledge of the charges against them, and had not had access to a fair trial.[47] The US Supreme Court found that the government had imprisoned the detainees for two years without affording them the chance to challenge the justification for their detainment and that their detentions were arbitrary owing to the fact that, amongst other things, the US never communicated the basis upon which it decides who is sent to Guantanamo Bay.[48]

The ECtHR has similarly supported the fundamental right of access to a hearing before a fair and impartial tribunal. In France, where some criminal

---

that '[n]obody may be deprived of the right to have his (her) case heard in the court and by the judge within whose competence the case is placed by law'.

43 Sixth Amendment to the US Constitution, 1787: 'In all criminal prosecutions, the accused shall enjoy the right to a speedy and public trial, by an impartial jury of the state and district wherein the crime shall have been committed'.

44 See arts V–X of the French Declaration of the Rights of Man and of the Citizen, 1789; art 20(1) of the Constitution of Portugal (n 41): 'Everyone shall be guaranteed access to the law and the courts in order to defend those of his rights and interests that are protected by law, and justice shall not be denied to anyone due to lack of financial means'; art 30 of the Constitution of Lithuania, 1992: 'The person whose constitutional rights or freedoms are violated shall have the right to apply to court'; art 31: 'A person charged with the commission of a crime shall have the right to a public and fair hearing of his case by an independent and impartial court.'

45 Art 24 of the Constitution of Italy, 1947: 'Anyone may bring cases before a court of law in order to protect their rights under civil and administrative law.' Art 5 of the Basic Law of Israel, 1958 provides that '[t]here shall be no deprivation or restriction of the liberty of a person by imprisonment, arrest, extradition or otherwise'; art 29(a) of Israel's Criminal Procedure (Enforcement Powers – Detention) Law, 5756–1996 states that a person who is detained by the officer-in-charge pursuant shall be brought before a judge as soon as possible, within 24 hours; art 24 of the Spanish Constitution, 1978 provides that '[a]ll persons have the right to obtain effective protection from the judges and the courts in the exercise of their rights and legitimate interests, and in no case may there be a lack of defence'.

46 Art 69 of the Constitution of Zimbabwe, 2013.

47 *Rasul v Bush* 215 F Supp 2d 55 (DC 2002); *Rasul v Bush* 124 S Ct 2686 (2004).

48 *Rasul v Bush* (2004) (n 47) IV.

proceedings in terrorist cases were extremely lengthy (up to nine years), the ECtHR found a violation of the right to a fair hearing within a reasonable time.[49] In the case of *Al Nashiri v Poland* the applicant, suspected of terrorism, alleged that he had been held at a US Central Intelligence Agency (CIA) 'black site' in Poland with Poland's knowledge, without any legal basis or any opportunity to contact his family.[50] He further argued that he had made every effort to engage the authorities in order to ensure an effective investigation of his allegations of torture during his detention at the site, but to no avail. A pending criminal investigation into CIA prisons in Poland was delayed for five years.[51] The ECtHR found a contravention of the right to an effective remedy by virtue of Poland failing to conduct an effective investigation and afford effective remedies with respect to the applicant's allegations of serious violations of the ECHR.[52] Arguably, the fact that the applicant did not have access to a court or tribunal to investigate allegations of torture or challenge his detention effectively denied him his right of access to a hearing.

Additionally, the fair trial guarantees set out in article 14 of the ICCPR are repeated almost word-for-word in article 21 of the ICTY Statute and article 20 of the ICTR Statute.[53] In *Prosecutor v Furundžija* the ICTY noted that the right to be tried before an independent and impartial tribunal is generally recognized as being an integral component of the requirement that an accused should have a fair trial.[54] The right to a fair trial was further supported by the ICTY in *Prosecutor v Tadić* and the Special Court of Sierra Leone in *Prosecutor v Norman, Kallon and Gbao*.[55]

It is argued that treaty law, state practice and international jurisprudence discussed in this section lend support to the notion that the right of an accused of access to a hearing before a fair and impartial tribunal is a core, non-derogable fair trial right, even in circumstances of public emergency. The next section will consider the right to be presumed innocent until proven guilty.

---

49 *Ekin Association v France* Application No 39288/98 ECHR (17 July 2001).

50 *Al Nashiri v Poland* Application No 28761/11 ECHR (24 July 2014) sec B.

51 Ibid., paras 342–3.

52 Ibid., para 598.

53 See *Tadić* (n 21) 46.

54 *Prosecutor v Furundžija* (Trial Chamber of ICTY, Judgment, 10 December 1998) IT-95-17/1-T10, 121 ILR 213, 260. The ICTY cited art 21(2) of the ICTY Statute and art 14 of the ICCPR.

55 See *Tadić* (n 21) and *Prosecutor v Norman, Kallon and Gbao* (2003) Special Court for Sierra Leone Case No SCSL-2003-09-PT, paras 7–11. See further Wolfgang Schomburg, 'The Role of International Criminal Tribunals in Promoting Respect for Fair Trial Rights' (2009) 1 Northwestern Journal of International Human Rights para 1–2.

2.2 *The Presumption of Innocence*

The presumption of innocence is guaranteed in terms of the UDHR as well as by various international and regional treaties, including the ICCPR and the ECHR.[56] Article 8(2) of the ACHR provides that '[e]very person accused of a criminal offence has the right to be presumed innocent so long as his guilt has not been proven according to law'.[57] Article 7(1) of the Banjul Charter states that '[e]very individual shall have the right to have his cause heard'. This comprises 'the right to be presumed innocent until proved guilty by a competent court or tribunal'.[58] In terms of article XXVI of the American Declaration on the Rights and Duties of Man (ACRDM) '[e]very accused person is presumed innocent until proven guilty'.[59] The ASEAN Human Rights Declaration similarly provides for a fair and public trial and the presumption of innocence.[60] Furthermore, the presumption of innocence is guaranteed in the Third Geneva Convention as well as in the war manuals of various states, illustrating that this right must be respected even in times of war.[61]

---

56 Art 11(1) of the Universal Declaration of Human Rights 1948 (UDHR) states that '[e]veryone charged with a penal offence has the right to be presumed innocent until proved guilty according to law in a public trial at which he has had all the guarantees necessary for his defence'. See art 6(2) of the ECHR (n 2). See further art 14(2) of the ICCPR which provides that '[e]veryone charged with a criminal offence shall have the right to be presumed innocent until proved guilty according to law'. The presumption of innocence is further guaranteed under Additional Protocols I and II to the Geneva Conventions 1949. Art 75(4)(d) of Additional Protocol I provides: 'Anyone charged with an offence is presumed innocent until proved guilty according to law.' See further art 6(2)(d) of Additional Protocol II; art 40(2)(b)(i) of the Convention on the Rights of the Child 1989; art 66 of the ICC Statute 1998; art 17(3) of the Statute of the Special Court for Sierra Leone 2002; arts 15 and 16 of the Statute of the Special Tribunal for Lebanon 2007; art 19 of the Cairo Declaration on Human Rights in Islam, 1990; art 8 of the ILC Draft Code of Crimes against the Peace and Security of Mankind 1996; Article 21(3) of the ICTY Statute, 1993; art 20(3) of the ICTR Statute, 1994; art 48(1) of the EU Charter of Fundamental Rights 2000.

57 Art 8(2) of the ACHR (n 9).

58 See the African Charter on Human and Peoples' Rights 1981 (Banjul Charter).

59 American Declaration of the Rights and Duties of Man, 1948.

60 Art 20 of the ASEAN Human Rights Declaration (n 31).

61 Secs 3.30, 4.15 and 5.09 of Argentinia Law of War Manual 1989. In its chapters on non-international armed conflicts, Canada's LOAC Manual 1999 17–3 sec 29(d) states that 'accused persons shall be presumed innocent until proved guilty according to law' and its 2001 manual states that '[a]s a minimum, accused persons … (d) shall be presumed innocent until proved guilty according to law'. See further Sweden's IHL Manual 1999, 19 para 2.2.2.3. Djibouti's Manual on International Humanitarian Law 45 (2004) states: 'The fundamental principles concerning detention [include] … the presumption of innocence'; Mexico's Army and Air Force Manual (2009), in a section on the 1949 Geneva Convention III, sec 9.6 states: 'Judicial procedure must be regular, that is, it must include at least the

In addition to the above, various national constitutions provide for the presumption of innocence.[62] The right to be presumed innocent is further supported in national legislation. Afghanistan's Interim Criminal Procedure Code states: 'From the moment of the introduction of the penal action until when the criminal responsibility has been assessed by a final decision, the person is presumed innocent.'[63] Poland's Constitution states: 'Everyone shall be presumed innocent of a charge until his guilt is determined by the final judgment of a court.'[64] In terms of Zimbabwe's Constitution, '[e]very person accused of an offence has the right to a fair and public trial within a reasonable time before an independent and impartial court' and '[a]ny person accused of an offence has the right to be presumed innocent until proved guilty'.[65] Furthermore, the right against self-incrimination is guaranteed in various international and regional treaties.[66] In terms of the US Constitution, an accused shall not be 'compelled in any criminal case to be a witness against himself'.[67]

---

following guarantees: … the accused must be presumed innocent.' The UK LOAC Manual (2004) states in its chapter on the protection of civilians in the hands of a party to the conflict: 'In the case of penal offences relating to the armed conflict, the basic principles of natural justice must be observed … These principles include the following: … anyone charged with an offence is presumed innocent until proved guilty according to law.' Peru's IHL and Human Rights Manual (2010) 251 sec 33(n)(4) states that a person charged with a criminal offence under international humanitarian law must be provided with certain guarantees, including '[p]resumption of innocence while culpability has not been proven'. New Zealand's Military Manual (1992) sec 1137(4)(d) provides: 'Anyone charged with an offence is presumed innocent until proved guilty according to law.'

62 Art 9 of the French Declaration of the Rights of Man and of the Citizen, 1789; art 32(2) of the Constitution of Portugal, 1976; art XXVIII(2) of the Constitution of Hungary, 2011; art 3(h) of the Constitution of South Africa, 1996 and art 11(1) of the Constitution of Cameroon, 1972.

63 Arts 3(1) and 4(1) of Afghanistan's Interim Criminal Procedure Code, 2004; see further art 35 of Cambodia's Law on the Establishment of the Extraordinary Chambers, 2001 (as amended).

64 Art 42(3) of the Constitution of Poland, 1997.

65 Art 69 of Constitution of Zimbabwe, 2013.

66 Art 14(3)(g) of the ICCPR; arts 8(2)(g) and 8(3) of the ACHR (n 9); art 57 of the Banjul Charter.

67 Fifth Amendment to the US Constitution, 1789. See further art 12 of China's Criminal Procedure Law, 1979 (as amended), art 29 of Colombia's Constitution, 1991 ('every person is presumed innocent until proven guilty by a court of law'; art 19(2) of Iraq's Law of the Supreme Iraqi Criminal Tribunal, 2005 and art 2 of Peru's New Code of Criminal Procedure, 2004.

The presumption of innocence has been supported in national case law. In Canada, the Supreme Court described the importance of the presumption of innocence as protecting 'the fundamental liberty and human dignity of any and every person accused by the state of criminal conduct in light of the grave consequences involved, including the loss of physical liberty and social stigma'.[68] In considering pre-trial detention of suspected terrorists, the Peru Constitutional Court held in the case of *Marcelino Tineo Silva & Others*:

> Justifying ... pre-trial detention solely with the reproachable nature and negative social consequences of the crime of terrorism would violate the principle of presumption of innocence because, as stated by the Inter-American Commission of Human Rights, justifying a person's detention based on the degree of danger or nature of the crime 'could be understood as being subjected to punishment in advance before the competent judge has had a chance to decide whether or not the person is guilty'. This situation may lead to an arbitrary and twisted application of preventive detention for purposes different from those considered in the law itself.[69]

In the UK, David Miranda, a journalist, was detained at Heathrow airport in 2016 for carrying files related to information obtained by the US whistle-blower, Edward Snowden. This sensitive journalistic information was seized and retained without any immediate *post-factum* judicial authorization being required.[70] The UK Court of Appeal held that the provisions of schedule 7 of the Terrorism Act of 2000, which allowed travellers to be detained at a port and questioned to find out whether they appeared to be terrorists and in terms of which they may be detained for up to nine hours, were incompatible with the

68 *R v Oakes* (1986) 26 DLR (4th) 200.

69 *Marcelino Tineo Silva & Others* Peru Constitutional Court Case No 010-2002-AI/TC (3 January 2003) para 122.

70 *Regina (David Miranda) v Secretary of State for the Home Department & Others* (2016) EWCA Civ para 6, 12, 15. The concern appeared to revolve around espionage and national security issues: 'Schedule 7 paragraph 8 in particular, permitted us to search him to ascertain whether he had the material in his possession to assist in the determination of whether or not he was a person concerned in the commission, preparation or instigation of acts of terrorism.' The Port Circulation Sheet completed by the Security Service read: 'We assess that Miranda is knowingly carrying material, the release of which would endanger people's lives. Additionally the disclosure, or threat of disclosure, is designed to influence a government, and is made for the purpose of promoting a political or ideological cause. This therefore falls within the definition of terrorism and as such we request that the subject is examined under Schedule 7.'

ECHR.[71] Arguably, the provisions of schedule 7 also infringes on the right of an accused to be presumed innocent.

The right to be presumed innocent is further supported in the jurisprudence of human rights courts and commissions. In *Gridin v Russia* the HRC found that a public declaration by officials presenting the accused as guilty before his conviction violated the accused's presumption of innocence.[72] In *Khalilov v Tajikistan* the accused was forced to admit guilt publicly on national television during the investigation phase, and the HRC found this to be a violation of his right to be presumed innocent.[73] In 1989 in *Acosta-Calderón v Ecuador*, the Customs Military Police arrested the complainant, a Colombian national, on suspicion of drug trafficking. It was alleged that the statement of the accused had not been received by a judge until two years after his detention, that he had not been notified of his right to consular assistance, that he had been in custody pending trial for over five years, condemned in 1994 without the alleged drugs being found, and released in 1996 after having served part of his sentence while he was in prison pending trial.[74] The IACHR found a violation of the right of the accused to be presumed innocent until proven guilty. It confirmed that 'the principle of presumption of innocence constitutes a foundation for judicial guarantees' and linked the presumption of innocence with the obligation of the state to 'not restrict the detainee's liberty beyond the limits strictly necessary to ensure that he will not impede the efficient development of the investigations'.[75]

In *Allenet de Ribermont v France* the ECtHR found a violation of the presumption of innocence where high-ranking officials referred to the accused as an instigator of murder and an accomplice before a finding had been made.[76]

---

71 See schedule 7 of the UK Counter-Terrorism and Security Act, 2015 para 114. See further statement by the Court that 'prior judicial or other independent and impartial oversight (or immediate post factum oversight in urgent cases) is the natural and obvious adequate safeguard against the unlawful exercise of the Schedule 7 powers in cases involving journalistic freedom'. See further *The Guardian* 'Terrorism Act Incompatible with Human Rights, Court Rules in *David Miranda* Case' <www.theguardian.com/world/2016/jan/19/terrorism-act-incompatible-with-human-rights-court-rules-in-david-miranda-case> accessed 21 October 2017.

72 *Gridin v Russia* Communication 770 UNHR Committee (20 July 2000) UN Doc CCPR/C/69/D/770/1997 (2000) para 8.3. See further *Saidova v Tajikstan* Communication 964/2001 UNHR Committee (20 August 2006) UN Doc CCPR/C/81/D/964/2001 para 6.6.

73 *Khalilov v Tajikistan* Communication 973/2001 UNHR Committee (13 April 2005) UN Doc CCPR/C/83/D/973/2001 para 7.4.

74 *Case of Acosta-Calderón v Ecuador* IACHR (24 June 2005) Ser C No 129 para 3.

75 Ibid., 111.

76 *Allenet de Ribermont v France* Application No 15175/89 20 EHRR 557 (judgment of 10 February 1995) para 41.

In *Funke v France* the European Commission (EC) held that fairness embraced the right of anyone charged with a criminal offence 'to remain silent and not to contribute to incriminating himself'.[77] In *Murray v UK* the EC found that an individual's right to remain silent during police questioning and the privilege against self-incrimination are 'generally recognized international standards which lie at the heart of the notion of a fair procedure under Article 6' and are guaranteed in the ECHR.[78]

In *Pagnoulle v Cameroon* the ACHPR further found that the five-year imprisonment of a Cameroonian national by a military tribunal violated his presumption of innocence.[79] The IACtHR, in its report on Argentina, also found that an excessive period of pre-trial detention violates the presumption of innocence as it fails to assign blame within a reasonable time and substitutes pre-trial detention for punishment.[80] The EC in *R v Saunders* further commented on the close link between the presumption of innocence and the freedom from self-incrimination.[81]The presumption of innocence reflects 'the expectation that the state bears the general burden of establishing the guilt of an accused, in which process the accused is entitled not to be required to furnish any involuntary assistance by way of confession'.[82] In *Mouesca v France* the ECtHR stated that a criminal procedure against a terrorist that lasted longer than two years and two months constituted a breach of the right to a hearing.[83]

Although this book deals with the right to a fair trial in peacetime, it is further illustrative of the fact that the right to a fair trial, as well as the right to be presumed innocent, is guaranteed even during armed conflict. For example, the UK Law of War Manual states in its chapter on the protection of civilians in the hands of a party to the conflict that the basic principles of natural justice must be observed, including the right to be presumed innocent until proven guilty.[84] Additionally, states have made statements before the HRC and the Counter-Terrorism Committee (CTC) supporting the right to be presumed in-

77 *Funke v France* (1993) 16 EHRR 297.

78 *Murray v UK* (1996) 22 EHRR 29.

79 *Pagnoulle v Cameroon* (2000) AHRLR 57 (ACHPR 1997).

80 *Jorge A Giménez v Argentina*, Case 11.245, Report No 12/96, Inter-AmCHR, OEA/Ser.L/V/II.91 Doc 7 (1 March 1996) IACHR 33; see further case of *Suárez Rosero v Ecuador* (12 November 1997) IACtHR Series C No 35, where the accused was detained from 23 June 1992 to 28 April 1996 and only ordered to be released on 10 July 1995. The Court held that preventative detention violated the accused's presumption of innocence.

81 *Saunders v UK* (1997) 23 ECHRR (ECHR) 313.

82 Ibid.

83 *Mouesca v France* Application No 52189/99 ECHR (judgment of 3 June 2003).

84 UK Law of War Manual 2004. See further Argentina's Law of War Manual 1983; Canada's LOAC Manual 1999 and 2001; Colombia's Basic Military Manual 1995; Djibouti's Manual on

nocent. For example, in 2007, in its third periodic report to the HRC, Azerbaijan stated that any person accused of an offence shall be presumed innocent until proven guilty, and the burden of proof of the charges and refutation of the arguments put forward in defence of the accused rests with the prosecution.[85] In 2006, in a report to the CTC, Finland stated that the Criminal Investigations Act provides that, in a criminal investigation of a suspected offence, circumstances and evidence against and in favour of the suspect must be examined and the suspect must be treated as being not guilty during the investigation.[86] Other states have also supported the presumption of innocence in reports to the HRC.[87] Furthermore, in a resolution adopted in 2007 on the strengthening of basic principles of judicial conduct, the UN Economic and Social Council (ECOSOC) recalled the UDHR and the ICCPR which enshrine in particular the principles of equality before the law; the presumption of innocence; the right to a fair and public hearing by a competent, independent and impartial tribunal; and the right to be tried without undue delay.[88] In light of the discussion above, therefore, it is argued that the right to be presumed innocent is a core fair trial right. The next section will discuss an accused's right to review.

2.3 *The Right to Review*

The right to review is guaranteed in international and regional treaty law.[89] Article 14(5) of the ICCPR states that '[e]veryone convicted of a crime shall have the right to his conviction and sentence being reviewed by a higher tribunal according to law'. Article 8 of the UDHR guarantees the right to an effective remedy by a competent national tribunal for acts violating fundamental rights granted by the constitution or by law.[90] It is argued that the right to review

---

International Humanitarian Law 2004; New Zealand's Military Manual 1992; the Manual of Pakistan Military Law 1987; Peru's IHL Manual 2004; Sweden's IHL Manual 1991.

85 Third Periodic Report to the Human Rights Committee, Azerbaijan, 10 December 2007, UN Doc CCPR/C/AZE/3 (submitted 4 October 2007) paras 376–8.

86 Finland Report to the Counter-Terrorism Committee of the UN Security Council, 15 May 2006, annexed to UN Doc s/2006/506 (19 July 2006).

87 Second Periodic Report to the Committee on the Rights of the Child, 24 May 2005, Hungary, UN Doc CRC/C/70/Add 25 (submitted 17 February 2004) para 508; Morocco, Fifth Periodic Report to the Human Rights Committee, 11 May 2004, UN Doc CCPR/C/MAR/2004/5 (submitted 10 March 2004) para 191.

88 UN Economic and Social Council, Res 2007/22, Preamble (26 July 2007).

89 See for example art 8(2)(h) of the ACHR (n 9); art of the ECHR (n 2); art 7(1) of the Banjul Charter; art 2(1) of the Convention for the Protection of Human Rights and Fundamental Freedoms; art 8(2)(h) of the ACHR.

90 Art 8 of the UDHR 1948 states that '[e]veryone has the right to an effective remedy by the competent national tribunals for acts violating the fundamental rights granted him by the constitution or by law'.

interacts with the right of access to a fair and impartial tribunal, as the absence of access to such a tribunal would make it impossible to exercise an effective remedy, including the right to review a judicial decision or allegations of contraventions of human rights while in detention. In regional treaty law, article 7(1)(a) of the Banjul Charter states that the right of every individual to have his cause heard includes 'the right to an appeal to competent national organs against acts of violating his fundamental rights as recognized and guaranteed by conventions, laws, regulations and customs in force'.[91] The ECHR and the IACHR similarly provide for the right to an effective remedy.[92]

The right to review is further guaranteed under the constitutions and national legislation of various states. The Constitution of South Africa, for instance, guarantees the right of appeal to, or review by, a higher court.[93] Cameroon's Constitution provides that every individual shall have the right to have his cause heard, which comprises *inter alia* the right to an appeal to competent national organs against acts violating his fundamental rights as recognized and guaranteed by conventions, laws, regulations and customs in force.[94] In the UK, article 5(1) of the Human Rights Act states that '[e]veryone who is deprived of his liberty by arrest or detention shall be entitled to take proceedings by which the lawfulness of his detention shall be decided speedily by a court and his release ordered if the detention is not lawful'.[95] The Philippines' Revized Rules of Criminal Procedure states that, in all criminal prosecutions, an accused shall be entitled to an appeal in all cases allowed and in the manner prescribed by law.[96] The Code of Criminal Procedure of Cambodia includes, under the right of appeal, the right to a full review.[97] The review must concern

91 See further *Constitutional Rights Project & Others v Nigeria* (2000) AHRLR 227 (ACHPR 1999) para 27–31, where the African Commission criticized the provisions of the Nigerian Robbery and Firearms (Special Provision) Decree as it did not provide a right to judicial appeal as a consequence of which several persons had been sentenced to death. It found that 'to foreclose any avenue of appeal to "competent national organs" in criminal cases bearing such penalties clearly violates article 7(1)(a) of the African Charter'.

92 Art 13 of the ECHR (n 2) and art 15 of the ACHR (n 9).

93 Art 35(3)(o) of the Constitution of South Africa, 1996.

94 Art 7(1)(a) of the Constitution of Cameroon (n 62); art 33 of the Constitution of Lithuania (n 44) provides that citizens shall be guaranteed the right to criticize the work of state institutions or their officials and to appeal against their decisions.

95 Art 5(1) of the UK Human Rights Act, 1998.

96 Philippines Revised Rules of Criminal Procedure, 2000.

97 Code of Criminal Procedure of the Kingdom of Cambodia, 2007.

both the legal and material aspects of the person's conviction and sentence.[98] In terms of the Constitution of the Russian Federation,

> any person convicted of a crime shall have the right to appeal against the verdict to a higher court in accordance with the procedure established by federal law, as well as to request pardon or mitigation of the punishment.[99]

Although the Sixth Amendment of US does not specifically refer to the right to review, US courts have stated that '[p]rocedural due process rules are meant to protect persons not from the deprivation, but from the mistaken or unjustified deprivation, of life, liberty, or property'.[100] Accordingly, the core elements of due process are those that minimize such substantively unfair or mistaken deprivations by enabling persons to contest the basis upon which a state proposes to deprive them of protected interests.[101]

In other cases, the ECtHR has repeatedly criticized France for allowing prolonged periods of detention on remand in relation to terrorist investigations. In one case detention on remand amounted to two years, 11 months and 13 days;[102] in another case to three years, nine months and 18 days;[103] and in another to over four years.[104] In 2006 the ECtHR dealt with the case of *Ramirez Sanchez v France*.[105] Sanchez complained about his solitary confinement for eight years pursuant to his conviction for terrorist-related offences. The Court found that Sanchez had been held in solitary confinement for eight years after his conviction on terrorism-related offences, had no means of challenging a decision to extend his detention in solitary confinement, and was deprived of his right of access to an effective remedy.[106]

The ACHPR Principles and Guidelines on Human and Peoples' Rights while Countering Terrorism in Africa further support the right to review. They provide that '[s]tates shall respect the principle of legality, non-discrimination,

98 See *Gómez v Spain* Communication No 701/1996 HRC (6 April 1998) UN Doc GAOR, A/55/40 (vol II) 109, para 11.1.
99 Art 50(3) of the Constitution of the Russian Federation, 1993.
100 *Mullane v Central Hanover Trust Co* 339 US 306, 313 (1950).
101 See *Carey v Piphus* 435 US 247, 259 (1978): 'Procedural due process rules are shaped by the risk of error inherent in the truth-finding process as applied to the generality of cases.'
102 *Gérard Bernard v France* Application No 27678/02, (judgment of 26 September 2006).
103 *Morgani v France* EComHR Application No 17831/91 (report of 30 November 1994).
104 *Debboub alias Husseini Ali v France* Application No 37786/97 (judgment of 9 November 1999).
105 *Ramirez Sanchez v France* Application No 59450/00 ECHR Grand Chamber judgment (4 July 2006) paras 165 and 179.
106 Ibid.

and procedural protection standards when it designates and sanctions an individual or entity as a terrorist', and state:

> States shall permit the listed individual or entity the right to apply for non-implementation or de-listing of the sanctions and a right to an independent, impartial adjudicative body to review the decision resulting from such application, with due process rights applying to such a review, including being able to provide a meaningful defense and ensuring that rules concerning the burden of proof are commensurate with the severity of the sanctions.[107]

3 Are the Core Fair Trial Rights *Jus Cogens*?

This section will consider whether the core fair trial rights discussed in section 2 above have attained the status of *jus cogens*. In order to evaluate this, regard must be had to the criteria and characteristics of *jus cogens* norms as discussed in chapter 3. The core fair trial rights will be discussed in light of the criteria for a norm to be a norm of *jus cogens* as set out in article 53 of the Vienna Convention on the Law of Treaties (Vienna Convention). As discussed in previous chapters, the criteria for elevation of a norm to *jus cogens* status are that it is a norm of general international law which is accepted and recognized by the international community of states as a whole as a norm from which no derogation is permitted.[108] This will be followed by a consideration of whether these core fair trial rights meet the characteristics of *jus cogens* norms, namely, that they reflect the fundamental rights of the international community of states as a whole, are hierarchically superior and are universally applicable.

3.1 *The Criteria under the Vienna Convention on the Law of Treaties*

3.1.1 A Norm of General International Law

General international law includes both rules of customary law and general principles of law.[109] As discussed earlier, the fact that the right to a fair trial is part of customary international law is beyond dispute and, as such, the right to a fair trial is part of general international law. In *Prosecutor v Aleksovski* the

107 ACHPR Principles and Guidelines on Human and Peoples' Rights While Countering Terrorism in Africa 28–29 <http://www.achpr.org/files/special-mechanisms/human-rights-defenders/principles_and_guidelines_on_human_and_peoples_rights_while_countering_terrorism_in_africa.pdf> accessed 21 October 2017.

108 See Ch 3 and art 53 of the Vienna Convention on the Law of Treaties 1969.

109 See eg sec 3.1.1 of ch 3.

ICTY stated that the right to a fair trial contained in article 14 of the ICCPR and article 21(4) of the ICTY Statute was 'of course' a requirement of customary international law.[110] Writers have further argued that both the UDHR and the provisions of article 14 of the ICCPR reflect customary international law.[111] It has been argued that 'the provision of article 14 on the right of an accused to a fair trial reflects customary international law is beyond dispute'.[112]

3.1.2 Accepted and Recognized

The next question is whether the core fair trial rights discussed in section 2 above, namely, the right of access to court, the presumption of innocence and the right to review, are accepted and recognized by the international community of states as a whole as norms from which no derogation is permitted. In other words, do states have the *opinio juris* that no derogation from these fair trial rights is permitted (*opinio juris cogentis*)?[113]

The inclusion of the right of access to a court, the presumption of innocence and the right to review in the national legislation and case law of various states,

---

110 *Prosecutor v Aleksovski* ICTY Case No IT-95-14/1-A (24 March 2000) 104, 113.

111 John Humphrey, 'The Universal Declaration of Human Rights: Its History, Impact and Juridical Character' in Bertrand Ramcharan (ed), *Human Rights: Thirty Years After the Universal Declaration* (Martinus Nijhoff 1979) 21, 37; Louis Sohn, 'The Human Rights Law of the Charter' (1977) 12 Texas International Law Journal 129, 133; Anthony d'Amato, *International Law: Process and Prospect* (Transnational Publishers 1986) 123–47; Michael Eidenmuller, 'Eleanor Roosevelt: On the Adoption of the Universal Declaration of Human Rights, 9 December 1948' <www.americanrhetoric.com/speeches/eleanorrooseveltdeclarationhumanrights.htm> accessed 11 March 2017, referring to the statement by Eleanor Roosevelt that the UDHR 'may well become the international Magna Carta of all men everywhere'. *Prosecutor v Duško Tadić* (n 21) 3; *Prosecutor v Aleksovski* (n 110) 104, 113 (stating that the right to a fair trial requirement contained in art 14 of the Covenant and art 21(4) of the ICTY Statute was 'of course' a requirement of customary international law); *Prosecutor v Furundžija* (n 54) 164 (commenting that the right to be tried before an independent and impartial tribunal was generally recognized as being an integral component of the requirement that an accused should have a fair trial, with reference to art 21(2) of the ICTY Statute and art 14 of the Covenant).

112 Patrick Robinson, 'The Right to a Fair Trial in International Law, with Specific Reference to the Work of the ICTY' (2009) 3 Berkeley Journal of International Law Publicist 6.

113 See draft Conclusion 11 Report of the International Law Commission (2014) 66th session (5 May–6 June 2014 and 7 July–8 August 2014) Supplement No 10 (A/69/10) 240. Examples of *opinio juris* include 'statements by States which indicate what are or are not rules of customary international law, diplomatic correspondence, the jurisprudence of national courts, the opinions of Government legal advisers, official publications in fields of international law, treaty practice and action in connection with resolutions of organs of international organizations and of international conferences. Inaction may also serve as evidence of acceptance as law.'

as discussed above, together with the absence of any provisions for derogation from these rights in national legislation, arguably support the view that these are norms of general international law that states accept and recognize as norms from which no derogation is permitted. However, states have in the past derogated from fair trial rights, in particular the prohibition on arbitrary arrest and the right to liberty. Between 1976 and 1984, and again from 1988 to 2001, the UK derogated from the ban on arbitrary arrest and detention in response to widespread murders, bombings and civil disturbances in Northern Ireland.[114] After the terrorist attacks in Paris, France stated that it 'may' derogate from the ICCPR, including from the right to liberty.[115] It has been argued that many of these provisions would be 'usual suspects' for derogation during a state of emergency and that none of the explicitly non-derogable provisions listed in article 4(2) of the ICCPR has been included. Furthermore, derogations did not seem specifically to reference rights such as the right to a fair trial or the presumption of innocence.

Turkey's notification of derogations from the ICCPR published by the United Nations (UN) in 2016 illustrated a different approach. Turkey's notification provided a list of articles from which Turkey may derogate, including the right to liberty, movement, privacy and family, but also the right to a remedy, the humane treatment of detainees and the right to a fair trial.[116] The derogation from the right to a remedy, the right to human treatment and the right to a fair trial have been criticized as ill-advised.[117] Martin Scheinin has noted that one of the items that appear to not be permissible in this list is the derogation from the right to a remedy, where HRC General Comment 29 makes it very clear that this right is not subject to derogation. Further, although countries have

114 *Ireland v the United Kingdom* Application No 5310/71 ECHR (1978) 602 Yearbook of European Convention on Human Rights (Judgment) para 212.

115 *Le Monde France* 'New Emergency Powers Threaten Rights Parliament Should Ensure New Powers Not Misused' <https://www.hrw.org/news/2015/11/24/france-new-emergency-powers-threaten-rights> accessed 21 May 2017, stating that 'President Francois Hollande declared a state of emergency following the November 13 attacks in Paris. Since the state of emergency was declared, *Le Monde* reported, on November 23, French authorities had conducted 1 072 searches without judicial warrants and 139 stops leading to 117 pre-charge detentions; placed 253 people under house arrest; and discovered 201 weapons.'

116 Martin Scheinin, 'Turkey's Derogation from Human Rights Treaties – An Update' <www.ejiltalk.org/turkeys-derogation-from-human-rights-treaties-an-update/> accessed 10 March 2017. Turkey also filed derogations in respect of various other articles of the ICCPR: the humane treatment of detainees (art 10); safeguards against expulsion (art 13); expression (art 19); assembly (art 21); association (art 22); political participation (art 25); equality and nondiscrimination (art 26); minority rights (art 27).

117 Scheinin (n 116).

derogated from the right to a fair trial in periods of public emergency, it has been argued that these states 'almost invariably represent that the procedures which they adopt are fair in the context of those exceptional circumstances'.[118] For example, Turkey appears to be keeping the Council of Europe informed of its measures taken pursuant to the state of emergency and that its measures will remain within the exigencies of the situation. During the drafting of the ICCPR the US delegation originally argued for an inclusion of the entire fair trial provision among the explicitly non-derogable rights in the ICCPR.[119]

Moreover, various declaratory instruments guarantee the right to a fair trial before an independent and impartial tribunal.[120] Guideline IX of the Guidelines of the Committee of Ministers of the Council of Europe on Human Rights and the Fight against Terrorism stipulates that a person accused of terrorist activities has the right to a hearing by an independent, impartial tribunal established by law.[121] This is echoed in article XXVI of the American Declaration of the Rights and Duties of Man (ADRDM) which similarly guarantees the right of everyone to a hearing by an independent and impartial tribunal.[122] The principle of consistency contained in article 4(1) of the ICCPR requires that derogation measures are consistent with a state's other international legal obligations. Based on the principle of consistency, it may be argued that those aspects of a fair trial that are common to the legal regimes dealing with international armed conflict, on the one hand, and internal armed conflicts, on the other, must be provided in all types of emergency, including in emergencies that fall short of the legal threshold of an armed conflict. Any derogation from these aspects would be inconsistent with the customary law which remains applicable even in the worst cases of emergency, and, therefore, would invalidate the derogation.[123] A recommendation by the Committee

118 Robinson (n 112) 7.

119 See Robinson (n 112) 36; Commission on Human Rights Summary Records of the 325th meeting E/CN4/325 (13 June 1949) for the proposal of the US that '[t]he rights and freedoms set forth in … article 13 [14], article 14 [15] and article 15 [16], of this Covenant shall not be subject to any limitation'. See further Draft International Covenant on Human Rights UN Economic and Social Council E/CN.4/SR.195 (29 May 1950) para 140. The United States were voting in favour of accepting the proposal to include the full fair trial provision among the non-derogable rights.

120 Art 20 of the Association of Southeast Asian Nations (ASEAN) Human Rights Declaration (n 31); American Declaration of the Rights and Duties of Man (ADRDM), 1949.

121 Council of Europe: Committee of Ministers Guidelines on Human Rights and the Fight against Terrorism, 11 July 2002 <https://refworld.org/docid/47fdfb220.html> accessed 21 May 2017.

122 Art XXVI of the ADRDM.

123 Robinson (n 112) 43.

to the Sub-Commission on the Prevention of Discrimination and Protection of Minorities concerning a draft third optional protocol to the ICCPR provided:

> The Committee is satisfied that states parties generally understand that the right to *habeas corpus* and *amparo* should not be limited in situations of emergency. Furthermore, the Committee is of the view that the remedies provided in article 9, paragraphs 3 and 4, read in conjunction with article 2 are inherent to the Covenant as a whole.[124]

In light of the above it is argued that the core fair trial rights of access to a hearing before a tribunal, the right to be presumed innocent and the right to a remedy meet the criteria for *jus cogens* norms, namely, that they are accepted and recognized by the international community of states as a whole as norms from which no derogation is permitted. The next section will consider whether core fair trial rights, in addition to meeting the criteria for a *jus cogens* norm, display the characteristics of *jus cogens* norms.

4 Core Characteristics

While meeting the criteria of the Vienna Convention is sufficient for the core elements of the right to a fair trial discussed above to qualify as norms of *jus cogens*, an analysis of the characteristics of *jus cogens* norms further support why certain elements of the right to a fair trial are regarded as non-derogable by the international community. This section considers whether the right to a fair hearing, the presumption of innocence and the right to review exhibit the characteristics of *jus cogens* norms.

The core elements of the right to a fair trial protect fundamental values, such as the right to freedom, the right to human dignity and equality before the law.[125] These values are encapsulated by the right to a fair hearing by an impartial tribunal, the presumption of innocence and the right to an effective remedy. Derogation from these core rights would entail the arbitrary deprivation of freedom without just cause and infringe upon the right to human dignity and the right to an effective remedy, as well as the substantive fairness of a hearing. It is further argued that the core fair trial rights are hierarchically

124 UN Doc A/49/40 paras 22–25.

125 Nsongurua J Udombana, 'The African Commission on Human and Peoples' Rights and the Development of Fair Trial Norms in Africa' (2006) 6 African Human Rights Law Journal 298–332 sec 2.1.

superior in that they nullify contradictory norms and are universally applicable. These rights apply in situations of both peace and armed conflict, and it would be difficult to imagine an agreement or legislation negating the right of an accused to be presumed innocent, to have access to a court and to have the right of review.

5 Core Fair Trial Rights and the *Jus Cogens* Prohibition of Terrorism

This section will consider the interaction between the core fair trial rights discussed above (the presumption of innocence, the right to a hearing before a fair and impartial tribunal and the right to review) and the *jus cogens* prohibition of terrorism. In considering a possible balancing of rights between the prohibition of terrorism and the right to a fair trial, it must be considered which underlying values are protected by these norms. Both norms aim to safeguard the underlying right to human dignity. In this regard, the prohibition of terrorism safeguards the right of human beings not to be used as a means to an end, and core fair trial rights guarantee the right not to be arbitrarily deprived of one's liberty.

This section will explore whether case law and legal doctrine support upholding core fair trial rights in the face of counter-terrorism measures.[126] With regard to the right of an accused to have his matter heard before a fair and impartial tribunal, the *Kadi* case will be used for illustrative purposes. *Kadi* concerned the regime based on UNSC Resolution 1267, which obliges UN member states to impose certain sanctions against the Taliban, al Qaeda and associated

126 Writers have confirmed that, at a minimum, the rights to be accorded to an individual should include the right to be informed of charges against him/her, the right to be heard, the right to judicial review and the right to an effective remedy. See Gavin Sullivan and Ben Hayes, 'Blacklisted: Targeted Sanctions, Preemptive Security and Human Rights: European Centre for Constitutional and Human Rights' <www.tni.org/files/Blacklisted%20-%20Executive%20summary.pdf> accessed 5 July 2017. See further Erika de Wet, 'Human Rights Considerations and the Enforcement of Targeted Sanctions in Europe: The Emergence of Core Standards of Judicial Review in Securing Human Rights?' in Bardo Fassbender (ed), *Securing Human Rights? Achievements and Challenges of the Security Council* (Oxford University Press 2011) who argues that the right to a hearing requires that the listed individuals or entities are provided with sufficient information to be able to adequately state their case. They must be notified of the evidence against them and provided with a statement of reasons for the decision to list them. De Wet stresses that (under European Law) the right to a fair hearing applies to all decisions that can culminate in a measure adversely affecting a person.

individuals and entities.[127] Sanctions are administered with reference to a list regulated by a Committee of the United Nations Security Council (UNSC) and states can propose the names of individuals and entities for inclusion in the list, without such affected parties having any right to challenge their inclusion on this list.[128] Kadi attacked this targeted sanctioning of individuals and argued that it constituted a violation of the right of listed individuals to be heard, as well as their property rights and rights to effective judicial review.[129] It was alleged that the 1267 regime infringed upon basic due process standards, specifically a lack of fairness with regard to listing and delisting procedures.[130] The ECHR held that the relevant legislation implementing the 1267 regime violated the right of listed individuals to be heard in that they were not provided with the opportunity to present their side of the case in a meaningful way.[131] Statements by certain states before the UNSC criticized the 1267 listing procedures. For example, Mr Adekanye, on behalf of Nigeria, stated that

> a situation in which a person or entities are included on a list before the affected states are informed is against both the peremptory norms of fair trials and the principle of the rule of law. Nigeria is therefore opposed to any breach of those peremptory norms.[132]

Although Nigeria did not stipulate to which specific fair trial norms it was referring, arguably inclusion on the list discussed above without having been afforded an opportunity to challenge such inclusion negates both the right of access to court as well as the right to review. In this regard it is argued that the ombudsperson procedure created in 2009 in terms of which individuals could

127 See SC/RES 1267 (1999). See further United Nations Global Counter-Terrorism Strategy, GA Res 288 (2006) para 15, Annex II; Dire Tladi and Gillian Taylor, 'On the Al Qaeda/Taliban Sanctions Regime: Due Process and Sunsetting' (2011) 10 Chinese Journal of International Law 771 para 5.

128 Tladi and Taylor (n 127) para 7; S/RES 1267 para 6.

129 *Kadi* (n 125); *Yusuf and Al Barakaat* (n 125); *Kadi v Commission* Judgment of the General Court (Seventh Chamber) (30 September 2010) Case T-85/09; De Wet (n 126) 141. See, eg, A Posch, 'The *Kadi* Case: Rethinking the Relationship between EU Law and International Law?' (2009) 15 Columbia Journal of Economic Literature 1; Johannes Reich, 'Due Process and Sanctions Targeted against Individuals Pursuant to Resolution 1267 of 1999 (2008) 33 Yale Journal of International Law 505; see further United Nations Global Counter-Terrorism Strategy (n 127) para 15, Annex II.

130 See, e.g., Posch (ibid.); Reich (ibid.); see further United Nations Global Counter Terrorism Strategy (n 127) para 15, Annex II (2008).

131 *Kadi* (n 125) para 334.

132 Statement by Nigeria, 5474th Meeting of the UN Security Council, 22 June 2006 (S/PV5474).

submit a request for delisting to the ombudsman, who would gather information from the state involved and make a recommendation to the CTC, introduced a form of review.[133] The importance of fair trial rights and continuing concerns over listing procedures is further evident in a 2017 resolution by the Institute of International Law Review of Measures Implementing Decisions of the Security Council in the Field of Targeted Sanctions. This resolution noted that judgments in national and regional courts have declared that 'national or European Union measures implementing targeted sanctions against individuals or entities have violated human rights, including the right to a fair trial, of those who have been targeted'.[134] It provided that targeted sanctions can be reviewed by national or regional courts and argued that, in the course of such review, those courts may interpret relevant UNSC decisions. It further states that sanctions committees shall fully respect the UN Charter, including the provisions protecting human rights. It further provides that the ombudsperson procedure, created in 2009, be applied to 'all such regimes, present and future, when providing for the prescription of targeted sanctions, that its procedure be rendered more transparent' and that 'considering the possible human rights consequences of listing, such a process shall respect international, regional and national human rights standards'.[135]

The right to be presumed innocent has further been upheld in the context of the prohibition of terrorism. In this regard, in the 1970s and 1980s parliamentary legislation gave special powers of arrest and detention to the police in light of the terrorism in Northern Ireland that caused thousands of deaths.[136] In *Heaney and McGuinness v Ireland* the two applicants were arrested on the suspicion of a serious terrorist offence, namely, a bombing at a British army checkpoint that killed five people.[137] After having been cautioned by police officers that they had the right to remain silent, they were nevertheless requested, under section 52 of the Offences Against the State Act of 1939, to provide details about their movements at the time of the relevant offences.[138] The ECtHR

133 See S/RES/1904 (2009) creating the Office of the Ombudsperson (ISIL and Al-Qaeda Sanctions List).

134 See Institute of International Law 'Review of Measures Implementing Decisions of the Security Council in the Field of Targeted Sanctions' Twelfth Commission Judicial Review of Security Council Decisions (9 September 2017) (on file with author).

135 Ibid., paras 4.2, 7.3 and 9(1)(b).

136 *Brogan & Others v the United Kingdom* ECHR (29 November 1988) Ser A No 145-B 1.

137 *Heaney and McGuinness v Ireland* (1996) 1 IR 580.

138 Sec 52 of the 1939 Act reads as follows: '1 Whenever a person is detained in custody under the provisions in that behalf contained in Part IV of this Act, any member of the [police] may demand of such person, at any time while he is so detained, a full account of such person's movements and actions during any specified period and all information in his

found that the security and public order concerns relied on by the government could not justify a provision that extinguishes the essence of the applicants' rights to silence and against self-incrimination guaranteed by the ECHR.[139]

Concerns were raised about the apparent erosion of the presumption of innocence and the notion that to be accused of terrorism is tantamount to being considered guilty.[140] In terms of the Guidelines on Human Rights and the Fight against Terrorism, '[a] person accused of terrorist activities benefits from the presumption of innocence'.[141]Human rights activists have been arguing that Guantanamo detainees must be brought to the US and tried in a federal court.[142] Further concerns have been raised regarding the failure to

---

possession in relation to the commission or intended commission by another person of any offence under any section or sub-section of this Act or any scheduled offence. 2 If any person, of whom any such account or information as is mentioned in the foregoing sub-section of this section is demanded under that sub-section by a member of the [police], fails or refuses to give to such member such account or any such information or gives to such member any account or information which is false or misleading, he shall be guilty of an offence under this section and shall be liable on summary conviction thereof to imprisonment for a term not exceeding six months.'

139 Ibid., paras 8–10.

140 Karen Greenberg, 'Guilty Until Proven Guilty: The Presumption of Innocence and the Trial of Ahmed Khalfan Ghailani' (11 October 2017) <www.motherjones.com/politics/2010/11/ahmed-khalfan-ghailani-verdict/.> accessed 22 October 2017. Greenberg is of the view that '[a]lthough it is increasingly politically incorrect to insist on this point, in the American system of justice, a trial – even in the context of terrorism – should not, in fact, have a foreordained verdict. That verdict should not be known in advance, nor should it, in essence, need to be announced by the Attorney General before the trial begins. A jury should consider all the facts that the law allows to be presented to them in the context of the presumption of innocence; and those 12 jurors should come up with their own determination of guilt or innocence. With terrorism trials, the more serious they get, the more the presumption of innocence seems to lie at the mercy of politics.' See further 'Will Accused 9/11 Architect Khalid Sheikh Mohammed Ever Come to Trial?' *The Guardian* <www.theguardian.com/us-news/2017/sep/11/will-khalid-sheikh-mohammed-come-to-trial-9-11-attacks> accessed 22 October 2017.

141 Ch IX(2) of the Guidelines On Human Rights And The Fight Against Terrorism adopted by the Committee of Ministers of the Council of Europe in 2002 at its 804th meeting (11 July 2002). Ch IX(2) further states that '[a] person accused of terrorist activities has the right to a fair hearing, within a reasonable time, by an independent, impartial tribunal established by law' and that '[t]he imperatives of the fight against terrorism may nevertheless justify certain restrictions to the right of defence, in particular with regard to (i) the arrangements for access to and contacts with counsel; (ii) the arrangements for access to the case-file; (iii) the use of anonymous testimony. 4 Such restrictions to the right of defence must be strictly proportionate to their purpose, and compensatory measures to protect the interests of the accused must be taken so as to maintain the fairness of the proceedings and to ensure that procedural rights are not drained of their substance.'

142 Greenberg (n 140).

bring Khalid Sheikh Mohammed, thought to be the operational mastermind behind the attacks of 9/11, to trial. It appeared that, owing to security and other concerns, the US government decided that it was too risky to try his case before a jury of civilians in a US federal court. It is, however, doubtful whether Mohammed will receive a fair trial via a military commission at Guantanamo Bay. The result is that, over two decades after 9/11, the accused will still be in Guantanamo Bay, preparing for his next pre-trial hearing, while his defence counsel are of the view that Mohammed may die before the matter is finally brought to trial.[143] This may infringe his right to innocence, as well as his right to a hearing.

With regard to the right to review, the ECtHR has supported this right in cases involving terrorism. For example, in the *Brogan* case four persons were arrested and detained under the Prevention of Terrorism Act of 1984 in terms of which persons could be arrested and detained without warrant or charge.[144] The Secretary of State further agreed to a police request for an extension of detention in the case of all the accused.[145] The accused were not brought before a judge nor were they charged after their release, which occurred after periods of detention ranging from between four to six days.[146] The UK government relied on the special security context of Northern Ireland to justify the length of the detention periods, but the Court found that even the shortest periods of detention would have resulted in consequences impairing the very essence of the right to a trial within a reasonable time as the applicants were neither promptly brought before a judicial authority nor promptly released following their arrest.[147] The Court concluded that the argument that the arrest and detention of the applicants were inspired by the legitimate aim of protecting the community as a whole from terrorism did not justify an infringement of the right to a trial within a reasonable time.[148] Similarly, in *A & Others v Secretary of State for the Home Department* the applicants alleged that they were detained under a UK statutory scheme which allowed for the indefinite detention of

143 Ibid.

144 *Brogan & Others v the United Kingdom* ECHR (29 November 1988) Ser A No 145-B 1.

145 Ibid.

146 Ibid.

147 Ibid., 6–7.

148 Ibid. Art 15 of the ECHR states: '1 In time of war or other public emergency threatening the life of the nation any High Contracting Party may take measures derogating from its obligations under this Convention to the extent strictly required by the exigencies of the situation, provided that such measures are not inconsistent with its other obligations under international law. 2 No derogation from article 2, except in respect of deaths resulting from lawful acts of war, or from articles 3, 4 (paragraph 1) and 7 shall be made under this provision.'

non-nationals certified by the Secretary of State as being suspected of involvement in terrorism.[149] The House of Lords declared this measure incompatible with the right to liberty and the prohibition of discrimination in the ECHR.[150]

In *Hamdi v Rumsfeld* the US Supreme Court held that detainees had the right of *habeas corpus* to challenge their detention.[151] Hamdi, an American citizen, was captured by the Afghan Northern Alliance forces allied with the US and detained indefinitely without charge, based on the government's assertion that he was an unlawful combatant and not a prisoner of war and, thus, did not enjoy the protection of the Geneva Conventions.[152] He was denied any opportunity to challenge the assertion that he was an unlawful combatant, and denied access to counsel.[153] The US Supreme Court held that a citizen detained by the government as an enemy combatant is entitled to a meaningful opportunity to contest the facts on which his detention is based before a neutral decision maker, and that Hamdi, therefore, could challenge his detention.[154] In *Hamdan v Rumsfeld*, the applicant, suspected of terrorism, was transported to Guantanamo Bay in 2002 and declared to be eligible for trial by military commission only a year later

149 *A & Others v Secretary of State for the Home Department* (2004) UKHL 56 (16 December 2004); Anti-Terrorism, Crimes and Security Act, 2001.

150 *A & Others* (n 149).

151 *Hamdi v Rumsfeld* 542 US 507 (2004). See further Report of the Special Rapporteur on the Promotion and Protection of Human Rights and Fundamental Freedoms While Countering Terrorism, Martin Scheinin, A/HRC/16/51 (10 December 2010) para 35(i), which provides for the protection of individual rights during counter-terrorism measures and states as follows: '(i) Intent: The sanctions against an individual or entity shall be based on reasonable grounds to believe that the individual or entity had knowingly and with intent carried out, supported, participated in, or facilitated a terrorist act. (ii) Notification: States shall promptly and fully inform the individual or entity of the accusations or charges; states shall provide the individual or entity with any decision taken and the reasons for that decision; and states shall inform the individual or entity of the consequences of the accusations or charges. If relevant, the listing state shall also promptly and fully inform the state to which the individual or entity belongs. (iii) Appeal and De-Listing: States shall permit the listed individual or entity the right to apply for non-implementation or de-listing of the sanctions and a right to an independent, impartial adjudicative body to review the decision resulting from such application, with due process rights applying to such a review, including being able to provide a meaningful defence and ensuring that rules concerning the burden of proof are commensurate with the severity of the sanctions. If relevant, the listing state shall also promptly and fully inform the state to which the individual or entity belongs if de-listing occurs. (iv) Reparations: States shall provide reparation for any violation of an individual's rights associated with listing laws and procedures.'

152 See *Hamdi v Rumsfeld*, 296F3d 278, 281 (4th Cir 2002); *Hamdi v Rumsfeld* (n 151).

153 *Hamdi v Rumsfeld* (2002) (n 152).

154 *Hamdi v Rumsfeld* 124 S Ct 2635 (2004) (plurality opinion) 2635.

for then unspecified crimes.[155] After another year, he was charged with conspiracy to commit offences triable by a military commission.[156] Hamdan alleged *inter alia* that the procedures adopted by the commission to try him contravened military and international law, including the principle that a defendant must be permitted to see and hear the evidence against him (he did not have access to such evidence).[157] The US Supreme Court held that the procedures of the military commissions had violated *inter alia* Common Article 3 of the Geneva Conventions.[158] Judge Stevens stated:

> When assuming that Hamden is a dangerous individual who would cause great harm or death to innocent civilians given the opportunity, the Executive nevertheless must comply with the prevailing rule of law in undertaking to try him and subject him to criminal punishment.[159]

It is argued that it is simply not possible to limit the core non-derogable fair trial rights in a manner that does not result in a 'flagrant denial of justice.'[160]

---

155 *Hamdan v Rumsfeld* 548 US 557 (29 June 2006).

156 Ibid.

157 Ibid., 49–52. Judge Stevens held that '[t]he Commission's procedures, set forth in Commission Order No 1, provide, among other things, that an accused and his civilian counsel may be excluded from, and precluded from ever learning what evidence was presented during, any part of the proceeding the official who appointed the commission or the presiding officer decides to "close". Grounds for closure include the protection of classified information, the physical safety of participants and witnesses, the protection of intelligence and law enforcement sources, methods, or activities, and "other national security interests". Appointed military defence counsel must be privy to these closed sessions, but may, at the presiding officer's discretion, be forbidden to reveal to the client what took place therein. Another striking feature is that the rules governing Hamdan's commission permit the admission of any evidence that, in the presiding officer's opinion, would have probative value to a reasonable person. Moreover, the accused and his civilian counsel may be denied access to classified and other "protected information", so long as the presiding officer concludes that the evidence is "probative" and that its admission without the accused's knowledge would not result in the denial of a full and fair trial.'

158 Ibid., 52–53. See further ibid., 62–68: Judge Stevens determined that Common Article 3 to the Geneva Conventions of 1949 applies as a matter of law to the conflict with al Qaeda and that the procedures of military commissions as constituted by the Department of Defence were not consistent with Common Article 3.

159 Ibid., 72.

160 *Othman (Abu Qatada) v The United Kingdom* Application No 8139/09 ECHR (17 January 2012) 183–184 para 260. In Qatada, the Court states that 'a flagrant denial of justice goes beyond mere irregularities or lack of safeguards in the trial procedures such as might result in a breach of article 6 if occurring within the contracting state itself. What is required is a breach of the principles of fair trial guaranteed by article 6 which is so fundamental as to amount to a nullification, or destruction of the very essence, of the right guaranteed

The ECtHR has stated that a flagrant denial of justice goes beyond mere irregularities or lack of safeguards in the trial procedures. What is required is a breach of the principles of fair trial guaranteed by article 6 which is so fundamental as to amount to a nullification, or destruction, of the very essence of the right guaranteed by that article.[161] These core fair trial rights are inextricably linked to substantive justice.[162]

Moreover, there is no legal antinomy between the prohibition of terrorism as a *jus cogens* norm, on the one hand, and core fair trial rights as *jus cogens* norms, on the other. The aforementioned norms are not contrary norms which cannot be applied in their entirety to the same situation or which require the invalidity or limitation of one of the norms in order to apply both to counter-terrorism measures. As was the case with the prohibition of torture and terrorism, it is impossible to justify that one competing norm should prevail over another, as these norms embody similar and equally important underlying values.[163] In this regard, with regard to a possible balancing of rights or a limitation of core fair trial rights in the context of the prohibition of terrorism as a *jus cogens* norm, the statement by Justice Sachs in the *Basson case* before the South African Constitutional Court of may be illustrative:

> [T]he effective prosecution of war crimes and the rights of the accused to a fair trial are not antagonistic concepts. On the contrary, both stem from the same constitutional and humanitarian foundation, namely the need to uphold the rule of law and the basic principles of human dignity, equality and freedom.[164]

---

by that article.' See, further, *Snyder v Massachussets* 291 US 97 (1934) 201. In *Snyder*, the US Supreme Court stated that 'due process of law requires that the proceedings must be fair, but that fairness is a relative, not an absolute concept: It is fairness with reference to particular conditions or particular results. As applied to a criminal trial, denial of due process is the failure to observe that fundamental fairness essential to the very concept of justice. In order to declare a denial of it [the Court] must find that the absence of that fairness fatally infected the trial.'

161 Ibid.

162 *Qatada* (n 160).

163 See further UNSC Resolution 2178 (2014) where the UNSC reaffirms that member states must ensure that any measures taken to counter terrorism comply with all their obligations under international law, in particular international human rights law, international refugee law, and international humanitarian law.

164 *S v Wouter Basson* (2004) (judgment) CCT 30/03 para 126.

6 Conclusion

This book aims to evaluate the role of *jus cogens* in the rules of international law relating to terrorism. The previous chapter considered the effect of the prohibition of terrorism as a *jus cogens* norm on the prohibition of torture, and it found that the prohibition of torture itself is a *jus cogens* norm, an absolute prohibition that is not subject to limitation, even in the context of another *jus cogens* norm such as the prohibition of terrorism.

The question addressed in this chapter has been whether counter-terrorism measures taken in support of the prohibition of terrorism can limit the right to a fair trial, and, in particular, those elements of the right to a fair trial that have been suggested as being non-derogable, namely, the right to a hearing before an impartial tribunal, the presumption of innocence and the right to review. While certain fair trial rights are capable of derogation in terms of article 4(1) of the ICCPR, such as the right to witnesses, the right to a public hearing and the right to legal counsel, it was found that the non-derogation of the core fair trial rights proposed are supported by treaty law, state practice and international jurisprudence.

Furthermore, this chapter has found that these core fair trial rights meet the requirements for a *jus cogens* norm under section 53 of the Vienna Convention as they are norms of general international law, accepted and recognized by the international community of states as a whole as norms from which no derogation is permitted. Even when states have filed notices of derogation from fair trial norms, this typically did not relate to the norms proposed in this chapter as non-derogable. The right to a hearing, the presumption of innocence and the right to review display the characteristics of *jus cogens* norms as they protect the fundamental values of the international community, are hierarchically superior and are universally applicable. Moreover, it was found that these core fair trial rights have been upheld in the context of terrorism. In light of the underlying value of human dignity protected by core fair trial norms and the prohibition of terrorism respectively, no limitation of either of these norms is necessary or possible, and both norms can be applied in their entirety in the context of anti-terrorism measures.

CHAPTER 5

The Prohibition of Terrorism and International Law Relating to the Use of Force

1 Introduction

This book aims to evaluate the role of *jus cogens* in the rules of international law relating to terrorism. Part I explored the prohibition of terrorism under international law and considered the elements of a definition of terrorism that have emerged under international law. Chapter 2 found that a rule prohibiting terrorism is supported in both treaty law and state practice. Chapter 3 illustrated that the prohibition of terrorism meets the criteria for a *jus cogens* norm as set out in the Vienna Convention on the Law of Treaties as well as possessing the core characteristics of a *jus cogens* norm, namely, the protection of the fundamental values of the international community, hierarchical superiority and universal applicability.

Part II explored the issue of whether the prohibition of terrorism may have led to the limitation of other norms of international law, norms which themselves may constitute norms of *jus cogens*, namely, the prohibition of torture, the right to a fair trial and the prohibition of the use of force. Chapter 4 found that the prohibition of terrorism and the prohibition of torture were both *jus cogens* norms from which no derogation is permitted. Chapter 5 illustrated that the non-derogable elements of the right to a fair trial are not capable of limitation in the context of counter-terrorism measures without compromising the overall right to a fair trial.

This chapter will explore the interaction between the prohibition of terrorism and the use of force. It will explore whether the fact that attacks against states are being committed by non-state actors, namely, terrorist organizations, affects the law on the use of force, and in particular whether the prohibition of terrorism as a *jus cogens* norm may expand the exceptions to the use of armed force in anticipatory self-defence against terrorists. The analysis in this chapter will follow a different structure from that of chapters 5 and 6. Unlike the prohibition of torture and the right to a fair trial, the *jus cogens* status of the prohibition on the use of force under international law is beyond dispute.[1]

1 *Armed Activities on the Territory of the Congo* (*DRC v Rwanda*), Preliminary Objections 2006 ICJ Reports 148 ('[t]he prohibition against the use of force is a cornerstone of the United

 | DOI:10.1163/9789004391543_007

Section 2 will therefore be limited to an overview of international law governing the use of force, in light of the general acceptance of the prohibition of the use of force as a *jus cogens* norm. Section 2 will consider the status of the prohibition of force as a norm of *jus cogens* under treaty law, focusing on the UN Charter, as well as its status under customary international law and international jurisprudence. Section 3 will discuss the scope of the prohibition of force under international law and attempt to clarify which uses of force are prohibited. In this regard, it will consider the concepts of the use of force, aggression, and armed attack. It will further consider whether the threat of the use of force and the use of force in self-defence in themselves constitute *jus cogens* norms. This discussion is important in order to evaluate whether a particular terrorist attack involves the use of force in respect of which states may use armed force in self-defence.

Section 4 will discuss the requirements for the use of force in self-defence and anticipatory self-defence against non-state actors. The requirements of the existence of an armed attack to justify self-defence under the UN Charter, the requirements of necessity and proportionality for the use of force in self-defence under customary international law and the attribution of the acts of non-state actors to states will be considered. This section will then discuss whether the prohibition of terrorism as a *jus cogens* norm has affected the scope of the use of force in self-defence against terrorists. In other words, does the prohibition of terrorism as a *jus cogens* norm influence the boundaries of what is considered to be an armed attack as well as possibly lower the standard of attribution in order to attribute the acts of non-state actors to a state, thus reducing the scope of the prohibition of the use of force? Does it result in a relaxation of the requirements of necessity and proportionality in responding to terrorist attacks? Finally, in considering the interaction between the prohibition of terrorism and the prohibition of force, section 5 will evaluate whether there is any normative conflict between these two norms and, if so, how such a conflict can be resolved. International instruments and court decisions will be used as primary sources, complemented by academic literature.

Nations Charter'); *Nicaragua v US* Merits (27 June 1986) (1986) ICJ Reports 14 153 (separate opinion of President Singh referring to the prohibition of the use of force as 'the very cornerstone of the human effort to promote peace in a world torn by strife'); *Case Concerning Oil Platforms* (*Islamic Republic of Iran v United States of America*) ICJ (6 November 2003) (2003) ICJ Reports 161 (dissenting opinion of Judge Elaraby) 291 ('[t]he principle of the prohibition of the use of force in international relations … is, no doubt, the most important principle in contemporary international law to govern inter-state conduct; it is indeed the cornerstone of the Charter'); separate opinion of Judge Simma 328; Christopher Joyner, *International Law for the 21st Century* (Rowman & Littlefield Publishers 2005) 165.

2 The Use of Force: an Overview

The ban on the use of inter-state force is widely held to be peremptory in nature, and it has often been described as the cornerstone of the modern international system.[2] The Kellogg-Briand Pact provided for the renunciation of war as an instrument of national policy.[3] Pledging to 'save succeeding generations from the scourge of war', decades later the framers of the UN Charter established a normative order prohibiting the unlawful use of force.[4] In terms of article 2(4) of the Charter, states were to 'refrain in their international relations from the threat or use of force against the territorial integrity or political independence of any state or in any other manner inconsistent with the purposes of the United Nations'. The Charter provided for only two explicit exceptions to this prohibition: the use of force authorized by the UNSC and the use of force in self-defence.[5] In this regard it has been argued that article 51 of the UN Charter was not intended to create a new right of self-defence, but rather recognized the inherent right of self-defence which states already enjoy under international law.[6]

2 Ibid.

3 General Treaty for Renunciation of War as an Instrument of National Policy of 1928 (Kellogg-Briand Pact), League of Nations, Treaty Series, Vol 94, 57 (No 2137). Art I provides that '[t]he High Contracting Parties solemnly declare in the names of their respective peoples that they condemn recourse to war for the solution of international controversies, and renounce it, as an instrument of national policy in their relations with one another'. Article II provides that '[t]he High Contracting Parties agree that the settlement or solution of all disputes or conflicts of whatever nature or of whatever origin they may be, which may arise among them, shall never be sought except by pacific means'. The prohibition applied to war and not to the use of force, and forcible measures 'short of war' were eliminated from consideration. This was addressed in the UN Charter which explicitly prohibited the use of force in art 2(4).

4 Preamble and arts 1, 2, 33, 39, 42 and 51 of the United Nations (UN) Charter, 1945. In terms of art 1 of the UN Charter, the purpose of the UN is 'to maintain international peace and security'. The general prohibition on the use of force is set out in art 2 of the UN Charter. Art 2(3) provides that UN members must settle international disputes by peaceful means; art 2(4) states that '[a]ll members shall refrain in their international relations from the threat or use of force against the territorial integrity or political independence of any state or in any other manner inconsistent with the purposes of the United Nations'. Art 51 provides that '[n]othing in the present Charter shall impair the inherent right of individual or collective self-defence if an armed attack occurs against a member of the United Nations'.

5 Ibid., art 51 and ch VII, arts 39 and 42.

6 Daniel Bethlehem, 'Self-Defence Against an Imminent or Actual Armed Attack by Nonstate Actors' (2012) 106 American Journal of International Law 771; James Green, 'Questioning the Peremptory Status of the Prohibition of the Use of Force' (2011) 32 Michigan Journal of International Law 215–216, 222; Hermann Mosler, 'The International Society as a Legal

Furthermore, United Nations General Assembly (UNGA) resolutions have confirmed the obligation of UN members to refrain from the threat or use of force subject to the exceptions on the UN Charter.[7] For example, the UNGA Declaration on the Enhancement of the Effectiveness of the Principle of Refraining from Threat or Use of Force in International Relations contains detailed provisions dealing with the prohibition of the use of force, subject to the fact that states have the inherent right of individual or collective self-defence if an armed attack occurs.[8] UNSC resolutions do not explicitly prohibit or authorize the use of force, but support the right to self-defence.[9]

Community' (1974) 140 1 Recueil Des Cours 1, 283; *Nicaragua* (n 1) 176; *Legality of the Threat or Use of Nuclear Weapons* ICJ (8 July 1996) (1996) ICJ Reports 226.

7 Universal Declaration of Human Rights 1948; Geneva Convention for the Protection of War Victims, 1949; International Covenant on Civil and Political Rights, 1966; Preamble and art 1 of the UNGA Declaration on the Inadmissibility of Intervention in the Domestic Affairs of states and the Protection of Their Independence and Sovereignty, A/RES/2131 (XX)(1965); Principles 1 and 2(3) of the UNGA Declaration on Principles of International Law Concerning Friendly Relations and Cooperation among States in Accordance with the Charter of the United Nations, A/RES/2625 (XXV)(1970), UNGA Definition of Aggression, A/RES/3314 (XXIX) (1974); UNGA Manila Declaration on the Peaceful Settlement of Disputes, A/RES/37/10 (1982); arts 1–4 and 13 of the Declaration on the Enhancement of the Effectiveness of the Principle of Refraining from Threat or Use of Force in International Relations A/RES/42/22 (1987); Preamble and arts 1(3) and 23 of the UNGA Declaration on the Prevention and Removal of Disputes and Situations which may threaten International Peace and Security and on the Role of the UN in this Field A/RES/43/51 (1988).

8 Arts 1–4 and 13 of A/RES/42/22 (1987): '1 Every state has the duty to refrain in its international relations from the threat or use of force against the territorial integrity or political independence of any state, or from acting in any other manner inconsistent with the purposes of the United Nations. Such a threat or use of force constitutes a violation of international law and of the Charter of the United Nations and entails international responsibility. 2 The principle of refraining from the threat or use of force in international relations is universal in character and is binding, regardless of each state's political, economic, social or cultural system or relations of alliance. 3 No consideration of whatever nature may be invoked to warrant resorting to the threat or use of force in violation of the Charter. 4 States have the duty not to urge, encourage or assist other states to resort to the threat or use of force in violation of the Charter.' Art 13 provides that states have the inherent right of individual or collective self-defence if an armed attack occurs, as set forth in the Charter. Art 16: 'States shall abide by their commitment to the principle of peaceful settlement of disputes, which is inseparable from the principle of refraining from the threat or use of force in their international relations.'

9 S/RES/1368 (2001), for instance, expresses the 'readiness' of the UNSC to take all necessary steps. S/RES/1373 (2001) adopted under ch VII of the UN Charter decides that all states shall 'take the necessary steps to prevent the commission of terrorist acts'. See *Legal Consequences for States of the Continued Presence of South Africa in Namibia (South West Africa).* Notwithstanding Security Council Resolution 276 (1970) Advisory Opinion ICJ (21 June 1971) (1971) ICJ Reports 15: 'The language of a resolution of the Security Council should be carefully analysed … having regard to the terms of the resolution to be interpreted, the discussions

Additionally, the prohibition of the use of force is set out in regional treaties.[10]

Moreover, by virtue of the near-universal application of the UN Charter and the fact that the prohibition of the use of force is an accepted rule of customary international law, the prohibition of the use of force is applicable to all states. Pursuant to art 103 of the UN Charter, the prohibition of the use of force trumps all other non-Charter obligations.[11] Jurisprudence of the International Court of Justice (ICJ) has further confirmed that all states are bound by the general requirement not to use military force in their international relations.[12] In the *Nicaragua* case, for example, the ICJ stated that the principle of the prohibition of the use of force is at 'the very cornerstone of the human effort to promote peace' and that it is part of 'peremptory rules of customary international law which impose obligations on all states'.[13] The US in its Counter-Memorial on the questions of jurisdiction and admissibility in the same case further pointed out that the prohibition on the use of force has *jus cogens* status, *inter alia* due to the fact that it was a 'universal norm'.[14] In the *Palestinian*

leading to it, the Charter provisions invoked and, in general, all circumstances that might assist in determining the legal consequences.' It is important to note that Resolution 1373 and the kinds of 'steps' identified do not include a ch VII authorisation for the use of force.

10 See art 18 of the Charter of the Organisation of American States 1948, which states that '[t]he American states bind themselves in their international relations not to have recourse to the use of force, except in the case of self defense in accordance with existing treaties or in fulfillment thereof'. Art 3(a) of the African Union Non-Aggression and Common Defence Pact, 2005 states that state parties undertake to resolve any differences by peaceful means in order to avoid endangering peace and security and to refrain from the use of force or threat to use force in their relations with each other and in any manner whatsoever, incompatible with the United Nations Charter. It further provides that no consideration whatsoever, be it political, economic, military, religious or racial, shall justify aggression.

11 Art 4 of the UN Charter states that '[m]embership in the United Nations is open to all peace-loving states which accept the obligations contained in the present Charter and, in the judgement of the Organization, are able and willing to carry out these obligations'. Art 103 of the UN Charter, the 'supremacy clause', states that '[i]n the event of a conflict between the obligations of the members of the United Nations under the present Charter and their obligations under any other international agreement, their obligations under the present Charter shall prevail'. For views that the near universal membership of the UN is evidence of the universal scope of the prohibition of the use of force, see Ian Brownlie, *International Law and the Use of Force by States* (Clarendon Press 1963) 113; Jai Singh, *Use of Force Under International Law* (Harnam Publications 1984) 210.

12 Art 53 of the Vienna Convention on the Law of Treaties, 1969.

13 *Nicaragua* case (n 1) 100–101, 199.

14 Ibid.; Counter-Memorial of the United States of America (Questions of Jurisdiction and Admissibility) para 313.

Wall case, Judge Elaraby in his separate opinion reiterated that the prohibition of the use of force is the most important principle that has emerged in the twentieth century and is 'undoubtedly' part of *jus cogens*.[15]

Furthermore, there is widespread academic acceptance of the prohibition of the use of force as *jus cogens*.[16] It has been argued that prohibition of the use of force 'as set out most crucially in article 2(4) of the UN Charter' is often seen as the archetypal example of *a jus cogens* norm.[17] Orakhelashvili argues that '[t]he prohibition of the use of force by states *undoubtedly* forms part of *jus cogens*', and the ILC states in its commentary to article 50 (which ultimately became article 53) of the Vienna Convention that 'the law of the Charter

---

15 See *Legal Consequences of the Construction of a Wall in the Occupied Palestinian Territory* (9 July 2004) (2004) ICJ Reports 136 paras 157 and 199; Judge Elaraby, Separate Opinion, para 3.1. See statement of Mr Suy (Belgium), UN General Assembly, 25th Session of the UN General Assembly, Sixth Committee, Agenda Item 96: 'Review of the role of the International Court of Justice' (1970). Mr Suy noted that the prohibition of the use of force in art 2(4) of the Charter 'was so fundamental that it had become a peremptory norm of international law'.

16 James Crawford, *The Creation of States in International Law* 146 (2nd edn, Oxford University Press 2006); Yoram Dinstein, *War, Aggression and Self-defence* (4th edn, Cambridge University Press 2005) 99–104; Lauri Hannikainen, *Peremptory Norms (Jus Cogens) in International Law* (Finnish Lawyers' Publishing Company 1988) 323, 356; Mohammad Karoubi, *Just or Unjust War?* (Ashgate Publishing 2004) 108–9; Lindsay Moir, 'Reappraising the Resort to Force: International Law, *Jus Ad Bellum* and the War on Terror (2010) 15 Journal of Conflict and Security Law 9; Alexander Orakhelashvili, *Peremptory Norms in International Law* (Oxford University Press 2008) 50; Jonathan Charney, 'Anticipatory Humanitarian Intervention in Kosovo' (1999) 93 American Journal of International Law 834, 837; Jochen Frowein, '*Jus Cogens*' in Rüdiger Wolfrum (ed), *Max Planck Encyclopaedia of Public International Law* (Oxford University Press 2009) 8; Carin Kahgan, '*Jus Cogens* and the Inherent Right to Self-Defence' (1997) 3 Comparative and International Law Journal of Southern Africa 767, 777–81; Dino Kritsiotis, 'Reappraising Policy Objections to Humanitarian Intervention' (1998) 19 Michigan Journal of International Law 1005, 1042–43; Karin Parker and Lyn Neylon, '*Jus Cogens*: Compelling the Law of Human Rights' (1989) 12 Hastings International and Comparative Law Review 411, 436–37; Natalino Ronzitti, 'Use of Force, *Jus Cogens* and State Consent' in Antonio Cassese (ed), *The Current Legal Regulation of the Use of Force* (Martinus Nijhoff 1986); Oscar Schachter, 'In Defence of International Rules on the Use of Force' (1986) 53 University of Chicago Law Review 113, 129; Egon Schwelb, 'Some Aspects of International *Jus Cogens* as Formulated by the International Law Commission' (1976) 61 American Journal of International Law 946, 952; Bruno Simma, 'NATO, the UN and the Use of Force: Legal Aspects' (1999) 10 European Journal of International Law 1, 3; Peter Stephens, 'A Categorical Approach to Human Rights Claims: *Jus Cogens* as a Limitation on Enforcement?' (2004) 22 Wisconsin Journal of International Law 245, 253–54; Alfred Verdross, '*Jus Dispositivum* and *Jus Cogens* in International Law' (1966) 60 American Journal of International Law 55, 60.

17 Green (n 6) 231.

concerning the prohibition of the use of force in itself constitutes a conspicuous example of a rule in international law having the character *of jus cogens*'.[18]

The discussion above further provides support for the acceptance of the prohibition of the use of force as a norm which is recognized by the international community as a whole as a norm from which no derogation is permitted and, thus, a rule of *jus cogens*.[19] However, the *jus cogens* status of the prohibition of the use of force presents certain doctrinal difficulties. These include definitional issues arising from the wording relating to the use of force in the Charter; uncertainty with regard to which part of the law on the use of force constitutes *jus cogens*; and the scope and effect of exceptions to the use of force. These issues will be addressed below.

3 The Prohibition of the Use of Force as a *Jus Cogens* Norm

The doctrinal issues that arise with regard to the prohibition of the use of force as *jus cogens* will be explored in this section. First, the scope of the prohibition of the use of force must be considered. This will include a discussion on definitional issues with regard to which conduct constitutes the use of force as contemplated in the UN Charter. In this regard, the meaning of the terms 'aggression', 'use of force' and 'armed attack' will be considered. In addition, the question of whether the prohibition of the threat of the use of force and the use of force in self-defence in themselves constitute *jus cogens* norms will be considered.

As set out in paragraph 2 above, the international community seeks to limit resort to the use of armed force, including the use of armed force in self-defence. It is therefore important to clarify which acts by non-state actors qualify as the use of force in respect of which the use of forcible actions in self-defence or anticipatory self-defence is allowed under international law. With regard to the scope of the prohibition of the use of force, it has been argued that the entire law on the use of force as set out in the UN Charter is *jus cogens*.[20] This is problematic as there are numerous rules that make up the *jus ad bellum* with different functions and levels of obligation.[21] For example, Chapter VII, when referring to the UNSC authorising the use of armed force, includes various ad-

18 Orakhelashvili (n 16); Draft Articles on the Law of Treaties with Commentaries' Yearbook of the International Law Commission (1966) Vol II 247.

19 Art 53 of the Vienna Convention on the Law of Treaties, 1969.

20 See Orakhelashvili (n 16) 51, stating that 'the *jus ad bellum* as a whole is peremptory'.

21 Green (n 6) 215–6.

ministrative procedures, and it would be nonsensical to regard the entire contents of this chapter as comprising *jus cogens* norms.[22] Article 51 of the UN Charter also requires members to immediately report measures taken in the exercise of this right of self-defence to the UNSC.[23] If the entire article 51 is regarded as *jus cogens*, the failure to report would entail a breach of *jus cogens* and trigger the international responsibility of the breaching state.[24] Such an interpretation would defeat the restriction of *jus cogens* norms to norms with certain fundamental characteristics, including the protection of fundamental values.[25]

The next question is which use of force is regarded as *jus cogens*. The UN Charter uses various terms relating to the use of force without defining them, namely, the use of force in article 4(2); aggression in article 39; and an armed attack in article 51.[26] With regard to aggression, article 1(1) of the Charter stipulates that the purpose of the Charter is the maintenance of international peace and security and provides for the suppression of acts of aggression or other breaches of the peace. The Charter further provides that where the United Nations Security Council (UNSC) determines the existence of any threat to the peace, breach of the peace, or act of aggression, it may decide on the application of non-forcible measures or, if it considers those to be inadequate, take forcible measures.[27] A further reference to aggression is found under regional arrangements relating to the maintenance of international peace and security. This refers to arrangements directed against the renewal of aggressive policy on the part of a state until such time as the UN may be charged with the responsibility for preventing 'further aggression' by such a state.[28]

---

22 See for example art 47 of the UN Charter which refers to the establishment of a Military Staff Committee to advise and assist the Security Council on all questions relating to the Security Council's military requirements. See, further, Green (n 6) 233: 'It is impossible to take the approach of throwing any and all associated rules into the supernorm mixture; to do so would mean elevating the threat of force or the reporting requirement or any number of other minor or procedural rules to fundamental peremptory status.'

23 See art 51 of the UN Charter (n 4).

24 See *Nicaragua* case (n 1) (noting that reporting to the Security Council is not a condition of lawfulness in the context of a purely customary international law claim of self-defence). See further Gordon Christenson, 'The World Court and *Jus Cogens* (1987) 81 Amercian Journal of International Law 93, 99: '[T]he requirement to report immediately to the Security Council any use of force in self-defence is not part of the customary norm of *jus cogens*.'

25 See ch 3.

26 Arts 39, 41 and 42 of the UN Charter.

27 Ibid., art 39.

28 See art 53(1) of the UN Charter.

With regard to the use of the word 'force', article 2(4) prohibits 'the threat or use of force against the territorial integrity or political independence of any state, or in any other manner inconsistent with the purposes of the UN'. While the ICJ in the *Nicaragua* case held that the 'principle of non-use of force' includes the prohibition of the threat of force, it did not explicitly hold that the threat of force is *jus cogens*.[29] It is arguably possible to separate the threat of force from the prohibition of the use of force so as to sustain only the latter as a *jus cogens* norm.[30] Moreover, scholars have asserted that states have not regarded the prohibition of the threat of force in the same light as the prohibition of the use of force. In state practice, threats of force occur without comment or censure.[31] If states tolerate the prohibition of the threat of force without legal comment, it is hard to sustain an argument that the prohibition of the threat of the use of force is a norm of general international law which the international community as a whole recognizes and accepts as a norm from which no derogation is permitted. It is, thus, argued that the threat of force is not a norm of *jus cogens*.[32]

As regards terms used to describe force, the Charter does not shed much light on the difference between the terms 'force' and 'aggression'. An analysis of the wording of the Definition of Aggression that followed the UN Charter is helpful in this regard.[33] The Definition of Aggression omits the reference to the threat of force prohibited by article 5(2) of the UN Charter.[34] It further requires an element of gravity in relation to an act of aggression, stating that aggression is 'the most serious and dangerous form of the illegal use of force'. The notion of aggression as armed force is reinforced in the examples of aggression provided in the Definition of Aggression, including an attack by the armed forces of a state on another state, as well as the sending by, or on

29 Brownlie (n 11) 364; Dinstein (n 16) 86, 64; *Legality of the Threat or Use of Nuclear Weapons* case (n 6) 47; *Nicaragua* case (n 1) paras 92, 227–228.

30 Green (n 6) para 229.

31 Hillaire Mccoubrey and Nigel White, *International Law and Armed Conflict* (Dartmouth 1992) 56 ('[t]he world community is generally, and quite rightly, more concerned with the use of armed force'); Kritsiotis (n 15) 302 (providing examples).

32 Green (n 6) 215–6, 227; Mark Weisburd, *Use of Force: The Practice of States Since World War II* (Pennsylvania State University Press 1997) 22, making the general point that '[i]f states violate the norm, and other states seem able to live with the violations, is it hard to see how the norm could be characterized as vital'; Parker and Nylon (n 16) 436–37 (noting only the 'international rule prohibiting the use of force' in art 2(4) as a norm of *jus cogens* according to ICJ case law); Simma (n 16) 3 (noting only 'the prohibition enunciated in article 2(4)' as a rule of *jus cogens*. See *Nicaragua* case (n 1) 100–101.

33 A/RES/3314 (XXIX)(1974) (Definition of Aggression).

34 Ibid.

behalf of, a state of armed bands, groups, irregulars or mercenaries which carry out acts of armed force against another state of such gravity as to amount to the acts of aggression listed in the article, or the state's substantial involvement therein.[35] Accordingly, it appears that aggression refers to armed force and requires an element of gravity.[36] This, in turn, implies that there are other uses of force that may be less serious and which may not amount to aggression.[37] The *travaux préparatoires* of the definition of aggression further illustrate that numerous states were of the view that only the most serious uses of force qualify as armed attacks.[38]

When does an act of aggression amount to an armed attack in respect of which a state can invoke the right to self-defence?[39] While article 2(4) of the Charter prohibits 'the threat or use of force' (*à la menace ou à l'emploi de la*

---

35 Art 3 states that '[a]ny of the following acts, regardless of a declaration of war, shall, subject to and in accordance with the provisions of article 2, qualify as an act of aggression: (a) the invasion or attack by the armed forces of a state of the territory of another state, or any military occupation, however temporary, resulting from such invasion or attack, or any annexation by the use of force of the territory of another state or part thereof; (b) bombardment by the armed forces of a state against the territory of another state or the use of any weapons by a state against the territory of another state; (c) the blockade of the ports or coasts of a state by the armed forces of another state; (d) an attack by the armed forces of a state on the land, sea or air forces, or marine and air fleets of another state; (e) the use of armed forces of one state which are within the territory of another state with the agreement of the receiving state, in contravention of the conditions provided for in the agreement or any extension of their presence in such territory beyond the termination of the agreement; (f) the action of a state in allowing its territory, which it has placed at the disposal of another state, to be used by that other state for perpetrating an act of aggression against a third state; (g) the sending by or on behalf of a state of armed bands, groups, irregulars or mercenaries, which carry out acts of armed force against another state of such gravity as to amount to the acts listed above, or its substantial involvement therein'. See further art 8(bis) of the Rome Statute of the International Criminal Court of 1998: The definition of the 'crime of aggression' refers to an act of aggression which, 'by its character, gravity and scale', constitutes a manifest violation of the UN Charter.

36 See *Nicaragua, Oil Platforms* and *Armed Activities on the Territory of the Congo (DRC v Rwanda)* (n 1). In these cases the ICJ found that an armed attack necessarily constituted aggression.

37 Declaration on Friendly Relations (n 7), Preamble.

38 Ibid.

39 See art 51 of the UN Charter: 'Nothing in the present Charter shall impair the inherent right of individual or collective self-defence if an armed attack occurs against a member of the United Nations, until the Security Council has taken measures necessary to maintain international peace and security. Measures taken by members in the exercise of this right of self-defence shall be immediately reported to the Security Council and shall not in any way affect the authority and responsibility of the Security Council under the present Charter to take at any time such action as it deems necessary in order to maintain or restore international peace and security.'

force in the French version), article 51 refers to an 'armed attack' (armed aggression, or *une agression armée* in the French version) required to trigger the right to self-defence. The implication is that, while every use of force against the territorial integrity or political independence of another state is prohibited, not every such use of force will constitute an armed attack which will trigger the right to self-defence.[40]

In the *Nicaragua* case, the ICJ found that the term 'armed attack' has a narrower meaning than the words 'threat or use of force' and 'aggression'.[41] This makes sense as the right to the use of force in self-defence is triggered by an armed attack and, therefore, the bar should be set high to avoid the unnecessary use of force by states.[42] In this regard, scholars have argued that an armed attack under article 51 must be of a relatively large scale, sufficient gravity and have a substantial effect.[43]

An example of an action which arguably did not constitute an armed attack triggering the right to self-defence was the US missile attack on Iraq in 1993 in response to a foiled assassination attempt on former President George H Bush while he was visiting Kuwait.[44] The US attack destroyed most of the Iraqi Intelligence Service building in Baghdad and caused many civilian deaths. The US Ambassador to the UN, Madeleine Albright, reported to the UNSC that 'we responded directly as we were entitled to do under article 51 of the United Nations Charter which provides for the exercise of self-defence in such cases'.[45] The US actions were criticized on the basis that an attempted assassination did not meet the threshold of gravity of an armed attack which would trigger the right to self-defence.[46]

The ICJ has further found that not every use of force in breach of article 2(4) can be designated as an armed attack.[47] In the *Nicaragua* case, the Court held that 'mere frontier incidents' do not have the necessary gravity to constitute armed attacks, and the Eritrea-Ethiopia Claim Commission confirmed

40 David Kretzmer, 'The Inherent Right to Self-Defence and Proportionality in *Jus Ad Bellum*' (2013) 24(1) European Journal of International Law 242.

41 *Nicaragua* case (n 1) 100.

42 Ibid.

43 Albrecht Randelzhofer and Georg Nolte, 'Article 51' in Bruno Simma, Hermann Mosler, Andreas Paulus and Eleni Chaitidou (eds), *The Charter of the United Nations: A Commentary'* (3rd edn, Oxford University Press 2013).

44 'US Strikes Iraq for Plot to Kill Bush' *Washington Post* (27 June 1993) <http://www.washingtonpost.com/wp-srv/inatl/longterm/iraq/timeline/062793.htm> accessed 9 August 2017.

45 Ibid.

46 Ibid.

47 *Nicaragua* case (n 1) para 195.

that 'localized border encounters between small infantry units, even those involving the loss of life, do not constitute an armed attack for purposes of the Charter'.[48] The level of gravity of the use of force was further mentioned in several ICJ cases. In the *Oil Platforms* case, the ICJ distinguished between 'most grave' and 'less grave forms' of the use of force, and it commented that not every illegal use of force warrants states to resort to self-defence.[49] In *DRC v Uganda* the ICJ contemplated the use of self-defence only if directed against 'large-scale attacks'.[50] Minor violations of the prohibition of the use of force falling below the threshold of an armed attack, therefore, do not justify the use of force in self-defence.[51]

Finally, it has been argued that the right to self-defence in article 51 is *jus cogens*.[52] The ICJ in the *Nuclear Weapons* case stated that the right of states to resort to self-defence follows from the fundamental right of every state to defend itself, and that this right is also part of *jus cogens*.[53] Orakhelashvili argues that 'if the very prohibition of the use of force is *jus cogens*, then every principle specifying the limits on the entitlement of states to use force is also a peremptory norm *of jus cogens*'.[54] The latter argument is not supported. The primary prohibition of the use of force includes exceptions to the use of force, such as self-defence. Furthermore, if both the use of self-defence and the prohibition

48 Ibid. See further *Jus Ad Bellum – Ethiopia's Claims 1–8, Eritrea and Ethiopia Partial Award of the Eritrea-Ethiopia Claims Commission* (2006) 45 ILM 430 Permanent Court of Arbitration para 11 <http://legal.un.org/riaa/cases/vol-XXV1/457-469.pdf> (accessed 12 August 2014), where the Commission held that '[l]ocalized border encounters between small infantry units, even those involving the loss of life, do not constitute an armed attack for purposes of the Charter'.

49 *Oil Platforms* (n 1) 147; Randelzhofer and Nolte (n 43).

50 *Armed Activities on the Territory of the Congo* (*Democratic Republic of the Congo v Uganda*) (19 December 2005) (2005) ICJ, Judgment, paras 146–7.

51 Enzo Cannizzaro, 'Contextualizing Proportionality: *Jus Ad Bellum* and *Jus In Bello* in the Lebanese War' (2006) 88 International Review of the Red Cross 779, 782. See further Oil Platforms (n 1) 72. The Court explicitly stated that it '[did] not exclude the possibility that the mining of a single military vessel might be sufficient to bring into play the "inherent right of self-defence"'.

52 Analytical Report of the Study Group of the International Law Commission finalised by Chairman Martti Koskenniemi *Fragmentation of International Law: Difficulties Arising from the Diversification and Expansion of International Law* UN Doc A/CN4/L682 (13 April 2006) 189; Erika de Wet, '*Jus Cogens* and Obligations *Erga Omnes*' in D Shelton (ed), *The Oxford Handbook of International Human Rights Law* (Oxford University Press 2013); see also International Law Commission, Draft Articles on State Responsibility, Commentary on Article 40, paras 4–6 Official Records of the General Assembly, Fifth-sixth Session (A/56/10) 283–284.

53 *Nuclear Weapons* case (n 6).

54 Orakhelashvili (n 16).

of the use of force are *jus cogens*, no derogation is allowed from the use of self-defence, which could not have been the intention of a regime aiming to limit the use of inter-state force.

In light of what has been said above, it is argued that it is the use of grave force or aggression, such as armed aggression, which constitutes *jus cogens*. In the light of the interests of the international community to limit resort to the use of armed force, including the use of armed force in self-defence, it is argued that less grave forms of aggression or threats of the use of force would rather justify the use of non-forcible measures to deter such an act.

4 The Use of Force in the Context of Terrorism

This section will discuss the requirements for the use of force in self-defence and will consider whether the status of the prohibition of terrorism as a *jus cogens* norm has resulted in the expansion of the scope of exceptions to the use of force in self-defence. It will be considered the requirements for conduct to constitute an 'armed attack' justifying the use of force in self-defence in light of ongoing low-level terrorist attacks. Furthermore, with regard to the use of force in anticipatory self-defence against non-state actors, it will be analyzed whether it can be argued that the requirements of necessity and proportionality may be relaxed in an effort to fight terrorist attacks. It will further be considered whether a less stringent standard for the attribution of the acts of non-state actors to states has developed in the context of the fight against and deterrence of terrorism. These issues will be discussed in light of relevant state practice and legal doctrine, supported by international jurisprudence.

4.1 *Armed Attack*

Traditionally, low-level, pin-prick attacks were not regarded as reaching the level of an armed attack or justifying the right to self-defence.[55] However, there are signs that, with the growing awareness that transnational terrorist attacks present states with a serious problem, the use of force in self-defence against ongoing low-level attacks it is not as widely rejected as it was in the past.[56] As Tams puts it, 'states seem to have shown a new willingness to accept

55 Michael Brody, 'Contemporary *Jus Ad Bellum* on Use of Force in Self-Defense by States Against Non-State Terrorist Groups – Limitations, Evolutions and Alternatives' 2011 <https://calhoun.nps.edu/handle/10945/5496> accessed 12 October 2017 81; Kretzmer (n 40) 244.

56 Theresa Reinold, 'State Weakness, Irregular Warfare, and the Right to Self-Defense Post 9/11' (2011) 105 American Journal of International Law 244.

the "accumulation of events" doctrine which previously had received little support'.[57] While the attacks would in themselves constitute less grave use of force, when these incidents form part of a chain of events they can, thus, be transformed into an armed attack triggering the right of self-defence.[58] In this regard the *Nicaragua* and *Oil Platforms* cases support the view that 'consecutive attacks linked in time, source and cause may constitute an armed attack, in particular when those attacks are part of a "continuous, overall plan of attack purposely relying on numerous small raids"'.[59] Both state practice and ICJ case law provide further support for this doctrine.[60]

In the age of terrorism, force is increasingly used constantly, at a low level, over extended periods of time and in various territories.[61] As discussed above, an armed attack is not defined in the UN Charter, neither does the Charter rule out the 'accumulation' doctrine. Tams describes the accumulation doctrine as 'a new understanding of the rules on force and a "protean" approach striking a new balance between the absence of force and the protection of common values, permitting states to disregard constraints of the Charter in defence of community goals'.[62] In *Nicaragua* the ICJ held that multiple small-scale attacks could together satisfy the threshold for an armed attack, even if none of the attacks on its own could satisfy the threshold.[63] In the US, Operation Enduring Freedom was at first justified on the basis of article 51 of the UN Charter, but it is unclear whether this ongoing operation now is based on the accumulation

57 Christian Tams, 'The Use of Force Against Terrorists' (2009) 20 European Journal of International Law 388.

58 *Nicaragua* (n 1) para 231; *Oil Platforms* (n 1) 64.

59 Ibid.

60 Ibid.; *Armed Activities on the Territory of the Congo (Democratic Republic of the Congo v Uganda)* (n 50); Christine Gray, *International Law and the Use of Force* (3rd ed, Oxford University Press 2008) 130, 155; Tams (n 57) 388 ('[s]tates seem to have shown a new willingness to accept the "accumulation of events" doctrine which previously had received little support'); Raphael van Steenberghe, 'Self-Defense in Response to Attacks by Non-State Actors in Light of Recent State Practice: A Step Forward?' (2010) 23 Leiden Journal of International Law 184 ('[a]ny armed attack must reach some level of gravity – which may be evaluated by accumulating minor uses of force – in order to trigger the right of self-defense').

61 Brody (n 55) 82.

62 Tams (n 57) 395.

63 See Gray (n 60) 136 (arguing that this language can be interpreted narrowly, to permit defensive force against non-state actors in other states); Tams (n 57) 388 ('[s]tates seem to have shown a new willingness to accept the "accumulation of events" doctrine which previously had received little support'); Van Steenberghe (n 60) 183, 184 ('any armed attack must reach some level of gravity – which may be evaluated by accumulating minor uses of force – in order to trigger the right of self-defense').

doctrine. From the outset, the US declared that the circumstances were exceptional, and that it was, essentially, at war. President Bush declared: 'Our war on terror begins with al-Qaida, but it does not end there. It will not end until every terrorist group of global reach has been found, stopped and defeated.'[64] The US viewed its response to the 9/11 attacks as a response to a larger, global conflict against any and all global, non-state terror groups, including, but not ending with, al Qaeda. Its notion of self-defence, in this context, thus, went far beyond the concept of a limited, necessary, immediate, and proportional response to an armed attack.[65]

Some writers argue that UNSC resolutions passed after 9/11 recognize that large-scale terrorist action could constitute an armed attack that would give rise to the right of self-defence.[66] Byers argues that the events of 9/11 set in motion a significant loosening of the legal constraints on the use of force, and this, in turn, will lead to changes across the international legal system.[67] It has been argued that if there is evidence of further imminent attacks by terrorist groups, states may use force in anticipatory self-defence, subject to the fact that such a use of force is a last resort and is proportionate and necessary in response to the attacks concerned. The prohibition of terrorism as a *jus cogens* norm and the need to deter terrorist attacks, therefore, has led to a willingness to accept that multiple small-scale attacks could together satisfy the threshold for an armed attack.

4.2 *Necessity and Proportionality*

It is further important to consider whether the prohibition of terrorism as a *jus cogens* norm and global efforts to fight increased attacks by terrorists justify an expanded notion of the requirements of necessity and proportionality. In other words, does the global threat of terrorist attacks and the status of the prohibition of terrorism as a *jus cogens* norm warrant the use of force in self-defence, even when it cannot be proven that a terrorist attack is necessarily imminent? Furthermore, does the scourge of terrorism warrant a response to an act of aggression which goes further than merely repelling an attack and preventing future attacks – a response which could be seen as disproportionate? These themes will be explored below, in particular in the context of anticipatory self-defence against 'imminent' terrorist attacks.

64 Jackson Maogoto, 'Battling Terrorism: Legal Perspectives on the Use of Force and the War on Terror' (Ashgate Publishing Ltd 2005) 115.

65 Brody (n 55) 44.

66 S/RES/1368 and 1373 (2001); Bethlehem (n 6) 772.

67 Michael Byers, 'Terrorism, the Use of Force and International Law After 11 September' (2002) 51 International and Comparative Law Quarterly 414.

While anticipatory self-defence is not guaranteed by the UN Charter, this doctrine has developed under customary international law. The requirements for necessity and proportionality in the use of anticipatory force in self-defence were established in the Caroline incident of 1837.[68] In this case, during an anti-British insurrection in Canada, the Caroline, a US ship, was allegedly being used to supply the rebels on the Canadian side of the Niagara River. British forces boarded the Caroline, killed several US nationals, set the ship on fire and sent it over the Niagara Falls, claiming that they were acting in self-defence.[69] During diplomatic communications between Lord Ashburton of the UK and the US Secretary of State, Daniel Webster, Webster asserted that a state that wished to use force in self-defence would need to show that the 'necessity of that self-defence is instant, overwhelming, and leaving no choice of means, and no moment of deliberation'.[70] Moreover, the use of force in self-defence must not be excessive and must be limited by the necessity of responding to the threat.[71] The UK agreed, and two criteria for self-defence emerged from this, namely, necessity and proportionality.[72] Although not explicitly referred to in the Caroline situation, it is argued that these criteria apply to anticipatory self-defence, as the UK did not react to an immediate attack. International jurisprudence has further supported the requirements of necessity and proportionality for the use of force in self-defence.[73]

---

68 History Central '1837 – Caroline Affair' <www.historycentral.com/ant/caroline.html> accessed 12 October 2017.

69 Dire Tladi, 'The Non-Consenting Innocent State: The Problem with Bethlehem's Principle 12' (2013) 107 Amercian Journal of International Law 573. Tladi notes that neither the UK nor the US questioned that the initial attack to which the UK responded was committed by non-state actors.

70 Letter from Mr Webster to Lord Ashburton, 6 August 1842, cited in Lori Damrosch (ed), *International Law: Cases and Materials* (West Publishing 2001) 923. See further Tladi (n 69) 573, noting that at that time, international law did not prohibit the use of force, so justification for the use of force on the grounds of self-defence was not advanced as a defence against wrongfulness.

71 Letter from Mr Webster to Mr Fox, 24 April 1841, cited in Damrosch (n 70).

72 See Robert Jennings, 'The Caroline and McLeod Cases' (1938) 32 Amercian Journal of International Law 82. See Brownlie (n 11) 701, who notes that, although the Webster formula may be of value as a formulation of anticipatory self-defence, the correspondence made no difference to the legal doctrine of the time. This suggests the existence of rules of customary international law governing self-defence and anticipatory self-defence even before the Caroline incident.

73 *Nicaragua* case (n 1) 194–5. The ICJ noted that because 'the issue of the lawfulness of a response to the imminent threat of armed attack has not been raised … the Court expresses no view on the issue'. In his dissenting opinion Judge Schwebel hinted at anticipatory self-defence, noting that art 51 of the UN Charter does not state that the use of force in self-defence is allowed 'if, and only if, an armed attack occurs'. In his dissenting opinion,

While necessity requires a temporal element as articulated in the Caroline case, the US has contended that the requirement of necessity (imminence) for the use of force in self-defence, including pre-emptive self-defence, should be relaxed in the context of anti-terrorist measures.[74] In its 2002 National Security Strategy, the US asserted a right of pre-emptive self-defence against non-imminent threats, in particular those by terrorist organizations.[75] The US further argued that '[t]he greater the threat, the greater is the risk of inaction – and the more compelling the case for taking anticipatory action to

Judge Elaraby expressed his disappointment that the ICJ had 'refrained from exploring refinements and progressive development of the existing doctrine of self-defence'. In Judge Simma's separate opinion, he noted the 'half-heartedness' and 'inappropriate self-restraint' with which the ICJ dealt with this area. *Oil Platforms* case (n 1). In the *Oil Platforms* case, the ICJ assessed the necessity and proportionality of the US attacks on Iranian oil platforms on the basis of attacks on US commercial and naval vessels which the US attributed to Iran, and concluded that neither of the attacks was a necessity as the platforms were not legitimate military targets. It confirmed that the right of individual self-defence is dependent on a state being the victim of an armed attack and that the force used in self-defence must be necessary and proportionate.

74 The terms 'pre-emptive self-defence' and 'anticipatory self-defence' have been used interchangeably, and for purposes of this study preemptive self-defence will be used as akin to anticipatory self-defence. See for example VAV Andreias, 'Anticipatory Self-defense in International Law: Legal or just a Construct for Using Force' <http://arno.uvt.nl/show.cgi?fid=122935> accessed 27 November 2017. The author refers to 'anticipatory self-defense (or pre-emptive self-defense' in his discussion. See further Megi Medzmariashvili, 'Pre-emptive Self-defence Against States Harbouring Terrorists' 2011 Research Papers 9 <uploads/research-papers-list/19/4-medzmariasgvili-final.pdf> accessed 27 November 2017. See further General Counsel of the Department of Defense 'Legal Distinction between Preemption, Preventive Self-Defense, and Anticipatory Self-Defense' 3 <http://library.rumsfeld.com/doclib/sp/2564/2002-10-16.pdf> accessed 16 November 2017, where the US Department of Defence states that '[i]nternational law recognizes no difference between "preemption", "preventive self-defense", and "anticipatory self-defense". These terms all refer to the right to use force based on the existence of an imminent threat but prior to an armed attack.' See, however, Michael Reisman and Andrea Armstrong, 'The Past and Future of the Claim of Preemptive Self-Defense' (2006) 100 Amercan Journal of International Law 526, stating that '[p]reemptive self-defense differs from anticipatory self-defense in that those contemplating the latter can point to a palpable and imminent threat'. The authors critisize the use of pre-emptive self-defence on the basis of the 'mere possibility of an attack at some future time'.

75 White House, 'The National Security Strategy of the United States of America 2002' 12–16 <https://georgebush-whitehouse.archives/gov/ns6/nss/2002/7> accessed 29 July 2017. See further Schachter (n 16) 314: 'If there had been a pattern of prior attacks and a substantial threat, the need to have definite knowledge of future attacks should be less demanding.' He argues that when it comes to terrorists, the imminence requirement for use of pre-emptive force is not judged by the imminence in time of the expected terrorist attack but 'by the extent to which the self-defense occurred during the last window of opportunity'.

defend ourselves, even if uncertainty remains as to the time and place of the enemy's attack'.[76] The 2004 report of the UN High-Level Panel on Threats, Challenges and Change, however, supports pre-emptive self-defence as self-defence against 'imminent' (and not non-imminent) threats of attack. This is confirmed by the UN Secretary-General's report 'In Larger Freedom' which states that a threatened state, 'according to long established international law, can take military action as long as the threatened attack is imminent'.[77]

An evaluation of whether the use of force in anticipatory self-defence is necessary given the facts is often difficult, as there is no prescribed evidentiary standard that may be used to assess the factual allegations upon which such a use of force is premised.[78] Notwithstanding this, it has been argued that a military response to a terrorist attack should, as a minimum, require that the state carefully evaluates the evidence to ensure a high degree of certainty that it has identified those responsible for an attack, that more attacks are imminent, that the facts relied upon are made public, and that these facts are subject to international scrutiny and investigation.[79] For example, when Israel destroyed an Iraqi nuclear reactor in 1981, its claim of self-defence was firmly rejected by other states.[80] Since a nuclear strike had not occurred, and was not imminent, the requirements of necessity and proportionality had not been fulfilled.[81] Similarly, in 1998 the US launched attacks in alleged self-defence against Afghanistan and Sudan just over two weeks after attacks on US embassies in Nairobi, Kenya and Dar es Salaam, Tanzania, on the basis that the US had 'convincing evidence' that Bin Laden was behind the embassy bombings.[82] Although the US allies expressed their support, the Arab Nations, China and Russia criticized the lack of evidence.[83]

---

76 Ibid.

77 Report of the Secretary-General's High-Level Panel on Threats, Challenges and Change 'A More Secure World: Our Shared Responsibility' 2 December 2004, UN Doc A/59/ 565 para 189. See White House (n 75) 12–16.

78 Jules Lobel, 'The Use of Force to Respond to Terrorist Attacks: The Bombing of Sudan and Afghanistan' (1999) 24 Yale Journal of International Law 538.

79 Ibid., 547.

80 Byers (n 67) 410; S/RES/487 (1981) (unanimous) (Iraq-Israel).

81 Ibid.

82 The UNSC had also condemned the embassy bombings as a threat to international peace and security, despite the fact that no clear indication of a state sponsor or direct state support for the attacks existed. See S/RES/1189 (1998) (bombings in Nairobi, Kenya, and Dar es Salaam, Tanzania); Maogato (n 64) 113, Brody (n 55) 41–42. 'US Strikes Back' *Newsday* (21 August 1998) <www.newsday.com> accessed 1 July 2017; Lobel (n 78) 537.

83 See 'Tribunal Allies Back US Strikes; Russia Among the Dissenters' *Minneapolis Star Tribune* (22 August 1998) 6A <www.startribune.com> accessed 1 July 2017; F Ching, 'China

The UK has supported the right to anticipatory self-defence under customary international law being subject to the requirement of necessity. In a debate in the House of Lords in April 2004, a question was put to the UK government as to whether it accepted the legitimacy of a pre-emptive armed attack as part of the inherent right of self-defence under article 51 of the UN Charter. The then Attorney-General emphasized the right to anticipatory self-defence under customary international law subject to the requirement of necessity, and stated that the UN Charter simply codified that existing right.[84] Military action should be used only as a last resort and it must be necessary to use force to deal with the particular threat that is faced.[85] The UK seemed to keep a door open, though, as it was at pains to point out that 'the concept of what constitutes an imminent armed attack will develop to meet new circumstances and new threats'. It was argued that self-defence is not a static concept and must be reasonable and appropriate to the threats and circumstances of the day.[86]

Once there has been a resort to force, the question arises as to whether the means used by the state acting in self-defence were necessary to achieve

Feels Let Down by US' *Far Eastern Economic Review* (24 September 1998) 38; see further Maogato (n 64) 114.

84 House of Commons Foreign Affairs Committee, 'Foreign Policy Aspects of the War Against Terrorism' 2002–03, HC 196, Parlementary Debate, HL (2004) 356 (Lord Thomas of Gresford, statement opening the debate on international self-defense) <www.publications.parliament.uk/pa/cm200304/cmselect/cmfsff/441/441.pdf> accessed 1 August 2017. Lord Goldsmith answered as follows: 'Article 51 of the Charter provides that "[n]othing in the present Charter shall impair the inherent right of individual or collective self-defence if an armed attack occurs against a member of the United Nations". It is argued by some that the language of art 51 provides for a right of self-defence only in response to an actual armed attack. However, it has been the consistent position of successive United Kingdom governments over many years that the right of self-defence under international law includes the right to use force where an armed attack is imminent. It is clear that the language of art 51 was not intended to create a new right of self-defence. Art 51 recognises the inherent right of self-defence that states enjoy under international law. That can be traced back to the 'Caroline' incident in 1837. It is not a new invention. The Charter therefore did not affect the scope of the right of self-defence existing at that time in customary international law, which included the right to use force in anticipation of an imminent armed attack. The government's position is supported by the records of the international conference at which the UN charter was drawn up and by state practice since 1945. It is therefore the government's view that international law permits the use of force in self-defence against an imminent attack but does not authorise the use of force to mount a pre-emptive strike.

85 Ibid.

86 Ibid.

the legitimate ends of self-defence in the specific context.[87]Did the action in self-defence meet the test of proportionality? This test is notoriously difficult to apply in practice.[88] Writers have different views with regard to the requirements for proportionality of a response in self-defence. Gray notes that proportionality historically involved the elimination of an enemy state's military assets, supply hubs or command and control structures.[89] It did not necessarily entail the annexation of large swaths of enemy territory, or attacking targets worldwide such as, arguably, can be applied to the US force in Afghanistan since 9/11.[90] Cassese argues that the force used must be judged both against the legitimate ends and the attack against which it is responding. To breach the proportionality norm under the *jus ad bellum*, the victim state must do more than is reasonably required in the circumstances to deter a threatened attack or defeat an ongoing attack.[91] Self-defence should be confined to the area of the attacks that they are designed to repel and should not continue

---

87 Christopher Greenwood, 'Self-Defence and the Conduct of International Armed Conflict' in Yoram Dinstein (ed), *International Law at a Time of Perplexity: Essays in Honour of Shabtai Rosenne* (Martinus Nijhoff 1989) 155.

88 Final Report to the Prosecutor by the Committee Established to Review the NATO Bombing Campaign Against the Federal Republic of Yugoslavia, para 48 <www.icty.org/sid/10052> accessed 27 January 2017: 'It is much easier to formulate the principle of proportionality in general terms than it is to apply it to a particular set of circumstances because the comparison is often between unlike quantities and values. One cannot easily assess the value of innocent human lives as opposed to capturing a particular military objective.'

89 Gray (n 60) 120, 160.

90 Ibid.

91 Michael Schmitt, 'Change Direction 2006: Israeli Operations in Lebanon and the International Law of Self-Defense' (2008) 29(2) Michigan Journal of International Law 154. Under international humanitarian law applicable in armed conflict the *jus in bello* proportionality involves assessing whether the expected collateral damage to civilians of an attack on a legitimate military target is excessive in relation to the direct military advantage anticipated. See art 51(5)(b) of Protocol I to the Geneva Conventions, 1949. See further Jean-Marie Henckaerts and Louise Doswald-Beck, *Customary International Humanitarian Law, i: Rules 46–50* (Cambridge University Press 2005); Françoise Hampson, 'The Principle of Proportionality in the Law of Armed Conflict' in Sarah Perrigo and Jim Whitman (eds), *The Geneva Conventions Under Assault* (Pluto Press 2010) 42. See further R Ago, 'Addendum to Eighth Report on State Responsibility' (1980) II Yearbook of the International Law Commission UN Doc A/CN4/318/ADD5-7 13, 69, stating that 'it would be mistaken … to think that there must be proportionality between the conduct constituting the armed attack and the opposing conduct. The action needed to halt and repulse the attack may well have to assume dimensions disproportionate to those of the attack suffered. What matters in this respect is the result to be achieved by the "defensive" action, and not the forms, substance and strength of the action itself.'

past the point in time that is necessary to deal effectively with the attack(s).[92] Furthermore, the purpose of anticipatory self-defence is to prevent future attacks from occurring.[93] If the pending attack is expected to be isolated and limited, the purpose of the force used in self-defence should be restricted to stopping that attack from occurring. If, however, the expected attack is one of a massive scale, amounting to war, an invasion of the victim state's territory or wide-scale bombardment of its territory, or is part of an 'accumulation of events', the victim state cannot be expected to restrict its anticipatory use of force to thwarting the imminent attack alone. It may act to remove the wider threat of reasonably foreseeable future attacks by the imminent aggressor.[94] This is illustrated by the reaction to Israel's use of force in self-defence against terrorist actors below.

In 1985 Israel's attack on the Palestine Liberation Organization (PLO) in Tunis killed at least 60 people and injured approximately 100 people.[95] Israel argued that this attack was in retaliation for the killing the previous week of three Israelis aboard a private yacht in Larnaca, Cyprus, as well as other acts of terrorism blamed on the PLO.[96] Israel was accused of using disproportionate force in self-defence.[97] There was, however, a different view when in 2006 and following rocket attacks against it by the Lebanon-based Hezbollah, Israel responded first with bombardments followed by an invasion of Lebanon.[98] Israel included in its use of force targeting lines of communication: It bombed Beirut International Airport, 109 Lebanese bridges and

92 Greenwood (n 87) 273–88. See further Kretzmer (n 40) 238. Kretzmer asserts that sometimes proportionality refers to the relationship between an act and the legitimate response to that act ('an eye for an eye' or 'tit-for-tat' proportionality) and, at other times, it relates to an assessment of the harm caused by the means used to further legitimate ends ('means-ends proportionality'). With regard to the use of force in self-defence, proportionality should be based on an assessment of the force used in relation to that end as the 'tit-for-tat' test would be inapplicable. The problem is the absence of consensus over what that end may be, in particular in response to an imminent attack. See further Antonio Cassese, *International Law* (2nd edn, Oxford University Press 2005) 355: 'The victim of aggression must use an amount of force strictly necessary to repel the attack and proportional to the force used by the aggressor.' See also Cannizzaro (n 51) 779.

93 Ago (n 91) 121.

94 Kretzmer (n 40) 271–2.

95 Andreas Zimmerman, 'The Second Lebanon War: *Jus Ad Bello, Jus In Bellum* and the Issue of Proportionality' (2007) 11 Max Planck University Yearbook of International Law 123.

96 Ibid.

97 Ibid.

98 Gray (n 60); Tams (n 57) 379.

137 roads and established air and naval blockades.[99] In this case it was argued that Israel's actions may have been proportionate. As noted by Judge Rosalyn Higgins, the former President of the ICJ, '[p]roportionality cannot be in relation to any specific prior injury – it has to be in relation to the overall legitimate objective, of ending the aggression or reversing the invasion'.[100] An action is disproportionate when a reasonably available alternative military course of action employing significantly lesser force would successfully have met the defensive aims.[101] There was a view that, under the *jus ad bellum* and at least *vis-à-vis* operations designed to stop rocket attacks, Israeli actions were proportionate and relative to Israel's defensive needs. This was evidenced by the fact that Hezbollah continued to conduct anti-Israeli attacks even after Israeli defensive action.[102]

This section illustrated that notwithstanding the global threat of terrorism and support for fighting terrorism, the status of the prohibition of terrorism as a *jus cogens* norm and the need to repel terrorist attacks have not led to a general expanded notion of the requirements of necessity and proportionality of an armed attack in anticipatory self-defence. It is further evident that whether these requirements have been met will depend on the facts of the particular matter.

4.3 *Attribution*

The concept of attribution is important in considering whether states are justified in using force in self-defence against non-state actors in the territory of another state in the fight against terrorism. In terms of the UN Charter, the use of force in self-defence requires an armed attack. Where the armed attack is carried out by a non state actor, it must be capable of being attributed to the state concerned in order to trigger the right of armed self-defence against such a state. Furthermore, in terms of customary international law, the use of force

99 'Israel Attacks Beirut Airport and Sets Up Naval Blockade' *New York Times* <http://www.nytimes.com/2006/07/13/world/middleeast/13cnd-mideast.html> accessed 24 October 2017. The effects of Israel's actions, according to the Lebanese government, were the deaths of 53 Lebanese with more than 103 being wounded. After the attacks, 'Lebanese hoarded canned goods and batteries as lines at gas stations stretched for blocks' and '[s]upermarkets and bakeries were flooded'. While the Lebanese government denied having anything to do with the raids, Israel said that the Lebanese government was responsible for the actions of Hezbollah.

100 Rosalyn Higgins, *Problems and Process: International Law and How We Use It* (Calrendon Press 1994) 232.

101 Schmitt (n 91) 156.

102 Ibid., 155.

in self-defence, including the use of anticipatory force, must meet the requirements of necessity and proportionality.

As discussed above, in terms of the UN Charter a state may use force in self-defence against an armed attack. In terms of the Charter an armed attack needs to be against a state to trigger the right to the use of force in self-defence. Nothing in the language of article 51, however, requires that such an attack be carried out by another state.[103] Accordingly, states may use force in self-defence where an armed attack originates from a non-state actor.

Where an armed attack originates from a non-state actor located on the territory of another state, however, the act of such a non-state actor would further need to be capable of being attributed to the state concerned before force can be used in self-defence against the latter state. An analysis of the effect of the status of terrorism as *jus cogens* on the rules of attribution is important due to arguments that force can be used in self-defence against states that simply harbour terrorists or fail to effectively restrain terrorists activities, which will be discussed in more detail below.

With regard to attribution, the ILC Draft Articles on State Responsibility (DARSIWA) provide that the conduct of a person or group of persons shall be considered to be an act of a state under international law when such a person or group of persons is 'in fact acting on the instructions of, or under the direction or control of, that state in carrying out the conduct'[104] (the effective control test). The ICJ in various judgments has upheld the need for attribution in line with DARSIWA. The effective control test for the attribution of the acts of a non-state actor to a state was shaped in the *Nicaragua* case where the ICJ accepted that the prohibition of the use of force could be violated by 'the sending by or on behalf of a state of armed bands, groups, irregulars or mercenaries,

103 Sean Murphy, 'Self-Defence and the Israeli Wall Opinion: An *Ipse Dixit* from the ICJ?' (2005) 99 Amercian Journal of International Law 62; Thomas Franck, 'Terrorism and the Right of Self-Defense' (2001) 95 Amercian Journal of International Law 839, 840; Sean Murphy, 'Terrorism and the Concept of "Armed Attack" in Article 51 of the UN Charter' (2002) 43 Harvard Journal of International Law 50; Jordan Paust, 'Responding Lawfully to International Terrorism: The Use of Force Abroad' (1986) 8 Whittier Law Review 711, 723; Ruth Wedgwood, 'Responding to Terrorism: The Strikes Against Bin Laden' (1999) 24 Yale Journal of International Law 559, 564. In the *Israeli Wall Opinion* (n 15) para 139, the ICJ observed that art 51 of the UN Charter recognises the existence of an inherent right of self-defence 'in the case of armed attack by one state against another state'.

104 See art 8 of the Draft Articles on Responsibility of States for Internationally Wrongful Acts with Commentaries, adopted by the ILC at its 53rd session (2001) Yearbook of the International Law Commission 2001 II 106–7.

which carry out acts of armed force against another state'.[105] For the conduct of irregular forces to be attributable to a state, that state had to exercise 'effective control [over] the military or paramilitary operations' in question. The ICJ found that, although knowing assistance by the US to the contras in the form of provision of weapons or logistical or other support might constitute an impermissible use of force leading to state responsibility, such acts would not constitute an armed attack for purposes of attribution for the acts of the contras to the US and trigger the right to the use of force in self-defence.[106] This test set a high threshold and required an instruction by a state to the non-state actor in respect of the conduct by such actor.[107]

The *Armed Activities on the Territory of the Congo* and *Tadić* cases similarly used the effective control test for attribution. The ICJ found that the necessary link of attribution was not present where Uganda relied on self-defence for its actions against the Democratic Republic of the Congo (DRC), pursuant to alleged attacks attributed by Uganda to the DRC. The ICJ concluded that there was no satisfactory proof of the involvement of the DRC in the attacks against

105 Art 3(g) of the Definition of Aggression (n 33); *Nicaragua* (n 1) para 195. See further the ILC 'Draft Code of Offences Against the Peace and Security of Mankind' (1954) 2 Yearbook of the International Law Commission UN Doc A/CN4/SER.A/1954/Add.I 149, 150, which labels 'the toleration of the organization of ... [armed] bands in its own territory, or the toleration of the use by such armed bands of its territory as a base of operations or as a point of departure for incursions into the territory of another state' an offence against 'the peace and security of mankind'.

106 *Nicaragua* (n 1) paras 18, 93–94, 228 (mere supply of funds is not a use of force); para 230 ('provision of arms' is not an armed attack). Even if the US participation in the contras' activities involved 'financing, organizing, training, supplying and equipping of the contras, the selection of its military and paramilitary targets, and the planning of the whole of its operation', the US did not exercise 'effective control' over the military and paramilitary operations and there was insufficient evidence that the United States 'directed or enforced the perpetration of the acts'. Consequently, attacks by the contras were not acts attributable to the US. See further dissenting opinion of Judge Jennings, para 543–4. Judge Jennings argued that 'it [became] difficult to understand what it [was], short of a direct attack by a state's own forces, that [might] not be done apparently without a lawful response in the form of ... self-defence'. See further *Prosecutor v Tadić* Opinion and Judgment, IT-94-1-T (7 May 1997) para 137, where the ICTY stated that 'in addition to financing, training and equipping or providing operational support' the state should have a 'role in organizing, coordinating or planning the military actions of the [non-state group]'.

107 Ibid., paras 109 and 115. See further separate opinion of Judge Ago, para 17. *Nicaragua* (n 1) 103, para 195. The majority opinion recognized that a state that sends 'armed bands, groups, irregulars ... [or others to] carry out acts of armed force against another state of such gravity as to amount to an actual armed attack' can be engaged in an armed attack that triggers the right of self-defence against such a state. See further *Tadić* (n 106) paras 115, 109–110 and 115.

Uganda, and these attacks were not undertaken on the instruction or on behalf of the DRC. Accordingly, as the initial attacks were not attributable to the DRC, Uganda could not justify a claim of self-defence.[108] The International Criminal Tribunal for the Former Yugoslavia (ICTY) Trial Chamber in the *Tadić* case similarly could not find a link to attribute the acts of a non-state actor to a state. In this case the ICTY considered whether the acts of genocide at Srebrenica by Bosnian Serb armed forces could be attributed to the Federal Republic of Yugoslavia (FRY).[109] The armed forces occupying Srebrenica officially belonged to a non-state actor, the Bosnian-Serb Republic or Republika Srpska. Republika Srpska had close ties to the FRY and consisted mainly of units from the former Yugoslavian national army, which was *de facto* controlled by Serbia. The Trial Chamber did not find a sufficient link between the armed forces and the FRY. It held that the effective control test required a direct order from the state to the non-state actor to commit the act in question.[110]

The strict standard of effective control was, however, relaxed by the Appeals Chamber to an 'overall control' test[111] for attribution of the acts of non-state actors to a state.[112] While the Appeals Chamber did not differ with regard to the test for effective control, it found that this test was suitable for the acts of individuals and unorganized groups, while the test for organized groups should be that of overall control.[113] The requirement for overall control is that an individual must be a member of an 'organized and hierarchically structured group'. This test is wide and includes military units or 'armed bands of irregulars or rebels' and 'any other hierarchically organized group'.[114] Overall control does not require any specific instructions by the controlling state concerning the commission of acts by a non-state actor. It is satisfied where there is support by the state as well as participation in the general direction, coordination and supervision of the activities and operations.[115] It has been argued that the

108 *Armed Activities on the Territory of the Congo* (*DRC v Uganda*) (n 50).

109 *Prosecutor v Tadić Judgment*, IT-94-1-A (7 May 1997).

110 Ibid., paras 605, 141, 584–585, 601–606.

111 *Prosecutor v Tadić* (n 109).

112 Ibid., 72 para 162. 'The Appeals Chamber therefore concludes that, for the period material to this case (1992), the armed forces of the Republika Srpska were to be regarded as acting under the overall control of and on behalf of the FRY.'

113 Ibid., para 132, 141. See further United States Diplomatic and Consular Staff in Tehran (*Hostages* case) (*US v Iran*) Merits (24 May 1980) (1980) ICJ Reports 3, 13, para. 17.

114 *Tadić* (n 109) paras 120, 125–128, 137, 146.

115 Ibid., para 131. See further para 137: 'when a state (or, in the context of an armed conflict, the Party to the conflict) has a role in organizing, coordinating or planning the military actions of the military group, in addition to financing, training and equipping or providing operational support to that group'.

organizational requirement adds some control in itself, as it is much easier to control an organized group than one made up of loosely-tied individuals without clear hierarchies.[116]

In the context of terrorism, the international community initially relied on the standards for attribution, that is, the effective control test, as set out in *Nicaragua*.[117] For example, in 1985 Israel attacked the headquarters of the PLO in Tunisia and claimed to have acted in self-defence.[118] Israel alleged that Tunisia was harbouring, supplying and assisting non-state actors that had committed acts of terrorism within Israeli territory and that the PLO headquarters housed key PLO leadership authorities.[119] Israel's raid was 'condemn[ed] vigorously' by the UNSC, which declared it an 'act of armed aggression ... in flagrant violation of the Charter of the United Nations', and the UNSC urged other states 'to take measures to dissuade Israel from resorting to such acts against the sovereignty and territorial integrity of all states'.[120] The Tunisian Ambassador to France, Hédi Mabrouk, called the raid 'state terrorism' which resulted in many civilian casualties as well as casualties among Tunisian security forces. Mr Mabrouk stated that Tunisia 'has never been a base for terrorists'.[121]

The greatest effect of the prohibition of terrorism as a *jus cogens* norm is felt in the customary international law rules of attribution. The rules of attribution are not *jus cogens*, but ordinary rules of customary international law. As a norm of *jus cogens*, the prohibition of terrorism would thus trump the rules of attribution. Article 51 of the Charter does not specify a certain approach with regard to attribution, and it has been argued that the rules of attribution are not set in stone.[122] The traditional approach requiring 'effective state control' as set out in *Nicaragua*, *Oil Platforms* and *DRC* was a standard developed by the ICJ.[123] Arguably, a move towards a more lenient standard of attribution is being shown under customary international law. Thus, while the focus of case law up to the time of the *Tadić* judgment by the ICTY Appeals Chamber has been on the effective control test, increasing arguments in favour of acts of

116 Ibid., paras 153, 155–156; Kokott (n 109).
117 Brody (n 55) 40.
118 Michael Byers, *War Law: Understanding International Law and Armed Conflict* (Grove Press 2007) 62; Gray (n 60) 161.
119 Maogoto (n 64) 112.
120 S/RES/ 573 (1985); S/RES/313 (1972), S/RES/508 and 509 (1982).
121 'Israeli Planes Attack PLO in Tunis, Killing At Least 30; Raid "Legitimate", US Says' *New York Times* (2 October 1985) <www.nytimes.com/1985/10/02/world/israeli-planes-attack-plo-in-tunis-killing-at-least-30-raid-legitimate-us-says.html?mcubz=3> accessed 28 August 2017.
122 Tams (n 57) 383–7.
123 Ibid., 386.

terrorists harboured by a state or where terrorist activities are not restrained by a state to be attributed to the state in question necessitates a reconsideration of this test.

In this regard, authors have been arguing in favour of a relaxation of the standard of attribution to address the increasing problem of terrorist groups being supported by states. This includes the argument that, if the host state does not act to curb the activities of the non-state actors in its territory, a state that has been a victim of an armed attack by those non-state actors may use force against them in that territory. Tams notes that contemporary practice suggests that a territorial state has to accept anti-terrorist measures of self-defence directed against its territory where it is responsible for complicity in the activities of terrorists based on its territory, 'either because of its support below the level of direction and control or because it has provided a safe haven for terrorists'.[124] In terms of the Common Defence Pact of the African Union (AU), 'the encouragement, support, harbouring or provision of any assistance for the commission of terrorist acts and other violent trans-national organized crimes against a member state' constitute acts of aggression.[125]

The author Bethlehem includes in the attribution of the acts of non-state actors to states, states' planning, threatening, and perpetrating armed attacks and those providing material support essential to those attacks, 'such that they can be said to be taking a direct part in those attacks'.[126] He also suggests that if a state is unable or otherwise unwilling to effectively restrain the armed activities of the non-state actor, it leaves the victim state with no other reasonably available effective means of addressing an imminent or actual armed attack than to act in self-defence.[127] The latter view has been criticized by Tladi. It would imply the lowering of the standard of attribution for an armed attack against a state not responsible for the terrorist attack and where there is no basis for attribution, in other words no objective basis for concluding that such a state is colluding with, or is otherwise unwilling to effectively restrain the armed activities of the non-state actor (referred to as a non-consenting innocent state).This would mean that consent may be dispensed with even where such a state takes reasonable but ineffective measures to prevent its territory

124 Ibid., 385.

125 Art 1(c)(xi) of the Common Defence Pact of the African Union 2005.

126 Bethlehem (n 6), Principle 6. Principle 7 states that '[a]rmed self-defence may also be directed against those in respect of whom there is a strong, reasonable, and objective basis for concluding that they are taking a direct part in those attacks through the provision of material support to the attacks'.

127 Bethlehem (n 6), Principles 11 and 12.

from being used to launch attacks.[128] Murphy argues in favour of broadening the standards of attribution of a state by including the concept of 'aiding and abetting' in terrorist activities.[129] Gray questions whether a wider right of self-defence has developed which allows for the use of force in self-defence against non-state actors in the territory of a third state that was not involved in the terrorist attack.[130]

Cassese acknowledges that the effective control standard is problematic when used to assess whether violent actions by terrorist groups may be imputed to states aiding and abetting terrorism.[131] He notes that the effective control test raises serious problems of evidence in these scenarios as the hidden nature and covert actions involved in terrorism make it virtually impossible to prove the issuance of instructions or directions by a state to a terrorist operation or proving that a particular terrorist group has acted upon instructions or directions, or is under the specific control of a state.[132] He argues in favour of the overall control test for attribution which would make it easier to hold such states responsible for terrorist acts. With regard to the conduct of organized armed groups, it is sufficient to show that the state to which they may be linked exercises 'overall control' over them in order for the conduct of those groups or units to be legally attributed to the state.[133] Notably, Cassese still requires an element of active involvement by the state. He states that it would be sufficient to demonstrate that certain terrorist groups are not only supported, armed, financed, equipped or trained by a specific state, but also that such a state generally speaking organizes or coordinates or, at least, participates in coordinating or planning its terrorist actions.[134]

In practice, there was general agreement that the US could resort to measures of self-defence in response to the 9/11 attacks and a notable absence of condemnation by states of the actions of the US.[135] In reality, however, the link

128 Tladi (n 69) 573.

129 Murphy (n 103) 51.

130 Gray (n 60); Christian Tams and James Sloan (eds), *The Development of International Law by the International Court of Justice* (Oxford University Press 2013).

131 Antonio Cassese, 'The *Nicaragua* and *Tadic* Tests Revisited in Light of the ICJ Judgment on Genocide in Bosnia' (2007) 18 European Journal of International Law 649–68.

132 Ibid.

133 Ibid.

134 Ibid.

135 See further Michael Schmitt, 'Counter-Terrorism and the Use of Force' in Fred Borch and Paul Wilson (eds), *International Law and The War On Terror* (Newport 2003) 161 <https://www.researchgate.net/publication/235160755_counter-terrorism-and-the-use-of-force-in International-Law> accessed 20 August 2017, where he argues that '[w]hile the legitimacy of translating the non-reaction into a new norm regarding state support of terrorism is

of attribution was tenuous, and it has been argued that there was no link of attribution to impute the acts of al Qaeda to Afghanistan as justification for the US to use force in self-defence against Afghanistan.[136] That the US admitted to using force against Afghanistan and not only to target al Qaeda was clear from a statement by the then President George W Bush immediately after the attacks. In announcing the war in Afghanistan, Bush said that the US 'will make no distinction between the terrorists who committed these acts and those who harbour them'; that by 'aiding and abetting murder, the Taliban regime is committing murder'; and that the 'Taliban must act and act immediately [and] … hand over the terrorists, or they will share in their fate'.[137]

The US attacks, therefore, were attacks on Afghanistan, and not on al Qaeda, and the basis of the attacks seemed to be a kind of attribution of blameworthiness to the Taliban government for harbouring and refusing to hand over terrorists.[138] The Taliban's provision of a safe haven to Bin Laden and its toleration of his terrorist training camps in areas generally controlled by the Taliban, as well as its receipt of monies and military support from Bin Laden for the Taliban's war against the Northern Alliance, would not constitute the Taliban's control of, or direct participation in, al Qaeda attacks and cannot be used to justify the use of military force against the Taliban. Indeed, Taliban support for al Qaeda fell far below the threshold set in either *Nicaragua* or *Tadić*.[139] For the conduct of irregular forces to be attributable to a state, that state had to exercise 'effective control [over] the military or paramilitary operations' in question. In *Nicaragua* where the ICJ found that, although knowing assistance by the US to the contras in the form of the provision of weapons or logistical or other support might constitute the non-permissible use of force leading to state responsibility, such acts would not constitute an armed attack for purposes of attribution of the acts of the contras to the US and triggering the right to use of force in self-defence.[140]

In earlier case law, in the *Corfu Channel* case, the ICJ stated that every state has the obligation to 'not knowingly allow its territory to be used for acts

questionable, it is certainly evidence of a community conviction that Afghanistan had not met its obligations to police its territory'. Franck (n 103) 839; SC Resolutions 1510 (2003); 1589 (2005); 1659 and 1707 (2006) and 1368 (2001).

136 Tladi (n 69) 574–5.

137 CNN 'Transcript of President Bush's Address to a Joint Session of Congress on Thursday night, September 20, 2001' http://edition.cnn.com/2001/US/09/20/gen.bush.transcript/ accessed 28 August 2017.

138 Tladi (n 69) 575.

139 Schmitt (n 91) 144.

140 See *Nicaragua* (n 1) paras 18, 93–94, 228.

contrary to the rights of other states'.[141] In the 1980 *Theran Hostages* case, the ICJ found that the authorities of one state are required to take appropriate action to protect the interests of a foreign state's officials and citizens, particularly while they have the means to do so.[142]

An example of whether the actions of a non-state actor can be imputed to a state was when, on 12 July 2006, Hezbollah launched Operation True Promise, involving the ambush and killing of Israel Defence Force (IDF) soldiers patrolling the border with Lebanon as well as rocket attacks against northern Israeli towns and IDF facilities. Israel quickly reacted with Operation Change Direction, which included a naval and air blockade of Lebanon, air strikes throughout the country, and a major ground incursion into Southern Lebanon.[143] Israel initially made statements attributing Hezbollah's actions to Lebanon owing to Lebanon's failure to control the south.[144] Moreover, the UN Human Rights Council report of November 2006 drew a close connection between Hezbollah and Lebanon, noting that in Lebanon, Hezbollah is a legally-recognized political party, has duly elected representatives in parliament, and is part of the government.[145] Therefore, it stated that Hezbollah

> integrates and participates in the constitutional organs of the state ... The effective behaviour of Hezbollah in South Lebanon suggests an inferred link between the Government of Lebanon and Hezbollah in the latter's assumed role over the years as a resistance movement against Israel's occupation of Lebanese territory ... Hezbollah had also assumed *de facto* state authority and control in South Lebanon in non-full implementation of Security Council Resolutions 1559 (2004) and 1680 (2006).[146]

141 *Corfu Channel* case (n 60) 22.

142 United States Diplomatic and Consular Staff in Tehran (n 113) paras 32–3, 44.

143 Schmitt (n 91) 127.

144 See the special Cabinet Communiqué issued the day of the Hezbollah attacks: by the Cabinet Secratariat, Israeli Ministry of Foreign Affairs <transcripts.cnn.com/TRANSCRIPTS/0607/15/se.01.html> accessed 3 September 2017. The Communiqué noted that 'Israel views the sovereign Lebanese government as responsible for the action that originated on its soil and for the return of the abducted soldiers to Israel. Israel demands that the Lebanese government implement UN Security Resolution 1559.'

145 UNGA HRC Commission of Inquiry on Lebanon 'Implementation of General Assembly Resolution 60/251 of 15 March 2006 entitled "Human Rights Council"': Report of the Commission of Inquiry on Lebanon pursuant to Human Rights Council Resolution S-2/1 UN Doc A/HRC/3/2 (23 November 2006) 55.

146 Ibid.

In letters to the UN Secretary-General and Security Council President, the Charge d'Affairs of the Permanent Mission of Lebanon to the UN claimed that 'the Lebanese government was not aware of the events that occurred and are occurring on the international Lebanese border' and that 'the Lebanese government is not responsible for these events and does not endorse them'.[147] Prime Minister Siniora similarly distanced himself from the attacks, denying any prior knowledge thereof.[148] By the end of the conflict Israel, however, refrained from arguments that Hezbollah actions amounted to a Lebanese armed attack.[149] Eventually Israel's self-defence justification was focused on Hezbollah as opposed to alleged actions by Lebanon.[150]

Notwithstanding the above, the question arises as to whether in the circumstances Hezbollah's acts could have been attributed to Lebanon for Israel to characterize these acts as an attack by Lebanon itself, on the basis of Hezbollah's participation in the Lebanese government and the government's apparent recognition of the organization as a legitimate resistance group. It has been argued that there was not enough evidence to impute the acts of Hezbollah to Lebanon on the basis of article 8 of DARSIWA, which provides that an action carried out 'on the instructions of, or under the direction or control of, the state' amounts to an 'act of a state'.[151] Despite the fact that Hezbollah had seats in the National Assembly and occupied two Cabinet posts, it is unsustainable to argue that virtually all Hezbollah members thereby became agents of the state.[152] There is no evidence that the Lebanese government controlled Hezbollah or directed its actions, either directly or indirectly, or that Hezbollah parliamentarians or cabinet members were otherwise involved in the attacks. It was further not an entity that exercised elements of the governmental authority in the absence of the official authorities pursuant to article 9 of DARSIWA.[153] Accordingly, it does not meet the overall control test for imputability.

It is important, however, to take into account the context in which the use of force in Operation Change Direction occurred. The situation in Lebanon

147 Charge d'Affairs of the Permanent Mission of Lebanon to the United Nations. Letters dated 13 July 2006 addressed to the Secretary-General and the President of the Security Council UN Doc A/60/938, S/2006/518 (13 July 2006).

148 Prime Minister Fouad Siniora Address to the Lebanese people, July 15, 2006 <transcripts.cnn.com/TRANSCRIPTS/0607/15/se.01.html> accessed 3 September 2017.

149 Schmitt (n 91) 139.

150 Ibid., 141.

151 See art 8 of DARSIWA (n 111).

152 Schmitt (n 91) 141.

153 Ibid., 142.

differed from that after 9/11. Until its expulsion from Lebanon in 1982, the PLO used Southern Lebanon as a base of operations against Israel.[154] In 1982 Israel invaded Lebanon and expelled the PLO and its leader, Yasser Arafat.[155] Israel established a buffer zone in the southern part of the country where the IDF remained for the next 18 years. In May 2000 Israel ended its occupation of Southern Lebanon.[156] The UN Interim Force on Lebanon and the Lebanese government failed to deter further Palestinian attacks. During this period Israel repeatedly called on Lebanon to establish control over the south. Likewise, the UNSC regularly stressed the importance of Lebanese action.[157] Not only did Lebanon fail to exert physical control over Hezbollah-controlled territory, but it also refused to freeze the organization's financial assets.[158] Following its withdrawal from Lebanon in 2000, both Israel and the international community repeatedly demanded that Lebanon move south to secure the area from Hezbollah and other terrorist attacks. Lebanon, however, failed to take any steps to prevent the misuse of its territory by Hezbollah.[159]

Accordingly, there was a history of Lebanon failing to take action to avoid the misuse of its territory by Hezbollah. Furthermore, Israel's Operation Change Direction was confined to a certain area in Lebanon. It lasted for a limited period of 34 days and, although Israel struck Lebanese military targets, it avoided striking Lebanese government facilities and equipment, at least those without an express link to Hezbollah.[160] There was, thus, cautious acceptance of the legitimacy of the Israeli defensive response to Hezbollah. Secretary-General Annan acknowledged Israel's right to defend itself under article 51 of the UN Charter.[161] UNSC Resolution 1702 indicated that Hezbollah's attacks of 12 July had precipitated the events that followed.[162] The US, Canada, Australia

154 Ibid., 130.

155 See Barry Feinstein, 'The Legality of the Use of Force by Israel in Lebanon – June 1982' (1985) 20 Israeli Law Review 362.

156 S/RES/1310 (2000) on the situation in the Middle East.

157 See Resolutions on Lebanon: S/RES/1310 (2000), S/RES/1337 (2001); S/RES/1365 (2001), S/RES/1391, 1428 (2002); S/RES/1461 and 1496 (2003); S/RES/1525, 1553 and 1559 (2004); S/RES/1583 and 1614 (2005); S/RES 1680 and 1655 (2006).

158 Audrey Cronin and others, Congressional Research Service Report, Foreign Terrorist Organsations, Report No RL32223, 6 February 2004 <https://fas.org/irp/crs/RL32223.pdf> accessed 26 October 2017.

159 Schmitt (n 91) 163.

160 Ibid., 139, 164.

161 The Secretary-General Statement to the Security Council UN SCOR 61st Session 5492 meeting UN Doc S/PV.5492 (20 July 2006) 3.

162 S/RES/1701 (2006) T11: The Council '[e]xpress[ed] its utmost concern at the continuing escalation of hostilities in Lebanon and in Israel since Hizbollah's attack on Israel on 12 July 2006'. See further The Secretary-General Report on the United Nations Interim Force

and the European Union supported Israel's actions.[163] Although Israel did not finally argue that its attacks had also been against Lebanon, it has been argued that Operation Change Direction serves as an example of the growing acceptability of cross-border counter-terrorist operations when the state in which terrorists are located fails to comply with the duty of policing its own territory.[164]

Although the status of the prohibition of terrorism as a *jus cogens* norm resulted in a movement towards a special standard of imputability in relations between terrorist groups and host states most closely resembling international rules against 'aiding and abetting' illegal conduct,[165] imputability still requires some level of complicity by the harbouring state. The use of force against such a state cannot be justified where a state has no active involvement in the terrorist conduct. A non-consenting innocent state which was not responsible for a terrorist attack and may have taken reasonable but ineffective measures to restrain terrorist activities in its territory, but had no additional level of direct involvement in terrorist activities, may thus not be subjected to an armed attack in self-defence. While on the one hand it should be appreciated that a state cannot passively accept that terrorists can freely use bases in other countries for attacks on states, any further dilution of the restrictions on the use of force in international law to allow for armed attacks in anticipatory self-defence against a non-consenting innocent state may, in itself, constitute a threat to international peace and security and may open the door to the misuse of military force.[166] It is thus argued that while the prohibition of terrorism

---

in Lebanon to the Security Council delivered to the Security Council UN Doc S/2006/560 (21 July 2006) 3: 'The crisis started when, around 9 am local time, Hizbollah launched several rockets from Lebanese territory across the withdrawal line (the so-called Blue Line) towards Israel Defence Forces (IDF) positions near the coast and in the area of the Israeli town of Zarit. In parallel, Hizbollah fighters crossed the Blue Line into Israel and attacked an IDF patrol. Hizbollah captured two IDF soldiers, killed three others and wounded two more. The captured soldiers were taken into Lebanon.'

163 See 'Israel Acting in Self-defence, Says Howard' Australian Broadcasting Corporation News Online <https://abc.net.au/news/2006/israel-acting-in-self-defence-say-howard/1802556> accessed 3 September 2017; Delegation of the European Commission to the United Nations, EU Council Conclusions on the Middle East, 17 July 2006, <www.europa-eu-un.org/articles/en/article_6125 en.htm> accessed 3 September 2017; US Department of State's Bureau of International Info Programs 'G8 Statement on Situation in Middle East' <https://2001-20-09.state.gov/p/us/rm/2006/69071.htm> accessed 3 September 2017.

164 Schmitt (n 91) 164.

165 Tams (n 57) 385.

166 Tom Farer, 'Beyond the Charter Frame: Unilateralism or Condominium' (2002) 96(2) American Journal of International Law 363; Frédéric Megret, 'War? Legal Semantics and the Move to Violence' (2002) 13(2) European Journal of International Law 384, 397–9;

as *jus cogens* has led to a relaxation of the standards of attribution to overall control rather than effective control, it still requires a level of complicity by the state concerned before force may be used against such state.

5 A Normative Conflict?

This section will investigate whether there is a normative conflict between the prohibition of terrorism and the prohibition of the use of force as *jus cogens* norms or whether it is possible for the two norms to co-exist without conflict. The threat of terrorism has called into question the basic paradigm on the law of the use of force as set out in the UN Charter and customary international law. The law of the Charter was aimed at addressing conventional threats posed by conventional actors, namely, states as opposed to non-state actors. Similarly, the criterion for anticipatory self-defence in customary international law as set out in the Caroline incident arguably is not geared towards attacks by non-state actors where there is no time to wait for the armed attack to become imminent. Terrorist tactics are often covert and almost impossible to detect until they are well advanced or finalized (as is illustrated by 9/11).[167]

The prohibition of terrorism and the prohibition of the use of force protect both the interests of international peace and security. The prohibition of terrorism further protects the underlying value of human dignity. Similarly, the use of inter-state force may have consequences for individuals and also impair human dignity, as the indiscriminate use of force may have grave consequences for individuals who may be treated as a 'means to an end'. The question arises as to whether a legal antinomy arises between the two *jus cogens* norms which would necessitate a limitation of one of the norms in order to apply both to a relevant situation (that is, counter-terrorism measures).

From a normative point of view, the norms of the prohibition of terrorism and the prohibition of force are not in conflict. In other words, both norms can be applied to a given situation without the need to limit one or both of the norms. In particular, it is important that the prohibition against the unilateral use of force is not diluted. Any illegal force in the furtherance of the fight against terrorism would retain its illegal character while the legal use of force in the pursuit of the prohibition of terrorism is allowed.

Michael Byers, 'The Shifting Foundations of International Law: A Decade of Forceful Measures Against Iraq' (2002) 13(1) European Journal of International Law 36, 38–9.

167 Anthony Clarke, 'International Law and the Pre-Emptive Use of Military Force' (2003) 26(2) The Washington Quarterly 89.

The law relative to the use of force (*jus ad bellum*), however, is evolving owing to a variety of strategic factors related to the advent of non-state terror actors.[168] This does not, however, affect the nature of the prohibition of the use of force as a norm from which no derogation is permitted. The prohibition of the use of armed force remains a *jus cogens* norm, but arguably there has been a development of the rules of customary international law pertaining to the definition of an armed attack and the rules of attribution of the acts of a non-state actor to a state. In this regard, an armed attack can consist of an accumulation of attacks, and overall control is increasingly being regarded as sufficient for the imputablity of the act of a non-state actor to a state. This has led to a normative drift affecting key limitations of the traditional doctrine of self-defence, which may increase the risk of abuse.[169]

6 Conclusion

As part of the evaluation of the role of *jus cogens* in the rules of international law relating to terrorism, this chapter has considered the interaction between the prohibition of force and the prohibition of terrorism. Section 2 provided an overview of the status of the use of force as a *jus cogens* norm under treaty law and customary international law. It was illustrated that the prohibition of the use of force as a *jus cogens* norm is uncontested under international law. Section 3 considered which uses of force are norms of *jus cogens*, and found that there must be an element of aggression and that non-armed use of force would not qualify as an armed attack or justify the use of armed force in self-defence. Section 4 considered the requirements for the use of force in self-defence, including an armed attack, attribution of the acts of non-state actors to a state and necessity and proportionality under customary international law. It found that the status of the prohibition of the use of force as a *jus cogens* norm has not led to a relaxation of the requirements of necessity and proportionality under customary international law. It has, however, led to the increased acceptance of the accumulation of events doctrine (a series of low-grade attacks constituting an armed attack), as well as a lower overall effective control test for attribution of the acts of non-state actors to a state.

Section 4 further found that the prohibition of the use of force as a jus co*gens* norm has not led to the imputability of acts of a non-state actor to a non-consenting innocent state, including where such a state has taken reasonable

168 Brody (n 55) 87.
169 Tams (n 57) 359.

but ineffective measures to address terrorism within its territory. Where, however, forcible action is taken against a non-state actor in a territory where the state in which the non-state actor resides has failed to take any measures to police its terroritory for a lenthy period of time, despite pleas by the UNSC and other states, such action by the victim state has enjoyed more acceptance.

The requirements of necessity and proportionality in relation to the use of force in anticipatory self-defence were considered in light of state practice and international jurisprudence. It is argued that these requirements have not been restricted by the prohibition of terrorism as a *jus cogens* norm. Section 5 found that the legitimate use of force is not antagonistic to counter-terrorism measures and that no normative weighing or limitation of either the prohibition of terrorism or the prohibition of the use of force is necessary.

Conclusion

This book considered the role of *jus cogens* norms in the context of international terrorism. The universal condemnation of terrorism gave rise to the question of whether the prohibition of terrorism has acquired *jus cogens* status. This was discussed in Part I of the book. Part I, in chapters 2 to 4, considered the regulation and prohibition of terrorism under international law and the elements of a definition of terrorism that have emerged from international law. It further discussed the criteria and characteristics for a *jus cogens* norm and whether the prohibition of terrorism has been elevated to a *jus cogens* norm as set out in the Vienna Convention on the Law of Treaties (Vienna Convention), namely, a norm of general international law accepted and recognized by the international community of states as a norm from which no derogation is permitted. Part II analyzed the effect of state responses to terrorism in light of other rules of international law which could also constitute *jus cogens*, such as the prohibition of torture, the right to a fair trial and the prohibition of the use of force under international law.

In Part I, chapter 1 discussed the prohibition and regulation of terrorism under international law and considered whether a definition of terrorism had emerged under customary international law, notwithstanding the fact that there is no agreed-upon international treaty definition of international terrorism. This chapter found that terrorism is prohibited under treaty law, state practice and the United Nations Security Council (UNSC) and United Nations General Assembly (UNGA) resolutions. While initially courts tended to treat acts of terrorism as ordinary crimes under domestic legislation or relied on the prohibition of specific terrorist acts under sectoral treaties, courts later condemned terrorism irrespective of the absence of an internationally agreed-upon definition of terrorism.

Furthermore, notwithstanding the absence of such a definition of terrorism, an analysis of international conventions illustrated that certain common elements have emerged with regard to the definition of terrorism, namely, criminal acts intended to terrorize populations or coerce an authority to do or abstain from doing any act, with a transnational element. Likewise, under regional conventions, definitions had in common: violence causing harm to persons or property, an element of terror or fear, a political purpose element and a transnational element. A review of national legislation revealed similar elements in the definitions of terrorism. Although there were semantic differences, the core elements that emerged from national legislation and jurisprudence were similar to the elements that had emerged from treaty law, namely,

 | DOI:10.1163/9789004391543_008

that a terrorist act is an act causing the death of or serious harm to a civilian, with the purpose of intimidating a population or for a political purpose and with a transnational element.

Furthermore, these elements found support in national and international jurisprudence. International criminal courts, such as the International Criminal Tribunal for the former Yugoslavia (ICTY), found that terrorism is a crime under customary international law with the elements of a criminal act, the intent of spreading fear among the population, a political motive and a transnational element. These elements are further supported in the Draft Comprehensive Convention on International Terrorism of 2006. With regard to this Convention, it is not the exclusionary elements that have prevented the finalization of this Convention, but rather whether acts of self-determination and activities by the military forces of a state should be excluded from the definition.

Moreover, an analysis of the prohibition of terrorism in various UNSC and UNGA resolutions illustrated the unequivocal condemnation of all terrorist acts, methods and practices of terrorism as criminal and unjustifiable, regardless of their motivation. The UNGA and UNSC resolutions further set out the elements of terrorism as containing a criminal act against civilians, committed with intent, requiring serious violence, and containing a political purpose and a transnational element. Resolutions such as UN Resolution 1373 of 2001 imposed binding, quasi-legislative obligations on member states to take certain actions to fight terrorism and to report on its counter-terrorism measures to the Counter-Terrorism Committee (CTC).

The evidence in this chapter supported the near-universal prohibition and condemnation of terrorism, as well as the view that an agreed definition of international terrorism has emerged under customary international law. Accordingly, terrorism indeed has attained, in international law, a core, objectively determinable meaning. The common elements of international terrorism reflected in treaties, state practice, UNGA and UNSC resolutions and international jurisprudence are an act of violence, committed with the intent to cause death or serious bodily injury to any person, or to spread fear among civilians, for a political purpose and with a transnational element. This chapter found that the absence of a comprehensive definition does not preclude the identification or prohibition of international terrorism.

Chapter 2 initiated a discussion of the criteria for a norm to be elevated to a *jus cogens* norm, and whether the prohibition of terrorism meets these criteria. In terms of article 53 of the Vienna Convention, a *jus cogens* norm is a norm of general international law which is accepted and recognized by the international community as a whole as a norm from which no derogation is permitted.

The evolution of the concept of *jus cogens* through the ages was discussed. It was found that *jus cogens* is steeped in the natural law tradition, and early writers were of the view that there are certain necessary principles of international law that are *jus scriptum* (obligatory law) and permit no derogation as they are derived from a higher source, namely, natural law. The idea of certain peremptory, non-derogable norms eventually received a positivist slant with its formal inclusion in the Vienna Convention. In this regard, the various debates in the International Law Commission (ILC) with regard to the wording of article 53 were discussed, and it was noted that, while there was support for the existence of *jus cogens* norms, the ILC was of the view that the content of the rule would be worked out in state practice and jurisprudence. Notwithstanding the fact that the precise nature of *jus cogens* norms remained a subject of debate, article 53 of the Vienna Convention did set out the criteria for norms of general international law to be elevated to *jus cogens* status. This chapter then evaluated whether the prohibition of terrorism meets these criteria.

As was established in chapter 1, the prohibition of terrorism is a norm of customary international law. Customary international law forms part of general international law and, accordingly, the prohibition of terrorism is a norm of general international law. Furthermore, general international law consists of norms that support the 'moral commandments of society', which are not consent-based and which are binding *erga omnes*. In addition to this, the support for universal jurisdiction in respect of terrorist crimes may also be evidence of its status as a norm of general international law. This chapter further found that the prohibition of terrorism is recognized by the international community as a whole, by way of *opinio juris*, as a norm already in existence and from which no derogation is permitted owing to the essential interests which that norm protects. Recognition by states of the prohibition of terrorism, therefore, is declaratory, not constitutive.

In addition to the above, it was found that the prohibition of terrorism meets the core characteristics of *jus cogens* norms. This chapter found that the core characteristics of *jus cogens* norms as have emerged from international law are that these norms protect the fundamental values of the international community, are hierarchically superior and are universally applicable. Although it is sufficient for its *jus cogens* status that the prohibition of terrorism meets the criteria in article 53 of the Vienna Convention, the possession of these characteristics provided further support for the prohibition of terrorism as a *jus cogens* norm.

It was found that the prohibition of terrorism protects certain fundamental values which are of such importance that they enjoy a superior hierarchical position. Acts of terrorism are committed with the intent of spreading fear amongst innocent civilians and using human beings as instruments for the furtherance of a political or ideological goal. This infringes upon the basic right to human dignity. Terrorism further enjoys near-universal condemnation and, owing to the nature of the values it protects, the prohibition of terrorism is hierarchically superior to other norms of general international law. Furthermore, the prohibition of terrorism is universally binding by its very nature and leads to *erga omnes* obligations.

On the basis that the prohibition of terrorism as a norm of *jus cogens*, Part II considered the effect of the prohibition of terrorism and counter-terrorism measures on other norms which may similarly be norms of *jus cogens*, namely, the right to a fair trial; the prohibition of torture; and the international law on the use of force. This included an evaluation of whether the aforementioned rights may be limited in the context of counter-terrorism measures.

Chapter 3 discussed the effect of the prohibition of torture on the prohibition of terrorism. It analyzed the prohibition of torture under international law and found that torture is widely prohibited under regional and international treaty law. The Convention against Torture (CAT) enjoys ratification by 161 state parties of 193 UN member states. In addition to this, it found that torture is prohibited in the national legislation of numerous states and that state practice similarly evidences the prohibition of torture. In order to consider which acts would amount to prohibited torture during counter-terrorism measures, this chapter further evaluated the elements of torture that appear from the sources of international law. The elements of intent, severe pain and suffering, purpose and the commission of the act of torture by a public official, as set out in the widely-ratified CAT, were discussed in the context of the national legislation of states.

This chapter found signs of evolution with regard to what is regarded as torture under international law. With regard to the degree or severity of torture, while the Declaration against Torture referred to torture as an aggravated or deliberate form of cruel, inhuman and degrading treatment or punishment, the CAT omitted this wording. National jurisprudence did not seem to support a requirement of severity for an act to constitute torture, but only the infliction of some form of pain and suffering, and the degree or severity of the pain and suffering was not a consistent element. The case law of regional treaty bodies further illustrated support for the prohibition of torture in the absence of physical violence (including the threat of violence, torture or mock executions and mental torture). This chapter found support for the evolution of a view that 'severity' is a relative concept and depends on all the circumstances of the case, including the duration of the treatment, its physical or mental effects, as well as the sex, age and state of health of the victim. Accordingly, certain acts which in the past had been classified as inhuman and degrading treatment and not torture as these acts purportedly lacked the requisite degree of severity, would now amount to torture. This would include the psychological 'stress and duress' techniques to which terrorist suspects have allegedly been subjected at Abu Graib and Guantanamo Bay in the United States, such as sleep deprivation, blindfolding or hooding and being bound in awkward painful positions.

In additionally, with regard to the requirement of the intent and purpose of the act of torture (for example obtaining information or a confession, punishment, intimidation or coercion or for any reason based on discrimination of any kind) and the commission of the act by a public official, this chapter found that prohibited torture under international law is often concerned with torture that is the result of state policy. Cruelty by private individuals unrelated to state activity, therefore, does not qualify as torture under international law. Furthermore, public officials (such as the US Central Intelligence Agency) are often accused of being the perpetrators of torture during counter-terrorism measures, such as torture inflicted on terrorist suspects at Abu Ghraib and Guantanamo Bay. The widespread use of torture and the consistency of torturous methods used in the war against terrorism may indicate a strategic element and support the requirement of state involvement as an element of torture.

With regard to national legislation, this chapter found that individual states have varied in implementing the intent, purpose and state official involvement requirements. The definitions of some states mirror the definition in the CAT while others do not require the intent of the perpetrator nor mention a specific purpose. The legislation of certain states includes torture for some purposes (for instance, to extract a confession) but not for others (for instance, for purposes of punishment or for discriminatory reasons). The public official requirement is not consistently reflected, although some definitions specifically refer to the torture of detainees which may point to some level of state involvement. In national jurisprudence, some support was found for the contention that a plaintiff must establish some governmental involvement in the torture or killing to constitute a prohibited act of torture. International jurisprudence supported torture for a prohibited purpose, including punishment, intimidation, extracting information or a confession and the commission of such act by a public official. It further found that the requirement of acquiescence by a state official in an act of torture would be met if such an official was aware of the torture and turned a blind eye towards it. Intent and purpose interacted, as the requirement of intent was met when the torture is committed for a prohibited purpose, often to extract a confession.

Although the elements of intent, purpose and involvement of a state official were not consistent in state practice, the majority of states are party to the CAT and, therefore, bound by the CAT definition of torture. Furthermore, in the context of terrorism and cases involving torture as part of counter-terrorism measures, some level of state involvement is required and an act of torture must be permitted with intent and for a prohibited purpose, or it would constitute a private act of torture.

This chapter further considered whether the prohibition of torture is a *jus cogens* norm in light of the criteria and characteristics of *jus cogens* norms as set out in chapter 2. It found that the prohibition of torture met both the criteria and characteristics of *jus cogens* norms. With regard to the criteria for a *jus cogens* norm, the prohibition of torture is a norm under customary international law and, therefore, a norm of general international law. Evidence of acceptance and recognition appeared from various universal and regional treaties, national legislation, statements by states before the UN that reject torture, as well as international jurisprudence. It was accordingly argued that there is no dissent about the fact that the prohibition of torture is a *jus cogens* norm and an absolute right that may never be derogated from, not even in a state of emergency. This chapter further found support in state practice and jurisprudence that the prohibition of torture meets the characteristics of a *jus cogens* norm. State practice supported the prohibition of torture as specific, universal and obligatory. The prohibition of torture has been described as a fundamental standard of the international community and superior to state power. It protects the right to the fundamental value of the right to human dignity, is hierarchically superior because of the importance of the values it protects and, linked to its superior status, is universally applicable.

As a norm of *jus cogens*, it was then considered whether the prohibition of torture could be limited in the context of anti-terrorism measures in support of another *jus cogens* norm, namely, the prohibition of terrorism. Jurisprudence dealing with torture in the context of the fight against terrorism was considered. This chapter found support for upholding the absolute prohibition of torture even in the fight against terrorism, and argued that no derogation from the prohibition of torture can be allowed. Under international jurisprudence, even lighter forms of torture, such as the shaking of suspected terrorists, was prohibited, as well as the deportation of suspected terrorists to a state where they may face torture. Arguments that if a state adduced evidence that a threat to national security existed, stronger evidence had to be adduced by the applicant to prove that he would be at risk of ill-treatment in the receiving country, were dismissed. It was further found that there is no legal antinomy between the prohibition of terrorism and the prohibition of torture – both norms therefore can be applied in the context of terrorism without any need for limitation of either norm. Both the prohibition of terrorism and the prohibition of torture protect the underlying value of human dignity, which cannot be limited.

Chapter 4 addressed the question of whether the right to a fair trial can be limited as part of counter-terrorism measures. While the right to a fair trial consists of numerous elements, this chapter suggested that there are certain core elements to the right to a fair trial. In this regard it found that, while certain fair trial rights are capable of derogation, such as the right to call witnesses, the right to a public hearing and the right to legal counsel, other elements of the right to a fair trial are non-derogable, namely, the right to a hearing before an impartial tribunal, the presumption of innocence and the right to review. These rights were suggested as core fair trial rights guaranteed in both civil and criminal proceedings, and the content of these rights was then discussed under international law.

With regard to the right of an accused to access to a hearing before a fair and impartial tribunal, this chapter found that treaty law, state practice and international jurisprudence supported this right as a core, non-derogable fair trial right, even in circumstances of public emergency. This right is further guaranteed in the International Convention on Civil and Political Rights (ICCPR) which has been widely ratified by 169 states parties. In addition to this, the right to a hearing is guaranteed in the constitutions of numerous states. Courts have further upheld this right where the accused is arrested on suspicion of terrorism, and the right is guaranteed even in times of armed conflict. Furthermore, human rights activists have been arguing that Guantanamo detainees must be brought to the US and tried in a federal court.

In addition to the above, the presumption of innocence was found to be guaranteed in terms of the various international and regional treaties, national constitutions and case law. States have further supported this right in statements before the Human Rights Committee (HRC) and the CTC. The presumption of innocence lies at the heart of a fair trial procedure and, thus, this chapter found that state concerns regarding terrorism cannot extinguish the right to innocence of terrorist suspects. For example, it has been found that a long period of pre-trial detention violates the presumption of innocence as it fails to assign blame within a reasonable time and it substitutes pre-trial detention for punishment.

Finally, the right to review was found to be guaranteed in international and regional treaty law as well as under the constitutions and national legislation of various states. In cases of long pre-trial detentions without access to a court it was found that the right to review was compromised. Furthermore, it was found that the listing procedures under the UNSC 1267 regime, where suspected terrorists are included on a list without the opportunity to challenge their inclusion, negated both the right of access to a hearing and the right to review.

It was then considered whether the core fair trial rights, namely, the right of access to court, the presumption of innocence and the right to review, are norms of *jus cogens* in terms of article 53 of the Vienna Convention. It was found that the fact that the right to a fair trial forms part of customary international law is beyond dispute and, as such, the right to a fair trial is part of general international law. Furthermore, the inclusion of the rights of access to court, the presumption of innocence and the right to review in the national legislation and case law of various states, together with the absence of any provisions for derogation from these rights in national legislation, support the view that these are norms of general international law that states accept and recognize as norms from which no derogation is permitted. This chapter further found *opinio juris* that states regard the core fair trial rights as *jus cogens* norms. Although countries have derogated from the right to a fair trial in periods of public emergency, these states have invariably argued that the procedures which they adopt are fair in the context of exceptional circumstances. Even when states have filed notices of derogation from fair trial norms, this typically did not relate to the norms proposed in this chapter as non-derogable.

Moreover, the chapter found that the core fair trial rights display the characteristics of *jus cogens* norms as they protect the fundamental values of the international community, are hierarchically superior and are universally applicable. The core fair trial rights protect fundamental values such as the right to freedom, the right to human dignity and equality before the law. These values are encapsulated by the right to a fair hearing by an impartial tribunal, the presumption of innocence and the right to an effective remedy.

Derogation from these core rights would entail the arbitrary deprivation of freedom without just cause and infringe the right to human dignity, the right to an effective remedy as well as the substantive fairness of a hearing. It was further argued that the core fair trial rights are hierarchically superior in that they nullify contradictory norms and are universally applicable. These rights apply in situations of peace and armed conflict. As there is no justification for derogation from fair trial rights in armed conflict, it would be difficult to argue that such derogations are allowed in other emergency situations, such as terrorism.

Finally, in the interaction and possible balancing of rights of the prohibition of terrorism and the right to a fair trial, it was found that both norms aim to safeguard the underlying right to human dignity. The prohibition of terrorism protects the rights of human beings not to be used as a means to an end, while core fair trial rights protect the right not to be arbitrarily deprived of one's liberty. Core fair trial rights of persons suspected of terrorism have been upheld in international jurisprudence. It was found that detainees suspected of terrorism had the right of *habeas corpus* to challenge their detention and that lengthy pre-trial detentions of suspected terrorists infringe upon the right of access to a hearing, the presumption of innocence and the right to review. In addition, concerns were raised about the fact that measures implementing targeted sanctions against individuals or entities suspected of terrorism have violated fair trial rights. In this regard, no limitation has been allowed in respect of the right to a hearing, the presumption of innocence and the right to review.

In light of the underlying value of human dignity protected by both the prohibition of terrorism and core fair trial rights, no limitation of either norm is necessary or possible, and both norms can be applied in their entirety in the context of anti-terrorism measures. It is simply not possible to limit the core non-derogable fair trial rights in a manner that does not result in a flagrant denial of justice. Moreover, there is no legal antinomy between the prohibition of terrorism as a *jus cogens* norm and the *jus cogens* norms of core fair trial rights. The prohibition of terrorism and core fair trial rights does not consist of contrary norms that cannot be applied in their entirety to the same situation or which require the invalidity or limitation of one of the norms in order to apply both norms in the context of counter-terrorism measures. As was the case with the prohibition of torture and the prohibition of terrorism, it is impossible to justify that one competing norm should prevail over another, as these norms embody similar and equally important underlying values.

Chapter 5 dealt with the prohibition of force in the context of the fight against terrorism. Unlike the prohibition of torture and the right to a fair trial, the *jus cogens* status of the prohibition on the use of force under international law is beyond dispute. There is widespread support for the prohibition of the use of force as a *jus cogens* norm under international treaty law, various UNGA and UNSC resolutions and international jurisprudence as well as extensive academic acceptance of the prohibition of the use of force as *jus cogens*. In addition to this, by virtue of the near-universal application of the UN Charter and the fact that the prohibition of the use of force is an accepted rule of customary international law, the prohibition of the use of force is applicable to all states.

The next question that was addressed related to which use of force is *jus cogens*. It was found that, although various terms are used in connection with force, such as aggression, force and an armed attack, the use of force which is prohibited as a *jus cogens* norm requires an element of gravity and relates to the use of armed force. While every instance of the use of force against the territorial integrity or political independence of another state, thus, is prohibited, not all such use of force will constitute an armed attack which will trigger the right to self-defence. For example, assistance to rebels in the form of the provision of weapons or logistical support was found not to constitute an armed attack, and international jurisprudence has distinguished between more grave and less grave forms of the use of force. The UNSC Definition of Aggression supported the use of grave force or aggression, such as armed aggression, as *jus cogens.*

This chapter also considered whether the status of the prohibition of terrorism as a *jus cogens* norm has resulted in the expansion of the scope of exceptions to the use of force in self-defence. This was considered in the context of the use of force in anticipatory self-defence against non-state actors. In the age of terrorism, force is increasingly used constantly, at a low level, over extended periods of time and in various territories. It was found that states seem to have shown a new willingness to accept the 'accumulation of events' doctrine. While less grave incidents, such as ongoing pin-prick attacks by terrorists, thus, in themselves could constitute less grave uses of force, when these incidents form part of a chain of events they can be transformed into an armed attack triggering the right of self-defence.

The chapter further found that necessity and proportionality remain requirements for an armed attack in self-defence in response to an initial attack, including the use of force in anticipatory self-defence. This was supported by international jurisprudence. While there is no prescribed evidentiary standard by which to assess whether an attack is 'necessary', it was argued that a military response to a terrorist attack should, as a minimum, require that the state carefully evaluates the evidence to ensure a high degree of certainty that it has identified those responsible for an attack, that more attacks are imminent, that the facts relied upon are made public and that these facts are subject to international scrutiny and investigation. With regard to proportionality, it was found that the victim state must do no more than is reasonably required in the circumstances to deter a threatened attack or defeat an ongoing attack. Examples such as Israel's alleged use of disproportionate force in self-defence in response to actions by the Palestine Liberation Organization (PLO) and Hezbollah illustrated that the evaluation of proportionality of the use of force in self-defence often is contentious.

This chapter found that the greatest effect of the prohibition of terrorism as a *jus cogens* norm is felt in the customary international law rules of attribution. The rules of attribution are not *jus cogens,* but rather ordinary rules of customary international law. As a norm of *jus cogens*, the prohibition of terrorism would, thus, trump the rules of attribution. Article 51 of the Charter does not specify any certain approach with regard to attribution, and it has been argued that the rules of attribution are not set in stone. The traditional approach requiring 'effective state control' was a standard developed by the International

Court of Justice (ICJ). Arguably, a move towards a more lenient standard of attribution is being illustrated. The effective control test initially set a high threshold and required an instruction by a state to the non-state actor in respect of the conduct of such an actor. This chapter found that the strict standard of effective control had been relaxed in favour of the overall control test. The overall control test does not require any specific instructions by the controlling state concerning the commission of acts by a non-state actor. The test is satisfied where there is support by the state for the non-state actor as well as its participation in the general direction, coordination and supervision of the activities and operations. Imputability still requires some form of complicity by the harbouring state. Therefore, it cannot be argued that a non-consenting innocent state which has taken ineffective measures to restrain terrorist activities in its territory but is not responsible for a terrorist attack nor actively involved in same, may be subjected to an armed attack in self-defence. This was illustrated by the criticism regarding the attribution to the Lebanese government by Israel of attacks by the Hezbollah, on the one hand, and acts by the PLO to Tunisia, on the other, where these attacks were argued to be justification for Israel's use of armed force against Lebanon and Tunisia respectively. Furthermore, it was found that even the Taliban's provision of a safe haven to Bin Laden, its toleration of his terrorist training camps in areas generally controlled by the Taliban and the receipt of monies and military support from Bin Laden for the Taliban's war against the Northern Alliance, did not constitute the Taliban's control of, or direct participation in, attacks by al Qaeda. As such, the attacks by al Qaeda against the US on 11 September 2000 could not have been used by the US to justify the use of military force against Afghanistan.

Furthermore, it was considered whether there is a normative conflict between the prohibition of terrorism and the prohibition of the use of force as *jus cogens* norms or whether it is possible for the two norms to co-exist without conflict. It was found that both norms protect the interests of international peace and security and the value of human dignity. The use of inter-state force may impair human dignity as well, as the indiscriminate use of force may have grave consequences for individuals who are 'casualties' of this use of force.

This chapter further found that no legal antinomy arises between the two *jus cogens* norms of the prohibition of the use of force and the prohibition of terrorism. As long as the use of force is legitimate (that is, in terms of the UN Charter as well as the requirements of customary international law), force may be used as a counter-terrorism measure. Any illegal force in the furtherance of the fight against terrorism would retain its illegal character while the legal use of force in the pursuit of the prohibition of terrorism is allowed. As discussed above, there has, however, been some development in the rules of customary international law pertaining to the definition of an armed attack and the rules of attribution to a state of the acts of a non-state actor. The international community has, furthermore, during the last two decades increasingly recognized the right of states to use anticipatory force against terrorists, which may ultimately have the effect of diluting the requirement of necessity for the use of force in self-defence. This has led to a normative drift affecting key limitations of the traditional doctrine of self-defence, which could increase the risk of abuse.

In summary, the research undertaken in this book has found that the prohibition of terrorism is a crime that shocks the conscience of humankind and has become the *jus cogens* norm of our time: a norm accepted and recognized by the international community of states as non-derogable in all circumstances. It thus illustrates that *jus cogens* norms can emerge in response to contemporary challenges. Furthermore, notwithstanding a universally-agreed treaty definition, terrorism has attained, in international law, a core, objectively determinable meaning. Terrorism is an act of violence, committed with the intent to cause death or serious bodily injury to any person or to spread fear among civilians, for a political purpose and with a transnational element. Notwithstanding this, the prohibition of terrorism as a *jus cogens* norm does not justify the limitation of other norms which were also found to be *jus cogens*. These are the absolute prohibition of torture; core fair trial rights (the right of access to a hearing, the presumption of innocence and the right to review); and the prohibition of the use of illegitimate force. Any such limitation would have the ultimate effect of destroying the very rights that the fight against terrorism seek to protect.

Bibliography

Books

Alexy R, *A Theory of Constitutional Rights* (Oxford University Press 2010) 64–68

Avrich P, *Anarchist Voices: An Oral History of Anarchism in America* (Princeton University Press 1996) 13–33

Bluntschli J and Scott J (eds), *Le droit international codifié* (2nd edn, Librairie de Guillaumin et Cie 1874) 238–240

Brownlie I, *International Law and the Use of Force by States* (Clarendon Press 1963) 113

Brownlie I, *Principles of Public International Law* (6th edn, Oxford University Press 2003) 15

Burgers H and Danelius H, *The United Nations Convention Against Torture: A Handbook on the Convention Against Torture and Other Cruel, Inhuman or Degrading Treatment or Punishment* (Martinus Nijhoff 2008) 41

Byers M, *War Law: Understanding International Law and Armed Conflict* (Grove Press 2007) 62

Cahin G, *La Coutume Internationale et les Organisations Internationales: L'incidence de la Dimension Institutionnelle sur le Processus Coutumier* (Pedone 2001) 615

Cassese A, *International Law* (Oxford University Press 2005) 199, 355

Cassese A, '*Jus cogens*' in Cassese A (ed), *Realizing Utopia: The Future of International Law* (Oxford University Press 2012) 159

Chimimba T, 'United Nations Security Council Resolution 1373 as a Tool for Criminal Law Enforcement' in Maluwa T, Du Plessis M and Tladi T (eds), *The Pursuit of a Brave New World in International Law: Essays in Honour of John Dugard* (Brill Nijhoff 2017) 535–526

Christófolo J, *Solving Antinomies Between Peremptory Norms in Public International Law* (Schulthess 2016) 7

Conquest R, *The Great Terror: Stalin's Purge of the Thirties* (MacMillan 1968) 251

Costelloe D, *Legal Consequences of Peremptory Norms in International Law* (Cambridge University Press 2017)

Crawford J, *The Creation of States in International Law* (2d edn, Oxford University Press 2006) 146

D'Amato A, *International Law: Process and Prospect* (Transnational Publishers 1986)

Damrosch L (ed), *International Law: Cases and Materials* (West Publishing 2001) 923

Dershowitz A, 'Tortured Reasoning' in Levinson S (ed), *Torture: A Collection* (Oxford University Press 2004) 266

Dershowitz A, *Why Terrorism Works: Understanding the Threat, Responding to the Challenge* (Yale University Press 2002) 131–134

De Groot H, *De Jure Belli Ac Pacis Libri Tres* (Clarendon Press 1625) Book 1 Chapter 1

De Vattel E, *Le Droit des Gens, ou Principes de la Loi Naturelle, Appliqués à La Conduit et aux Affaires des Nations et des Souverains* (Neufchatel 1758) 1

De Wet E and Vidmar J (eds), *Hierarchy in International Law: The Place of Human Rights* (Oxford University Press 2012) 2, 11, 17

De Wet E, 'Human Rights Considerations and the Enforcement of Targeted Sanctions in Europe: The Emergence of Core Standards of Judicial Review' in Fassbender B (ed), *Securing Human Rights? Achievements and Challenges of the UN Security Council* (Oxford University Press 2011)

De Wet E, '*Jus Cogens and Obligations Erga* Omnes' in Shelton D (ed), *The Oxford Handbook of International Human Rights Law* (Oxford University Press 2013) 541–561

Dinstein Y, *War, Aggression and Self-defence* (4th edn, Cambridge University Press 2005) 99–104

Dugard J, *International Law: A South African Perspective* (4 edn, Juta 2011)

Elshtain J, 'Reflection on the Problem of Dirty Hands' in Levinson S, *Torture: A Collection* (Oxford University Press 2004)

Fauchille P and Bonfils H, *Traité de Droit International Public* (Rousseau 1921) 1

Fine H, *Human Rights and Wrongs: Slavery, Terror, Genocide* (Paradigm Publishers 2007) 63–76

Frowein J, '*Jus cogens*' in Wolfrum R, *Max Planck Encyclopaedia of Public International Law* (Oxford University Press 2009) 8

Gray C, *International Law and the Use of Force* (Oxford University Press 2008) 130, 136, 155

Greenwood C, 'Self-Defence and the Conduct of International Armed Conflict' in Dinstein Y (ed), *International Law at a Time of Perplexity: Essays in Honour of Shabtai Rosenne* (Martinus Nijhoff 1989) 155, 237–288

Guggenheim P, *Traité de Droit International Public* (Georg & Co 1953) 57–58

Gur-Arye M, 'Can the War against Terror Justify the Use of Force in Interrogations? Reflection in Light of the Israeli Experience' in Levinson S (ed), *Torture: A Collection* (Oxford University Press 2004)

Hampson F, 'The Principle of Proportionality in the Law of Armed Conflict' in Perrigo S & Whitman J (eds), *The Geneva Conventions Under Assault* (Pluto Press 2010) 42

Hannikainen L, *Peremptory Norms (Jus Cogens) in International Law* (Finnish Lawyers' Publishing Company 1988) 323, 256

Henckaerts, Jean-Marie & Doswald-Beck, Louise (eds), *Customary International Humanitarian Law i: Rules, 46–50* (Cambridge University Press 2005)

Higgins R, *Problems and Process: International Law and How We Use It* (Clarendon Press 1994) 232

Humphrey J, 'The Universal Declaration of Human Rights: Its History, Impact and Juridical Character' in Ramcharan BG (ed), *Human Rights: Thirty Years After the Universal Declaration* (Martinus Nijhoff 1979) 21, 32

Jones H, *Kant's Principle of Personality* (University of Wisconsin Press 1971) 127

Joyner C, *International Law for the 21st Century* (Rowman & Littlefield Publishers 2005) 165

Karoubi M, *Just or Unjust War?* (Ashgate Publishing 2004) 108–109

Kelsen H, *Principles of International Law* (Rinehart 1952) 188, 344

Knuchel S, *Jus Cogens: Identification and Enforcement of Peremptory Norms* (Schulthess 2015) 52

Kolb R, 'Conflits Entre Norms de Jus Cogens' in Salmon, J *Droit de Pouvoir, Pouvoir de Droit, Mélanges offerts à Jean Salmon* (Bruylant 2007)

Kolb R, *Peremptory International Law Jus Cogens – A General Inventory* (Hart 2005)

Koskenniemi M, *From Apology to Utopia: The Structure of International Legal Argument* (2nd edn, Cambridge University Press 2006) 363

Krauthammer C, *The Truth About Torture* in Levinson S (ed), *Torture: A Collection* (Oxford University Press 2004)

Lemkin R, 'Les actes Constituant un Danger General Interétatique Consideres comme Delits du Droit des Gens' in López-Rey M (ed), *Actes de la Vème Conférence Internationale pour l' Unification du Droit Pénal* (Madrid 14–20 October 1933) (A Pedone 1935) 48–56

Maogoto J, *Battling Terrorism: Legal Perspectives on the Use of Force and the War on Terror* (Ashgate Publishing Ltd 2005)

McCoubrey H and White N, *International Law and Armed conflict* (Dartmouth 1992)

McNair A, *The Law of Treaties* (2 edn, Clarendon Press 1961)

Nicto-Navia R, 'International Peremptory Norms (*Jus Cogens*) and International Humanitarian Law' in Vorah C, Pocar F, Featherstone Y and others (eds), *Man's Inhumanity to Man: Essays on International Law in Honour of Antonio Cassese* (Kluwer Law International 2003) 613–615

O'Connell M, 'International Law's Higher Ethical Norms' in Childress D (ed), *The Role of Ethics in International Law* (Cambridge University Press 2011) 94

Oppenheim L, *International Law: A Treatise, vol I: Peace* (2nd edn, Longman, Green & Co 1912)

Orakhelashvili A, *Peremptory Norms in International Law* (Oxford University Press 2008)

Pati R, *Due Process and International Terrorism: An International Legal Analysis* (Martinus Nijhoff 2009)

Perelman C, 'Les Antinomies en Droit, Essay de Synthèse' in Perelman CH (ed), *Les antonomies en droit* (Bruylant 1965) 393

Posner R, 'Torture, Terrorism, and Interrogation' in Levinson S (ed), *Torture: A Collection* (Oxford University Press 2004) 294

Randelzhofer A and Nolte G, 'Article 51' in Simma B, Mosler H, Paulus A and Chaitidou E (eds), *The Charter of the United Nations: A Commentary* (3rd edn, Oxford University Press 2013)

Rivier R, *Droit International Public* (2nd edn, Pedone 2013) 566

Ronzitti N, 'Use of Force, *Jus Cogens* and State Consent' in Cassese A (ed), *The Current Legal Regulation of the Use of Force* (Martinus Nijhoff 1986)

Rubin A, *The Law of Piracy* (2nd edn, Transnational Publishers 1998) 1, 17

Saul B, *Defining Terrorism in International Law* (Oxford University Press 2006)

Schlüter B, *Developments in Customary International Law* (Martinus Nijhoff 2010)

Schmid, A 'The Problems of Defining Terrorism' in Crenshaw M and Pimlott J (eds), *Encyclopedia of World Terrorism* (ME Sharpe 1997) 12, 13

Schmid A and Jongman A, *Political Terrorism: A New Guide to Actors, Authors, Concepts, Data Bases, Theories and Literature* (Transaction Publishers 1984) 75

Shaw M, *International Law* (5 edn, Cambridge University Press 2003) 92

Singh J, *Use of Force under International Law* (Harnam Publications 1984) 210

Tams C and Sloan J (eds), *The Development of International Law by the International Court of Justice* (Oxford University Press 2013)

Thirlway H, *International Customary Law and Codification: An Examination of the Continuing Role of Custom in the Present Period of Codification of International Law* (Martinus Nijhoff 1972) 67

Tomuschat C, 'The Security Council and *Jus Cogens*' in Cannizzaro E (ed), *The Present and Future of Jus Cogens* (5th edn, Cedam 2015)

Vidmar J, 'Norm Conflicts and Hierarchy in International Law: Towards a Vertical International Legal System?' in De Wet E and Vidmar J (eds), *Hierarchy in International Law: The Place of Human Rights* (Oxford University Press 2012)

Walzer M, *Just and Unjust Wars: A Moral Argument with Historical Illustrations* (3 edn, Basic Books 2000)

Walzer M, *Political Action: The Problem of Dirty Hands* in Levinson S, *Torture: A Collection* (Oxford University Press 2004)

Weeramantry C, *Universalizing International Law* (Martinus Nijhoff 2004) 267–268

Weisburd M, *A Use of force: The Practice of States Since World War II* (Pennsylvania State University Press 1997) 22

Whitman J, 'On Nazi "Honour" and the New European "Dignity"' in Joerges C and Ghaleigh NS (eds), *Darker Legacies of Law in Europe: The Shadow Of National Socialism And Fascism Over Europe And Its Legal Traditions* (Hart Publishing 2003)

Wolff C, 'Jus Gentium Methodo Scientifica Pertractatum' in Scott J (ed), *The Classics of International Law* (Clarendon Press 1764)

Journal Articles

Amet A, 'Terrorism and International Law: Cure the Underlying Problem, Not Just the Symptom' (2013) 19 Annual Survey of International and Comparative Law 17

Arasly J, 'Terrorism and Civil Aviation Security: Problems and Trends' (2005) The Quarterly Journal 75

Aydinli E 'Before Jihadists There Were Anarchists: A Failed Case of Transnational Violence' (2008) 31 Studies in Conflict and Terrorism 903

Bagchi A, 'Intention, Torture, and the Concept of State Crime' (2009) 114(1) Pennsylvania State Law Review 41

Bassiouni M, 'A Functional Approach to "General Principles of International Law"' (1990) 11 Michigan Journal of International Law 768

Beckett J, 'The Greek Case Before the European Rights Commission' (1970) 1 1 Human Rights 98

Bellal A, 'The 2009 Resolution of the Institute of International Law on Immunity and International Crimes: A Partial Codification of the Law?' (2011) 9 Journal of International Criminal Justice 227

Bellamy A, 'No Pain, No Gain? Torture and Ethics in the War on Terror' (2006) 82 (1) International Affairs 121–148

Bennoune K, 'Terror/Torture' (2008) (26) Berkeley Journal of International Law 11

Bethlehem D, 'Self-Defense Against an Imminent or Actual Armed Attack by Non-State Actors' (2012) 106 American Journal of International Law 770

Bianchi A, 'Enforcing International Law Norms against Terrorism: Achievements and Prospects' in Bianchi A and Naqvi Y (eds), (2004) Enforcing International Law Norms Against Terrorism 491, 526

Bin Cheng, 'United Nations Resolutions on Outer Space: "Instant" International Customary Law?' (1965) 5 Indian Journal of International Law 23

Bufacchi V and Arrigo J, 'Torture, Terrorism and the State: A Refutation of the Ticking-Bomb Argument' (2006) 23 Journal of Applied Philosophy 355

Burgess, D, 'Hostis Humani Generi: Piracy, Terrorism and a New International Law' (2006) 13 University of Miami International and Comparative Law Review 298

Byers M, 'Conceptualising the Relationship between *Jus Cogens* and *Erga Omnes* Rules' (1997) 66 Nordic Journal of International Law 211

Byers M, 'The Shifting Foundations of International Law: A Decade of Forceful Measures against Iraq' (2002) 13(1) European Journal of International Law 36, 38–9

Byers M, 'Terrorism, the Use of Force and International Law After 11 September' (2002) 51 International and Comparative Law Quarterly 414

Cannizzaro E, 'Contextualizing Proportionality: *Jus ad Bellum* and *Jus in Bello* in the Lebanese War' (2006) 88 International Review of the Red Cross 779

Cantegreil J, 'The Audacity of the Texaco/Calasiatic Award: René-Jean Dupuy and the Internationalization of Foreign Investment Law' (2011) 22 European Journal of International Law 441

Charney J, 'Anticipatory Humanitarian Intervention in Kosovo' (1999) 93 American Journal of International Law 834, 837

Cassese A, 'Terrorism is Also Disrupting some Crucial Legal Categories of International Law' (2001) 12 European Journal of International Law 993

Cassese A, 'The *Nicaragua* and *Tadic* Tests Revisited in Light of the ICJ Judgment on Genocide in Bosnia' (2007) 18 European Journal of International Law 649–668

Cheng B, 'United Nations Resolutions on Outer Space: "Instant" International Customary Law?' (1965) 5 Indian Journal of International Law 23

Cherneva, I, 'The Drafting History of Article 2 of the Convention Against Torture' (2012) 9(1) Essex Human Rights Review 1

Christenson G, '*Jus Cogens*: Guarding Interests Fundamental to International Society' (1987–88) 28 Virginia Journal of International Law 585

Christol CQ, 'Judge Manfred Lachs and the Principle of *Jus Cogens*' (1994) 22 Journal of Space Law 33

Clarke A, 'International Law and the Pre-Emptive Use of Military Force' (2003) 26(2) The Washington Quarterly 89

Conklin W, 'The Peremptory Norms of the International Community' (2012) 2 European Journal of International Law 837

Criddle E and Fox-Decent E, 'A Fiduciary Theory of *Jus Cogens*' (2009) 34 Yale Journal of International Law 331

Danelius H, 'Torture and Cruel, Inhuman or Degrading Treatment or Punishment' (1989) 58 Nordic Journal of International Law 172

Danilenko GM, 'International *Jus Cogens*: Issues of Law-Making' (1991) 2 European Journal of International Law 42

Dershowitz A, 'The Torture Warrant: A Response to Professor Strauss' (2003) 48 New York Law School Law Review 275

De Wet E, 'The Prohibition of Torture as an International Norm of *Jus Cogens* and its Implications for National and Customary Law' (2004) 15 European Journal of International Law 106

Dolzer R, 'Clouds on the Horizon of Humanitarian Law? (2003) 28 Yale Journal of International Law 337

Emerson S, 'The Lockerbie Terrorist Attack and Libya: A Retrospective Analysis' (2004) 36 Case Western Journal of International Law 487

Evans A, 'Aircraft Hijacking: Its Cause and Cure' (1969) 63 American Journal of International Law 695

Ezeani, E, 'The 21st Century Terrorist: Hostis Humani Generis?' (2012) Beijing Law Review, 158–169

Farer T, 'Beyond the Charter Frame: Unilateralism or Condominium' (2002) 96(2) American Journal of International Law 363

Feinstein B, 'The Legality of the Use of Force by Israel in Lebanon-June 1982' (1985) 20 Israeli Law Review 362

Fitzpatrick J, 'Speaking Law to Power: The War Against Terrorism and Human Rights' (2003) 14 European Journal of International Law 241

Focarelli C, 'Promotional *Jus Cogens*: A Critical Appraisal of jus cogens' Legal Effects (2008) 77 Nordic Journal of International Law 429

Franck T, 'Terrorism and the Right of Self-Defense' (2001) 95 American Journal of International Law 839

Gert B, 'Justifying violence' (1969) 66 The Journal of Philosophy 623

Green J, 'Questioning the Peremptory Status of the Prohibition of the Use of Force' (2011) 32 Michigan Journal of International Law 215–216

Hathaway O, Nowlan A and Spiegel J, 'Tortured Reasoning: The Intention to Torture under International Law' (2012) 52 Virginia Journal of International Law 802, 836

Henkin L, 'Remarks on Draft Restatement of the Foreign Relations Law of the United States (Revized)' (1982) 76 American Society of International Law Procedure 184, 190

Horsley R, 'The Sicarii: Ancient Jewish "Terrorists"' (1979) 59 Journal of Religion 435

Hossain K, 'The Concept of *Jus Cogens* and the Obligation under the UN Charter' (2005) 3 Santa Clara Journal of International Law 72

Hurd I, 'The UN Security Council and the International Rule of Law' (2014) Chinese Journal of International Politics 6

Janis M, 'The Nature of *Jus Cogens*' (1988) 3 Connecticut Journal of International Law 359, 361

Jennings R, 'The Caroline and McLeod Cases' (1938) 32 American Journal of International Law 82

Kahgan C, '*Jus Cogens* and the Inherent Right to Self-Defence' (1997) 3 Comparative and International Law Journal of Southern Africa 767, 777–81

Kleinlein T, '*Jus Cogens* as the "Highest Law"? Peremptory Norms and Legal Hierarchies' (2015) Netherlands Yearbook of International Law 173, 195

Kola F, 'Torture and Terrorism – A Case Study' (2007) 85 Supplement UCL Jurisprudence Review 97

Kretzmer D, 'The Inherent Right to Self-Defence and Proportionality in *Jus Ad Bellum*' (2013) 24(1) European Journal of International Law 242

Kritsiotis D, 'Reappraising Policy Objections to Humanitarian Intervention' (1998) 19 Michigan Journal of International Law 1005, 1042–43

Levitt G, 'Is "Terrorism" worth Defining?' (1986) 13 Ohio Northern University Law Review 97

Linderfalk U, 'The Effect of *Jus Cogens* Norms: Whoever Opened Pandora's Box, Did You Ever Think About the Consequences?' (2007) 18 European Journal of International Law 853

Linderfalk U, 'The Creation of *Jus Cogens* – Making Sense of Article 53 of the Vienna Convention' (2011) 71 Zeitschrift für Ausländisches Öffentliches Recht und Völkerrecht 359

Lippman M, 'The Development and Drafting of the United Nations Convention Against Torture and Other Cruel Inhuman or Degrading Treatment or Punishment' (1994) 17 Boston College International and Comparative Law Review 275

Lobel J, 'The Use of Force to Respond to Terrorist Attacks: The Bombing of Sudan and Afghanistan' (1999) 24 Yale Journal of International Law 537–557 540

MacMaster N, 'Torture: From Algiers to Abu Ghraib' (2004) 46 Race and Class 1

Marks S, 'Branding the "War on Terrorism": Is there a "New paradigm" of International Law?' (2006) 14 Michigan State Journal of International law 72

Meron T, 'International Criminalization of Internal Atrocities' (2005) American Journal of International Law 571

Megret F, 'War? Legal Semantics and the Move to Violence' (2002) 13(2) European Journal of International Law 384, 397–9

Moir L 'Reappraising the Resort to Force: International Law, *Jus Ad Bellum* and the War on Terror' (2010) 15 Journal of Conflict and Security Law 9

Morris M, 'Terrorism: The Politics of Prosecution' (2005) 5 Chicago Journal of International Law 405

Mosler H, 'The International Society as a Legal Community' (1974) 140 1 Recueil Des Cours 1, 283

Mujuzi J, 'Evidence Obtained through Violating the Right to Freedom from Torture and Other Cruel, Inhuman or Degrading Treatment in South Africa' (2015) 15 African Human Rights Law Journal 89–109

Murphy S, 'Self-Defence and the Israeli Wall Opinion: An *Ipse Dixit* from the ICJ?' (2005) 99 American Journal of International Law 62, 64

Murphy S, 'Terrorism and the Concept of "Armed Attack" in Article 51 of the UN Charter' (2002) 43 Harvard Journal of International Law 50

Parker K and Neylon L, '*Jus Cogens*: Compelling the Law of Human Rights' (1989) 12 Hastings International and Comparative Law Review 411, 436–37

Paust J, 'Responding Lawfully to International Terrorism: The Use of Force Abroad' (1986) 8 Whittier Law Review 711, 723

Posch A, 'The *Kadi* Case: Rethinking the Relationship between EU Law and International Law?' (2009) 15 Columbia Journal of Economic Literature 1

Rama Rao TS, 'International Custom' (1979) 19 Indian Journal of International Law 515, 520

Reich J, 'Due Process and Sanctions Targeted Against Individuals Pursuant to Resolution 1267 of 1999' (2008) 33 Yale Journal of International Law 505

Reinold T, 'State Weakness, Irregular Warfare, and the Right to Self-Defense Post 9/11' (2011) 105 American Journal of International Law 244

Reisman M, 'Unilateral Action and the Transformations of the World Constitutive Process: The Special Problem of Humanitarian Intervention' (2000) 11 European Journal of International Law 3

Reisman M and Armstrong A, 'The Past and Future of the Claim of Preemptive Self-Defense' (2006) 100 American Journal of International Law 526

Robinson P, 'The Right to a Fair Trial in International Law, with Specific Reference to the Work of the ICTY' (2009) 3 Berkeley Jorunal of International Law Publicist 6

Rodley N, 'The Definition(s) of Torture in International Law' (2002) 55 Current Legal Problems 467, 468

Rodley N, 'The Prohibition of Torture: Absolute Means Absolute' (2006) 34 Denver Journal of International Law and Policy 145–160

Schachter O, 'In Defense of International Rules on the Use of Force' (1986) 53 University of Chicago Law Review 113, 129

Scharf M, 'Seizing the "Grotian moment": Accelerated Formation of Customary International Law in Times of Fundamental Change' (2010) 43 Cornell International Law Journal 440

Scheuner U, 'Conflict of Treaty Provisions with a Peremptory Norm of General International Law' (1969) Zeitschrift für Ausländisches Öffentliches Recht und Völkerrecht 28

Schmitt M, '"Change Direction" 2006: Israeli Operations in Lebanon and the International Law of Self-Defense' (2008) 29(2) Michigan Journal of International Law 154

Schomburg W, 'The Role of International Criminal Tribunals in Promoting Respect for Fair Trial Rights' (2009) 1 Northwestern Journal of International Human Rights paras 1–2

Schwarzenberger G, 'International *Jus Cogens*?' (1965) 43 Texas Law Review 455

Schwelb E, 'Some Aspects of International *Jus Cogens* as Formulated by the International Law Commission' (1967) 61 American Journal of International Law 946, 952

Segesser D and Gessler M, 'Raphael Lemkin and the International Debate on the Punishment of War Crimes (1919–1948)' (2005) 7 Journal of Genocide Research 453

Shelton D, 'Normative Hierarchy in International Law' (2006) 100 American Journal of International Law 291

Simma B, 'NATO, the UN and the Use of Force: Legal Aspects' (1999) 10 European Journal of International Law 1, 3

Simma B and Alston P, 'The Sources of Human Rights Law: Custom, *Jus Cogens*, and General Principles' (1995) 6 European Journal of International Law 43

Smith M, 'Zealots and Sicarii: Their Origins and Relation' (1971) 64 Harvard Theological Review 1

Sohn L, 'The Human Rights Law of the Charter' (1977) 12 Texas International Law Journal 129, 133

Stephens P, 'A Categorical Approach to Human Rights Claims: *Jus Cogens* as a Limitation on Enforcement?' (2004) 22 Wisconsin International Law Journal 245, 253–54

Strauss M, 'Torture' (2003–2004) 48 New York Law School Law Review 48

Strydom H, 'From Mandates to Economic Partnerships: The Return to Proper Statehood in Africa' (2007) 7 African Human Rights Law Journal 74–75

Subedi S, 'The UN Response to International Terrorism in the Aftermath of the Terrorist Attacks in America and the Problem of the Definition of Terrorism in International Law' (2002) 4 International Law Forum du Droit International 159

Tams C, 'The Use of Force Against Terrorists' (2009) 20 European Journal of International Law 388, 359

Tladi D, 'The Non-Consenting Innocent State: The Problem with Bethlehem's Principle' (2013) 107 American Journal of International Law 570, 573

Tladi D and Dlagnekova P, 'The Will of the State, Consent and International Law: Piercing the Veil of Positivism' (2006) 21 South African Public Law 111

Tladi D and Taylor G, 'On the Al Qaida/Taliban Sanctions Regime: Due Process and Sunsetting' (2011) 10 Chinese Journal of International Law 771

Trindade A, '*Jus Cogens*: The Material and the Gradual Expansion of its Material Content in Contemporary International Case Law' (2008) 35 Curso de Derecho International Organizado por el Comité Jurídico Interamericano 3, 27

Tunkin G, '*Jus cogens* in Contemporary International Law' (1971) 1–2 University of Toledo Law Review 107

Udombana N, 'The African Commission on Human and Peoples' Rights and the Development of Fair Trial Norms in Africa' (2006) 6 African Human Rights Law Journal 298–332

Van Steenberghe R, 'Self-Defence in Response to Attacks by Non-State Actors in Light of Recent State Practice: A Step Forward?' (2010) 23 Leiden Journal of International Law 183

Vargas E, 'In Quest of the Practical Value of *Jus Cogens* Norms' (2015) 46 Netherlands Yearbook of International Law 211, 214

Verdross A, 'Forbidden Treaties in International Law: Comments on Professor Garner's Report on "The law of treaties"' (1937) 31 American Journal of International Law 571

Verdross A, '*Jus Dispositivum* and *Jus Cogens* in International Law' (1966) American Journal of International Law 55

Walker C, 'Irish Republican Prisoners – Political Detainees, Prisoners of War or Common Criminals?' (1984) 19 Irish Jurist 189

Weatherall T, 'The Status of the Prohibition of Terrorism in International Law: Recent Developments' (2015) 46 Georgetown Journal of International Law 589

Wedgwood R, 'Responding to Terrorism: The Strikes against Bin Laden' (1999) 24 Yale Journal of International Law 559, 564

Weisburd M, 'The Emptiness of the Concept of *Jus Cogens* as Illustrated by the War in Bosnia-Herzegovina' (1995) 17 Michigan Journal of International Law 1

Weissbrodt D and Hallendorff M, 'Travaux Préparatoires of the Fair Trial Provisions – Articles 8 to 11 – of the Universal Declaration of Human Rights' (1999) 21 Human Rights Quarterly 26

Williams S, '"Your Honor, I Am Here Today Requesting the Court's Permission to Torture Mr Doe": The Legality of Torture as a Means to an End v The Illegality of Torture as a Violation of *Jus Cogens* Norms under Customary International Law' (2004) 12 University of Miami International and Comparative Law Review 325

Wilson R, 'Prosecuting Pinochet: International Crimes in Spanish Domestic Law' (1999) 21 Human Rights Quarterly 927

Zimmerman A, 'The Second Lebanon War: *Jus Ad Bello, Jus In Bellum* and the Issue of Proportionality' (2007) 11 Max Planck University Yearbook of International Law 123

International Law Commission

Ago R, 'Addendum to Eighth Report on State Responsibility' (1980) II Yearbook of the International Law Commission UN Doc A/CN4/318/ADD5–7 13, 69

Documents of the Second Part of the Seventeenth Session and of the Eighteenth Session including the Reports of the Commission to the General Assembly' Yearbook of the International Law Commission (1966) vol 2

Draft Articles on the Law of Treaties, with Commentaries, 1966, Vol II Yearbook of the International Law Commission, 38

Draft Articles on Responsibility of States for Internationally Wrongful Acts with Commentaries, adopted by the ILC at its 53rd session (2001) Yearbook of the International Law Commission 2001 II 106–107

International Criminal Court Elements of Crimes Official Records of the Assembly of States Parties to the Rome Statute of the International Criminal Court, First session, New York, 3–10 September 2002 part II B

International Law Commission 'Draft Code of Offences Against the Peace and Security of Mankind' (1954) 2 Yearbook of the International Law Commission UN Doc A/CN4/SER A/1954/Add I 149

International Law Commission 'First Report on Subsequent Agreements and Subsequent Practice in Relation to Treaty Interpretation' (19 March 2013) UN Doc A/CN4/660 para 111

International Law Commission 'Fragmentation of International Law: Difficulties Arising from the Diversification and Expansion of International Law' (13 April 2006) A/CN4/L682

International Law Commission 'Second Report on Subsequent Agreements and Subsequent Practice in Relation to Treaty Interpretation' (26 March 2014) UN Doc A/CN4/671 para 119

Measures to Eliminate International Terrorism (1972) Summary of Work of the Sixth Committee A/63/100

Official Records of the General Assembly, 71st Session, Supplement No 10 (A/71/10)

Report of the International Law Commission on the Work of its 28th session (3 May–23 July 1976) A/31/10 Supplement No 10

Report of the International Law Commission on the Work of its 46th session (2 May–22 July 1994) A/49/10 Supplement No 10

Report of the International Law Commission on the Work of its 48th session (6 May–26 July 1996) A/51/10 Supplement No 10

Report of the International Law Commission on the Work of its 50th session (20 April–12 June and 27 July–14 August 1998) A/53/10 Supplement No 10

Report of the International Law Commission on the Work of its 52nd session (1 May–9 June and 10 July–18 August 2000) A/55/10 Supplement No 10

Report of the International Law Commission on the Work of its 53rd session (23 April–1 June and 2 July–10 August 2001) A/56/10 Supplement no 10

Report of the International Law Commission on the Work of its 57th session (2 May–3 June and 11 July–5 August 2005) A/60/10

Report of the International Law Commission on the Work of its 63rd and 65th sessions (6 May–7 June and 8 July–9 August 2013) A/68/10 Supplement No 10

Report of the International Law Commission on the Work of its 66th session (5 May–6 June 2014 and 7 July–8 August 2014) A/69/10 Supplement No 10

Report of the International Law Commission on the Work of its 67th session A/RES/70/236 (2015)

Summary Records of the Seventeenth Session and of the Eighteenth Session, Yearbook of the International Law Commission (1966) II 26

Summary Record of the 682nd meeting A/CN4/SR682 Yearbook of the International Law Commission (1963) vol 1

Summary Record of the 683rd meeting A/CN4/SR683 Yearbook of the International Law Commission (1963) vol I
Summary Record of the 828th meeting A/CN4/SR828 Yearbook of the International Law Commission (1966) vol I (part 1)
Summary Record of the 877th meeting A/CN4/SR877 Yearbook of the International Law Commission (1966) vol I (part 2)
Summary Records of the Plenary meetings and of the meetings of the Committee of the Whole A/CONF39/11 UN conference on the law of treaties, first session, Vienna (26 March–24 May 1968)
Summary Records of the meetings of the Sixth Committee, 2nd, 27th–30th & 32nd–34th meetings (A/C6/52/SR2) 1997
Summary Records of the meetings of the Sixth Committee 64th session, 3rd Meeting A/C6/64/SR3 (2009)
The Obligation to Extradite or Prosecute (*Aut Dedere Aut Judicare*) Final Report of the International Law Commission (2014) Yearbook of the International Law Commission vol II (part 2)
Vienna Conference on the Law of Treaties (26 March–24 May 1968) Summary Records of the Plenary Meetings Fourth Plenary Meeting (8 May 1968) Official Records of the General Assembly para 2

Special Rapporteur Reports

Fifth Report of the Special Rapporteur on the Law of Treaties, Sir Humphrey Waldock (15 November 1965, 4 December 1965, 20 December 1965, 3 January 1966 & 18 January 1966) A/CN4/183 & Add 1–4
Fourth Report of the Special Rapporteur on the Law of Treaties 1964, vol II, A/A/CN4/177 & Add 1 and 2; 1966, vol II
First Report of the Special Rapporteur on the Law of Treaties, Sir H Waldock (26 March 1962) A/CN4/144 & Add 1
Interim Report of the Special Rapporteur on Torture and Other Cruel, Inhuman or Degrading Treatment or Punishment, Manfred Nowak (28 July 2008), A63/175 para 46
Report of the Special Rapporteur on the Law of Treaties, Sir H Lauterpacht (24 March 1953) A/CN4/63 93
Report of the Special Rapporteur on Torture and Other Cruel, Inhuman or Degrading Treatment or Punishment, JE Méndez, on his mission to Mexico (21 April to 2 May 2014) A/HRC/28/68/Add para 13–14
Report of the Special Rapporteur on Torture and Other Cruel, Inhuman or Degrading Treatment or Punishment, JE Méndez, Addendum: Follow up report: Missions

to the Republic of Tajikistan and Tunisia, A/HRC/28/68/Add2 (27 February 2015) para 64

Report of the Special Rapporteur on the Promotion and Protection of Human Rights and Fundamental Freedoms while Countering Terrorism, Martin Scheinin (6 August 2008) A/63/223

Report of the Special Rapporteur on the Promotion and Protection of Human Rights and Fundamental Freedoms while Countering Terrorism, Martin Scheinin (22 December 2010) GA HRC 51

Report of the Special Rapporteur on Torture and Other Cruel, Inhuman or Degrading Treatment or Punishmen, P Kooijmans (19 February 1986) UN Doc E/CN4/1986/15 1

Report of the Special Rapporteur on Torture and Other Cruel, Inhuman or Degrading Treatment or Punishment, Nils Melzer A/HRC/34/54 (14 February 2017)

Second Report of the Special Rapporteur on the Law of Treaties, Sir Humprey Waldock (20 March, 10 April, 30 April and 5 June 1963) A/CN4/156 & Add 1–3

Sixth Report of the Special Rapporteur on the Law of Treaties, Sir Humphrey Waldock, Special Rapporteur (11 March, 25 March, 12 April, 11 May, 17 May, 24 May, 1 June and 14 June 1966) A/CN4/186

Third Report by the Special Rapporteur on the Law of Treaties, Sir Humphrey Waldock (3 March, 9 June, 12 June and 7 July 1964) A/CN4/167 & Add 1–3

Third Report by the Special Rapporteur on the Law of Treaties, Sir GG Fitzmaurice (18 March 1958) A/CN4/115 & Corr 1 26–27

Tladi D, 'First Report on *Jus Cogens*' in the Report of the International Law Commission 68th session (2 May–10 June & 4 July–12 August 2016) A/CN4/693 36

Tladi D, '*Jus cogens*' in the Report of the International Law Commission 66th session (5 May–6 June and 7 July–8 August 2014) A/69/10 Annex

Tladi, D 'Second Report on *Jus Cogens*' in the Report of the International Law Commission 69th session (1 May–2 June and 3 July–4 August 2017) A/CN4/706

UN Economic and Social Council Resolutions

Draft International Covenant on Human Rights UN Economic and Social Council E/CN4/SR195 (29 May 1950)

Question of the Human Rights of All Persons Subjected to Any Form of Detention or Imprisonment, Summary Prepared by the Secretary-General in Accordance with Commission Resolution E/CN4/l314/Add 2 (31 January 1979)

Report of the Working Group on a Draft Convention against Torture and Other Cruel, Inhuman or Degrading Treatment or Punishment E/CN4/L1470 (12 March 1979)

UN Economic and Social Council Res 2007/22 (26 July 2007)

United Nations General Assembly Resolutions

Measures to Prevent International Terrorism

A/RES/40/61 (1985) para 1
A/RES 42/159 (1987) para 1

Measures to Eliminate International Terrorism

A/RES 46/51 (1991) Preamble
A/RES/49/60 (1994) (Measures to eliminate international terrorism)
A/RES 50/53 (1995) para 1
A/RES 51/210 (1996) para 1
A/RES 52/165 (1997)
A/RES 54/110 (2000) para 1.
A/RES 55/158 (2001) para 1
A/RES/69/127 (2014)
A/RES/69/17 (2014)

Resolutions Supporting the View That Terrorism Must Be Eliminated, While Respecting Human Rights

A/RES 48/122 (1993) para 1
A/RES 49/185 (1994) para 1
A/RES/50/186 (1995) para 2
A/RES/52/133 (1997) para 3
A/RES 54/164 (2000) para 2
A/RES 57/219 (2003) Preamble
A/RES 58/81 (2004) para 1
A/RES 59/153 (2005)
A/RES/60/288 (2006)

Resolutions Reaffirming the Right to Self-Determination, Yet Offering an Unqualified Condemnation of Terrorism

A/RES 44/29 (1989) 301–302
A/RES/46/51 (1991) 15

Further Resolutions

A/RES/2131(XX) (1965) Declaration on the Inadmissibility of Intervention in the Domestic Affairs of states and the Protection of their Independence and Sovereignty
A/RES/2625(XXV) (1970) Declaration on Principles of International Law concerning Friendly Relations and Cooperation among States in accordance with the Charter of the United Nations

A/RES/3034 (XXVII) (1972) Establishment of the *Ad Hoc* Committee on International Terrorism

A/RES/3314 (XXIX) (1974) Definition of Aggression

A/RES/34/145(1979) (agree on co-operative measures for the elimination of international terrorism and unequivocal condemnation of terrorism). Re-endorsed in A/RES/36/109 (1981) & A/RES/38/130 (1983)

A/RES/37/10 (1982) Manila Declaration on the Peaceful Settlement of Disputes

A/RES/37/194 (1982) Principles of Medical Ethics relevant to the Role of Health Personnel, particularly Physicians, in the Protection of Prisoners and Detainees against Torture and Other Cruel, Inhuman or Degrading Treatment or Punishment

A/RES/42/22 (1987) Declaration on the enhancement of the effectiveness of the principle of refraining from threat or use of force in international relations

A/RES/43/51 (1988) (UNGA Declaration on the Prevention and Removal of Disputes and Situations which may threaten International Peace and Security and on the role of the UN in this field)

A/RES 51/210 (1996) (Ad Hoc Committee on International Terrorism)

A/RES 59/153 (2005) (Strengthening international cooperation and technical assistance in promoting the implementation of the universal conventions and protocols related to terrorism within the framework of the activities of the United Nations Office on Drugs and Crime)

Security Council Resolutions

S/RES/313 (1972), A/RES/508 & 509 (1982) & A/RES/ 573 (1985) (Israel)

S/RES/487 (1981) (Iraq-Israel)

S/RES/731 & 748 (1992) (on Libya)

S/RES/51/210 (1996) (regarding ad hoc and special committees established on the recommendation of the Sixth Committee)

S/RES/1044 & 1054 (1996) condemning assassination attempt against President Mubarak of Egypt

S/RES/1189 (1998) (bombings in Nairobi, Kenya, and Dar es Salaam, Tanzania)

S/RES/1368, 1373 & 1377 (2001) (Threats to international peace and security caused by terrorist acts)

S/RES/1333 (2000) & 1390 (2002) on Afghanistan

S/RES/1438 (2002) (condemnation of bombings in Bali)

S/RES/1440 (2002) (condemnation of hostage-taking in Moscow)

S/RES/1450 (2002) (condemnation of terrorist attacks in Kenya)

S/RES/1465 (2003) (condemnation of bomb attacks in Bogota, Colombia)

S/RES/1510 (2003); 1589 (2005); 1659 & 1707 (2006) (right to self-defence)

S/RES/1516 (2003) (condemnation of bombings in Istanbul)

S/RES/1530 (2004) (condemnation of bomb attacks in Madrid)

S/RES/1566 (2004) (threats to international peace and security)
S/RES/1611 (2005) (condemnation of bomb attacks in London)
S/RES/1618 (2005) (condemnation of bomb attacks in London)
S/RES/1624 (2005) (Counter-Terrorism Implementation Task Force)
S/RES/1310 (2000), S/RES/1337 (2001), S/RES/1365 (2001), S/RES/1391, 1428 (2002); S/RES/1461 & 1496 (2003); S/RES/1525, 1553 & 1559 (2004); S/RES/1583 & 1614 (2005); S/RES 1680 & 1655 (2006) (on Lebanon)
S/RES/1701 (2006) (Israel)
S/RES/1904 (2009) creating the Office of the Ombudsperson Office of the Ombudsperson (ISIL & Al-Qaida Sanctions List)
S/RES/ 1267 (1999), 1989 (2011) and 2253 (2015) concerning ISIL (Da'esh), Al-Qaida, and associated individuals, groups, undertakings and entities
S/RES 2249 (2015) (unequivocal condemnation of terrorist acts)

United Nations Documents and Reports

Charge d'Affairs of the Permanent Mission of Lebanon to the United Nations Letters dated 13 July 2006 addressed to the Secretary-General and the President of the Security Council UN Doc A/60/938, S/2006/518 (13 July 2006)
Conclusions of the Work of the Study Group on the Fragmentation of International Law: Difficulties arising from the diversification and expansion of international law Yearbook of the International Law Commission (2006) vol 2 part 2
Finland Report to the Counter-Terrorism Committee of the UN Security Council, 15 May 2006, annexed to UN Doc S/2006/506 (19 July 2006)
League of Nations Committee of Experts for the Progressive Codification of International Law, Replies of Governments League of Nations (1927) Doc C 196 M 70 1927 V
Meeting of the 6th Committee during the 69th session of the GA, AC 6/69/SR 28 (7 October–14 November 2014)
Official Records of the General Assembly, 49th session, Supplement No 40 (A/49/40) vol I annex XI para 2 – the Committee's Concluding Observations on Israel (1998) (CCPR/C/79/Add93) para 21
Report of the Ad Hoc Committee established by General Assembly Resolution 51/210 of 17 December 1996, sixth session (28 January–1 February 2002) A/57/37
Report of the *Ad Hoc* Committee established by the General Assembly resolution 51/210 of 17 December 1996 ninth session (28 March–1 April 2005) A/60/37, Annex I
Report of the *Ad Hoc* Committee established by General Assembly Resolution 51/210 of 17 December 1996 11th session (5, 6 and 15 February 2007) A/62/37 Annex to the Report

Report of the *Ad Hoc* Committee established by General Assembly Resolution 51/210 of 17 December 1996 14th session (12–16 April 2010) 62nd session A/62/37 Supplement No 37

Report of the *Ad Hoc* Committee established by General Assembly Resolution 51/210 of 17 December 1996 16th session (8–12 April 2013) 65th session A/65/37 Supplement no 37

Report of the Secretary-General's High-level Panel on Threats, Challenges and Change 'A More Secure World: Our Shared Responsibility' 2 December 2004, UN Doc A/59/565 para 189

Report of the Sixth Committee 'Measures to Eliminate International Terrorism' (2008) 64th session A/64/37 Supplement No 37

Report of the Special Committee on the Question of Defining Aggression (1968) A/7185/Rev1

Second Periodic Report to the Committee on the Rights of the Child, 24 May 2005, Hungary, UN Doc CRC/C/70/Add 25 (submitted 17 February 2004)

The Secretary-General Report on the United Nations Interim Force in Lebanon to the Security Council delivered to the Security Council UN Doc S/2006/560 (21 July 2006) 3

The Secretary-General Statement to the Security Council UN SCOR 61st Session 5492 meeting UN Doc S/PV 5492 (20 July 2006) 3

United Nations General Assembly 56th session, 12th plenary meeting (1 October 2001) A/56/PV12

Websites and Online Sources

Ad Hoc and Special Committees established on the Recommendation of the Sixth Committee <http://legal.un.org/committees/terrorism/> accessed 6 January 2016

ACHPR Principles and Guidelines on Human and Peoples' Rights while Countering Terrorism in Africa 28–29 <http://www.achpr.org/files/special-mechanisms/human-rights-defenders/principles_and_guidelines_on_human_and_peoples_rights_while_countering_terrorism_in_africa.pdf> accessed 21 October 2017

Al Jazeera 'At Least 11 Civilians Killed in Boko Haram Attack' <http://www.aljazeera.com/news/2017/09/11-civilians-killed-boko-haram-attack-170902043943431.html> accessed 1 October 2017

Al Jazeera (9 July 2017) 'Kenya: Nine Beheaded in Suspected al-Shabab' <http://www.aljazeera.com/news/2017/07/kenya-attack-170708103555604.html> accessed 1 October 2017

Amnesty International 'Spain: Civil Guards Convicted of Torture' (10 January 2011) <https://www.amnesty.org/en/library/asset/EUR41/002/2011/en/60b24c89-1115-4124-aa36-68f3705efc84/eur410022011en.html> accessed 1 May 2017

Amnesty International 'Torture in 2014: 30 Years of Broken Promise <https://www.amnestyusa.org/sites/default/files/act400042014en.pdf> accessed 12 April 2016

Andreias V, 'Anticipatory Self-Defence in International Law: Legal or Just a Construct for Using Force?' <http://arno.uvt.nl/show.cgi?fid=122935> accessed 27 November 2017

Article 15–6 Investigation of the 800th Military Police Brigade – The Taguba Report: a Report Prepared by Maj Gen AM Taguba on Alleged Abuse of Prisoners by Members of the 800th Military Police Brigade at the Abu Ghraib Prison, Baghdad' <https://fas.org/irp/agency/dod/taguba.pdf> accessed 16 April 2017

Association Internationale de Droit Pénal (1928) 5 Revue Internationale de Droit Pénal 1 <http://gallica.bnf.fr/ark:12148/bpt6k12550937.textelimage> accessed 9 August 2017

BBC News 'Israel Admits Torture' (2000) <http://news.bbc.co.uk/2/hi/middle_east/637293.stm> accessed 12 August 2017

BBC News 'London Bridge Attack: Timeline of British Terror Attacks' <www.bbc.com/news/uk-40013040> accessed 1 October 2017

Belluck P, 'Threats and Responses: The Bomb Plot; Unrepentant Shoe Bomber is Given a Life Sentence for Trying to Blow Up Jet' *New York Times* (31 January 2003) <https://www.nytimes.com/2003/01/31/us/threats-responses-bomb-plot-unrepentant-shoe-bomber-given-life-sentence-for.html> accessed 16 November 2017

Beri R, 'Rise of Terrorism in Africa Institute for Defence Studies and Analyses' <www.idsa.in/idsacomments/rise-of-terrorism-in-africa_rberi_130417> (13 April 2017) accessed 1 October 2017

Brody M, 'Contemporary *Jus Ad Bellum* on Use of Force in Self-Defense by States against Non-State Terrorist Groups – Limitations, Evolutions and Alternatives' (2011) <https://calhoun.nps.edu/handle/10945/5496> accessed 12 October 2017, 81

Brownlie I, (editor's preface) in D McGoldrick (1994) 'The Human Rights Committee: Its Role in the Development of the International Covenant on Civil and Political Rights' <https://global.oup.com/academic/product/the-human-rights-committee-9780198258940?cc=za&lang=en&> accessed 18 August 2017

Burke D, 'Muslim Leaders: 'We Will Not Allow the Extremists to Define Us' CNN (15 June 2016) <https://pressroom/2006/pages> accessed 3 September 2017

CNN 'Transcript of President Bush's address to a Joint Session of Congress on Thursday night, 20 September 2001' (21 September 2001) <http://edition.cnn.com/2001/US/09/20/gen.bush.transcript/> accessed 28 August 2017

Commission of Inquiry into the Methods of Investigation of the General Security Service Regarding Hostile Terrorist Activity (1989) <https://www.cambridge.org/core/journals/israel-law-review/article/commission-of-inquiry-into-the-methods-of-investigation-of-the-general-security-service-regarding-hostile-terrorist-activity/2FEEB59B40B66A41E9FF3633C0D3BF69> accessed 13 August 2017

Consideration of Reports submitted by States Parties under article 19 of the Convention pursuant to the optional reporting procedure, Bahrain (16 June 2016) CAT/C/BHR/3 <www.refworld.org/publisher/CAT.html> accessed 23 October 2017

Consideration of Reports submitted by States Parties under Article 19 of the Convention, Croatia, UN Doc CAT/C/54/Add3 12, <docstore.ohcr.org.SelfServices/FilesHandler.ashx.enc.> accessed 1 May 2017

Consideration of Reports submitted by States Parties under Article 19 of the Convention, Egypt, UN Doc CAT/C/34/Add 11 49, <docstore.ohcr.org.SelfServices/FilesHandler.ashx.enc.> accessed 1 May 2017

Consideration of Reports submitted by States Parties under Article 19 of the Convention, Greece, UN Doc CAT/C/61/Add 1 <docstore.ohcr.org.SelfServices/FilesHandler.ashx.enc.> accessed 6 May 2017

Consideration of Reports submitted by States Parties under Article 19 of the Convention, Guatemala, UN Doc CAT/C/49/Add 2, 9, <docstore.ohcr.org.SelfServices/FilesHandler.ashx.enc.> accessed 13 August 2017

Consideration of Reports submitted by States Parties under Article 19 of the Convention, Iceland, UN Doc CAT/C/59/Add 2 58, <docstore.ohcr.org.SelfServices/FilesHandler.ashx.enc.> accessed 13 August 2017

Consideration of Reports submitted by States Parties under Article 19 of the Convention, Indonesia, UN Doc CAT/C/47/Add 3 66, <docstore.ohcr.org.SelfServices/FilesHandler.ashx.enc.> accessed 10 August 2017

Consideration of Reports submitted by States Parties under Article 19 of the Convention, Latvia, UN Doc CAT/C/21/Add 4, Latvia, <docstore.ohcr.org.SelfServices/FilesHandler.ashx.enc.> accessed 12 August 2017, 6

Consideration of Reports submitted by States Parties under Article 19 of the Convention, Luxembourg, UN Doc CAT/C/SR 517, 7 <docstore.ohcr.org.SelfServices/FilesHandler.ashx.enc.> accessed 6 May 2017

Consideration of Reports Submitted By state Parties under Article 19 of the Convention, Spain, UN Doc CAT/C/55/Add 5 16, <docstore.ohcr.org.SelfServices/FilesHandler.ashx.enc.> accessed 10 August 2017

Convention against Torture and Other Cruel, Inhuman or Degrading Treatment or Punishment, Reservations, Understandings and Declarations Made by the United States of America CAT/C/28/Add5 <https://www.unhchr.state.gov/documents/organization/100296.pdf> accessed 12 August 2017

Council of Europe Committee of Ministers 'Guidelines on Human Rights and the Fight against Terrorism' 11 July 2002 <https://refworld.org/docid/47fdfb220.html> accessed 23 October 2017

Country Reports: East Asia and Pacific Overview <www.state.gov/j/ct/rls/crt/2015/257515.htm> accessed 23 October 2017

Cronin A and others, 'Congressional Research Service Report, Foreign Terrorist Organzations, Report No RL32223 (6 February 2004) <https://fas.org/irp/crs/RL32223.pdf> accessed 26 October 2017

Delegation of the European Commission to the United Nations, EU Council Conclusions on the Middle East (17 July 2006) <www.europa-eu-un.org/articles/en/article_6125.en.htm> accessed 3 September 2017

De Man P, 'State Practice, Domestic Legislation and the Interpretation Of Fundamental Principles of International Space Law' (2017) Leuven Centre for Global Governance Studies Working Paper No 181 <https://ghum.kuleuven.be/ggs/publications/working_papers/new_series/wp-171-180/wp181deman.pdf> accessed 2 October 2017

Department of State's Bureau of International Info programmes G8 Statement on Situation in Middle East (16 July 16, <https://2001-2009.state.gov/p/us/rm/2006/69071.htm> accessed 3 September 2017

Dictionnaire de l'Académie Française online 5 ed (1798) <http://portail atilf fr/cgi-bin/getobject_?p.16:40./var/artfla/dicos/ACAD_1798/IMAGE/> accessed 4 February 2017

Eidenmuller M, 'Eleanor Roosevelt: On the Adoption of the Universal Declaration of Human Rights' (9 December 1948) <www.americanrhetoric.com/speeches/eleanorrooseveltdeclarationhumanrights.htm> accessed 11 March 2017

Eighth BRICS Summit – GOA Declaration (16 January 2017) <https://brics2017.org/English/Documents/Summit/201701/t20170125_1410.html> accessed 26 October 2017) para 57

Federal Bureau of Investigation 'Terrorism' <www.fbi gov/about-us/investigate/terrorism/terrorism-definition> accessed 27 May 2017

Final Report to the Prosecutor by the Committee Established to Review the NATO Bombing Campaign Against the Federal Republic of Yugoslavia <www.icty.org/sid/10052> accessed 27 January 2017 para 48

Fox News 'Al-Shabab fighters attack African Union Convoy in Southern Somalia, Killing at Least 8' (30 July 2017) <www.foxnews.com/world/2017/07/30/al-shabab-fighters-attack-african-union-convoy-in-southern-somalia-killing-at-least-8.html> accessed 1 October 2017

General Counsel of the Department of Defence 'Legal Distinction between Preemption, Preventive Self-Defense, and Anticipatory Self-Defense' 16 October 2002, 3 <http://library.rumsfeld.com/doclib/sp/2564/2002-10-16.pdf> accessed 16 November 2017

G20 Statement on the Fight against Terrorism (2015) <http://www.consilium.europa.eu/en/meetings/international-summit/2015/11/g20-statement-on-the-fight-against-terrorism_pdf/> accessed 7 August 2016

Greenberg K, 'Guilty until Proven Guilty: The Presumption of Innocence and the Trial of Ahmed Khalfan Ghailani (19 November 2010) <www.motherjones.com/politics/2010/11/ahmed-khalfan-ghailani-verdict/> accessed 22 October 2017

Guide on Article 6 of the European Convention on Human Rights Rights to a Fair Trial (civil limb) <www.echr.coe.int/Documents/Guide_Art_6_ENG.pdf> accessed 20 August 2017

History Central '1837- Caroline Affair' <www.historycentral.com/ant/caroline.html> accessed 12 October 2017

House of Commons Foreign Affairs Committee, Foreign Policy Aspects of the War Against Terrorism, 2002–03, HC 196, Parlementary Debate, HL (2004) 356 (Lord Thomas Of Gresford, statement opening the debate on international self-defense) <www.publications.parliament.uk/pa/cm200304/cmselect/cmfsff/441/441.pdf> accessed 1 August 2017

International Law Association Committee on Formation of Customary (General) International Law 'Final report of the committee: Statement of principles applicable to the formation of general customary international law' (2000) <http://www.ila.hq.org/index.php/committees> accessed 1 September 2017

International Law Commission, 69th session (1 May–2 June & 3 July–4 August 2017) Peremptory Norms of General International Law (Jus Cogens) Statement of the Chairman of the Drafting Committee Mr Airuddga Rajput http://legal.un.org/ilc/documentation/english/statements/2017_dc_chairman_statement_jc.pdf> accessed 3 November 2017

Islamic Statement against Terrorism <www.mafhoum.com/press5/747529.htm> accessed 11 November 2017

'Israel Acting in Self-Defence, Says Howard,' Australian Broadcasting Corporation News Online (16 July 2006) <www.abc.net.au/news/newsitems/2006/Israel-acting-in-self-defence-says-Howard/1802556> accessed 3 September 2017

Joint Statement of the BRICS leaders (26 January 2017) <https://brics2017.org/English/Documents/Summit/201701/t20170125_1403.html> accessed 29 August 2017

Jus Ad Bellum – Ethiopia's Claims 1–8, Eritrea and Ethiopia Partial award of the Eritrea-Ethiopia Claims Commission (2006) 45 ILM 430 Permanent Court of Arbitration <http://legal.un.org/riaa/cases/vol-XXVI/457-469.pdf> accessed 12 August 2017 para 11

Kokott K, 'The Impact of 9/11 on the South African Anti-Terrorism Legislation and the Constitutionality Thereof' unpublished LLM dissertation, University of the Western Cape, 2005 <http://etd.uwc.ac.za/xmlui/bitstream/handle/11394/1673/Kokott_LLM_2005.pdf?sequence=1> accessed 13 July 2017

Lepard BD, 'The Necessity of *Opinio Juris* in the Formation of Customary International Law' (12–13 July 2013) <http://law.duke. edu/cicl/> accessed 9 August 2017

Letter dated 17 March 2004 from the Permanent Representative of France to the United Nations addressed to the Chairman of the Counter-Terrorism Committee S/2004/226 (29 March 2004) <https://www.refworld.org/docid/46dcleb5c.html> accessed 23 October 2017

Letter dated 26 January 2006 from the Permanent Representative of the United States of America to the United Nations addressed to the Chairman of the Counter-Terrorism Committee (s2006/69) (3 February 2006) <https://www.refworld.org/docid/46de6022d.html> accessed 23 October 2017

Letter dated 22 December 2001 from the Chargé d'Affaires of the Permanent Mission of the People's Republic of China to the United Nations addressed to the Chairman of the Security Council Committee established pursuant to resolution 1373 (2001) concerning counter-terrorism S/2001/1270 (27 December 2001) <https://www.refworld.org/docid/46d5712f8.pdf> accessed 23 October 2017

Le Monde France: New Emergency Powers Threaten Rights Parliament Should Ensure New Powers Not Misused 24 November 2015 <http://www hrw.org/news/2015/11/24/france-new-emergency-powers-threaten-rights> accessed 21 May 2017

Levin M, 'The Case for Torture' <http://people.brandeis.edu/~teuber/torture.html> accessed 5 September 2017

'Lockerbie Suspects Ask for Reduced Charges: 2 Libyans are Charged in Deaths of 270 People' *Deseret News* (7 December 1999) <www.deseretnews.com/article/731811/Lockerbie-suspects-ask-for-reduced-charges.html?pg=all> accessed 5 September 2017

'Lockerbie: The 270 Victims' Aljazeera 11 March 2014 <www.aljazeera.com/programmes/lockerbie/2014/03/lockerbie-270-victims-201431075240135389.html> accessed 2 February 2017

Lyons M, 'The Grotian Moment: Hugo Grotius and the Invention of International Law' (2011) <https://mathewlyons.wordpress.com/2011/10/12/the-grotian-moment-hugo-grotius-and-the-invention-of-international-law/> accessed 2 April 2017

Medzmariashvili M 'Pre-Emptive Self-Defence Against States Harbouring Terrorists' 2011 RGSL Research Papers <uploads/research-papers-list/19/4-medzmariasgvili-final.pdf> accessed 27 November 2017

McCain J, 'Torture's Terrible Toll' *Newsweek* (21 November 2005) <www.newsweek.com/tortures-terrible-toll-115193> accessed 28 October 2017

Miller G, 'Defining Torture' Floersheimer Centre Occasional Papers <https://cardozo.yu.edu/sites/default/files/Defining%20Torture.pdf> (2006) accessed 23 October 2017, 14

Minneapolis Star Tribune 'Tribunal Allies Back US Strikes; Russia Among the Dissenters' 22 August 1998 <www.startribune.com> accessed 1 July 2017, 6A

Newsday 'US Strikes Back' 21 August 1998, A38 <www.newsday.com> accessed 1 July 2017

New York Times 'Israel Attacks Beirut Airport and Sets Up Naval Blockade' (13 July 2006) <www.nytimes.com/2006/07/13/world/middleeast/13cnd-mideast.html> accessed 24 October 2017

New York Times 'Israeli Planes Attack PLO In Tunis, Killing At Least 30; Raid "Legitimate", US Says' 2 October 1985 <http://www.nytimes.com/1985/10/02/world/israeli-planes-attack-plo-in-tunis-killing-at-least-30-raid-legitimate-us-says.html?mcubz=3> accessed 28 August 2017

Oechmichen A, 'Terrorism and Anti-Terrorism Legislation: The Terrorised Legislator?' Doctoral thesis, Leiden University (2009) <http://hdl.handle.net/1887/13852> accessed 1 July 017 338–342

Office of the United Nations High Commissioner for Human Rights Human Rights Fact Sheet: No 4 Combating Torture 34 (May 2002) <www.un-documents.net/ohchr/factsheet04rev.1en.pdf> accessed 26 October 2017

Paredi, L, 'The War Crime of Terror: An Analysis of international Jurisprudence' <www.internationalcrimesdatabase.org/upload/documents/20150610T161544-Laura20%Paredi20%Brief_final.pdf> accessed 11 November 2017

Pollock D and Abdelaziz M, 'Arab States condemn "terrorist" Paris attacks' <https://english.alaribiya.net/en/News/middle-east/2015/11/14/Arab-states-denounce-Paris-attacks-as-violation-of-human-values.html> accessed 1 December 2016

Pramono A, 'Aircraft Hijacking: A Legal Perspective' (2014) 43 Masalah-Masalah Hukum 487 <http://portalgaruda.org> accessed 9 August 2017, 491

Prime Minister Fouad Siniora Address to the Lebanese People (15 July 2006), <transcripts.cnn.com.TRANSCRIPTS/0607/15/se.01.html> accessed 3 September 2017

Primoratz I, 'Terrorism' in EN Zalta (ed), *Stanford Encyclopedia of Philosophy* (2007) <http://plato.staford.edu> accessed 1 May 2017

Report of the Inter-American Commission on Human Rights Right to Humane Treatment <http://cidh.oas.org/Terrorism/Eng/exe.htm> accessed 3 October 2017

Report of the International Committee of the Red Cross 'Customary IHL' re France: Practice Relating to Rule 90; art 222–3 of the Criminal Code <https://ihl-databases.icrc,org/customary-ihl/eng/docs/v2_cou_fr_rule90_sectionb> accessed 9 August 2017

Report of the International Committee of the Red Cross on the Treatment by the Coalition Forces of Prisoners of War and Other Protected Persons by the Geneva Conventions in Iraq During Arrest, Internment and Interrogation' (2004) <www.derechos.org/nizkor/us/doc/icrc-prisoner-report-feb-2004.pdf> accessed 7 October 2017, 8

Report of the International Committee of the Red Cross 'Report on the Treatment of Fourteen "High Value Detainees" in CIA Custody' (2007) <https://assets.nybooks.com/media/doc/2010/04/22/icrc-report.pdf> accessed 7 October 2017, 12

SC Counter-Terrorism Committee Country reports: Resolution 1373 (2001) <www.un.org/en/sc/ctc/resources/countryreports.html> accessed 4 January 2017

Scheinin M, 'Turkey's Derogation from Human Rights Treaties – An Update' <www.ejiltalk.org/turkeys-derogation-from-human-rights-treaties-an-update/> accessed 10 March 2017

Schmitt M, 'Counter-Terrorism and the Use of Force in International Law' in Borch F and Wilson P (eds), *International Law and The War On Terror* 2003) <https://www.researchgate.net/publication/235160755-counter-terrorism-and-the-use-of-force-in-International-Law> accessed 20 August 2017, 161

Schwikkard P, 'A Constitutional Revolution in South African Criminal Procedure?' (2015) <https://lawexplores.com/a-constitutional-revolution-in-south-african-criminal-procedure/> accessed 26 August 2017

Sixty Eighth General Assembly Plenary Reiterating Unequivocal Condemnation of Terrorism in all Forms, General Assembly Adopts Resolution Reaffirming Global Commitment to Combating Threat (2014) 96th and 97th meetings, GA/11523 <www.un.org/press/en/2014/ga11523 doc.htm> accessed 13 March 2016

Special cabinet Communiqué issued by the Cabinet Secratariat, Israeli Ministry of Foreign Affairs <transcripts.cnn.com/TRANSCRIPTS/0607/15/se.01.html> accessed 3 September 2017

Statement by Israeli representative at 18th Session of United Nations Committee against Torture, Geneva, Switzerland (7 May 1997) <http://mfa.gov.il/MFA/InternatlOrgs/Speeches/Pages/STATEMENT%20BY%20ISRAELI%20REPRESENTATIVE%20TO%20UN%20COMMITTE.aspx> accessed 4 September 2017

Sullivan G and Hayes B, 'Blacklisted: Targeted Sanctions, Preemptive Security and Human Rights European Centre for Constitutional and Human Rights' (2010) <www.tni.org/files/Blacklisted%20-%20Executive%20summary.pdf> accessed 5 July 2017

Summary Records of the Sixth Committee, 28th meeting Official Records of the General Assembly, 69th Session, A/C6/55/SR28 (7 October–14 November 2014) <https://papersmart.unmeetings.org/ga/69th-session/general-debate/statements/> accessed 8 August 2017

The Guardian 'Israeli Government Report Admits Systematic Torture of Palestinians' <www.theguardian.com/world/2000/feb/11/israel> accessed 13 August 2017

The Guardian 'Terrorism Act Incompatible with Human Rights, Court Rules in David Miranda case' (19 January 2016) <www.theguardian.com/world/2016/jan/19/terrorism-act-incompatible-with-human-rights-court-rules-in-david-miranda-case> accessed 21 October 2017

The Guardian 'Torture Techniques Endorsed by the Bush Administration' (2009) <www.theguardian.com/world/2009/apr/17/torture-methods-interrogation-george-bush-approved> accessed 12 August 2017, stating that torture and coercion were openly sanctioned as tools of interrogation at the highest levels of the Bush administration.

The Guardian 'Trump Claims Torture Works but Experts Warn of its 'Potentially Existential' Costs' (26 January 2017) <www.theguardian.com/us-news/2017/jan/26/donald-trump-torture-absolutely-works-says-us-president-in-first-television-interview> accessed 13 August 2017

The Guardian 'Will Accused 9/11 Architect Khalid Sheikh Mohammed Ever Come To Trial?' (11 September 2017) <www.theguardian.com/us-news/2017/sep/11/will-khalid-sheikh-mohammed-come-to-trial-9-11-attacks> accessed 22 October 2017

The New York Times 'Donald Trump May be Seeking to Reinstate Torture Methods for Detained Terrorist Suspects' <www.news.com.au/finance/work/leaders/donald-trump-may-be-seeking-to-reinstate-torture-methods-for-detained-terrorist-suspects/news-story/7d265cf92958ef86c9258391c60e6116> accessed 12 August 2017

The Telegraph 'How the World Reacted to the Barcelona Terror Attack' 18 August 2017 <http://www.telegraph.co.uk/news/2017/08/17/world-reacted-barcelona-terror-attack/> accessed 27 August 2017

The Telegraph 'Theresa May's Downing Street Statement on Manchester Terror Attack in Full' (23 May 2017) <www.telegraph.co.uk/news/2017/05/23/theresa-mays-downing-street-statement-manchester-terror-attack/> accessed 27 August 2017

Time Magazine 'A Timeline of Recent Terror Attacks in Europe' (20 December 2016 <http://time.com/4607481/europe-terrorism-timeline-berlin-paris-nice-brussels/> accessed 1 October 2017

Toronto Sun 'Theresa May "Absolutely" Condemns Torture Ahead of Trump Visit' <www.Torontosun.Com/2017/01/26/Theresa-May-Absolutely-Condemns-Torture-Ahead-Of-Trump-Visit> accesssed 2 August 2017

Transcript of US Joint Congressional hearing 'Extraordinary Rendition in US Counterterrorism Policy: The Impact on Transatlantic Relations' of Subcommittee on International Organizations, Human Rights and Oversight and Subcommittee on Europe, and in particular the arguments of Republican Congressman Rohrabacher: <http://fas.org/irp/cpngress/2007_hr/rendition.pdf> accessed 16 April 2017

US Department of State's Bureau of International Info programs G8 Statement on Situation in Middle East (16 July 16), <https://2001-2009.gov/p/us/rm/2006/69071.htm> accessed 3 September 2017

United Nations 'International Instruments related to the Prevention and Suppression of International Terrorism' (2008) <www.un-ilibrary.org/peacekeeping-and-security/international-instruments-related-to-the-prevention-and-suppression-of-international-terrorism_6866fb0e-en> accessed 26 October 2017, 190

United Nations Treaty ratifications <https://treaties.un.org> accessed 6 January 2016

United States Department of State 'United States condemns terrorist attack on Istanbul's Ataturk airport' 28 June 2016, <http://www.state.gov/r/pa/prs/ps/2016/06/259153.htm> accessed 2 February 2017

Washington Post 'US Decries Abuse but Defends Interrogations) (26 December 2000) <www.washingtonpost.com/> accessed 3 October 2017

Washington Post 'US Strikes Iraq for Plot to Kill Bush' 27 June 1993 <www.washington-post.com/wp-srv/inatl/longterm/iraq/timeline/062793.htm> accessed 13 August 2017

White House 'The National Security Strategy of The United States Of America' (2002) 12–16 <https://georgebush-Whitehouse.archives.gov/nsc/nss/2002> accessed 29 July 2017

Working document submitted by India on the Draft Comprehensive Convention on International Terrorism <http://www.satp.org/satporgtp/countries/india/document/papers/India_IntConv.htmSee> accessed 11 September 2017

Zemanek K, 'The Vienna Convention on the Law of Treaties' (2009) United Nations Audiovisual Library of International Law <http://legal.un.org/avl/ha/vclt/vclt.html> accessed 5 July 2017

Zenović P, 'Human Rights Enforcement via Peremptory Norms – A Challenge to State Sovereignty' (2012) Riga Graduate School of Law Research Papers No 6 <https://www.rgl.edu.lv/uploads/files/RP_6_Zenovic_final.pdf> accessed 12 July 2017

Index